Bauwelt Berlin Annual

Bauwelt Berlin Annual

Chronology of Building Events 1996 to 2001: 1996

Edited
by Martina Düttmann
and Felix Zwoch

Bauwelt Berlin

Birkhäuser Verlag
Basel · Berlin · Boston

The Bauwelt Berlin Annual is indebted to a number of persons and firms
working in Berlin and commited to the city.
Through sponsoring and advertising they contributed to the making of this Berlin chronology.
The editors would like to thank

Adler & Schmidt, GrafikBüro, Berlin
BauNetz, Bertelsmann Fachinformation GmbH, Berlin
Bauwert GmbH, Allgemeine Projektentwicklungs- und Bauträgergesellschaft mbH, Munich/Berlin
Berlin Hyp, Berlin-Hannoversche Hypothekenbank AG
BLEG Berliner Landesentwicklungsgesellschaft mbH
CEDC American Business Center GmbH & Co Checkpoint Charlie KG, Berlin
debis Gesellschaft für Potsdamer Platz Projekt und Immobilienmanagement mbH, Berlin
Entwicklungsgesellschaft Rummelsburger Bucht mbH/Wasserstadt Berlin Oberhavel GmbH
FSB Franz Schneider Brakel
GeSoBau – Gesellschaft für sozialen Wohnungsbau gemeinnützige Aktiengesellschaft, Berlin
GROTH + GRAALFS Industrie- und Wohnbau GmbH, Berlin
HANSEATICA Unternehmensgruppe, Berlin/Hamburg
HEWI Heinrich Wilke GmbH, Arolsen
ITAG Immobilien Treuhand- und Vermögensanlage AG, Berlin
Jagdfeld FriedrichstadtPassagen Quartier 206 Vermögensverwaltung KG, Berlin
Dr. Peter and Isolde Kottmair Berlin/Munich
LBB Grundstücksentwicklungsgesellschaft mbH, Bau- und Projektentwicklungen, Berlin
MetaDesign Berlin
se'lux, Semperlux GmbH, Berlin
STADT UND LAND, Wohnbauten – Gesellschaft mbH, Berlin
TishmanSpeyer Properties Deutschland GmbH, Berlin

Editorial Staff	Martina Düttmann and Haila Ochs
	with Michael Goj, Hildegard Loeb-Ullmann, Galina Rave
English Editor	Jackson Bond
Translations	Jackson Bond (p. 8, 14, 48, 70, 134, 141, 178, 181, quotes), Ian Cowley (p. 88, 96, 108, 120, 139, 152, 168, quotes),
into English	Peter Gilbert (p. 154), Nick Kumanoff (p. 20, 22, 30, 74, 102, 150, 156, 165), Ursule Molinaro (p. 159),
	Jeremiah M. Riemer (p. 130–179), Melissa Thorson Hause (p. 10, 82, 142, 145, 149, quotes), Lynnette Widder (p. 38)
Design	MetaDesign Berlin
Lithography/Setting	CitySatz & Nagel, Berlin
Printing	Ruksaldruck, Berlin
Binding	Heinz Stein, Berlin

A CIP catalogue record for this book is available from the Library of Congress, Washington, D.C., USA

Deutsche Bibliothek Cataloging-in-Publication Data

Bauwelt Berlin Annual: Chronology of Building Events 1996 to 2001/
ed. by Martina Düttmann and Felix Zwoch.
(Transl. into Engl.: Jackson Bond ...). — Basel; Berlin; Boston: Birkhäuser.

NE	Düttmann, Martina (Ed.)
	(Engl. Ed.).
	1996. – (1997)
	ISBN 3-7643-5664-2 (Basel ...)
	ISBN 0-8176-5664-2 (Boston)

© 1997   Bertelsmann Fachzeitschriften GmbH, Gütersloh, Berlin, und
          Birkhäuser-Verlag für Architektur, P.O. Box 133, CH 4010 Basel, Switzerland

World distribution by Birkhäuser Publishers

Printed on acid-free paper produced from chlorine-free pulp. TCF ∞

Printed in Germany   ISBN 3-7643-5664-2
                      ISBN 0-8176-5664-2

          9 8 7 6 5 4 3 2 1

Berlin combines the disadvantages of a big American city with those of a small German town.

Its advantages are listed in Baedeker.

Kurt Tucholsky, 1926

Content

Berlin. One Year

If there were one ultimate model for the Bauwelt Berlin Annual, it would have to
be the magazine "Querschnitt," published in Berlin between 1924 and 1933. It
bore the incredible subtitle "The Magazine of Current Eternal Values," which
more or less meant: be wary of comfortable opinions, collect anything found in
time and reality, consider things as of equal importance, pass over nothing, and
take life as it is, unedited. In other words, shying away from life helps no one
find their rightful place in Berlin, nor does Berlin help anyone to settle down in
one place for a lifetime. Could this be the reason why the decision is so difficult
for those moving here from Bonn? One city — one year, but no more; year book is
taken literally. The concept is very simple, but very strict. What is happening
now, in this moment, what would you like to know, as someone moving through
this city. There is no reason for selecting certain facts or avoiding others, there is
no need to euphemize or beautify, there is above all, no submission to the zeitgeist. You will not find rash judgements, nor architecture criticism and certainly
not mythos. But should a new Berlin mythos evolve, then Bauwelt Berlin Annual
— tracking events through the year 2001— might have provided some of the
material. What you have in your hands is a year's account, and the last photos
were taken just before our printer's deadline (despite icy rain and snow). There
are views from the S-Bahn window, with explanations of what you are seeing.
You will find the arguments of one of those controversial developers. There is a
portrayal of the industrial hinterland Oberschöneweide, revealed as something
of a historic counterpart to all the imposing new construction. And parallel to

the report about the gigantic subterranean urban renewal there are the images of those workers descending every morning into the earth. This debut publication of Bauwelt Berlin Annual had no time to lose. The first new buildings in Berlin-Mitte have either just opened or are nearing completion. The residential communities on the edge of the city are rising rapidly from the ground, already claiming their place in next year's book. Construction work on Potsdamer Platz will never again possess such theatrical qualities, and on the former stretch of border along the Görlitzer Railway, the features which once distinguished East from West are quickly disappearing. Meanwhile, the first buildings appear on Pariser Platz ...

The Bauwelt Berlin Annual consists of three independent parts, beginning with the main documentary section, offering the initial chapters of the city's narrative, which will be continued next year. The building chronology is the center-piece and best fulfils the editor's claim for equality and simultaneity. On one page in July, for example, you find noted: the Love Parade of 750,000 people, the future of the American bases, the light sculptures on the cranes on Potsdamer Platz, and the redirection of the Spree river near the Reichstag. It may be hard to imagine how often these sober texts had to be revised, since the facts true today read differently one month later. The third section, at the end of the book, offers a list of the new buildings throughout Berlin, registering who built what and when, thus keeping ordinary curiosity about the city's transformations well nourished. *Martina Düttmann*

Wings of Desire: The Sky Above Berlin

Der Himmel über Berlin. Film book by Wim Wenders and Peter Handke, Filmstrips Road Movies

I can't find Potsdamer Platz!
No, I think it was here …
But that can't be. The Café Josti was on Potsdamer Platz …
I used to sit there in the afternoons, talking and drinking coffee, watching the people,
and before that I would smoke my cigar at Löhser & Wolff, the famous tobacco shop, right across from here.
No, Potsdamer Platz can't be here!
And I don't see anyone I could ask …
But I'm not giving up 'til I find Potsdamer Platz!

Is it ever cold! My hands were always warm. A good sign, actually. It crunches so under my feet.
I wonder what time it is?
The sun is already going down. In the West, well, of course.
I used to take the subway east whenever I wanted to go home. Bought a 10-card, saved a mark. The sun was at my back,
the Stern to the left. Pretty good, actually: a sun and a star.

Actually, Berlin means nothing to me … Havel, is that a river or a lake? I never quite got that. Back there, back there is
Wedding district, or what? In the East? Actually, the East is everywhere.

I couldn't say who I am.
I don't have the slightest notion of myself. I am someone without origin, without a country, I insist on it!
I'm here, I'm free, I could imagine anything, anything is possible. The moment I look up I become the world.
Now, in this place, this feeling of happiness I could keep forever.

… Then I'll buy a newspaper
and read it from the headlines
to the horoscope. On the first day
I'll just let myself be waited on.
If anyone wants anything from me, I'll send him
on to the next man. Whoever
trips over my outstretched legs
will excuse himself politely.
I'll let myself be jostled and I'll
jostle back. The head waiter
in the full restaurant
will find me a table right away. On the street
an official car will stop next to me,
and the mayor will let me ride
for a while …

I'll seem familiar to everyone, and suspicious to no one.

First it was yesterday, then it was a couple days ago, and then it was a month ago.
After that comes another year.
Before that comes another week.
And a year.

© Wim Wenders: Potsdamer Platz, taken from the roof of the Staatsbibliothek with a panoramic camera early 1996
© Filmstrips: Road Movies Filmproduktion, Berlin
"Der Himmel über Berlin," quotations from the film book by Wim Wenders and Peter Handke, Suhrkamp 1987

Site-seeing on Potsdamer Platz

... it's been proven, that the Potsdamer Platz,
as a named point upon this barren body earth,
in central Europe, set slightly to the east,
in the "P−9" quadrant on the map of Berlin,
served Albert Einstein in 1916 as an exact site specification,
comparing the relationship between the Platz
and the cloud floating overhead with his
"special and general theories of relativity,"
explaining and making the point generally understandable
that in a four dimensional time/space continuum
we are at home, where time plays a role equal to
length, width and depth ...

Dawning, grey morning and the visitors' bus
balances between cranes and bull dozers,
stops where it disturbs the least,
shoes sinking in grey-whitish marl,
please pull your pants up a bit,
I can give you my arm, now careful,
we have laid out beams and planks, making the way
more secure, no nails, only the
slightly too steep visitors' stairs, here is room,
one moment, for your cold feet
we have something warm in the tent, the Imperial Room
will glide over air cushions and Wim Wenders
will speak to you; because
the sky over Potsdamer Platz,
once only Einstein's cloud,
which glided, balled itself up, pulled apart, and floated away
became Wim Wender's skyscape over Berlin
as an undivided, reliable constant

Construction site, where nothing but the moment exists,
the instant record, once and forever, gone;
because never again will the artificial lakes be so large
as today on Potsdamer Platz, that one might heed maritime law,
never again will you see a mobile container
frozen temporarily on the surface of fresh concrete;
the white liquid over the submerged pipes
will glisten tomorrow in another place,
a bundle of steel bars, a bamboo garden,
here still visible, there covered by floor slabs,
the piles of sand toward the perimeter have long since been filled up.
The steel support studding, here criss-crossed, there upright,
is rammed into the earth the next morning.
The Y-supports in the light-colored sand,
as long as there is nothing to support,
border what looks to be a beach promenade.
Months later the silhouette of a city of offices
will tower along the Landwehr Canal.
If not now, than you will never comprehend
the facade sections with their complex structures,
the bent cogs upon which they hang,
separators for air flow, channeled backsides,
which later become those smooth, inaccessible,
reflecting surfaces on the facades,
the balancing act of the blue mobile cranes lasts only minutes,
soon moving on to another construction site,
which resembles the one we see now, as all construction sites
do resemble each other like circuses all seem the same.
Nuances of distinction lie merely in the height of cranes,
the depth of the lakes, the speed and amount of change,
yet the danger of crashing remains the same.

Careful of
Contractual confines
Changing utilization obligations
Comings-short of any sort
Of
Counteracting infiltration and metallic accumulation regulations
Capacities of tolerance
Cancelled codes
Contention about taxation and sampling
Of
Connivance of conclusive caring
Cost of insurance proceedings
Conveyors for water from ground and bilge
Of coincidental compatibility, cautious circumventions,
of cooling-off periods, counterfeits, corrigenda

And in between are those dark blue container basins,
swung around and carefully lowered,
collecting what remains of today,
which will tomorrow be sorted out as

Rubble
Dry sand
Wet sand, desiccated, solid, stored in mounds,
As glacial till, excavated dry,
As limnetic peat, calcareous mud,
As silt and sand,
As soil contaminated or suspected of contamination,
As waste, plastic, wood, reinforcing steel and all that,
Which accumulates through filtering and smashing the rubble,
"Yet the deliverer must show proof of its very nature."

Classifying movables and immovables
for wagon classes:
Building machines
Building cranes
Construction site container
Precast concrete parts
Rods in bundles
Insulation material
Facade components
Ventilation shafts
Plastic pipes
Diaphragm wall units
Shuttering panels
Stones in cranable bundles
Girders
Tubing
Cement

"Some 2.1 million tons of excavated material have been loaded onto trains at Gleisdreieck since 1993. Lined up, their combined length would equal 532 kilometers, or the distance between Potsdamer Platz and Dortmund. You could dump the material on a soccer field to a height of 365 meters, or load it onto four rows of freight trucks bumper to bumper stretching from Berlin to Madrid."

Material fractions strength grades separate collection transfer consistancy
Freight type classification risk transition power-quantity check-system
Construction site waste sorting plant bulk goods dump truck
Supplementary charge for specified delay intermediate buffer disposition fees settlement principles
Conflict management

"Framework of overall guidelines"

... attention is drawn to the fact, that ...
... additional need is to be reported immediately, if ...
... evidence must be produced in case ...
... is to announce, that ...
... the subsequent demand beyond closed contracts is only possible, if ...
... application forms are due at least a day in advance ...
... waiving of contractor's rights is limited to ...
... is binding in cases of disagreement ...
... is to be reported immediately ...
... is to be activated promptly ...
... it is advisable to procede gradually, according to the amount of interest in each case ...

Prices and costs are to be gathered from
Conditions will be listed
For utilization apply
A summary gives
Liability would
See
Revised drafts go into effect immediatly

Smoke colors, sulphury, chalky white,
Vapor blue, sand pale, evening sky red,
Pond colors below, signal colors above,
Yellow for nearly everything that moves,
Green visions,
Crusty shoes,
Rosy speeches

17

Diving manoeuvres at Potsdamer Platz
in the Daimler-Benz construction pit.
The excavation waters turn cloudy 50 cm under the surface.
The work day takes place at 17 meters down.
80 professional divers working in temporary lakes.
Erik is one.
His fixed point on this stiff body earth
is a floating pontoon
with a walkie-talkie, an oxygen supply, a signal line,
the second diver maintains contact from above,
and a third is there, in case of emergency.
With 2000 anchors the concrete sole holds
the groundwater uplift in check
17 meters under the earth's surface.
The anchors are installed first, then the 1.2 meter thick sole
out of steel fiber underwater concrete. This takes about 6 weeks.
The concrete is mixed with short steel fibers
5 cm long, 1 mm thick,
that make it tough, workable, and resistant.
The process is new, though the Egyptians,
says the inventor from Braunschweig,
somewhat reserved,
mixed their clay with straw for the same purpose.
The divers find their way only by touch,
a decompression chamber is ready for emergencies,
each single post withstands a tensile force of 150 tons,
equivalent to the weight of approx. 100 E-class Mercedes,
according to reports.

All photos from the debis site on Potsdamer Platz by Rudolf Schäfer, Berlin

Pile up, pressing, devoluminize,
Pull at, weigh down, slowly ease off,
Set down, measure out, carefully solve,
Flow, wash, rinse and coagulate,
Solidify, harden up, smooth out, darken,
Blacken

Optional, mandatory, indispensable
Delivered, established, expedient
Daily, compulsory, comprehensive, consistent
Smoothly, urgent, on-time
Additionally agreed, specially enforced
Partially applicable, delayed at a charge
Insured, taxed, temporarily stored
Legitimately claimed, falsely weighed
Punished properly

Literally:
"Surveillance of disposal procedures implies those additional services, which occur when a third party is involved in the control of the groundwater discharger by the groundwater manager. The unit price is computed monthly and per connection point, beginning with the set up of the connection until the start of it's dismantling."

or
"The relevant rules and contractual regulations, which influence the construction logistics, are requested to be compiled and updated, especially those concerning the dynamics of site management , including the flow of materials with regard to the storage, transport and handling capacities."

From: Baulog Manual Potsdamer Platz
Baulog remix by Martina Düttmann

2

The FriedrichstadtPassagen

It was once Berlin's premier address: Friedrichstrasse. If the hopes of the city and of those who invest here come true, it will become that again, with the FriedrichstadtPassagen as its centerpiece. The name and the project are not new. In 1987, the East German government began an ambitious construction project of the same name in the same place. Around the time the Wall fell, this massive Thing was finished in some places, and a ruin in others. It had caused both sidestreets — Taubenstrasse and Mohrenstrasse — to simply vanish. It sealed off the former Platz der Akademie and retreated a step from the Friedrichstrasse's profile, only to focus more attention on its precast concrete facade.

The only thing to do was demolish it and plan something new. All 22 competitors for the huge property, who in the autumn of 1990 took part in a complicated procurement procedure, had committed themselves to this. The Berlin city government selected 5 groups of developers, giving them three conditions. Each had to present three different architectural projects and vouch for an immediate realization of the proposal selected by an independent jury. They had to agree to maintain the present street grid, to respect the Berlin eaves height of 22 meters, and to stick to a maximum building height of 30 meters, which was achieved with staggered top stories. Furthermore, they had to include a north-south subterranean passageway parallel to Friedrichstrasse in their plans.

The developers offered many of the best and most prestigious names in architecture, from the United States, Japan, France, Germany, and Berlin. The architects Skidmore, Owings & Merrill had not one but two proposals, for different developers, one of them in an amazing alliance with Coop Himmelblau. It was tough going for the jury, which had reached the understanding it would award the property to three developers with three maximally divergent architects. The final selection produced a neighborhood by Ungers, Pei, and Nouvel. The Galeries Lafayette had long decided on Jean Nouvel, whose glass house quickly won. He came and went as victor.

The awards jury decided on April 18th 1991. The demolition of the East German FriedrichstadtPassagen began the following autumn. For years thereafter, Berliners had an imposing construction site with a "vue du chantier." The three prominent buildings have been basically finished since early 1996, but it was not until November that the FriedrichstadtPassagen opened to the public. So much for the common history.

In the following pages, the story of each of these three big city blocks will be told and illuminated: Jean Nouvel's kaleidoscopic department store, the Europeanized "Architecture of Joy" by the New York office of Pei, Cobb, Freed & Partners, and the rational aesthetics of the construction site and building by Oswald Mathias Ungers.

2.1

Architect	Jean Nouvel, Paris
Competition Manager	Barbara Salin
Project Manager	Laurence Daude
Construction Managers	Viviane Morteau, Judith Simon
Structural Design	Polónyi and Fink, Berlin
Facade Planning	IBS Schalm, Berlin/Munich
Developers	Galeries Lafayette, Roland Ernst
Clients	Dresdner Bank
	Roland Ernst
	SGE Société Générale d'Entreprise
	CBC Compagnie Générale de Batiment et de Construction

Kaye Geipel
The FriedrichstadtPassagen – Quartier 207
The Department Store Kaleidoscope of the Galeries Lafayette

Ever since the grand opening of the Galeries Lafayette on February 29th 1996, the glass block in Friedrichstrasse has drawn a profusion of comments. On the one hand, there is the enthusiasm about the futuristic architecture, about the feeling of pioneering times this building, like no other, now symbolizes. There is also the praise for the entrepeneur's courage, being the first to open here. But these sentiments are mixed with laments about the seeming ease with which the project ignored normal budget restraints; that it boasts a double-layered all-glass facade, which may itself be ventilated and is equipped with sun-protection between layers, yet all this still does not lead to a conclusive energy concept for the entire building. The voices measuring Nouvel's building against the standards set by the other new office and commercial buildings in the Friedrichstrasse forget that the department store is the heart of this block. This type of inner-city department store has been stuck in a profound crisis for years. In the mind of the French entrepeneur, only a radical rethinking seemed to guarantee a reversal of the trend.

So the Galeries Lafayette wagered solely and consciously on seducing through architecture. In any case, this seems the only explanation for the owner's willingness to adopt the design concept, which seemed to contradict every aspect of construction logic. The design's basic idea, of lighting the department store's central atrium through a truncated cone, which at its upper tip in the roof measures only a few meters in diameter, seemed

just as preposterous as the concept of lighting the surrounding offices with fifteen smaller cones turned on their heads, so that as one descends from story to story the glass-roofed courts grow narrower.

But the arguments for conceding to such light-technical idiosyncrasies lie at a completely different level. The cones piercing the department store from above and below create large areas which bisect the space, transforming it into a kaleidoscope, by reflection, refraction, and coloration. They lure and grip the visitors, giving them a dazzling display and drawing them in toward the center. The department store's strategy is to seduce through architecture, through an architecture which retreats, removes itself, dissolves in pictures, and pushes the boundaries of the immaterial and the virtual.

Yet the store's entrance is rather nondescript. One reaches it almost without noticing, under a slim aluminum roof lightly turned upwards, which accompanies the pedestrian all the way on his walk around the building. Compared with the other new buildings along Friedrichstrasse, Nouvel's building has surely found the softest transition from the street to the interior. On the ground floor there is a whole phalanx of concentrically-ordered revolving doors, so that one needs only to leave the curb to be transported to the building's center. Had the architect been able to push through his original concept, then already here at the periphery there would have been deep cuts downward,

To create the sense of irritation within the space, the glass panels are printed or coated with translucent or reflective material

*Photos:
Philippe Ruault*

a vertical interlocking of spaces, and thus an irritation for the visitors the moment they enter the building. Now the visitors hesitate. The Lafayette standard furnishings of light wood and the colorful jumble of goods for sale stand in their path, as well as their line of vision. But after only a few steps — the building's interior is surprisingly small — visitors reach the two huge, reflective, glass cones converging at their bases in the middle of the building. They turn the ground floor into the irridescent crux of this temple of consumerism. The larger cone rises past the shopping and office floors to the roof, up to the blue fixed star of a narrow, daylight-bathed opening. The smaller cone pierces through the French gourmet market and touches the basement with its tip.

These two cones are the building's actual raison d'être.

The initial impression is truly amazing, because the building's actual function fades completely away. Anyone grown accustomed to the numerous colors and tricks of light might say the grandiose space displays the strolling shoppers better than the wares for sale. The whole production allows visitors to appear in a number of guises: as figures or shadows behind plates or as anonymous doubles, because one finds one's image and that of others on the cone's reflective surfaces again and again. The cone grows smaller with each floor, and everywhere, new searchers and observers appear, reflecting themselves and simultaneously looking down on those streaming in. The whole set-design

structurally resembles Peter Handke's legendary Insulting of the Audience. The more spectators who come, the more interesting the play becomes, although in the depth of the performance the viewer sees only his or her own reflection.

No doubt, in its spatial disposition, Nouvel's cone has learned from both interactive theater and museum concepts of the 1980s, which incorporate visitors as "actors." If one looks at the visitors in the Galeries Lafayette and how, with their elbows resting on the black balustrade, they watch themselves while watching others, thus forming part of the spectacle on display, one is reminded of Franco Purini's Teatro scientifico in Rome, or of the presentations in the Museum of Technology at the Porte de la Villette in Paris.

Such parallelism between concepts of department store, theater, and museum hardly comes as a surprise. Today, marketing specialists from department stores freely admit they adapt systems of conveyance from contemporary culture. Small productions take place in new atria, pianists play, champagne is served, all in artificial consumer worlds; from French bistro streets to underground basements, various kinds of public life are simulated. All these concepts make use of an illusion once discovered by the Surrealists: that one can switch directly from reality to the realm of dreams and wishes, and thereby in this "waking dream" remain a protagonist.

However, anyone who has spent time in the mirrored game house of the Galeries Lafayette

knows Nouvel's concept is more detached and sarcastic, perhaps more honest as well. While department store and galeria concepts are there to maintain the illusion of active participation, Nouvel's conditions have been dispassionately adjusted to a purely optical participation. In Nouvel's panopticon, as on the TV screen, one becomes the spectator of an exciting, moving, but in its self-organization, unalterable world behind thick glass. The flashing lights, the shadows without depth, the tempting reflexes are nothing more than an unusually attractive foreground for the wares draped further back. A glance upwards, past the shopfloors to the office space overhead, best reveals the full import of this two-dimensional public. In a soundless participation, all are visually present in the forty-meter-high air-space without being required to encounter or communicate with each other.

Such a space contradicts, to a certain extent, Nouvel's own and repeatedly invoked principle of being ephemeral, immaterial, and permanently in a state of flux, but this obvious inconsequence is quite secondary. Nouvel redirects, as it were, the development of the virtual facade back to its point of departure, to the simple idea of capturing the human disorientation in electronic space within an adequate architectural framework. Yet the architectural means by which he achieves these effects are surprisingly simple, if one disregards the expensive "hardware" and the large-scale construction, pushing the limits of engineering,

The double-layered glass facade has a structure thickness of 22 cm and is ventilated naturally floor by floor

Photos:
Lukas Roth (2),
Philippe Ruault (3)

with its inclined pillars and its inner soundproof glass facade. He works with seriographically coated patterns or foils which are then attached to the glass. The combination of layers of printed and reflective glass, of holography and complete transparency, produces the iridescent impression.

The inclined plates in the atrium, leaning forward like an observation post, also contribute to the spatial disorientation. One of the house's irritating experiences is, in the upper floors of the store, to lean over into the cone so as to be able to look all the way down. One touches the twenty-millimeter-thick insulating glass sooner with one's foot than with the upper body, and in doing so easily loses balance. Only the strong dark railing offers a measure of security.

The architect's selection of materials is rigorous. Besides various glass-forms, he prefers to use only stainless steel. The palette of colors is similarly narrow, black and grey dominate. Colorlessness or the practically immaterial nature of a reflective surface are, for him, just like glass. Outside, in bright sunlight, the gently curved, all-glass facade almost looks black. Jean Nouvel does not accept any photographs that show his glass facade as a reflective wall. Reflection would eliminate the building's transparency, the glass would become opaque, solid, and the no-longer immaterial house would become banal.

"Glass is transparency" is his motto. But Jean Nouvel's transparency is more than a generation removed from the dogma of modernism, which

interpreted transparency as permeability, openness from all sides, and rejection of hierarchy. Transparency for Jean Nouvel is abstraction. With his buildings he wants to provoke a way of perception which fabricates ideal structures; or in reverse, he creates structures which approach as near as possible the abstract concept of those structures. For Jean Nouvel, who always dresses in black and yet looks like a Fassbinder character, transparency is a form of sensuality which grows more effective the more it removes itself, an erotica based in the world of thoughts.

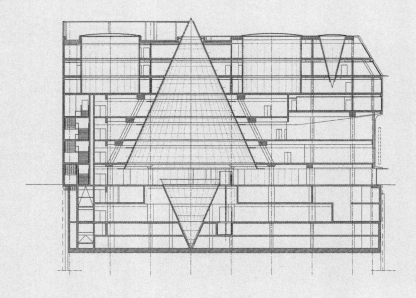

Subbasement
(passageway),
ground floor and section
1:750.
The Friedrichstrasse
entrance is on the right.
The bottom is north

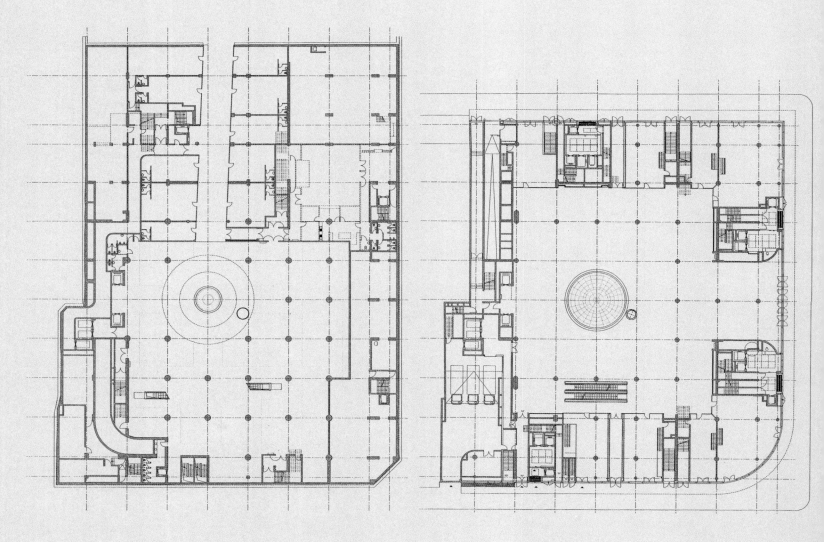

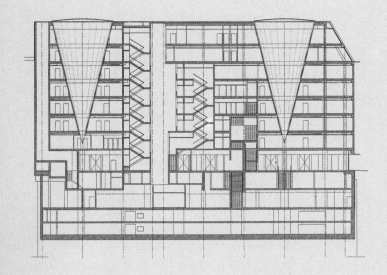

3rd floor,
top floor (offices),
and section
1:750

5 m   10 m

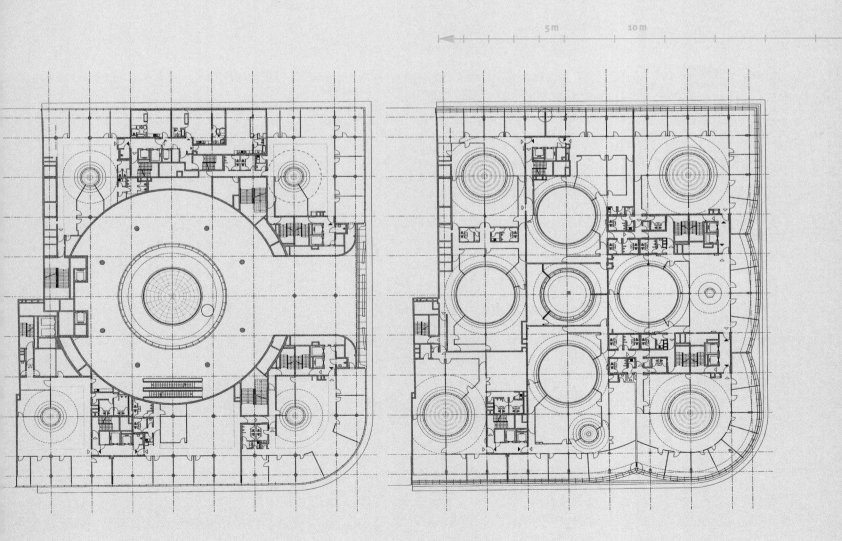

2.2

Architects	Pei, Cobb, Freed & Partners, New York
	Henry N. Cobb
	George H. Miller
Project Managers	Theodore J. Musho
	Brian P. McNally
	Georg Jell
Contact Architect	Hein & Partner, Berlin
Structural Design	Polónyi und Partner, Berlin
Curtain wall	Fritz Sulzer
Client	Jagdfeld FriedrichstadtPassagen
	Quartier 206 Vermögens-
	verwaltungs KG Berlin

Martina Düttmann
The FriedrichstadtPassagen – Quartier 206

Mozart at Place Voltaire

Dear Morris Lapidus, I've just been reading in the Architectural Record about another late honor to your person and your architecture. In Berlin, going down Friedrichstrasse, there is a house along the way, an American house, by Pei, Cobb, Freed & Partner, which seemed to me an homage to your "Architecture of Joy." At least that's how I see it, knowing you as well as I do.

It was finished a short while ago and has, until now (now being September), only once been open to the public. As part of the summer festival called "Berlin Site-Seeing," a small ensemble performed here. They played Mozart's musical comedy "Bastien and Bastienne," which he based on an intermezzo by the name of "Le devin du village," which basically means "the village fortune-teller," and was written and scored in 1752 by none other than Jean-Jacques Rousseau. It was such a success that it was revived in 1753 and performed in the Comédie Italienne under the title "Les amours de Bastien et Bastienne," as a parody in which the arcadian characters give way to boorish ones; only to be translated for Mozart by a Mr. Weiskern and used for the former's musical delicacy, which, by the way, then premiered in 1768 in the garden house of Dr. Friedrich Anton Mesmer, yes, that mesmerism-magician.

This little opera was staged on the marble floor—almost entirely modelled after the floor in the church of San Marco—which adorns the playful foyer of the new, and somehow unusual office building "Quartier 206" on Friedrichstrasse. The

foyer is known as Place Voltaire because Voltaire once lived in the area for a short while. In any event, everyone there expected to see the shephards play transformed back into its arcadian setting by the sophisticated surroundings. Which is why all were dumbfounded to see a Bastienne singing of her little sheep while wearing glasses and tennis socks and holding a college folder, riding up and down the new escalator. The production could have, with equal justification, made use of the marble spiral staircase just off to the side, which is a complete and utter descendant of your hotel staircase in Fontainebleau. It could have also used the small, half-oval platform on the mezzanine, which swings out like a theater balcony awaiting the entrance of the guest or customer, as you have done a thousand times in your hotels and shops. But no, they decided against all expectations in favor of an American college atmosphere and staged it within a space that is bursting with references to European history and its relaxed American adaptations.

In this long description of that short evening at the opera, you might be wondering why nothing has yet been said about the house itself. On the contrary, the important points have almost all been covered. The house is a grand, amazing, confusing game. I can begin anywhere, but I always come back to the same thing.

Naturally, the facade is an allusion to the 1920s, especially to the bands of light on department store facades. They were new at the time, but designed as a flat, integral part of the wall, because it was

precisely the depth of the stucco walls they wanted to get rid of back then. But here, depth is expressly desired. The facade has at least three layers which cannot definitely be considered separate from each other; in fact, quite the opposite is true. Initially, the ceilings of each floor appear to push their way outward, supporting the meandering alcoves, then the ceilings recede and the alcoves float freely, jutting through the facade from their interiors. Then the alcoves fill out into spearheaded balconies at the top. Toward the middle level, small, illuminated platforms protrude occasionally, and it is difficult to discern their origin and their purpose. At night I am thankful for the bright bands of light which, in contrast to the twenties, extend horizontally and vertically, crossing over one another. They remain mostly plane with the frontmost layer of the facade, except at the entrances, where they recede diagonally inward.

The house exhibits that wonderfully naive, American approach to history, as you have demonstrated so well (you will surely forgive me for using the term naive). Because only an American architect is capable of transforming a historical citation into a collection of stories, into dreams, as you always pointed out, of "happiness and delight," into an architecture of seduction, of illusion.

Let us go inside. A luxurious entrance, naturally with views, a necessity today. The stately staircase, steep and tall (this would be impossible in your buildings), seems to me like an escalator. Yet I enjoy the amazement. The balustrade on the

Friedrichstrasse entrance. The number of the city block becomes a signature of the house: 206 appears over the entrance and as ornament in the floor pattern

Place Voltaire
à l'Americaine:
folded skylight
over the foyer,
straight escalator
next to a baroque
spiral staircase,
San Marco marble
floor, pyramidal-
shaped light
fixtures, dots of
light

*All photos:
Jörn Vanhöfen,
Agentur Ostkreuz*

ground floor provides a view out over the foyer
with its San Marco marble. From there you can take
either the escalator or the winding baroque staircase down into the foyer. The balustrade is lens-
shaped, a very popular form these days, but it
doesn't appear more than once. Overhead, the
glass roof is raised over an eight-pointed star,
which is extended lengthwise and, like an exquisite hotel napkin, folded so as to stand up in the
air. The shape of the inner court is neither star-
nor lens-shaped, but a highly original geometric
invention made out of a rectangle, whose long
sides contain a central outward bulge, while the
short sides are slightly bowed, each with one
corner pushed inward. It is such an extraordinary
outline that the architect, or the client, or the lady
of the house deemed it a melody of recognition for
the interior. It reappears in the profile on the handrails and in the cross-section of the casings for the
ceiling lights in the offices. The handrail is a successful transformation and feels good; but the
profile of the light casings seems excessive; first
because it is not readily evident (unless one's
attention is expressly called to it), and second, it
does not make the lamps any better.

But this house is about storytelling, the lights
tell stories about the handrails and these in turn
tell stories about the unique shape of the atrium.
Yet in this regard, you Morris, remain, with your
beanpoles and woggles and cheeseholes, the more
original, the more practiced, the more expressive
storyteller.

Contradictory, once again, but somehow very pleas-
ing are the silent rows of facade lining the court.
In the floor plan, there are rows of simple spaces
for rent. Separating the offices facing the street
from those facing the courtyard is a hallway, which
runs all the way around the courtyard. I do not
know which side I would prefer, because the views
of Friedrichstrasse and of the Gendarmenmarkt,
the higher the office, grow ever more exciting,
more Berlin, more urbane, one would never want
to work anywhere else. Yet, the view inward to the
courtyard has something convincingly peaceful,
contemplative, despite the glass hotel napkin in
the middle.

As for the long, curving middle halls, how
well they remind me of your tricks: your inner hall
enlivened with sinewy strips in black and white or
with wave-like and light-spotted sawtooth ceilings. Here the solution is a hierarchy of doors
corresponding to a hierarchy of rooms; you enter
an important space through a door with intricate
woodwork inlaid with dark marble, a less important space through one with only intricate woodwork. A simple space has a simple frame.

Kindly follow me once again downward, to the
foyer with its Venetian floor, with its rows of pyra-
mid-shaped lights along the walkways, the glass
ceiling, and the shop entrances, with their dark,
circular ventilation exhausts which, though added
later, do not disturb in the least, because of the
degree of extravagance, diversity, and festivity of
the decor.

This foyer distinguishes itself extremely from its more severe neighbors (on the main subbasement level all three neighboring buildings are connected by a passageway) through a marketplace atmosphere and a playful lightness, which a few black holes above the encircling bands of light cannot change. The darkly tinted glass of the shop windows, the vertical, dark strips to the right and left of recessed entrances into which, of course, the marble strips extend, are quite obviously a stage-directed luxury, a gold-brick luxury, and the house freely admits it.

If I could leaf through the floor plans with you, even you, who thinks so highly of play, would follow the dance-steps of the pillars astonished. One row of pillars traces the lens-shaped glass roof — so far so good — but then there are a couple of additional pillars which nobody, aside from the structural analyst, knows anything about. And in general, when one looks at the various floor plans, the layout is dotted and dabbed with pillars, and it is not possible to say, with any precision, where they draw their necessity and their picturesque arrangement. But in this confusion of forms and inventions, of foldings and bendings, of quotes and self-quotes — what is the real point? Perhaps the pillars follow a musical rhythm, to which the structural engineer capriciously surrendered.

What I actually wanted to say is this: You, Morris, were the first, who, having really experienced European architectural history from the originals in a drafting course, sketched, tamed, Americanized and cinematically refined Europe for those clients who ordered baroque ambiance and just a little more, who wanted to see the Loire chateaux transplanted to America, but a bit more luxurious if you please, who wished for glamor and glitz, but with European roots. What was that title of your recent autobiography, "Too Much Is Never Enough?" Exactly. Today, with you long acknowledged as the source of it all, a new kind of luxury is in demand, which can no longer be fully satisfied by the ingenuity of imitation. In the late 1990s we have come full circle: the marble floor at the Place Voltaire, drawn by the hand of New York architects, equals the original from the church on the Piazza San Marco.

With many warm regards from Berlin,
Yours Martina

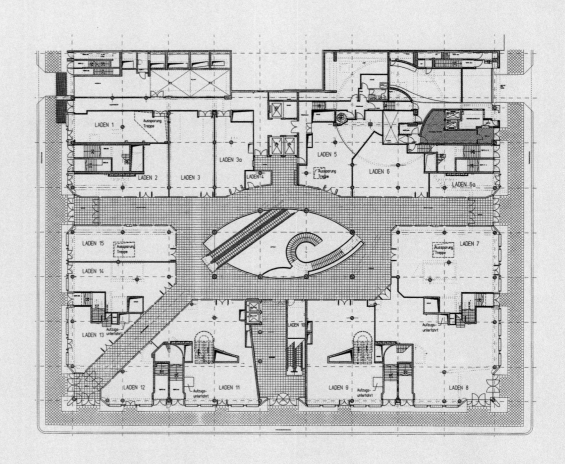

**Ground floor and
subbasement
(shopping area)
1 : 750. The
Friedrichstrasse
entrance is toward
the bottom, north
is to the left**

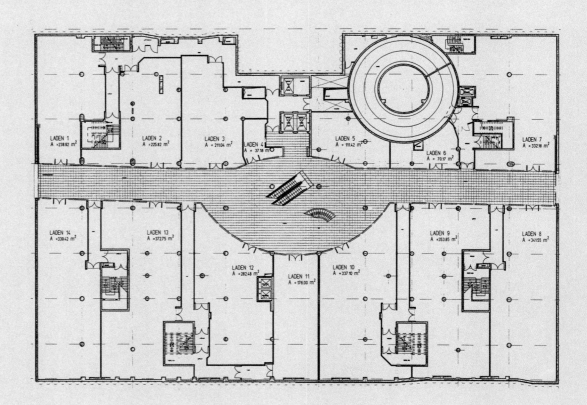

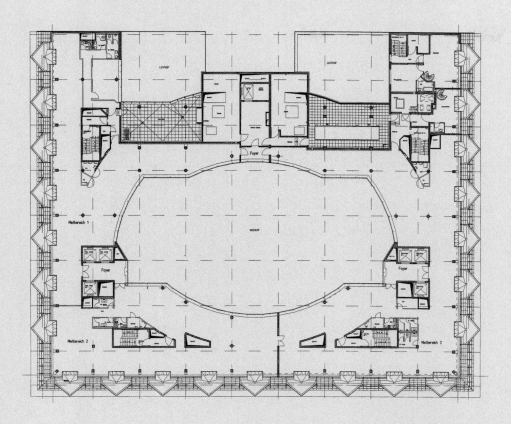

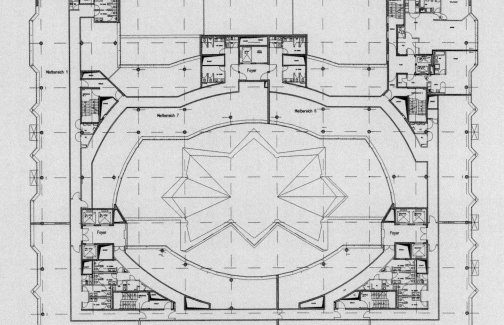

4th floor, 8th floor.
Flexible office
space (apartments
in the southeast
corner) 1:750

2.3

Architect	O.M. Ungers & Partner, Berlin
	Oswald Mathias Ungers
Project Managers	Sebastian Klatt
	Karl Heinz Winkens
Structural Design	IPP Köln, Polónyi/Styn
Project Coordination	Steiner Infratec GmbH
Client	TishmanSpeyer Properties
	Deutschland GmbH, Berlin

Paula Winter
The FriedrichstadtPassagen – Quartier 205
The Rational Aesthetic of Building Site and Structure

Lot number 3 and the final component of the Friedrichstadtpassagen is Quartier 205 by Oswald Mathias Ungers. Unlike its neighbors, the building occupies an entire city block of its own, it extends from Friedrichstrasse to the Gendarmenmarkt. It could as easily define itself as the neighbor of the Schauspielhaus by Schinkel on the Gendarmenmarkt, or as street-front architecture along Mohrenstrasse and Taubenstrasse, or as the third piece of the FriedrichstadtPassagen. In fact, the solipsistic volume dissolves the bonds tying it to its neighborhood. It sets itself apart by virtue of the geometry it establishes for itself, and devotes itself to a game of numbers, to the magic of the square.

Two atria penetrate the deep block's interior; one is roofed in glass, the other, paved and furnished with greenery. A system of paths measuring 6 meters in width traverses the building at ground level. The glazed atrium is positioned at their point of intersection, from which two steep escalators lead to the level of the FriedrichstadtPassagen below. 17,000 sq.m of retail floor area comprises the ground floor (with overflow area on the floor above) and the frontage along the Friedrichstadt-Passagen in the subbasement. 32,000 sq.m of flexible office space occupies every story but the uppermost. The building's circulation is subservient to the overall geometry: central corridors connect the six cores, ring corridors encircle them. 36 apartments occupying a total of 2,800 sq.m are located in the ninth top story.

The architect's first decision, the absolute precondition to his architectural language is the square grid. The site's dimensions, 109.60 x 76.61 meters, had to be binding for the design. The planning grid therefore measures 1.51 meters instead of the usual 1.50 meters. From this basic subdivision, a structural grid of 7.55 meters and a joint grid of 30.2 cm are derived; these remain consistent in the vertical and horizontal throughout the entire building. The fenestration grid which relentlessly traverses the facade seems independent of the structural grid. By necessity, the column grid of 6.04 meters in the street arcade and in the atria is subordinated to the fenestration grid.

These two differing systems of measure—the structural and the fenestration grids—overlap only in the basic 1.51 meters module. Even the column grid on the office floors deviates from the structural grid, if symmetrically.

The grid which is visible on the exterior demands a number of clever tricks to transfer the loads from above through the office and retail floors to the parking garage below. Heavily-reinforced hammerhead columns and spur walls, which conjoin or stiffen bearing columns, are responsible for the segue between the two different grids.

The design is based upon a conceptual part of a central building surrounded by six perimeter buildings. The eight-story high, light-toned block which houses the two atria is thus the core building, around which the six-story, darkly-clad

perimeter block buildings are grouped. With this organization, the architect intended to underline the reference he makes to the site's former parcel structure. The individual buildings are separated by deep indentations in the facade, which recede to the plane of the core building's facade. A pedestrian should be able to recognize this subdivision of the ensemble by virtue of the massive porte-cochères over the cavernous entranceways.

Nonetheless, the pedestrian would read the building differently, despite its differentiated coloration and deep indentations. The homogeneous facade cladding is stronger. Its almost immaterial precision, its unmodulated jointing, its relentless square gridding, transport the building to the realm of the abstract. This effect is amplified by the numerical games played in the facade subdivisions, which insinuate the building's self-referentiality. The viewers sense this. If one were to try to quantify the effect in calculations, one would establish the following: the 25 bays on the short side (or 40 on the long side) are subdivided into 10 fenestration bays per perimeter building plus 5 fenestration bays per indentation. The core building towers above the surrounding buildings. It is recessed on all sides, leaving mid-sections of 10 bays each. A series of axes or centers play a game of their own: the indentations are centered between the perimeter buildings, the next level of volumes are centered on them—no, wait, that cannot be, and in fact, it isn't exactly so. The next-higher volumes are, in accordance with

symmetry, shifted $2\,^1/_2$ bays from the corners, and the 10 bays spanning the mid-section comprise 9 full and 2 half bays.

It is almost a relief to see that the building rebels against its own rules at this point: for since its completion, since the last remnants of construction were cleared away from its base, the building begs the question whether it is to be perceived as architecture or as an intellectual construct, which threatens to disappear as soon as the gaze moves away from it. Moreover, it is precisely its own self-referentiality in the surrounding historical context that is so successful; accentuating the Schauspiel-haus or the Deutscher Dom like never before, depending on the perspective.

In order to alleviate any doubts, the entire building process will be recapitulated on these pages—but also in order to unveil many of the building's secrets which the virtual (and, in the Berlin tradition, stony) facade belies. And because this construction site was the clearest and most impressive around Friedrichstrasse. And, finally, because the construction process was, fortuitously, documented completely in photographs.

August 6, 1993

Excavated site, view towards Friedrichstrasse. Site area: 8,396.46 sq.m. A portion of the 1 meter deep sole has been poured. To the right, the primary waste water main in Taubenstrasse, beneath which the garage ramp and the entry ramp to Block 206 must be inserted. Parallel to Friedrichstrasse in the shuttering is the 110 kv electrical main for Berlin-Mitte

December 14, 1993

Floorslab above parking level. Beginning of the ramps (in and out separated) to the underground garages at −10.75 and −13.45 meters. The garages of Blocks 205, 206 and 207 are connected. The building is a reinforced concrete frame with six cores as stiffening

Building Diary

April 5, 1994

Construction site at street level. The ramps, the two atria and the six circulation cores are visible

May 31, 1994

The construction rises above street level. The indentations, which differentiate core building from perimeter buildings, become visible

July 13, 1994

Various stages of construction in the individual buildings

September 6, 1994

The small step from rough construction to finished building is accomplished with the mounting of the facade panel elements

January 31, 1995

Basic volume with curtain wall facade completed. Final stages of work on the roof structures with technical spaces. Grounding work in Charlottenstrasse

Construction of the Sole

The caterpillar belt indicates the depth of the excavations. In the background, the waste water main. Sole construction in 15 meters depth. The entire excavated area was enmured at a height of −2.00 meters to that of −45.00 by a perimeter diaphragm wall of waterproof steel sheet pile, which was used as lost shuttering. The building's foundation is a 1 meter thick sole made from water-impenetrable concrete

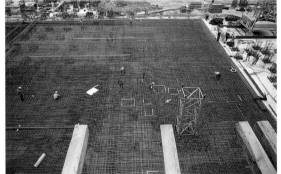

The Beauty of Bending Steel

Grid transition/column transfer:
Floor slab between ground and first floor. Reinforcing baskets for the hammerhead columns with the vertical reinforcement bars for the rows of columns in the office floors

All photos of construction site: Peter Zolcsak

Shuttering for the heavily-reinforced hammerhead columns

Detail of the reinforcing for a hammerhead column

Hammerhead column with shuttering removed

The facade cladding comprises a self-bearing curtain wall gridded in 3.02 x 3.30 meters units. The joints between panel elements, which measure the same as the joints between the stone elements incorporated into the panel, are practically invisible, and the dark gray coated aluminum windows incorporate themselves into the mesh of the facade by virtue of the artificially (and painstakingly) added transverse chamfers. All windows are operable. Roof terraces above 6th story

The dark sand-colored stone which characterizes the six individual buildings is French sandstone from the Val de Nod; the lighter-colored stone cladding core and atria is German Jura marble from the Altmühl valley. In the retail area, the matte tone of bronze building elements is the third color introduced

Photos: Stefan Müller

Facade Construction, Colors, Finishes

The core walls (concrete or masonry) are lavishly smoothed and varnished or plastered with stucco lustro. The 30 cm high base is clad in natural stone. The corridor walls (fire coded) and the partition walls (gypsum board) in office and commercial spaces are painted. The 15 cm baseboard is made of wood and set off using a reveal

All floors in the core area are natural stone in a mortar bed. The offices have raised floors, the retail areas screed, to be finished by the tenant. In the corridors, wooden doors with glass openings; otherwise, solid door frames in dark stained beechwood with flat saddles were used

45

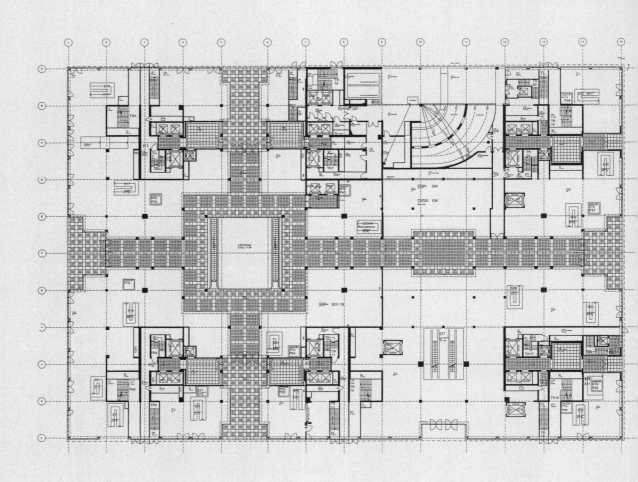

Ground floor, subbasement (shopping area) 1:750.
The Friedrichstrasse entrance is to the left, north is toward the top

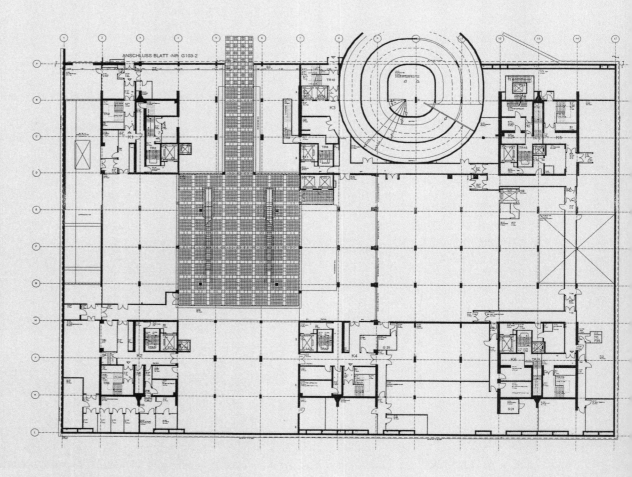

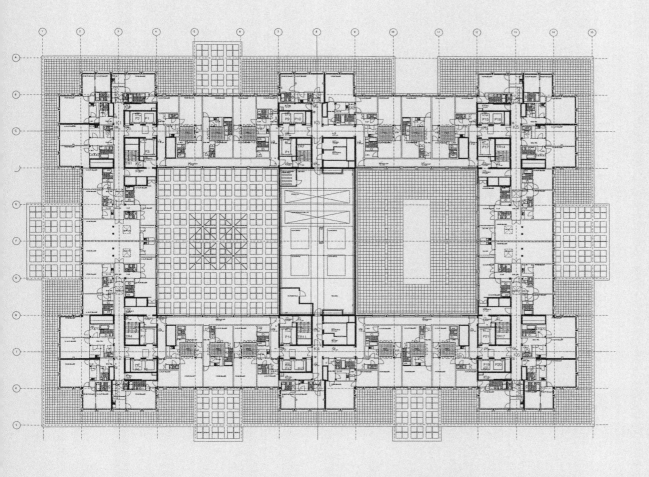

5 m   10 m

3rd floor (offices),
9th floor (apartments)
1:750

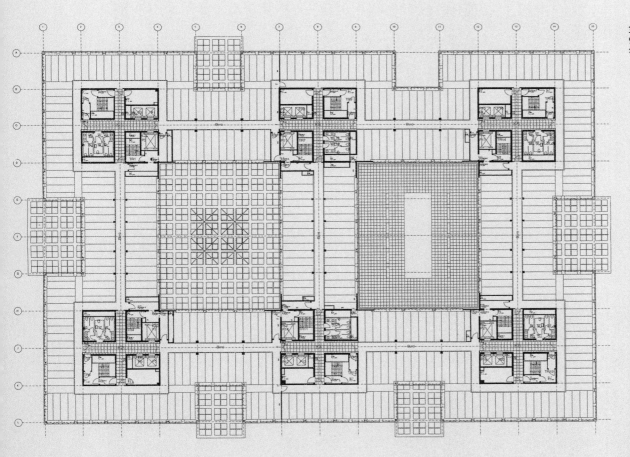

Philipp Moritz Reiser
New Buildings around the Gendarmenmarkt and Friedrichstrasse

A quick inventory along Friedrichstrasse, from south to north, from Kreuzberg to Mitte. It's not very far, and the pedestrian notes that the street frontages are almost complete and the building facades all more or less finished and aligned obediently with the city ground plan. Only the roof edges tower a little here and there above the midtown silhouette, and some of them still have tarps hanging from them. It's just that the bases of the buildings, their supports, arcades, the shop fronts, the entrances — finally all that which will flatter the public, spoil them, cover them in light and entice them inside — are mostly all still covered up or else caked in mud. Yet the impressions along the way and the findings from the map clearly demonstrate that the city is replenishing its center and reaching completion.

Hardly a year ago that book of perfect computer simulations was released, "Berlin — Visionen werden Wirklichkeit" ("Berlin — Visions Becoming Reality"), which claimed to offer a true-to-reality look at the future city skyline. Rightly so it did. If it weren't for the mud, pedestrians wouldn't be able to distinguish the real buildings from their simulated images. Fully aware of this, the building clients therefore only ever offer the simulations instead of the desired photographs. The similarity is baffling, as is the speed with which the images were transformed to stone. The stones competing for attention in the facades are: Kirchheimer shell limestone, Westenzeller sandstone, Roman travertine and varieties of granite, Bianco Castello, Verde Savanna or Ebony Black, bushhammered, ground, and polished. The buildings themselves and their floor plans do not compete with each other. They keep, sometimes more, sometimes less, to that "monotony without irony," as the well known newspaper Frankfurter Allgemeine Zeitung wrote. Therefore the floor plans here remain minute (scale 1 : 1000), too small to deserve any attention. The tiny signatures reveal only when and where the parcels of land, as determined by the city's "block division concept," were matched with various architects and how large or small the commissions really were.

The pedestrian tells himself, "If I observe properly, then it's not architecture I see, but rather a filled in city plan, urban design on a scale of 1 : 1. It impresses me against my will, as long as I alter my perspective and start looking for city blocks instead of architecture." The buildings are very closely related. All of them of the same height, not one stands out because of its details, and all of them are finished in expensive stone.

"By reducing its form, I am attempting to emphasize the individuality of the building within its historical surroundings, and at the same time to incorporate it into the context of the new buildings now being constructed," said one of the architects about his building, but he could have said it about any of the buildings around.

© SenBauWohnVerk / GrafikBüro Adler & Schmidt

3.13 Hotel Metropol/Maritim proArte
Architect: Holger Nettbaum

3.12 Haus Dussmann
Architect: Miroslav Volf

3.15 Office building
Deutscher Bundestag
Unter den Linden
Architect: Alexander Kolbe

3.11 Haus Pietzsch
Architect: Jürgen Sawade

3.14 Office building
Deutscher Bundestag
Wilhelmstrasse
Architect:
Gehrmann Consult

3.10 Lindencorso
Architect: Christoph Mäckler

3.9 Hofgarten at Gendarmenmarkt
Architects: Josef Paul Kleihues, Jürgen Sawade,
Max Dudler, Hans Kollhoff
2.1 Quartier 207 Galeries Lafayette
Architect: Jean Nouvel
2.2 Quartier 206
Architects: Pei, Cobb, Freed & Partners
2.3 Quartier 205
Architect: O. M. Ungers

3.8 Deutscher Dom at Gendarmenmarkt
Architect: Jürgen Pleuser
3.7 Office building (conversion)
with Jugendstil facade
Architect: Regina Schuh
3.6 Carré at Gendarmenmarkt
Architects: Josef Paul Kleihues,
Max Dudler, Hilmer & Sattler

3.5 Kontorhaus Mitte
Architects:
Josef Paul Kleihues, Theo Brenner,
Walter Stepp, V. M. Lampugnani

3.3 Atrium
Friedrichstrasse/
Leipziger Strasse
Architects: von Gerkan,
Marg und Partner

3.4 Corner office building
Leipziger Strasse/
Charlottenstrasse
Architect: Christoph Kohlbecker

3.2 Triangle
Architect: Josef Paul Kleihues

3.1 Checkpoint Arcades
Architect: Josef Paul Kleihues

3.1

Checkpoint Arcades
Architect	Josef Paul Kleihues, Berlin
Clients	GSW Gemeinnützige Siedlungs- und Wohnungsbaugesellschaft mbH, Berlin
	KapHag Unternehmensgruppe, Berlin
	Württembergische Hypothekenbank, Stuttgart
Address	Friedrichstrasse 45–46
	Zimmerstrasse 20–25
	Charlottenstrasse 81 (Kreuzberg)
Facade	Green glazed terra cotta tiling

Checkpoint Arcades

It is an ideal building site for an architect, the entire block of Zimmerstrasse including both corner properties. The resulting block thus acquires a unique form, with ship-shape structures at both corners, jutting out of the otherwise calm street-side facade. Stairwells are contained within, and conference rooms are placed behind the glass-fronts. The seven story building (plus four underground floors) presents itself as one of those effective multi-use complexes: shops on the ground floor, offices on the five stories above and apartments on the seventh floor. The room depth is 5.95 meters; a grid of 0.90 meter and 1.80 meter makes the floor space divisible (raised flooring) into office units of 171 and 527 sq. m.

Photos of the streeets, blocks, buildings (40) and facades (10): Erika Barahona Ede Photos of facades: Christian Gahl (6), Andreas Löhlein (3)

Typical floor plan for office levels
1:1000

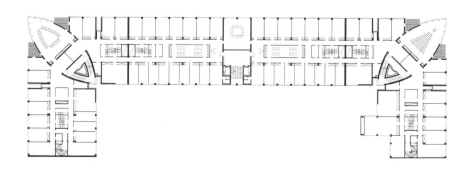

3.2

Triangle
Architect   Josef Paul Kleihues, Berlin
Client   TCHA-Grundstücke Berlin GbR Berlin
Address   Friedrichstrasse 204
Facade   Bianco Castello Granite, Portugal

Triangle

The property could be considered a remnant within
the orthogonal order of the Friedrichstadt district
which was bisected by the former customs wall.
This is what lends the building its charm. The
design has kept to the historical alignment, while
totally exploiting the regulation eaves height of
22 meters, topping off the building with residential
space, which is recessed and includes roof decks.
The architect's ambition was to develop a design
grid which could convert the odd-angled shape of
the property into a right triangle. One major advantage of the building could be its small dimensions
— it contains only 4 shops, 6 apartments, and
94 offices of limited size (20 – 50 sq. m).

**Planning grid, typical
floor plans for office
levels 1:1000**

Atrium Friedrichstrasse
Architects   von Gerkan, Marg und Partner, Aachen
Client   Grundstücks KG Kullmann & Co Quartier
              203 Berlin
Address   Corner of Friedrichstrasse/Leipziger Strasse
Facade   Kirchheimer shell limestone

Atrium

The name of the building characterizes its interior.
Lying parallel to Leipziger Strasse, it offers visitors
and occupants alike a 45 meter long hall, which
extends through the whole building and is covered
with a glass roof. The mezzanine level within the
hall serves as the main access floor. Two-story high
arcades run along Leipziger and Friedrichstrasse.
There is also a second glass-roofed atrium in the
section facing Kronenstrasse. The atria at once
provide the luminosity for the offices, which run
along central hallways (8.50 meter column grid,
1.50 meter planning grid). Room for apartments
(two per floor) is located in the Kronenstrasse
section. They are laid out (south/north, south/
west) toward the open courtyard between the new
building and the old corner building at Friedrichstrasse and Kronenstrasse.

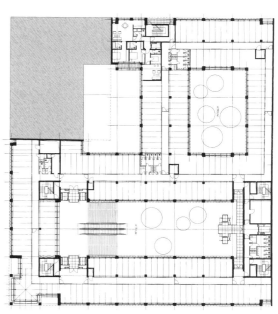

**Typical floor plan with
planning grid for office
levels 1:1000**

3.4

	Office and commercial building
Architect	Christoph Kohlbecker, Gaggenau
Client	HEFTER KG, Frankfurt am Main
Address	Leipziger Strasse 96/Charlottenstrasse 66
Facade	Westenzeller sandstone, ground

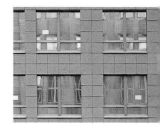

Corner Building at Leipziger and Charlottenstrasse

The same is true here as with the neighboring
Atrium building: the property gains area because
of the city's decision to narrow the Leipziger
Strasse to its historic width. Though much smaller,
this corner building extends the two-story high
arcade further along the Leipziger Strasse. It incorporates offices and apartments around two cores,
each with a double storied entrance hall. In the
middle is a garden courtyard, which brings natural
air circulation to the offices. The second to the
sixth floors each contain four divisible office units
(8.10 meter column grid, 1.35 meter planning grid).
Eleven apartments are located on the seventh floor
with small terraces in front. The architect decided
against building a second staggered floor which
city planning would have allowed for, thus avoiding
high-rise building regulations. With a one-story
high steel pergola he continues the ridge line of
the neighboring buildings.

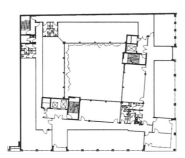

**Typical floor plan
for office levels
1:1000**

3·5

	Kontorhaus Mitte
Architects	Josef Paul Kleihues, Berlin (overall design)
	Theo Brenner, Berlin, Walter Stepp, Berlin
	Vittorio Magnago Lampugnani/Marlene Dörrie, Milan
Clients	Argenta Internationale Anlagengesellschaft mbH, Munich
	Hanseatica Unternehmens Consulting GmbH & Co KG, Hamburg
Address	Friedrichstrasse 185–190
	Mohrenstrasse 13–16
	Kronenstrasse 60–65
Facades	Roman travertine (Kleihues)
	Serpentine (Brenner)
	African granite, red, flame patterned (Stepp)
	Oberkirchner sandstone (Lampugnani)

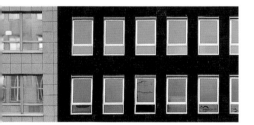

Kontorhaus Mitte

One city block, divided and built according to the "block division concept," in other words, one organizational and sales strategy, but four architects and six plots (including the historic building on the Kronenstrasse). All building sections share the main entrance on Friedrichstrasse and the 1,000 sq.m glass-roofed courtyard. The complex offers retail space on the ground floor and lower levels, offices from the second to the ninth floor and, as a novelty, a boarding house in the additional wing between Kronenstrasse and Mohrenstrasse with 84 "Madison City Suites." Here the more affluent, long-term visitors can order everything they might desire, including tailored shirts. All the architects kept to the urban design regulations of seven stories plus two staggered stories. They agreed on a common facade plane, and, although it's not readily evident, on a uniform window grid of 1.60 meters. Prerequisite here, as with all other new buildings in Mitte, is the divisibility of all office space, according to demand (with raised floors and suspendet ceilings). The smallest room unit has a width of 2.90 meter, with an average depth of 5.50 meter.

After the overall design was determined, all that was left for individual architects to do were facades, window proportions, the selection of the facade material and the detailing.

Block division concept: "the plot strategy." Typical floor plan for offices and apartments 1:1000

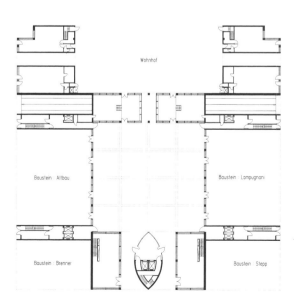

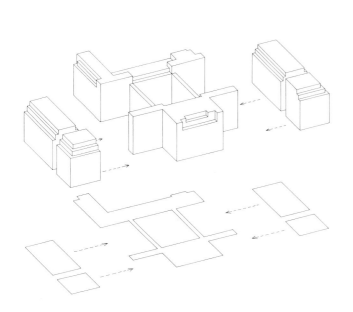
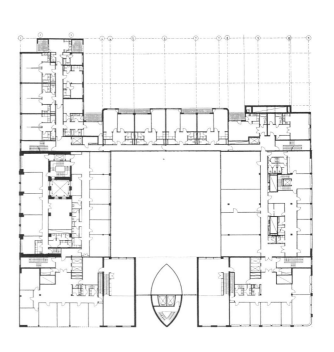

3.6

	Carré at Gendarmenmarkt
Architects	Josef Paul Kleihues, Berlin (Markgrafenhaus)
	Max Dudler, Berlin (BEWAG)
	Heinz Hilmer & Christoph Sattler, Munich
Clients	Hertie-Stiftung, BEWAG AG, Berlin
	Roland Ernst Städtebau, Berlin
Developer	Roland Ernst Städtebau, Berlin
Address	Markgrafenstrasse 34–36
	Mohrenstrasse 45
	Taubenstrasse 19
Facades	Cannstatter travertine/yellow band;
	Trim: Serpentine, ground (Kleihues)
	Pietra Serena, Ebony Black granite (Dudler)
	Bateig, spanish limestone (Hilmer/Sattler)

Carré at Gendarmenmarkt

Once again the Deutsche Dom is located between two prominent buildings: O.M.Ungers's Quartier 205, as the exceptional backdrop, and that of the "Carré" across from it. The name of the Carré building, with its three sections, derives from the developmental phase of the project. Now the individual sections each have their own street address. Only the corner building by J.P.Kleihues was given a name, Markgrafenhaus, and a corner tower, which (though still covered in scaffolding) strives for a dialogue with the Dom. Meanwhile, its pendant, the corner building on Taubenstrasse by the architects Heinz Hilmer & Christoph Sattler, does without. Otherwise the two corner edifices resemble each other in both use and floor plan: shops in the ground floor, offices along central halls in the five floors above and apartments on top. The facades are banded in cautious alignment. The corner building on Taubenstrasse has winter windows to the street to avoid air conditioning. Between the two lies the central office of the BEWAG (Berlin's electricity company) by Max Dudler. It acts as a middle with a gabled facade and balanced window formats, emphasizing neither height nor width. The floor plan is designed symmetrically around the central entranceway. Here again, apartments (maisonettes) are located in the two staggered floors.

**Typical floor plans
for office levels
1:1000**

 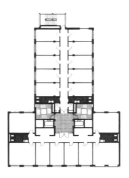 

3·7

	Conversion of two abutting buildings
Architect	Regina Schuh, Munich
Client	Roland Ernst Aufbaugesellschaft
	Taubenstrasse GbR
Developer	Roland Ernst Städtebau, Berlin
Address	Taubenstrasse 20
	Mohrenstrasse 42
Facade	Limestone, Jura,
	Marble quarry (Dittfurt)

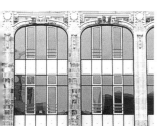

Office Building Taubenstrasse/Mohrenstrasse

The task here was the conversion and redesign of two buildings, including the construction of two additional stories. The existing buildings— one from the 50s on Taubenstrasse and the other from c. 1900 on Mohrenstrasse—are connected by wings extending across the courtyard. Despite their poor conditions, the buildings were preserved to save their distinct styles within the cityscape. Both of them were first reduced to their basic structures and then given new facades and turned into office buildings. They now contain some 18,000 sq. m of total floor space, including the additional stories. A surprise was discovered during remodelling the Mohrenstrasse building: hidden under the plain facade were Jugendstil fragments, which provided the basis for a recon- struction, as true to the original as possible.

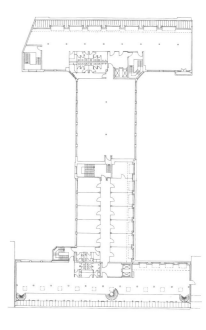

Floor plan of the
heightened story
1:1000

3.8

Architect
of Renovation

Client

Address

Deutscher Dom
Jürgen Pleuser, Berlin

Federal Republic of Germany:
Federal Building Ministry/
Federal Building Authority
Gendarmenmarkt

Deutscher Dom

The former East Berlin government began renovating the Dom into an art museum as early as 1983. Work was interrupted and its purpose redefined, when city officials declared it an adequate new home for the exhibition "Questions for the History of Germany," previously located in the Reichstag. Progress was again slowed in 1994 when the cupola caught fire, but renovations were finally completed in October 1996. The Dom, with traces of its 300 year old history—its most recent being the concrete framework in the cupola room—is both exhibition space and an exhibition in itself. Bearing this in mind, the architect uncovered the building's history: freeing the walls of concrete, clearly separating reinforced concrete sections from the historical structures, opening up the previously walled off niches and conchae and revealing the interior of the tower.

**Floor plans of 1st floor
and 6th floor, 1:1000.
Entrance level, stairwell
in tower with lantern,
ambulatories**

*Photos:
Ivan Nemec*

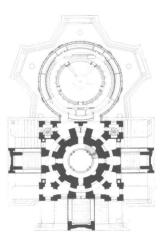

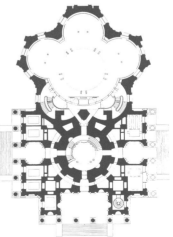

3·9

	Hofgarten at Gendarmenmarkt
Architects	Hans Kollhoff, Berlin
	Jürgen Sawade, Berlin
	Josef Paul Kleihues, Berlin
	Max Dudler, Berlin
Client	Hofgarten Real Estate B.V. Amsterdam
Developer	HINES Grundstücksentwicklung GmbH, Berlin
Address	Friedrichstrasse, Französische Strasse,
	Charlottenstrasse, Behrenstrasse
Facade	Granite, grey-green flame-patterned (Kollhoff)
	Ebony Black granite, polished (Sawade)
	Roman travertine Classico, serpentine,
	bushhammered, polished, ground (Kleihues)
	Granite, Verde Savanna, Ebony Black (Dudler)

Hofgarten at Gendarmenmarkt

When planning began, the originally densely built city block 208 contained only four, partially landmarked buildings. Yet the original small parcel structure was supposed to be restored. As a result, five compact new buildings were planned to fill the block around a common sparsely planted garden courtyard. The buildings were designed by four architects and remain effectively individual, and yet the block returns to a recognizable unity through the city's prevailing building regulations of a 22 meter maximum eaves height and two staggered floors. They are also related to each other through their use of natural stone for the building's outer cladding. The required amount of residential space is satisfied for the entire block in the segment designed by Max Dudler.

Segment by Hans Kollhoff

The three building sections along Friedrichstrasse are connected internally with one another. The middle section, Friedrichstrasse 79/80, was originally a historic building, whose facade and first layer of rooms were supposed to be integrated into the new building. The old edifice collapsed in the last phase of construction and the new one was then forced to imitate the proportions of the old facade. After all, the fenestration grid of the new buildings' facades (the wider unit spacing of the corner structure and the narrower of the urban infill) was based on the old edifice in the middle. Corner building and urban infill have separate accesses, but their relatedness is clearly manifest in the choice of grey-green flame patterned granite for both facades.

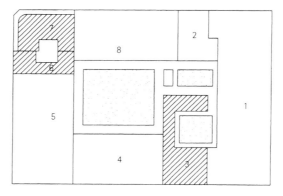

1, 2   **Kleihues Segment**
3   **Existing building with**
      Restaurant Borchardt
4   **Sawade Segment**
5   **Kollhoff Segment**
6, 7   **Existing buildings**
8   **Dudler Segment**

Segment by Jürgen Sawade

The adjacent building on Französische Strasse
continues the same vertical organization: two-
storied base, facade alignment over four stories,
topped with two staggered floors. The building
with its dark surface and horizontal windows, flush
with the facade, virtually hides itself, thus focusing
attention on its neighbor, the historical section,
home to the Restaurant Borchardt. It is not immediately evident that the facade follows a square
grid: vertical bands with a width of one square,
a window width of four squares with a height of
two squares and one square for lintel, ceiling and
height of the window sill. The typical floor plan
accommodates only office space and is organized
by a ring hallway around an access and sanitary
core.

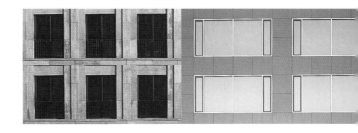

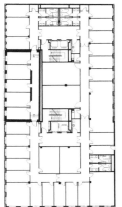

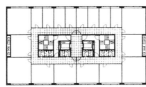

Typical floor plans
for office levels
1:1000

61

Segments by Josef Paul Kleihues

The five star hotel, "Four Seasons," fills the entire frontage along the Charlottenstrasse. The facade is clad in small shingles and extends around both corners of the block. The oddly curved bay windows were originally designed for hotel suites, but the building client had something else in mind and had the interior designed to his wishes: bold wood paneling, ornamental molding on Styrofoam, furniture à la "Art et Décoration," heavy velvet curtains and marble baths. Exceptional is the hotel's cuisine. All total, there are 204 rooms (Double = DM 430 – 645) and 42 suites (DM 750 – 2,500). Adjoining the hotel on Behrenstrasse is a small office building, which varies the hotel facade. With the same materials, the relationship between closed and open areas is virtually reversed; the bays become narrow openings. Each floor contains two office units (divisible in 2 x 3 if neccessary) sharing service and sanitation areas.

Hotel, 8th floor with
guest rooms.
Flexible floor plan
for office use
1:1000

Segment by Max Dudler

This block segment with its enormous 21 meter depth contains the required residential space for the entire block, spread between the second and ninth floors, a total of 46 apartments ranging in size between 45 and 210 sq. m each. Those apartments and maisonettes are oriented north-south, with access from a middle hallway. In the central part of the apartments are the halls, baths and side-rooms. The apartments between the second and sixth floors each include at least a small sunroom, while those in the upper two floors have terraces. On the street and courtyard side the architect was allowed, along a width of four fenestration bays, to aligne the normally staggered upper stories with the facade plane. The horizontal steel windows are recessed in the facade. Max Dudler also designed the two-story top addition to the historic corner building (dating from the late 19th century) at the intersection of Behrenstrasse and Friedrichstrasse. With his two new staggered floors he curved the otherwise beveled corner.

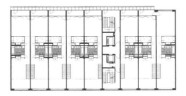
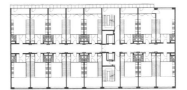

Typical floor plans for maisonettes 1:1000

3.10

Lindencorso
Architect — Christoph Mäckler, Berlin/Frankfurt am Main
Client — Lindencorso Grundstücks GmbH, Berlin
Address — Unter den Linden 19
Facade — Basalt, shell limestone

Lindencorso

At the intersection Unter den Linden and Friedrich-strasse stood the renowned Café Bauer until it was destroyed in the Second World War. It wasn't until the 60s that the site was redeveloped and housed the famous Building Academy of East Germany. This building was then demolished in 1993. Linden-corso, a German-French culture and shopping center now offers some 9,000 sq. m of retail space in the second floor, ground floor and in the lower levels. The shops are grouped around a central hall, while the main entrance faces Unter den Linden. From the third to the seventh floor office cells are arranged along a middle hallway and receive natur-al light from the glass-roofed courtyard. Luxury apartments are on the eighth floor. A two-story high arcade runs along Friedrichstrasse.

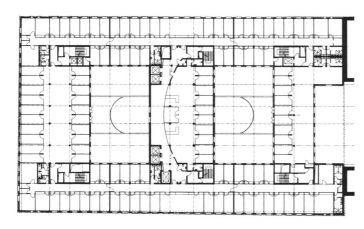

Typical floor plan
for office levels
1 : 1000

3.11

	Haus Pietzsch
Architect	Jürgen Sawade, Berlin
Client	Wert-Konzept GmbH
Address	Unter den Linden 42
Facade	Oberkirchner sandstone

Haus Pietzsch

The first building completed in the historic center after the fall of the Berlin wall stands on a surprisingly small site (15.71 meter x 52.96 meter), originally intended for the widening of the street. The seven story commercial building with its 780 sq. m of shops and 3,320 sq. m of office space is separated from the adjacent Unter den Linden building by a glazed gap. Between the fire wall of the historic building and the new edifice there now exists a slender, glass covered light-well, which is visible from the street and which houses the art collection of the building's client. A branch of Berlin's famous Café Einstein opened in the ground floor. The building also includes a fully computerized parking system in the subbasement, with a capacity for 36 cars over 760 sq. m. A modern climate control system uses water instead of air for cooling and heating, thereby saving up to 50% on energy costs. Access to the offices is extravagantly designed to occur from both the long glass gallery and a parallel hallway through the length of the building. The office rooms look out onto Neustädtische Kirchstrasse.

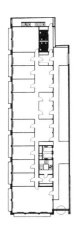

**Typical floor plan
for office levels
1:1000**

3.12

	Hotel Metropol/Maritim proArte
Architect	Holger Nettbaum, Berlin
Client	Hotel Metropol Berlin Grundstücks GmbH
Address	Friedrichstrasse 150–153
	Dorotheenstrasse
	Mittelstrasse
Facade	Impala, polished/Impala, flame patterned
	Sheeting metal (RAL 9006)

Hotel Metropol/Maritim proArte

The remodeling and the extension of the former Hotel Metropol was also used to partly restore the historic block structure. Construction work therefore began with filling out the building's base and lining it up along Dorotheenstrasse, and at the same time setting up an eight story building against the eleven story firewall. The new office building with two-story high arcades closes the block frontage towards Friedrichstrasse. In a second building phase the block front on the other side, towards Neustädtische Kirchstrasse, will be closed by an atrium building containing apartments and offices. At the end of construction work the high-rise slab will be clamped between two block-closing building volumes.

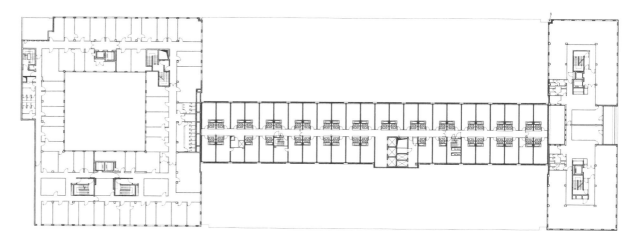

Typical floor plan for hotel guest rooms and office use 1:1000

3.13

	Haus Dussmann
Architect	Miroslav Volf, Saarbrücken
Client	Peter Dussmann, Munich
Address	Dorotheenstrasse
	Friedrichstrasse
	Mittelstrasse
Facade	Untersberger marble, bushhammered
	Precast concrete slabs,
	acid washed surface

Haus Dussmann

The building complex is set along the east side
of Friedrichstrasse and integrates—virtually swal-
lows—the historic buildings on Dorotheenstrasse
into the total structure. The main facade along
Friedrichstrasse acquired a two story arcade with
shops. Two narrow walkways lead to the inner
courtyard covered by a glass cupola. They are to
become part of a passageway between Unter den
Linden and the Friedrichstrasse Station. The facade
of the narrow courtyard, entirely made of glass,
opens and expands upward, while adjustable
industrial blinds direct daylight into the office
spaces.

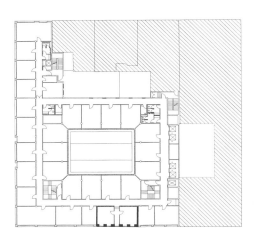

**Typical floor plan
for office levels
1:1000**

3.14

	Conversion for the German Bundestag
Architect	Alexander Kolbe, Berlin
Client	Federal Republic of Germany:
	Federal Building Ministry/
	Federal Building Authority
Address	Unter den Linden 44–60
Facade	Roman travertine

Conversion for the German Bundestag

The former East German Ministry for Foreign Trade will soon house 400 offices for parliamentary representatives, 90 offices for different political parties and some 20 secretarial offices. The building was gutted, save for the load-bearing structure; the roof level was converted into a functional floor and the facade received a new cladding. A new entrance hall faces out onto Unter den Linden with slender, lens-shaped supports and an elliptical glass room for the door personnel. From the first floor to the sixth floor offices are lined along a middle hallway.

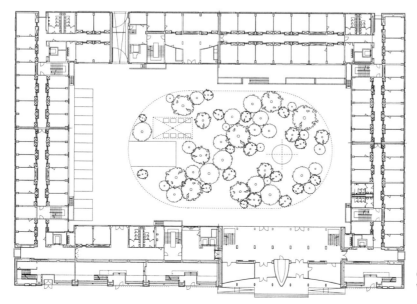

**Ground floor plan
with offices 1:1000**

3.15

Architects	Conversion for the German Bundestag
Client	Gehrmann Consult, Wiesbaden
	Federal Republic of Germany:
	Federal Building Ministry/
Address	Federal Building Authority
Facade	Unter den Linden 71
	Schönbrunner sandstone

Conversion for the German Bundestag

The five story complex was built in 1961/62 as a reinforced concrete skeleton filled with precast concrete slabs. It was used by the East German Ministry for the Education of the People. Here it was also necessary to first reduce the structure to its pre-existing load-bearing frame and then redesign the rest. The first floor columns create an arcade-like presence on the sidewalk and outline the plate glass windows and entranceways. The adjacent historic building in the Wilhelmstrasse was built between 1901 and 1903 for the Prussian Ministry of Education and has recently been restored. The two adjoining buildings share a courtyard and will house offices for parliamentary representatives, as well as part of the administration for the Bundestag.

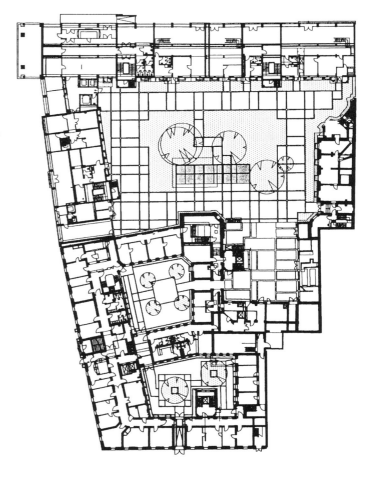

**Ground floor plan
with offices 1 : 1000**

4

Johann Wilhelm Anton Carstenn, Wilhelm August Ferdinand Riehmer and Georg Haberland were once well known speculators in Berlin. Wilhelm Carstenn, for example, on the opening day of the Anhalter railway station in 1868, decorated the entire stretch between the station and his Pavilion Restaurant in his country house colony Lichterfelde with hundreds of laurel trees in large buckets. Wilhelm Riehmer won his fight with city officials over his now famous private street in Kreuzberg by, among other tactics, refusing to sign his building proposals himself after 1880. Instead, he began calling himself "Riehmer, Rentier." In 1911 Georg Haberland succeeded in having the building code for the Rheinisches Quarter changed and an additional design regulation established for his row houses.

Historians have revealed the facts behind these figures, their initiatives and methods, which were highly controversial in their time. Now is the age of developers. Rather than wait for historians, Bauwelt Berlin Annual would like to provide portraits of certain people today, who are active in Berlin on a comparable level as those speculators of yore—and thereby offer its readers a brief introduction into the art and business of developing.

Investing in Berlin

Interview with Hans-Karl Herr, ITAG Aktiengesellschaft, on 11.1.1996

You have worked as a building developer in Berlin for some time now? What has changed for you and your work since the fall of the Wall?

The shift for me did not come first in 1989. The situation in Berlin had already begun to change in the mid-80s. Economic development was showing a clear positive trend. This was a signal for me, and I decided to become active in commercial real estate. Compared to cities like Frankfurt, commercial real estate in Berlin was for the most part underdeveloped. Nonetheless, an industry-specific demand existed and I responded to it by developing, as you know, the concept for FOCUS Teleport in Moabit.

Almost ten years have passed since the start of those plans. Would you recount the beginnings?

What's happening there, which prompted my action back then, is the result of a structural change I observed in the economy. Not only have the dimensions of technological products shrunk, but also the structure of companies has changed. Increasing automation is forcing large corporations to rationalize. Smaller, innovative companies can react with more flexibility, and succede with new products out on the market. Before we begin our own planning, we first try to read the market and understand it in detail. During the planning of FOCUS Teleport we held talks with large and small companies, with experts in the field, as well as with fledgling firms, all in the field of information technology and communication. We polled them about their expectations for Berlin, while at the same time conducting nationwide market research.

This resulted in the concept of a localized community of technologically oriented companies. We built densely—initially a source of much criticism—and also insisted on the idea of flexible space, which has since proven advantageous. We can meet almost all new or revised spacial needs of our tenants. Despite this flexibility inside, the house's exterior remains unchanged. It does not reveal the changes within. It is, how should I say, a reliable building block of the city.

The demand for office and commercial space, as calculated just after the fall of the Wall, has not materialized. There is talk of enormous miscalculations ... The calculations of demand, that is, the oft repeated comparisons between cities, with regard to available and needed office space, depict a false picture. The firms that were prepared to invest in this market segment in Berlin did not have access to any other data. The demand that everyone perceived and the tax advantages were the two biggest reasons for the massive production of commercial space. Nevertheless, I wouldn't call it an erroneous development, but a series of single bad investments. You may be surprised to know, commercial buildings are also delicate additions to an environment, depending on the location. And they themselves are delicately dependant on their environment. This is often considered to be the reason for the success or failure of a specific object. And I'm not just thinking of criteria such as access to public transport, site development or the like; there is also the social and cultural surroundings. Very few firms base their decision for a certain location only on the costs.

How would you describe your management philosophy? The goals of the ITAG Aktiengesellschaft can be summed up as: architecture and service. That means, we involve ourselves in projects that are particularly interesting in an urban design context. We then give form to these in an architecture that excites debate, outfitting it with services for future use. Beyond their competitiveness with other providers, our solutions must also offer the majority of advantages for the future tenant and the future surroundings, as well as for the community.

Would the term Public Private Partnership be applicable here? What is that exactly? Didn't Herr Haberland in 1912 also have to run his own bus route in the Rheinisches Quarter? What is so novel about the cooperation between private and public investors that warrants a new term for it? I am fundamentally in favor of partnerships, partnerships also in the sense of a Public Private Partnership. One such project is the center for the district of Hellersdorf, which we are developing together with four other Berlin firms. There we have to take care of everything: from the public transport infrastructure to the complete development. When all is finished, Hellersdorf will possess a functional center, with all the facilities of urban life. This development of Hellersdorf is a good example of Public Private Partnership.

We will certainly not be running our own bus route, as Hellersdorf is connected to the city center via subway. But we will provide parking decks and thus offer the possibility to park in the midst of this huge center and from there take the subway. Also, we are designating an area for a market, where local products can be sold. A disco will be built, restaurants, bistros, as well as facilities for senior citizen care.

Without these 3 Ps Hellersdorf couldn't have been developed. Public Private Partnership, by the way, is not so novel. In Anglo-Saxon countries there has been a stronger tradition of public services being turned over to the private sector. As the saying goes: the state shouldn't do that which the privat sector can do. The state just has to make sure that if private investors do take over public tasks, then they must also be responsible for high standards of quality.

Are you serving the city?
I wouldn't call it that. If others see my work that way, then I would be happy.

Could you work in another city? Yes, naturally, it is important for a businessman, sometimes even existentially, not to become too regionally dependant. And even though the real estate market, unlike other markets and products, is not experiencing a globalization, one needs to have single areas of concentration in other cities, perhaps even including diverse product lines. We are doing this, for example, in southern Germany and in Mecklenburg-Vorpommern.

When the newspapers report on the major foundation stone ceremonies, they sometimes talk about building costs and sometimes about development costs. Even in the "Chronology" in this book we sometimes have one, sometimes the other. Could you explain this ...

With the amount of information available on construction in this city, it is indeed difficult to keep track of it all, even for an insider. But these two terms are relatively simple: Building costs include the material costs, that is, all expenses which apply exclusively to erecting the building. Development costs include all other costs, like the cost of the property, planning, financing and, in some cases, as with hotels for example, also opening costs, advertising costs, etc.

Then what is the difference between the client, the investor and the project developer?

These names cannot be so easily and clearly distinguished from each other. To add to the confusion, there is sometimes even the additional title of building contractor. For me the contractor is not someone who runs the building, but rather someone who offers services to the building client. The building contractor is building for the client and his architect. For my position, I would use the term building client. This implies such a breadth of responsibilities, such that all our activities are also included in the term. We are a building client in situations where we establish an ownership collective initiated either for or from us.

A building client is that entity which, above all, identifies with its projects over an extended period of time and maintains them as its property. In this context, standards of quality are established as a priority in both the design and building phases.

Developing a concept for utilization, researching the market, selecting the site, juggling the financing, dealing with the architects and above all, communicating with the city, those are the tasks and challenges of a building client.The work during the project's development phase and then later during the building's financial management affect the consideration of the floor plans, the materials and finishes, and the quality and life expectancy of the structure.

So you manage your projects yourself ...

Once the building is completed an entirely new and equally interesting phase begins. Does the building satisfy the demands of the tenants? How long will the intended use continue? How often does the building require renovations or a total revitilization? Such questions need to be examined within a reasonable financial framework, particularly for commercial buildings.

Today one can hardly expect, that—as was true earlier—buildings will remain the same from their completion until they are old enough to qualify as historical monuments. Unless of course, we continually lower the "historical" qualifying age. Not even the ostensible security of a long-term lease can be considered a reliable basis any more. The pressure on a company is often so great, that it forces the company to change and accommodate market trends. There are a host of reasons for this, including the shortening product cycles, the methods of manufacturing and the marketability of the company's size. The common thread though, is that such changes usually directly affect the utilization of the building and thus also challenge any change to the real estate.

What do you expect from architects?

In short, a partner who is capable of critical dialogue and of critically examining the wishes of the clients. They must be able to penetrate the clients' concept to the same degree as the clients themselves.

From architects I also expect—and I make it possible for them—to thoroughly inform themselves about the planned use and the users, that these architects familiarize themselves with both the real and imaginary needs of the users—what type of workplace they envision, what they actually need, what sort of external appearance is appropriate, and so on. For the time being, the FOCUS Mediport project in Berlin-Steglitz is a concrete example of these types of challenges.

For years you were active in housing projects. Have you given that up?

No, not at all. The continual development of residential buildings is both desirable and advantageous for the market, yet for the moment it's hardly realistic. In the not-so-distant future we will once again be hearing complaints about the lack of housing space. If you listen closely, you can already hear them. For example, Berlin has failed to settle on a specific quota for affordable one-family residences. There just aren't enough appropriate and accessible properties. In this situation, the politicians and city administrators need to react fast, because the demand is there, and it's been there for some time, but nobody wanted to listen. Now that more property is available in the outlying areas, we are seeing people in Berlin moving out of the city, though the city would rather keep them for itself.

But to your original question: in terms of the present possibilities, we will remain active in residential projects. A housing project in the center of the city would be tempting. Berlin must want people moving to it, people who would like nothing more than to live in the center of the city for, let's say, adequately moderate prices.

How would that work, privately financed apartments in the middle of the city, that are moderately priced?

Centrally located apartments are just as much of a market as are single family homes in the suburbs. Moderate prices cannot be set so generally. Certainly the market will determine how prices develop in town and match demand with supply. Perhaps we just need to get used to the idea, that not all demand requires special attention in the form of some set of directives. In the past it was precisely this sort of overprotectiveness that regulated and complicated the market.

But if you're looking for those cost-reducing building concepts, I think they're extremely theoretical, and hardly realizable ... You can save money with building logistics, with a well prepared building process, with a perfect organization of the building site ...

What are your expectations for Berlin, that is, are expectations still even possible in a climate dominated by cutbacks ...

I believe we are gradually settling down in a totally normal and positive direction. One has the impression that it's ostensibly all about saving, but only ostensibly. We shouldn't be focusing only on cutting back. Savings should be part of the design phase, which implies a readiness to set priorities and commit to them. Saving also means redirecting and initiating. I consider cutbacks totally wrong, if projects that have been started are delayed or left incomplete. That might protect liquidity, but it won't save it ...

What will improve when the government moves to Berlin?

Mostly the atmosphere in the city. The resulting effect should not be underestimated. Generally speaking, I believe the atmosphere at the moment is worse than the real situation. And if that's the case, if the atmosphere does have such a strong effect, as I think it does, than it's especially important that the government's move to Berlin keep strictly to schedule. Embassies, institutions, lobbyists already have their feelers out for new locations, both in residential sectors as well as in commercial areas. Naturally, this still does not mean there is a great demand for real estate, but it does cause a shift in the atmosphere and accelerates decisions that others still have to make.

What sort of a future vision should the city develop for itself?

That which corresponds to its position in central Europe, which is actually not so new.

You mean an eastward perspective?

Yes, and not to look elsewhere, just because the markets don't quite match our expectations. They are just beginning to build themselves up, and offer good prospects. The shifting job market in eastern countries should not be seen as short-term and detrimental. The economic situation in central and eastern Europe is growing more stable through these shifts, and as a result, new markets are emerging. In this context, Berlin can take advantage of its key role in central Europe, yet that also requires preparation, because any vision has to be a major step ahead of reality ...

Photos: Erik-Jan Ouwerkerk

5

Development
Spreeknie
Client   BLEG
              Berliner Landes-
              entwicklungs GmbH
              & Co Grundstücks KG
Start of project   1994

Alexander Haeder
The Oberschöneweide Industrial Area

The Potsdamer Platz of the last turn of the century was the industrial district of Oberschöneweide, which lies southeast of the city center. What is today considered a unique testament to Berlin's industrial history, due to its size, its still-intact concentration of buildings, and its astounding silhouette towards the Spree, arose quite suddenly from the ground. As late as 1880 Oberschöneweide was still an idyllic place of meadows, wetlands, and flower gardens. By 1894 it was just one big construction site. In 1896, AEG built Germany's first three-phase power station here for the Berlin Electricity Works, and in 1898 production began in the finished or half-finished halls of the Oberspree Cable Works. If you walk just beyond Treskow Bridge and a small distance along Edisonstrasse — named after the famous Thomas Edison, from whom Emil Rathenow bought the license for the production and sale of electrical lighting systems in 1882 — you already find yourself dwarfed between two of these giant yellow brick buildings. To the left stands the former Frister Lamp Factory from 1897, now almost completely restored and with the new name Spreehöfe; to the right, the gable of the transformer hall built by Ernst Ziesel in 1925. And further on, around the corner to the right, along Wilhelminenhofstrasse, but remaining on the south side, gables, walls, and bays stand in line, imposing or dignified, richly or sparsely decorated, flat halls and multi-story buildings. It is quite obvious that various architects at different times built, added, or modified here, piece for piece, and yet

one feels a unifying trait among the designs. It is not the yellow brick, but a shared quality of impressiveness, if not intimidation. On the other side of the street and equally impressive, a row of three and four-story apartment buildings closes off the street space. This is interrupted at nearly regular, short intervals by intersecting streets leading north into a residential area, which, as one might surmise, arose on the ground of a very ambitious development plan of 1902. The view back from the residential streets offers glimpses of the yellow industrial facades, frames them, and underscores their sumptuousness.

If there was ever a golden age of German industry, it was in the period between 1895 and the outbreak of World War One. Large industries left the city center and resettled in waterside locations where further expansion was possible. The arguments that spoke for resettlement along this bend in the Spree were convincing. For quite a long time, Schöneweide had had access to a rail line, which since the 1890s was also part of the city's commuter rail network.

Construction of the power station was followed by that of the Oberspree Cable Works, which began production in 1897 as a subsidiary of AEG. Besides giant, multi-naved production halls, further multi-story factory buildings for the production of conductive and insulative materials were built within a very short time. What is particularly impressive is the logical consistency with which the complex was developed from the beginning.

Photos at the Spreeknie in spring 1994. View across the Spree from Niederschöneweide, with the great Spree hall and behind it the roofs of buildung A 8 by Ernst Ziesel

Photo: Michael Scholz

Right: aerial photo of the KWO property around 1930

Construction began immediately at the border of the power station site and progressed in an easterly direction. Axes and buildings were laid at right angles between Wilhelminenhofstrasse and the Spree. This form of development not only insured a high degree of building use, but was also ideal from a logistical perspective. The river lay to one side as a means of transport for raw materials, and the street and railway were on the other side, for transporting finished goods. The industrial railway which led along the Wilhelminenhofstrasse parallel to the tram line linked up to a series of connecting rails which gave every factory access to the long-distance rail lines. On the opposite side of the street began the residential settlement of late 19th-century apartment houses, which grew in step with the progressive industrialization along the Spree's bank towards the Wuhlheide meadows. Industry took advantage of the street-front facades. Opposite the plaster and stucco-faced apartment buildings it created a grandiose design of yellow brick and windows as high as in churches, decorated on the visible sides with reliefs of natural stone and terra cotta, with allegorical scenes celebrating the age of electricity. Behind these facades was a system of spatial subdivision inspired in its efficiency and logic by the pragmatism of American mass production. Among the post-1900 buildings, this mentality also acquired a corresponding attitude towards decoration, as artistic trimmings were gradually dropped in favor of more spartan ornamental patterns, making

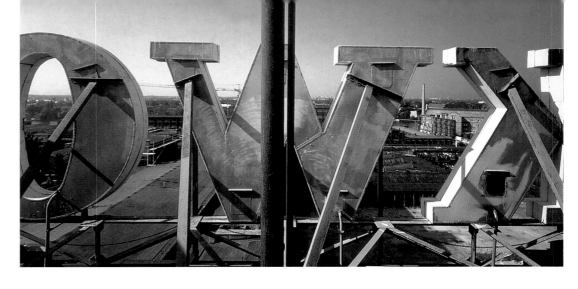

South view from the
water tower on the roof of
the factory building A4

*All photos:
Michael Scholz*

Views in the industrial
complex: management
building and the former
wire factory. Renovations
began with buildings
facing Wilhelminenhof-
strasse

Section of the facade of
building A2: the former
wire factory is connected
to the management
building by a "Bridge
of Sighs"

no attempt to hide their serial character. Peter Behrens created the most striking building in 1917, a production and administration building for the Nationale Automobilgesellschaft, a subsidiary of AEG. With a height of nearly 70 meters, the tower at the end of the Wilhelminenhofstrasse rises significantly above the surrounding buildings. Slightly turned on a diagonal, it marks the termination of this axis. Simultaneously, one of its wings continues the alignment of Ostendstrasse, opening up this area for possible further industrial development.

For generations, Oberschöneweide was a concept, a tacit understanding, that needed no explanation. It was synonymous for the heavy industry of the East German capital, an inhospitable piece of Berlin that seemend to belong exclusively to industry and yet boasted almost 24,000 residents. A city within a city, and site of one of the extreme high-performance plants set up in the wake of economic reform in East Germany in the late 1960s.

Besides the Oberspree Cable Works, the giant within this industrial agglomeration, several other major companies had their main plants on this site, including the equally well-known television electronics works WF and the Oberspree transformer works TRO. The number of jobs exceeded that of inhabitants, with nearly 25,000 on the right bank of the Spree alone. And there were thousands more in the engineering works in the district of Niederschöneweide on the opposite bank of the river.

These major companies of the state-controlled economy also played a central role in the social lives of employees. With their daycare centers, vacation homes, culture houses, sport clubs, and company clinics, they constituted nearly the entire cultural infrastructure of the area. They were part of a comprehensive system of maintenance and care for workers, employees, and their families, which also existed beyond the factory walls. These unbreakable ties between the factories and their people are known in the coal and steel industries between the Rhine and Ruhr. In fact, Oberschöneweide had a whole series of similarities with the Ruhr district.

The rude awakening in the land of the D-mark came as a shock to these factories spoiled by success. The Soviet Union, the number one customer, whose unquenchable thirst for machines and equipment of all kinds nearly exhausted the factories' capacity, dropped out, at least temporarily, as a trading partner or reduced its orders to a fraction of their accustomed volume. Prospects hardly looked brighter on the international market. The fact that products were exported to over 100 countries in the past was due to a fortuitous gap between soft socialist monies and hard currency. This disappeared overnight. Subject to the conditions of an aggressive and, especially in cable and electrical goods production, at times brutal market, poor competitiveness was immediately exposed.

Consultants entered the scene. Higher productivity and lower costs was the irresistible logic of

View from the WF building over the grounds on the Spreeknie, in the foreground is Peter Behrens' munitions factory

Views in the industrial complex: east facades of buildings A2 and A4 on the grounds of the Wilhelminenhof before the renovations, halls, crane tracks, and annexes in the foreground were torn down in 1995

their recommendations. Everything not immediately pertaining to production was dug up, cut out, removed, and melted down. Huge parts of the property and entire production sectors fell victim to the liquidators. The same was true for the sporting grounds, cultural houses and kindergartens. Although economically inevitable, the end of the accustomed social and cultural network came at a time when it was needed more than ever before.

The cuts were hard, even brutal. Nearly four-fifths of the workforce lost its jobs, meaning for many the termination of their careers. Some breathing space seemed to have been achieved around 1994/1995, since the big three appeared to have survived by concentrating on their core production. But it became obvious that this respite was only temporary when AEG-TRO announced the final liquidation of its plant for the end of 1996. Yet the industrial cores of two of Oberschöneweide's three major companies appeared intact. The former television electronic works were taken over by the Korean Samsung group, which purchased further production sectors over the past year and is modernizing them as it promised the city government it would. The former cable works, now called KWO-Kabelwerke GmbH, became a subsidiary of Britain's BICC, a cable group with worldwide operations. It is the most important British investment in the former East Germany, but this also meant that half the former cable work grounds had to be jettisoned.

The difficult task of preserving, separating, and subdividing the historic industrial buildings into smaller and more flexible production sites, and simultaneously making use of the chances offered by this district in terms of industry and residential space, fell into the hands of the newly founded Berlin State Development Association (BLEG). The BLEG, a joint subsidiary of the city-state of Berlin and the Landesbank Berlin, has since bought about 300,000 sq. m in the area, mainly from the state privitization agency of former East German industrial properties, the Treuhand. It acquired large areas of the core industrial sectors next to an extensive tract between Tabbert- and Nalepastrasse at the northern end of the complex, which was completely renovated and restored. Belonging to this was the quarter on Ostendstrasse, which had been rather neglected in the past. For several months a technology and entrepeneur center has been under construction here. Its architect is the Danish firm of C.F. Möller.

But the most important task lies in the 130,000 sq. m property at the southern end of Wilhelminenhofstrasse, which had to be separated from the Oberspree Cable Works during the process of restructuring. It can be seen as constituting the core of the Spreeknie region, where the river changes course from east to north, towards the city center. The property must be regarded as the key to the development of the entire district, and not only because of its geographical location. It is the only relatively expansive terrain along the

Oberschöneweide
industrial belt. From the
Treskow bridge eastward
along the Spree: factory
sites of TRO-AEG, KWO-
BICC (light colored),
BLEG (dark colored), and
Samsung. North of the
Wilhelminenhofstrasse:
The residential districts
with housing blocks from
the late 19th century and
from the 1920s and 30s.
Below left: the Schöne-
weide train station for
inner-city and long-
distance travel, and the
Adlergestell

entire bank of the Spree on which a future urban
infrastructure can be prepared today.

The problems facing BLEG are gigantic and
grow the closer you look at them. They begin with
the subdivision of the complex into smaller properties which have to be determined according to
changed ownership conditions. This process, which
appears simple at first glance, turns out to be highly complex and sensitive, with the actual problem
lying far beneath the ground surface. The cable
works, with a size of nearly 250,000 sq. m, are
equipped with an array of underground supply systems which were built in the course of decades.
Pipes from company-owned wells, conducting
thousands of cubic meters of water, criss-cross the
area, as do high-pressure steam pipes. Industrial
gases produced in their respective plants are lead
through a system of conduits. Underground tanks
contain chemicals and solvents of all kinds. High-
tension wires run through the complex toward
transformer stations, from which cables thick as a
man's arm lead toward faraway destinations. All
these systems are obviously kept running, as they
are needed for continuing production. Disentan-
gling such systems of heating pipes, drinking
water and sewage canalization, reconstructing the
steam pipes, and bringing into service new deep
wells alone constitutes a multi-year investment
program.

In addition, there is the virulent problem of
environmental contamination. The Spree's wetlands and marshes have always proved to be

Gabled fronts of KWO's
boiler house and steam
center, of the center nave
of Behrens' hall, of the
former automobile
factory NAG. Running
across the grounds are
crane tracks, high-
pressure lines, high-
powered electrical
cables, steam lines,
transformer stations…

Photos: Michael Scholz

difficult ground to build on. Halls and multi-story edifices had to be erected using an extensive system of pillars set deep in the soft ground. To secure the foundations, large tracts of the ground were filled in the years before 1914 with industrial slag, the origin of which remains unclear to this day. It was sludge strongly contaminated with heavy metals such as arsenic, mercury, copper, etc. Water extraction fell with production levels, causing the water table to rise and previously stationary pollutants to be set in motion towards the water works' pumping stations. The installation of new pumps inhibited this process but hardly represented a solution to the problem. This can only consist in the exchange and cleansing (or disposal) of the contaminated ground, which gives an idea of the scale of such an industrial clean up.

Nevertheless, the "Craftsmen's and Trade Center Wilhelminenhof" has been growing on the Spreeknie. The name harks back to an older farmstead along the Spree which was already referred to in the choice of street name. The complex includes a series of historic buildings which have changed usage several times since their construction between 1902 and 1911. One of the five-story factories with the name A2, whose rhythmic western facade recalls the Hamburg Speicherstadt, was originally constructed as storage space for the cable works. Later, through the annexation of a third wing and the addition of a story, the building served as a wire factory with hundreds of wire-winding machines, some of them several storys

high and apparently in use until 1990. Parallel to this and likewise in a north-south direction between Wilhelminenhofstrasse and the Spree stands the five-to-seven story building A4. With its 200 meter length it is probably the largest industrial edifice in the area after the Behrens building. In between, the half-decrepit five naved factory halls of the automobile subsidiary NAG stretch over the same distance. NAG operated here until 1916/17, when it moved into the new building opposite by Peter Behrens. The main building A4 and the remains of the halls belong to the first phase of construction of the Spreeknie complex, while the rebuilding of the wire factory A2 is being prepared for the years 1997/98.

Now, in November 1996, the first phase of modernization work has been completed. The buildings were constructed for the BLEG with part of the costs being taken over by the European Fund for Regional Development. In the meantime, over 30,000 sq. m of floorspace have been restored according to historic regulations and subdivided into practical units. The architecture is thoroughly able to absorb these dramatic changes, a fact which underscores its quality. The heights and depths of the spaces may not correspond to contemporary norms, but the new units with their enormous window fronts can boast spectacular quantities of light.

A great variety of rental spaces have been created. They have been made utterly accessible via five exterior staircases, as well as many newly-installed personal and freight elevators and in-

Craftsmen's and
Trade Center
"Wilhelminenhof"
Completion of the
first renovation
phase
Client

Outdoor Planning

Building A4
Renovation
Planning

Project
Management

Reconstruction
of the former NAG
Auto Works

November 1996

BLEG
Berliner Landes-
entwicklungs GmbH
& Co Grundstücks KG
Landschaft, Planen &
Bauen, Berlin

Ingenieurbüro kba,
Berlin
Heery International,
European subsidiary
of the Balfour Beatty Group
Ulrich Wolff, Berlin

**Wilhelminenhof, first
construction phase, west
facade. Production floors
following modernization
and before their subdivi-
sion into rental units.
Below: The inner court-
yard before the start of
the second construction
phase. The automobile
halls are still standing**

Photos: Gerhard Zwickert

house technical centers, etc. The spaces are
equipped in such a way, that their basic order
remains simple and that building changes are
possible at all times. The supply of spaces is
intended for mixed usage between handicrafts,
trade, and services, namely for those businesses
divorced from the pattern of large-scale companies and operating within the framework of local
industry. The building structure perfectly accommodates this mixture of uses, as the various parts
were used by the cable works both for production
and administration. The diversity of former usage
can also be identified on the exterior in the
changes in window design.

The comprehensive interior reconstruction
is combined with a meticulous treatment of the
historical substance. Modesty reigned in the renovation of the brick exterior: cleaning, fixing, and
reworking without erasing the traces of postwar
construction, which had to depend on lower-quali-
ty stone. There was never any doubt about keeping
the industrial windows. Their classical runged
subdivision, their steel-blue color, and the warm
yellow tone of the bricks form the constitutive
element of the building's exterior appearance.
A second, inner window, had to be added in most
cases to provide the necessary insulation. Facade
sections, as well as windows and gateways, were
only adapted to the new usage concept where
the factory directly leads into the halls.

The lower sections of the building between
the wings A4 and A2 can be handled more freely.

Ernst Ziesel's A8 building, Peter Behrens' WF tower in the background

Photo: Michael Scholz

The former NAG fitting factory had been partially converted to a rubber factory, leaving indescribable remains, while in other parts precast elements were inserted destroying much of its original character.

Urban development considerations were mainly responsible for the reconstruction of these decaying fitting halls' facades and trimmings. For in this way, part of the inner street system could be preserved and used by the public. The entire building behind the historic facade is being restored in keeping with the original dimensions of the hall wing. Small units of business space emerge as maisonettes, offering workshop and retail space on the ground floor as well as office and recreational space on the gallery level. The inner facades are to be glassed in and, after completion, will look out on a courtyard with a fountain fed by a giant cistern. Also bordering this green yard is the terrace of a cafeteria, currently taking shape in the ground floor of the gate construction on Wilhelminenhofstrasse. One of the surviving wings in the southern part of the property will be occupied by the driveway for a needed parking garage, which, hardly noticable from the outside, will provide some 300 parking spaces when complete.

The next redevelopment projects in the protected area Spreeknie have already been decided. Simplest to redesign and reutilize are the buildings from the 1920s. This third generation of buildings is represented chiefly by the extended factory building by Ernst Ziesel, one of Berlin's most im-

portant, if little-known, industrial architects. The four-story building, now freed from its provisional additions, was built within a matter of months in 1928 as one of the first steel-frame buildings in Germany. An addition of four or five floors was already planned at the time. With its staircase-towers, their corners in glass, and its horizontally running bands of windows divided by muntins still preserved on its south facade, the building known as A8 is undoubtedly one of the high points of modernist architecture in Berlin.

The restoration plans are alrady finished, and the Berlin office for the Protection of Historic Monuments has approved a planned expansion. In the first phase, a decentralized heating power station, which would supply the entire complex with heat and electricity, is planned in cooperation with the GASAG utilities company. It is to be built on the site of a demolished hall annex.

6

Wolfgang Kil
Along the Görlitzer Railroad

Some paths are to be tread only once. Like the rain-drenched path of dreams in Winfried Mateyka's photographic series: nothing but uncertain, blurry scenes of street lamps under rusty bridges, empty sidewalks, and crookedly parked cars under murkily lit shop signs: "… when I leave Neukölln at night on foot and suddenly end up in Treptow …" The series was photographed at the end of November 1989 and represents an irreplaceable document of the most recent turn of events in Berlin.

But there are also paths that preserve the aura of unexpected contact for a longer period of time. You can tread them again and again, and each time you get a new glimpse under the skin of the city, between the yellowed layers of its contradictory chronology. Mostly they are forgotten alleyways transecting politically significant points of the compass, slicing through the organizational patterns of modern bureaucracy. They are the concealed communications between alien worlds, passageways between times, populations, and cultures. If it is true that Berlin is really many cities, then such paths are probably the most "Berlinian" of all.

One of these paths is the track of the old Görlitzer railroad. The route to Görlitz, built 1865–67, was part of the radiating fan-like network of railway connections, intended to elevate the expanding metropolis of late 19th century Berlin into the transportation capital of the Kaiserreich. Tracks pushed in toward the city from all directions, each received by its own main station. Soon afterward, these terminus stations were completed by an inner distributing network of rail lines around and through the city, creating one of the most intelligent and efficient urban transit systems in Europe.

The Görlitzer Bahnhof, located in what was then open field at the edge of the city outside the Hallesches Tor, was responsible for travels and transports in the southeasterly direction—via Königs Wusterhausen to Cottbus, Görlitz, Silesia, and Bohemia. As usual, military considerations also played a role in the building of the railroad, but the primary significance of the route for Berlin lay in its function as a main transport line for grain and, above all, for brown coal from Lausitz. Building activity also benefited from the new transport arteries: the southeastern suburbs of Schöneweide, Adlershof, Glienicke, Johannisthal, Schmöckwitz, Grünau, and Zeuthen owe their rapid growth in those years to the railroad. Block by block, new land was developed for housing; but industry, too, sought locations near the tracks. By the turn of the century, an urban landscape thickly interspersed with factories and other commercial tracts had begun to develop directly behind the station grounds, on the other side of the Landwehr canal.

To this day, the existing remains of that townscape have continued to shape the image and social milieu of one of Berlin's least known neighborhoods: old Treptow. The blocks between Lohmühlenstrasse and Elsenstrasse, Heidelberger Strasse and Treptower Park, compactly built up in the manner of those earlier times, form the historic nucleus of the Treptow district of Berlin. While the Wall still stood, this neighborhood—tightly wedged in between the West Berlin districts of Neukölln and Kreuzberg—was essentially severed from the rest of Treptow, almost entirely a zone unto itself, subject to the surveillance regulations as a "border area." Even in the consciousness of East Berliners it had basically disappeared until 1989.

**Treptow rail tracks
and Alt-Treptow**

To facilitate the crossing of the Landwehr canal and the Lohmühlen-, Bouché-, Elsen-, and Puderstrassen, the Görlitzer railroad was built on a three to four-meter high embankment. After the war only one track was repaired; in 1951, the route was put entirely out of commission, and the rest of the tracks were later dismantled. The gravel bed remains to this day, and now provides an ideal elevated path crosswise through the colorful hodgepodge of old Treptow. Since the fall of the Wall, the through-streets have begun to function like a series of needle's eyes in the hectic rush of automobiles between Lichtenberg, Friedrichshain, and Treptow in the east and Neukölln, Tempelhof, and the city autobahn in the west. Here, however, on the quiet path hidden behind thick shrubbery, one can stroll northward at a leisurely pace from the old Treptow rail junction in the south. Passing a variety of picturesque views of the back sides of houses and shop yards, the pedestrian finally reaches the popular park that was once the site of the Görlitzer Bahnhof, thus finding himself in Kreuzberg, in the midst of the turbulent district SO 36.

Our journey begins at the edge of Treptower Park, at the south entrance of the Soviet war memorial. The stocky, monumental white limestone portal behind the short driveway is not hard to find. The street Am Treptower Park at this point resembles a race track, which is a shame, for the impressive houses facing the park actually deserve unhurried observation. Such a collection of splendid facades—a mixture of bourgeois Romanticism, jutting corner towers, and Jugendstil decoration—is otherwise found only in the better neighborhoods of the former "New West." Fortunately, the local historic conservation agency declared the whole ensemble a "protected area."

Directly across from the portal are two small villas. The right-hand one, closer to the street, houses the law offices of Lothar de Maizière, the last minister president of former East Germany. On the corner lot to the left is a small post office, which will soon share its modest domicile with a new tenant, the Belarussian embassy. Continuing past this soon-to-be eminent address along the short Puderstrasse, we reach the railroad embankment.

Beyond the rusty girders of the underpass, the view opens out before us. In front are abandoned workshops, probably relegated to the triangular no-man's-land between the tracks, because of their hazardous contents: galvanization remains? batteries? paint and varnish? In any case, appallingly contaminated. To the left is a piece of urban prairie. On the right is the small garden allotment complex "Alte Sternwarte;" the name is a local reference to the venerable observatory in the middle of Treptower Park. (Two kilometers away, on the Neukölln side, there is a garden allotment complex named "Kolonie Freiheit," which means "Freedom Colony"—truly a surreal neologism, but likewise a piece of local history after three decades of gardening within view of the Wall.)

"Let's be realistic—let's attempt the impossible," a banner on a factory wall calls out to passing trains. The wall belongs to the "Media Center at Treptower Park," in former East Germany the publisher and printer of the union newspaper Tribüne. Now it is the seat of the media group Schmidt & Partner, a consortium around Elefantenpress-Verlag. The former left-wing publishers have since become proper landlords. They acquired the commercial premises from the federal privatization agency and now rent out spaces to editorial

All photos:
Wolfgang Kil

offices of periodicals like Titanic, Junge Welt, Freitag, or Berliner Linke, but also to printers, security services, vocational schools, and a fitness studio. Except for the editorial offices, this is a mixture we will encounter more than once along our way.

Between the arbors and the busy train and transit lines to Schöneweide, a comfortable path leads slowly upwards to a barren plateau. There we find only rubble, gravel, and weeds, but also an incomparable panoramic view. To the south one can see far beyond Adlershof and Neukölln; to the north is the silhouette of the city. A little closer are the fire walls and roofs of mass housing projects and factories, overshadowed by the cranes of the "Treptowers," those imposing concrete giants on the banks of the Spree. High overhead, planes prepare to land at Tempelhof airport.

A row of weathered concrete posts signals the beginning of the broken stone path atop the old Görlitzer railroad embankment. Following it, after only a few steps we notice a small residential structure to the left; it could easily be taken for a work of Bruno Taut, especially from the entrance side on Kiefholzstrasse. Inquiries at GEHAG, however, reveal that the architect of this complex, built in 1931, was Ladislaus Förster. Still, he was a pupil of the master, which is why the restoration of the housing group was carried out with such remarkable historical accuracy.

Immediately thereafter, two newer housing complexes present themselves for comparison. Parallel to the embankment but accessed from Elsenstrasse, the architects Klippel, DeBiaso & Scherrer have grouped six-story buildings with 125 subsidized apartments around a handsome courtyard. The architecture of violet-brown clinker with

white horizontals exudes a pleasurable sobriety. On the Kiefholz-strasse side, the courtyard is closed in by a housing block which, though itself staggered a number of times, receives a strong axial emphasis from a symmetrical driveway passing through to the court-yard. The architects Liepe and Steigelmann thus found a clever solution to a difficult urban design problem—the gradual transition from Förster's recessed building front to the time-honored property line along the sidewalk. Why they also had to add a postmodern touch to their buildings remains all the more mysterious in view of the fact that not far from here, at Schmollerplatz, they created a truly convincing, timelessly modern housing project for the same client, TRIGON.

In the background behind the new residential complexes, a great silver-gray monolith pushes itself repeatedly into view; a stranger in the neighborhood, bursting out of the surrounding structures to liberate itself. There, on an extension of the grounds of the former VEB Signal- und Sicherungstechnik (previously Ehrich & Graetz, petroleum lamps), the Siemens real estate division together with the architect Douglas Clelland erected a new building in 1993–94 for its traffic technology division. It was a challenging attempt to consoli-date and upgrade the remnants of the defunct industrial complexes through a silvery exterior, though the result may seem dubious. The interior is also experimental: the storage warehouse is placed in the middle of the production area.

On the other side of the railroad embankment, things are more austere. Here a group of architecture and engineering firms has acquired a commercial location with an ever changing history. Built

STEREMAT factory grounds
and **BEWAG** administrative
complex

shortly after the turn of the century, the trade quarters at Elsen-strasse 106/107 first produced pianos, then aeronautics apparatus, and finally precision mechanics and communications equipment. Today the zeitgeist occupies the former factory floors: the building planners have been joined by computer specialists, recycling engineers, and ecological consultants. Beneath the blue fire escape, a small bar called "Mambo-Club" has built a wooden terrace over the narrow ditch between the fire wall and the railroad embankment. There one finds upscale Italian food for lunch, and in the afternoon, quietude and sun. But the basement levels in the extensively modernized commercial tracts, with their ingenious overhead lighting, stand empty. A banner over the entrance gate announces vacant office space. The "Mambo-Club," originally planned as a hot tip for tango fans, unfortunately closes at 6:00 p.m.

Elsenstrasse, on the other hand, poses as plebeian. "The ELSE – a lot of stuff under one roof," promises the inscription over the entrance to the bizarre shopping street. It would surely like to call itself a "shopping mall," but it is essentially just one of the last makeshift creations of post-war Berlin. The old bus depot diagonally opposite was torn down in early 1996, because here, along the "Beermann-Ritze," Dr. Braschel from Böblingen is planning a "Shopping Center at Treptower Park." The small shop owners from here to Karl-Kunger-Strasse await it with mixed feelings. The new "Zweite Hand" building (local advertising paper) is already finished and jammed in between two hectic intersections, along with an adjacent apartment building for the elderly. Here the offices of Patzschke, Klotz & Partner did the planning, and in fact the three-wing building

complex gives every appearance of being blessed by tradition.

While traffic and construction sites rumble below, the bridge girders on our way stand quietly rusting, and locust trees, birches, even walnut trees take over the old railroad land. From Elsenstrasse to the Landwehr canal, the embankment is a registered historic moument. Along Kiefholzstrasse, abandoned workshops await new life after legal settlements. Spreading out to the right are the extensive grounds of the old barracks, still built in patriotic imperial brick Romantic. In former East Germany they housed a border regiment and the army printing office. Now the property belongs to the federal government, which uses a few of the handsome buildings along Bouchéstrasse to accommodate asylum seekers and war refugees.

Once we have crossed Bouchéstrasse on the one-lane emergency bridge, there is relief for the feet: from this point on, following the example of Kreuzberg, the parks commission has buried the old gravel path under a firm layer of coarse sand.

The factory to the right is the former VEB STEREMAT. Here East Germany developed industrial robots. Today, all that remains are a couple of whitewashed, windowless concrete halls. In the middle of the grounds, two enormous and strangely expressionistic cathedral gables recall a time when factory work bore the insignia of higher culture. The administrative tract on Bouchéstrasse, whose brick Neo-Gothic was refurbished at considerable expense, is leased to real estate, construction, and technology firms. But there is also a billiard club here, as well as the cheapest discount store in the whole neighborhood, in front of which ageless alcoholics spend their surplus of free time.

"Laternen-Weber"
and AGFA factory

Now and then, beyond the STEREMAT grounds, an immense, gray-violet block comes into view. Finished in 1995, it now houses the administration of BEWAG (Berlin's electricity company). Despite its colossal proportions, the architects Liepe and Steigelmann managed to place it quite unobtrusively on the edge of Schlesischer Busch. From the stoic row of sharp-edged cubes to the powerful cornice and accentuated attic story, the four-winged administrative complex openly alludes to monumental models from early industrial modernism. Perhaps it is here, in these harsh industrial surroundings, that the ideal vision of an ongoing architectural tradition for Berlin still has its greatest chance.

Around a gentle curve, there appears in the distance for the first time the destination of our journey—the tower of the Emmauskirche at Lausitzer Platz. And promptly the route acquires drama. Walls move in closer on either side, as if to form a kind of "city gate." The generously curved factory to the left, built 1936–40, once belonged to "Laternen-Weber," a hardware manufacturer who once produced bomb and torpedo parts as well as antipersonnel and antitank mines. Consequently, the business was expropriated after the war and later transferred to the VEB Werkzeugmaschinenwerk BWF. Now the brown-black clinker building with the long ribbon windows is an architectural monument, but a largely empty one. On the other side, at the corner of Lohmühlenstrasse and Jordanstrasse, the "Aktiengesellschaft für Anilinfabrikation" (AGFA) was established in 1873 through the merger of two dye manufacturers, to which an inscription on the foremost fire gable bore witness until this summer. As a part of the corporation IG Farben, this factory complex was likewise expropriated in 1945; thereafter it served for sales and distribution of chemical products and from 1960 on, as a wholesale center for sporting goods. At present, the landlords have settled on a mix of computer offices, real estate and technological consultants, construction firms, fitness studios, and of course architectural offices.

On the back side of the former AGFA factory the windows are bricked up, and the courtyard walls facing the railroad are topped with barbed wire. Until 1989, this zone was strictly off limits, being only about 50 meters from the "western border of the state." The bridge over Lohmühlenstrasse to Kreuzberg was not torn down, but all access to it was blocked. Up until the spring of 1990, a piece of the Wall stood directly on the bridge, at the height of the eastern bank of the canal, where the narrow footpath now separates from the remains of the old rusted girders. A careful observer can still recognize the exact boundary line, even in the profiles of the railing: the never-replaced original iron indicates East, the round painted pipe is West.

From this dramatic bridge site, the many cities of Berlin can be perceived in an intensity seldom experienced elsewhere. Behind us is the sober, even strict quietude of the old workers' town of Treptow. Beneath us to the left, the anarchic chaos of a trailer shanty town. To the right, the Schlesischer Busch, whose gently rolling meadow landscape has already effaced all reminders of the death strip below. And in front of us, the noisy, colorful leisure oasis of Görlitzer Park.

The last of the great terminus stations in West Berlin (after the Potsdamer, Lehrter, and Anhalter stations), the Görlitzer Bahnhof stood for almost exactly a hundred years before it was torn down

Görlitzer Park

between 1962 and 1976. The modest structure was built by August Orth, 1865–67, "in a sturdy raw-cinderblock construction covered in Birkenwerder clinker with narrow bands of violet and white-bordered clay panels." Today all that remains of the building are two freight sheds and an "Expeditionsbureau" in the Görlitzer Strasse. In 1980, the 18 hectare area was transferred from the East German railway administration to the West Berlin Senate in a vague contract deal; suddenly a giant open space was available in a district with a shortage of parks. As part of a program of gentle renovation in Kreuzberg, Görlitzer Park was created, with lawns, sledding hill, sports field, children's zoo, and an overly-designed botanical corner, but also with many naturally proliferating islands of trees and shrubbery, in whose shadows hundreds of pounds of grilled meat spread their smoky aroma on weekends.

Indirect traces are now all that remain of the significance the railway station once had for the nearby residential areas: the old pedestrian tunnel running crosswise, once connecting Oppelner Strasse with Liegnitzer Strasse underneath the tracks, or the spires of the corner houses on the adjacent streets, calling attention to their well-to-do address in the then up-and-coming station area. And finally, the street names: the whole "rear" area known as SO 36 reads like a list of the landscapes and destinations to which people once traveled from here: Spreewald, Lausitz, cities in Silesia and Bohemia, finally even Vienna.

The grandfathers' geography has little meaning for the Kreuzberg of today, which has meanwhile assumed the exemplary role of an immigrant town and is accomplishing amazing things. The ease with which the Turkish community is given precedence in Görlitzer Park is one of the indisputable merits of a district often reproached for being difficult. The park's newest attraction is a great water terrace "modeled after the natural limestone terraces near the city Pamukkale in Turkey."

So our walk comes to an end among bikers and skaters, Turkish families, leather jackets and stray dogs. Whoever wishes can stay on the central axis of the old railroad line to the end, stride through the 14 meter high steel gate by Rüdiger Preisler, and finally reach the plateau that August Orth once raised for his Görlitzer Bahnhof. Concealed under the hill is the swimming pool on the Spreewaldplatz, built by Christoph Langhof in 1984. Directly opposite, the trains of the subway line "Linie 1" clatter by every few minutes.

Perhaps one should follow this path in the opposite direction, treading eastward and leaving behind a city already once thought to be at the limits of its perfection, and, from bridge to bridge, dive deeper into neighborhoods sunk in the confusion and uncertainty of upheaval. From this sharpened perspective, looking back, westward, might then reveal the threat and uncertainty hidden within such an ostensibly solid image. Forward looking would then mean looking eastward. From where the wind blows into the city ...

7

Hans Stimmann
Invisible Urban Development

"For those who pass it without entering, the city is one thing; it is another for those who are trapped by it and never leave. There is the city where you arrive for the first time; and there is another city which you leave never to return. Each deserves a different name …"
Italo Calvino, Invisible Cities,
translated by William Weaver, London 1979

Berlin is debating vehemently about the city which has been known by this name at various difficult periods in history, and about the future city with the same name which is supposed to be new and different, about its center, its identity, and about architecture and urban development. Over the last five years, "critical reconstruction"—the guiding model in the historical city center—has received much praise and some attacks.

There was a similarly contradictory response to the concept of "reestablishing the European city" for the large new buildings on Potsdamer Platz, on Alexanderplatz, and around the new Lehrter Bahnhof train station. Public attention concentrated—and concentrates—mainly on the visible, the quality of public areas, and in particular the effect and meaning of facades and their materiality. Architects, historians, and citizens are all aroused by the question of whether and how much glass, stone, and concrete will produce how much classicalness or modernity, and how much is wished for. Important though the debate is—even politically—for this city's appearance and its identity,

it fails to see what first has to be done out of sight, before one can start talking about such images. Fifty years ago Ernst Randzio coined the term "underground urban development." In doing so he made two observations. First, that underground structures had suffered relatively little war damage; as a result, the old city layout could for the most part be retained. Second, that the value of this "underground urban development" was around one third of that which was above ground and visible in a city. This relationship still holds today, considering the concentration of urban engineering and simultaneous modernization.

The long division of Berlin by the Wall meant that this indispensable city beneath the city was in most parts sliced up, largely decrepit, and badly in need of repair and renovation. After reunification, it was perfectly obvious to everyone that the city had to return to functioning order quickly and perfectly. Such were the expectations of Berliners and of the millions of visitors, but above all of those investors from western Berlin and western Germany. The modernization of the urban engineering infrastructure to match that of former West Germany was expected to take place at the same speed as the introduction of the Deutschmark into former East Germany. Expectations like this from an affluent society ignore the enormous efforts of planning and logistics involved, not to mention the unimaginable financial dimensions for the state and the partially state-run firms operating in this sector (as the gas and electricity providers, the city

*Photos from the
underworld by
Erik-Jan Ouwerkerk*

transport authority, the national railways, and
Deutsche Telekom).

People don't talk about that which they cannot
see. Media interest is not sparked by something
you can hardly show. Nevertheless, what has happened in this short pioneering phase is sensational. I can only try and roughly sketch the measures
taken in the individual urban engineering sectors
in order to give a feeling about what had to be done,
and what has been done so far.

The most obvious was also the easiest: closing the gaps and reconnecting the old roads which
used to link East and West Berlin. In a short space
of time some 189 roads had to be joined up and
completed. Above ground that was no problem
because during the years of division very few of
the severed streets had been built over with new
buildings, though this was not due to any mutual
agreement between East and West Berlin. Exceptions include Jerusalemer Strasse, which is blocked
by the Springer newspapers building, and the junction of Lindenstrasse and Spittelmarkt.

But recreating the road network did not just
involve the visible part of the street where people
walk and drive. It also meant a completely new
construction for urban engineering below the
surface: for pipes, canals, and cables. The financial
dimensions involved are reflected in the following
example: the construction department of the city
government maintained a road-building budget
for 1994 (just main roads) of DM 55 million. In the
same period, spending on urban engineering

infrastructure, for renewing and laying supply
lines and waste disposal systems, was more than
double that, at around DM 120 million.

In many places, where the Spree river had
served as border between the two Berlins, reconstructing the road network also included building
bridges. Seven bridges total were either reconstructed or newly built: the Sandkrugbrücke across
the Berlin-Spandau ship canal re-linking the
districts of Mitte and Tiergarten; the Kronprinzenbrücke north of the Reichstag; the Weidendammer
Brücke crossing the Spree as part of Friedrichstrasse; Grünstrassenbrücke across the Spree-
kanal; Michaelbrücke between Mitte and Friedrichshain which completes the axis through the
historical Luisenstadt area; Schillingbrücke linking
Kreuzberg and Friedrichshain; and the famous
Oberbaumbrücke which completes the inner-city
ring road. The city demanded high design standards for these bridges and insisted upon cooperation between architect and engineers within the
guiding principle of "critical reconstruction." An
outstanding example of these standards is the
Kronprinzenbrücke designed by Santiago Calatrava.

The quickest restorations were those of the
east-west subway (U-Bahn) connections cut by the
Berlin Wall. In the short term, rail connections were
repaired and important inner-city stations reactivated. For years these had been ghost stations,
watched over by armed guards, whom subway
passengers from West Berlin passed by like colorful fish in an aquarium. The first underground

**Maintenance work in
the motorway tunnel
near Tegel Airport**

stations to be re-opened included the famous ones at Stadtmitte and Potsdamer Platz (architect: Alfred Grenander). The two lines through the historical city center were restored, the north-south route from Tegel to Mariendorf, and the east-west route from Pankow to Charlottenburg. Berlin's U1 line, or "Linie 1," which was celebrated in a 1980's hit musical of the same name, no longer travels from Ruhleben to Schlesisches Tor in Kreuzberg but from Krumme Lanke to Warschauer Brücke in the former East. This link over the rebuilt Oberbaumbrücke provides a connection with the Stadtbahn, the main east-west inner-city railway route. Trains from Ruhleben now travel along the U2 line to Vinetastrasse in Pankow via Alexanderplatz.

These new linkages are changing the city's topography. Districts formerly detached are now more accessible with new station stops on central lines. An example of this was the reconstruction of Oberbaumbrücke, which met with vigorous resistance from a Kreuzberg neighborhood ill-prepared to exchange its former location on the periphery with its present (and historical) central location. Another example is the possibility nowadays for day-trippers in Pankow to travel all the way to Westend on the underground. It's a case of two leafy suburbs discovering one another.

In addition to this modernization and reactivation, necessary extensions to the underground network were also planned. These included the line linking Alexanderplatz, Leipziger Strasse and Potsdamer Platz with the Kulturforum in the former West (U3), and the so-called "Chancellor's Line" from the Town Hall to the Reichstag and to the new central station at Lehrter Bahnhof (U5). But both lines, despite their importance for Berlin's role as a metropolis and capital city, are out of the question in light of Berlin's current fiscal and budgetary situation (though construction of the north-south tunnel between Lehrter Bahnhof and the Brandenburg Gate also includes tunnels for a future subway line). For the moment, the most recent extension of the subway network is the 320 meter long stretch between Leinestrasse and the Hermannstrasse railway station.

However, subway planning means more than just extending lines and link-ups. Whoever expects, as the city government does, in the not-too-distant future to be able to convince 80 % of all people traveling in the city to decide to choose public transportation, then they have to offer the future passenger more than they do now: more daylight, more comfort and security, and more architectural quality. It was exactly these demands which the plans for the new subway line U5 were supposed to meet with its spacious stations flooded with daylight. For its bridges, a close cooperation with renowned architects was envisaged. Axel Schultes, Max Dudler, Axel Oesterreich and Richard Rogers were to guarantee the sought-for quality.

These new demands on Berlin's public transport system are approved and supported by the local transport authority, the BVG. But so far the

Work in the Telekom cable tunnel under Potsdamer Strasse in Zehlendorf

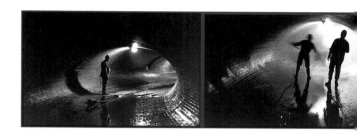

only visible sign of this is in the new information and guidance system created by MetaDesign. The system helps both visitors and regular passengers find the right train, make connections, and recognize links.

Perhaps the most typical transportation system for Berlin and environs is the city rapid line or S-Bahn. Electrification of the system began as early as the end of the last century. Its famous inner-city ring, the so-called "dog's head," not only links the various districts in east and west, but also links Berlin with the towns around it via radial routes. Königs Wusterhausen, Potsdam and Oranienburg are just three of these towns. The building of the Wall split the S-Bahn system, cutting off West Berlin from its surroundings. Another hard blow came when the BVG took over the remaining rump S-Bahn network in West Berlin in 1984. But now since the Deutsche Bahn AG (German Railway Company) owns the S-Bahn, and a separate Berliner S-Bahn Company was established, the organizational structure is back to its original state. Important routes are nearing completion, including the inner-city ring and the Tegel–Hennigsdorf line, to join other historical routes already back in service like Charlottenburg–Potsdam, Friedrichstrasse–Lichterfelde–Wannsee (the so-called "bankers' route"). It will cost even more billions of marks to recreate the old state of things and to satisfy tomorrow's demands. Meanwhile, the BVG has made a first gesture: since March 5th 1996 passengers on the S7 between

Potsdam-Stadt and Hauptbahnhof on the main east-west line are being offered special services entitled "S-presso." Trained staff travel in the trains offering snacks, helping with changing trains, passing on information, and giving the passengers a greater feeling of security. Coffee costs DM 1.40, a roll with drippings DM 1.50.

So far almost 300 km of the original 335 km of routes are back in service. It sounds easy, but the financial and logistical dimensions should not be underestimated. Along the way, many S-Bahn stations covered with spontaneous vegetation and forty-year-old robinias were re-discovered, woken from their ecological doze, and brought back to everyday life in the big city. The reconstruction and modernization of stations, outfitting them with elevators for disabled passengers, etc. have on the whole taken place at a modest aesthetic level. This is hardly surprising considering the organizational and financial difficulties. Nevertheless, the S-Bahn still has an undiminished fascination for Berliners. It's a way of really experiencing Berlin above ground with all its discontinuities and aesthetic appeal. This fascination is also demonstrated in the nightly after-hours broadcasts of S-Bahn travels on the local television channel SFB. Originally planned as something to fill the early morning broadcast gaps, they even became cult viewing for a while.

The S-Bahn's transformation into a modern, city-wide transport system has also led to a new topographical perception of particular places in

Cleaning rain water
drainage tunnels under
Martin-Luther-Strasse
in Schöneberg

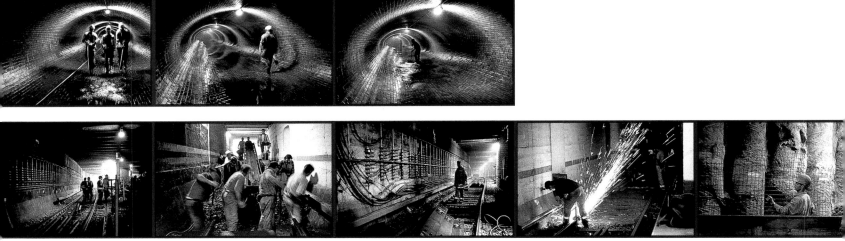

the former West. One example is the trade fair grounds, which to the amazement of many former West Berliners is now suddenly not just accessible from the city motorway but also with a wonderful S-Bahn connection. The middle class area of Friedenau on Bundesallee also now once again has its own convenient S-Bahn station. The reconstruction of the S-Bahn has helped return the old city feeling to Berlin. Now the long-distance trains bring you into Berlin, not to any particular terminus station, but rather to one of the many stations of the Berlin S-Bahn, from where residents can then return to their respective districts.

What we envisage is to build Berlin into a "city of railways." If we again take one step back in history, we can see that before the city was reunified, long-distance trains were basically unimportant in West Berlin. People traveled by plane or by car to West Germany. The East German railway system had been maintained but was in a wretched state. The tearing down of the former termini stations around the historical city center, and especially the destruction of Anhalter Bahnhof, Görlitzer Bahnhof, and Lehrter Bahnhof, is not only regrettable but above all irreversible. The tracks have long since been torn up and city parks laid out in their place.

For this reason, the railway company and the city have agreed to a completely new rail plan: a combination of features known as the "mushroom concept." The mushroom's outline is formed by the east-west line bringing the trains along the inner-

city route via Charlottenburg, Zoo, Friedrichstrasse and Hauptbahnhof (the mushroom's brim), and by an 8 km long stalk coming from the south. The two will cross at the planned new central station Lehrter Bahnhof. The top of the mushroom is formed by the northern half of the inner-city ring, a stretch reserved until now mainly for S-Bahn and freight traffic. Here trains can be brought around and led into the future tunnel so that they are able to travel in a variety of directions, such as southwest for instance.

The decision to build a new central station just a few minutes away from the German Chancellor's Office and the Reichstag is meant to signal the renaissance of Berlin as a railway city in the middle of the European railway network. The station, currently being designed by the office von Gerkan, Marg & Partner, will be the only station in Germany where high speed train routes cross. We hope that one day the utopia of a rapid, modern, ecologically-sound, European transport system will become a reality, and that you can change here for Moscow, Paris, Copenhagen or Vienna.

The planning of the new central station is linked with the decision to build other new stations. Especially important here are the main-line stations in the district of Spandau and in Papestrasse, which is to serve all of southern Europe.

Berlin's trams reflect a strange chapter of the city's division. Here it is not a question of re-creating and re-activating old connections, but in the treatment of a situation unique in the world. In one

Construction in the
U-Bahn tunnel along
the U6 line and in
the U-Bahn stations
Hermannstrasse,
Oranienburger Tor,
and Stadtmitte

half of the city—West Berlin—trams were completely swept away in the 1960s as a traffic hindrance. At the same time, in the other half—East Berlin—the system was maintained and expanded as a result of completely opposite aims in traffic planning. Trams were especially used to provide transport to the large new residential areas on the city's eastern outskirts.

In the meantime, the worn out East Berlin tram network with its out-dated trams has been technologically modernized by the newly-reunified BVG and converted to a low-body system. The city's reunification also signaled the start of the similarly unusual, successive re-introduction of trams in the western half of the city. The plans have already borne fruit: anyone who wishes can travel by tram from the new "in" district of Prenzlauer Berg in the east to the "red" district of Wedding in the west. In future, a passenger will be able to travel by tram from the city's most eastern extremity, the large housing projects of Marzahn, down to Alexanderplatz and on to Potsdamer Platz—or even as far as the Philharmonic.

Favorable hydrogeologic conditions mean that the Berlin area has never had a problem with its water supply in terms of quality or quantity. The water systems in the two halves of the city were separate up until reunification. The West Berliners drew their water from their own wells. The East Berliners did likewise. The problems have nothing to do with the water itself but with the quality of the underground pipes. These have to be renewed

by the year 2003, with investments totaling DM 3.5 billion.

With the drainage system it is a different story. For technological reasons there was never a complete separation. This was the result of the topography: sloping pipes can only run down to the pumping station at the respective lowest point of the Spree river. From there they are pumped out to sewage farms far from the edge of the city using the system introduced by James Hobrecht in the last century. This system continued to function up until reunification with just a few modifications (construction of sewage plants). Since then the main aim has been the thorough modernization of the drainage system in former East Berlin. The main pipe network, dating back to the beginning of this century, needed renewing. The sewage farm system—which worked right up until recently—is now being converted to a sewage plant system. The investment necessary comes to almost DM 10 billion. But it wasn't just a matter of technological reunification and modernization, but also of the fusion of two separate water and drainage firms. To this aim, the old headquarters of the Berlin waterworks in the historic city center is being reactivated and the former main headquarters for West Berlin, in Wilmersdorf, will be downgraded to a subsidiary.

Where the supply of energy in the form of electricity and gas is concerned, the former island of West Berlin has again become part of the German mainland. While conversion to natural

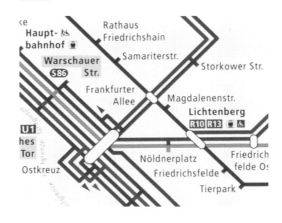

Chains of bubbles and
the inner-city train
network provide infor-
mation about which lines
run where and intersect
which other lines

gas—mainly from Siberia—is now complete in eastern Berlin, it is still being carried out in the western half of the city. Since 1985 western Berlin has been supplied with a separate pipeline from Siberia. The political situation and security reasons meant that this gas had to be converted at great effort into gas for the city. In addition, West Berlin also had to continue producing additional gas. One of the legacies of the city's former island state is a project for an underground town gas-holder near the Olympic Stadium, intended to ensure emergency supplies for West Berlin in the event of any intervention. The project had reached an advanced stage but will be completed at a smaller scale.

West Berlin's island-like conditions were much more evident in its electricity supply. After the Berlin blockade ended in 1949, new power plants were built in the city—a completely atypical approach for normal electricity supplies in Western Europe. The fundamentals of this system have changed since reunification and Berlin is now integrated in the western European electricity network.

However, the way residents became used to this remarkable supply structure might prove to be a possibly unique precondition for the introduction of new energy supply systems, such as small block thermal power stations. Small plants will also be necessary for the still seemingly utopian idea of supplying large parts of the city with solar energy. The Berlin Senate's Department for Urban Development, Environmental Protection and Technology

has initiated a solar energy decree which would make electricity production via solar cells obligatory for particular investments. In this way, the city's former island-like conditions enable a step in another dimension, in a manner more radical than anything tried anywhere else so far.

Moving on to telecommunications, parts of the East Berlin equipment dated back to 1922/26. A double line for two or more users was the rule. It is now hard to imagine just how difficult it was to communicate between the two halves of the city. There were a modest 72 lines from East to West— and 460 in the opposite direction. The systematic rebuilding of the whole telecommunications network in the east of the city took place at a rapid pace. Between 1991 and 1994 320,000 new connections were activated, so that now both halves are equally well supplied. The modest West Berlin telephone directory, and paper back-sized East Berlin directory have been replaced by three thick volumes for the entire city. These together weigh more than the directories for Munich, Stuttgart, Frankfurt and two or three small towns combined.

But there is no stagnation in telecommunications. The Deutsche Telekom invested DM 7 billion between 1990 and 1995, and will be investing the same again until the year 2000. A glass fiber network, replacing the old copper cables, is being installed in the 14 sq. km area between the Ku'damm, Alexanderplatz, Potsdamer Platz and Friedrichstrasse. And thanks to a large-scale test

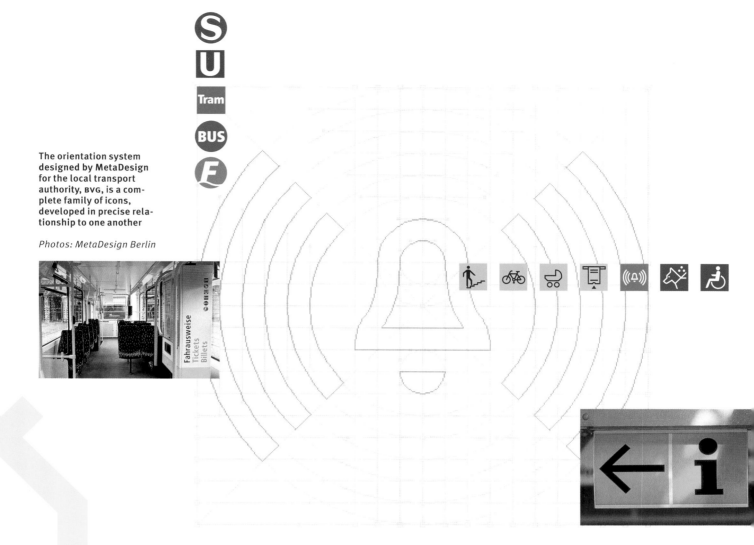

using ATM (asynchronous transfer mode) broad-
band technology, the German Chancellor's Office,
the Federal Government's Press and Information
Office, and a few ministries in Bonn are already
present in Berlin, at least virtually. The latest
multimedia technology means that in the future
not only the ministries remaining in Bonn can be
linked with Berlin, but Berlin itself with the whole
world.

Another change which shouldn't be forgotten
is the timing of traffic lights in former East Berlin.
Those infamously slow lights are being accelerated
to accommodate the tempo of a modern big city. In
the course of this accommodation the green man
also had to be exchanged. Now people are pleased
if they can still find one of the old-style lights in the
east with their charming green man wearing a hat
and optimistically striding across a zebra cross-
walk.

All of this changing and perfecting is connected
with time. Time needed to be caught up because
East Germany had a different sense of time than
the West. Speed for speed's sake was always characteristic of Berlin and is now true for both halves
of the city. The time-savings, which will never really
exist, could be achieved with faster trains, with the
perfect supplying of all forms of energy, and with
the use of video conferences.

Is it surprising that when the West Berlin electricity system switched over to the citywide system
all electrically synchronized clocks fell out of synch?
When, in a society where everything is measured in
time, yet where no one has any time, the measurement of time itself fails, due to some small invisible problem like electrical fluctuations, only then
does it become clear what the unification of two
completely different worlds really means.

8

Manfred Kühne
New Bridges over the Spree and Havel

The building activity currently in progress in Berlin includes numerous bridges. Some of these are still under construction or are already finished, others can be visualized with the aid of their winning competition entries. The projects are concentrated along the Spree river in the Mitte district, Berlin's historical city center. Many bridges there were only provisionally reconstructed after the war, some have been damaged by inadequate maintenance, others were not rebuilt after 1945 or were torn down when the Wall was built. Examples of this include the Kronprinzenbrücke and Alsenbrücke in the Spreebogen area, Ebertsbrücke and Waisenbrücke in Mitte, and Brommybrücke between the districts of Kreuzberg and Friedrichshain. The collection of historical bridges can be expanded with additional ones in the government quarter and at Hauptbahnhof.

Basic Conditions
One of the reasons for constructing and altering the bridges is the series of specifications for so-called "Europaschiffe" (Euro Ships). These affect the width of the channel, clearance height, and safety barriers around piers. Their effect can be seen with the example of the Marschallbrücke. A river width of 55 meters between the abutments means a clearance profile with a channel width of 30 meters is required—more than double what it was before. In addition, the river bed has to be deepened and, as a result, the foundations re-secured.

The "roadway gradient," which determines the course of the height of the bridge's deck, is also being altered in the process. Historical bridges used to have decks which rose in straight lines to their centers, resulting in creases where the road met the bridge and at the deck's vertex. Today this would only hinder vehicles, so transitions between road and bridge are smoothed out with rounded seams. Additionally, in case of further alterations, the height of the bridge's deck has to be adapted visually to its urban context, otherwise surrounding buildings appear to sink in comparison with the newly elevated bridge, thus detracting from the buildings' proportions.

The roadway over a bridge determines the bridge's width. In the old city center, historical conditions are generally taken into account. The only prominent exceptions to this are the bridges on the future inner-city ring, Sandkrugbrücke and Oberbaumbrücke.

In inner-city areas there is an especially high number of underground pipes and cables to be incorporated into the bridges' structures. These include those for heating, drinking water, gas, electricity, sewage, telecommunications and light signals, and other pipes and lines, such as those for the fire department and for parliament. There is only a narrow space available for these on the underside of the bridge, where the load-bearing construction is located—unless a decision is made to use an overhead support system, such as a truss system, suspension constructions, or some other

Oberbaumbrücke

such solution. But this, in turn, would contradict the historical inner-city "bridge typology." Instead, larger pipes and cables are subdivided and lain out next to each other. The plate, girder and truss systems are broken through in several places, or have to be slender enough that the cables and mains can be safely hung underneath them. Having them run underneath the river bed requires expensive manhole installations. These would have to be accessible on both sides of the river, which is not possible on many of the narrow riverside roads.

Typologies

The width, depth and current of the Spree in the historic city center have always been too modest to pose a serious challenge to construction. Only above the present-day locks at the old Mühlenstau (Mill Dam) does the river broaden considerably. For centuries, simple wooden constructions were used for crossing the Spree. It wasn't until around 1700 that the Lange Brücke (Long Bridge) was built in the baroque capital. Located where the unimpressive Rathausbrücke (Town Hall Bridge) stands today, the bridge was a prestigious stone construction and royal monument following the example of Pont Neuf in Paris. It set a creative standard, and had a determining influence on royal bridge construction up until Schinkel's Schlossbrücke (Palace Bridge). Nineteenth century industrialization allowed new cast iron and steel arch constructions, but had no great influence on the proportionality and ornamentation of the city's bridges.

The urban space surrounding the bridges prevented them from becoming symbols of the city. This is because the river is relatively narrow compared to prominant boulevards such as Unter den Linden, and the streets along the river are also small compared to those of the surrounding Friedrichstadt quarter. Furthermore, the medieval urban layout of those districts has been extensively lost, thus contributing to the declining importance of the Spree and its bridges in the cityscape.

The urban planning model of "critical reconstruction" favored in Berlin, aims to regain the historical proportionality, and prefers traditional typologies in bridge building. Piers frame the boats' underpass, structure the river area and moderate the span lengths. These solid, crash-resistant piers contrast with the slightly curved, narrow road plates, thus emphasizing the tectonic fittings. Ornamental details on the abutments, piers, railings, and masts, make the bridges more attractive for pedestrians. Delicate undersides offer boat passengers a pleasant sight. Diverse lighting designs accentuate the details by night.

Procedure

Constructive and creative expertise are united through cooperation between architects and engineers. To this end new methods were tried in the last few years. In the competitions, teams between architects and engineers were favored. In direct contracts, design advice from the architect has become a minimum standard.

Oberbaumbrücke	
Planning and Design	Berlin Building, Housing, and Traffic Dept., Bridge Building Section with WKP, Planning Office for Construction; ABKB, Architecture Office for Landmark and Art Conservation; IfS, Institute for Urban Renewal Architect: Santiago Calatrava (Zurich/Barcelona)
Built	1894–95
Restoration	1992–95
Total Length	approx. 150 m
Total Width	approx. 28 m
Effective Span	7.50 – 16 – 19 – 22 – 19 – 16 – 7.50 m
Building Cost	approx. DM 70 million

Michaelbrücke	
Planning and Design	Berlin Building, Housing, and Traffic Dept., Bridge Building Section Architects: Dörr, Ludolf, Wimmer (Berlin)
Built	1993–95
Total Length	72 m
Total Width	20.65 m
Effective Span	19.69 – 30.80 – 19.13 m
Building Cost	approx. DM 19 million

The Oberbaumbrücke

is exceptional among the inner-city Spree bridges because of its size. At this point the river is unusually wide, broadening still further upstream to form the scenic greenery between Treptow and Stralau. The bridge's name serves as a reminder of its historical role as a gate in the old baroque excise wall. In a later Berlin Wall it served a dual role, simultaneously dividing the city, while helping people maintain contact across the border between East and West. Its function today is in complete contrast to this — it is now part of a ring road designed to relieve the city center.

This combination bridge for tram and elevated railway lines — unique in Berlin — was built using the stylistic devices of historicism. It was a blend of historical architectural details with the most contemporary transportation technology. During the Second World War, only the center of the bridge was destroyed. A temporary reconstruction quickly followed.

A wide-ranging protection of the surviving structure was agreed to, along with a completely new construction of the center, railings and lighting masts, as well as the reconstruction of the top of the towers, which had been dismantled.

The complete historical reconstruction of the tram and elevated train bridge was not possible, because boat clearance in the center had to be raised. A prestressed concrete construction was chosen with sloped frames, cancelling out the vault thrust of the connecting arches. This form was also used in the steel construction of the elevated railway. The road surface had to be laid up to 26 cm higher than the walkways, thus compensating for the different construction heights over the shared bottom edge. The light, organic, new construction asserts itself powerfully within the bridge's structure. As a result, similar to the original design, a synthesis of historical forms and new construction and design methods is achieved.

The Michaelbrücke

lies on an axis which starts in Luisenstadt in the Mitte district. The axis extends from the neo-classical Michaelkirche over the bridge and through the underpass beneath the S-Bahn tracks on the northern bank of the Spree, thereby entering the Friedrichshain district. The new bridge construction had to raise the boat clearance, integrate district heating pipelines, and keep the height of the roadway in line with the opening under the S-Bahn. A new river footpath planned for the south bank of the Spree meant that the abutment had to be moved and the bridge's south pier built on a new site. Though the new bridge was laid symetrically, its vertex was set slightly south of the river's center point. All that remains of the old Michaelbrücke are parts of the north abutment and the granite base of the north pier.

The combination of massive hull shaped piers and a lighter steel construction is reminiscent of the old bridge. The piers are made of granite and exposed concrete and get lower toward their ends, so as to emphasize the floating effect of the steel construction, whose slightly arched gridwork has replaced the three original trussed arches. It has been broken through several times length-wise so as to accomodate numerous mains and pipes. This supporting structure cantilevers out under the bridge's deck, employing tapered cross-girders to give the sides of the bridge an especially narrowed edge profile. Filigree railings rise from these cantilevers. At night these are emphasized by illuminated handrails. The slender lighting masts rest on steel brackets at the ends of the piers. The prow-shaped brackets thus fulfill three functions simultaneously: they protect, illuminate, and denote structural divisions. The new Michaelbrücke's very liberal reinterpretation of its predecessor — a classic nineteenth century Spree bridge — makes it into one possible example of what "critical reconstruction" can mean in bridge building.

Sandkrugbrücke	
Planning and Design	Berlin Building, Housing, and Traffic Dept., Bridge Building Section
	Grassi Engineer's Office
	Architects:
	Thomas Baumann and Birgitt Welter (Berlin)
Built	1993–94
Total Length	34 m
Total Width	29 m
Effective Span	32.60 m
Building Cost	approx. DM 10 million

Kronprinzenbrücke	
Planning	Berlin Building, Housing, and Traffic Dept., Bridge Building Section
Design	Santiago Calatrava (Zurich/Barcelona)
Built	1993–96
Competition	1991
Total Length	73 m
Total Width	23.40 m
Effective Span	14.20 – 44 – 14.20 m
Building Cost	approx. DM 40 million

The Sandkrugbrücke,

like Oberbaumbrücke, lies on the historic boundaries around the baroque city and between East and West. It traverses the Berlin-Spandauer Canal at the northern exit of Humboldthafen (Humboldt Harbor), amid an ensemble of listed historic buildings, including a quayside, railway station, and hospital. A completely new bridge needed to be built for several reasons: the foundations' load-bearing capacity was at risk, the clearance for boats needed to be expanded, and a barrier to prevent boats crashing into the eastern abutment behind the bend in the canal had been deemed essential. The roadway had to be raised by one meter—both across the bridge and approaching it. The clearance and the bridge needed widening to 29 meters. The old bridge was dominated by abutments pushing out perpendicularly into the canal as curved extensions to the quay walls with stair exits. The heavy natural stone surfacing made the abutments seem very solid. By contrast, the finely structured steel truss arches stretched between them seemed especially light. The arches were provisionally replaced after the war by right-angled solid web girders. On the new bridge, the shortened abutments are no longer the dominant motif, despite the fact that the design uses elements from the previous bridge in the stair exits, the railings, and the natural stone parapets. The steel frame constructions have been placed in front of the abutment walls and particulary dominate the visible underside. The load-bearing structure appears to be lighter; tapered, secondary girders support the walkways like consoles. The railings and light masts have been developed as finely structured steel elements, emphasizing the construction while lending a subtle accent.

The Kronprinzenbrücke

has symbolic importance for Berlin. It was torn down to make way for the Wall, and has been rebuilt to be part of the future government quarter. As such, it represents Berlin's division, reunification, and development into the new German capital. EU subsidies demonstrate that this symbolism is also understood internationally; resulting in a Europe-wide competition won by Santiago Calatrava.

A carefully designed arch construction disbands into slanting braces and is spread out over underwater piers close to the banks. The bridge's outline is reminiscent of the nearby Weidendammbrücke. In both cases the short cantilevers have to be fastened to the supports with tie rods. The light Kronprinzenbrücke looks as if it is a unified whole. The girder construction and the details appear to be stretched into elegant curves, while the massive crash barriers in front of the bridge are more an eye-sore. They were not foreseen during the competition, but the bridge's slender support system is especially vulnerable to collisions. The whole sculptural impression with its light surfaces and elevation ensures a strong presence for the bridge in the as-yet, unbuilt surroundings. The height was possible through the absence of neighboring buildings, which otherwise would have pre-determined the appropriate dimensions.

Marschallbrücke
Planning | Berlin Building, Housing, and Traffic Dept., Bridge Building Section
Design | Pichler Ingenieure GmbH, Berlin
| Architect: Benedict Tonon, Berlin
Competition | January 1996
Built | 1997
Total Length | 64 m
Total Width | 19.2 m
Effective Span | 37.26 and 15.52 m
Building Cost | approx. DM 13 million

Südbrücke
Planning | Berlin Building, Housing, and Traffic Dept., Bridge Building Section
Design | Martin Krone
| (Leonhardt, Andrä and Partner)
| Architect: Walter Arno Noebel
Competition | December 1993
Built | 1995–97
Total Length | 270 m
Total Width | 22 m
Effective Span | 56 m mid-section
Building Cost | approx. DM 50 million

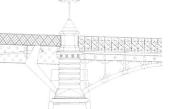

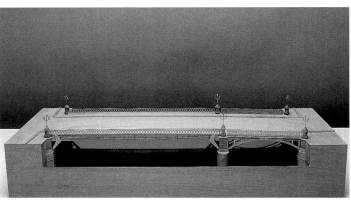

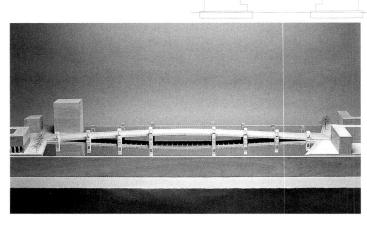

The Marschallbrücke

is one of the few remaining historic monuments in the parliamentary quarter. But at least two thirds of the historical substance has to be removed to allow for an increased boat clearance. The city's conservation authority insisted that one arch be preserved, but the construction department opposed combining old with new. The result was a procedural compromise: in a limited competition, four of the groups participating were to produce designs for completely rebuilding the bridge, four others were to produce construction designs incorporating the remnants of the bridge into the new one. The winner was a proposal from the "old/new" section, which divided the bridge not into two sections—old and new—but five. The roadway will be completely rebuilt, allowing it to become stronger and higher—albeit at the cost of tearing down the whole middle section of the arch, originally intended for preservation. However, two original, outside, load-bearing sections are being saved and transformed into footbridges. Their extensions are new, flat walkways, whose details incorporate the finely structured character of the rebuilt sections in a simplified way. The low level of the pedestrian areas still has to be resolved in the design. Nevertheless, its synthesis of historical and new building exemplifies the position of historic monument preservation in Berlin's bridge building.

Bridges in Wasserstadt Oberhavel

A new suburb with urban character is to arise in an industrial and warehouse area on both sides of the Oberhavel (Upper Havel) in Berlin's westernmost district of Spandau. Two bridges are intended to join the different halves across the river, not just in function but also in form.

There is a clear division of tasks between the two bridges. The narrower Südbrücke (southern bridge) is intended primarily for local traffic and is therefore more attractive for pedestrians. The Nordbrücke (northern bridge) will be very wide so as to be able to accommodate through traffic and a separate tram track. This has resulted in a typological distinction between a "fast bridge" and a "slow" one.

Competitions were held for both bridges: an open competition for the southern bridge, and a limited one for the northern bridge.

The Südbrücke

is being built according to a design which takes issue with its urban context and the pedestrian's perspective. A dense row of solid cubic pillars widens just around the central boat route. The clinker brick clad piers are durable and resistant to boat crashes, their volume allows the vertically vaulted concrete roadway construction to appear light. Small towers with illuminated cubes on top rise above the piers, emphasizing the continuation of the street. The bridge is still under construction and promises to become a symbol of the Wasserstadt.

Nordbrücke
Planning   Berlin Building, Housing, and Traffic Dept.,
                  Bridge Building Section
Design   Ingenieurbüro für Bauwesen
                  H.Fink GmbH
                  Architects: Dörr, Ludolf, Wimmer, Berlin
Competition   October 1995
Total Length   238.47 m
Total Width   33.60 m
Effective Span   32.41 – 43.21 – 54.02 –
                  68.42 – 50.41 m
Building Cost   approx. DM 70 million

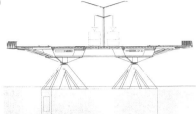

The Nordbrücke

is based on a completely different typological approach: a flat disc-like load-bearing structure is laid out like a dot on two (or four) supports which run to a point. It gives the impression of being a perfect continuation of the road surface. Rows of trees fill the ramp areas and optically narrow the street, making the bridge appear extremely wide, almost like a piazza. A narrow, middle row of combined overhead cable and lighting poles avoids even the slightest framing of the bridge's top surface. Along the whole length of the bridge, pedestrians are invited to enjoy the unhindered view of the river landscape. The visible underside dissolves into transverse girders, laid slightly at an angle, in line with the axis of the shipping channel. The taught deck construction appears to be floating on the piers, which have been removed of all their usual massiveness. They establish the river transport channels alongside each other — four piers for the main eastern channel, two piers

for the secondary western one. These also serve to accentuate the river's cross-section. The asymmetry loosens the composition and underlines the seperateness of the road level.

That represents the status report — but further construction will arise over the next few years. Footbridges will be needed between the government buildings and park areas. The building row north of the Spreebogen must first be completed before the Alsenbrücke can be rebuilt. Ebertsbrücke between Humboldt University and Oranienburger Strasse exists only in provisional form. The long-planned Bodebrücke at the tip of the Museum Island is still waiting to be carried out. Debate over Schlüter's equestrian monument seems inevitable during the forseeable rebuilding of the Rathausbrücke (formerly Kurfürstenbrücke and Lange Brücke) between Nikolaiviertel, the Marstall (former Royal Stables) and the Palast der Republik. Because of tram line construction there will also have to be a complete transformation of the old and new Gertraudenbrücke, located next to each other on Spittelmarkt. A further new bridge will also be needed for the tram line at Hauptbahnhof.

Unclear, however, is whether Waisenbrücke next to Köllnischer Park will be restored. Brommybrücke between Kreuzberg and Friedrichshain definitely stands a better chance because it helps relieve congestion on Oberbaumbrücke.

Library at
the Luisenbad
Architects   Rebecca Chestnutt and
                     Robert Niess, Berlin
Project Managers   Johannes Schulze-Icking,
                     Konrad Benstz
Client   City-State of Berlin,
                     represented by the District Wedding
Usable Area   1,764 sq. m
Opening   November 1995
Building Costs   approx. DM 30 million
Address   Travemünder Strasse 2,
                     Berlin-Wedding

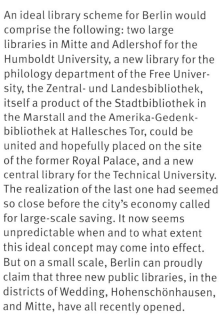

Ursula Flitner
New Libraries

An ideal library scheme for Berlin would comprise the following: two large libraries in Mitte and Adlershof for the Humboldt University, a new library for the philology department of the Free University, the Zentral- und Landesbibliothek, itself a product of the Stadtbibliothek in the Marstall and the Amerika-Gedenk-bibliothek at Hallesches Tor, could be united and hopefully placed on the site of the former Royal Palace, and a new central library for the Technical University. The realization of the last one had seemed so close before the city's economy called for large-scale saving. It now seems unpredictable when and to what extent this ideal concept may come into effect. But on a small scale, Berlin can proudly claim that three new public libraries, in the districts of Wedding, Hohenschönhausen, and Mitte, have all recently opened.

This is all the more amazing when one considers that not only did Berlin's budget cuts make working in libraries harder — reduced new acquisitions, fewer periodicals, hardly any new media — the libraries' whole social mission of providing the common people with comprehensive and free information, culture, and entertainment seems to be endangered by a growing number of private and profit-oriented competitors. Therefore, various

new processes and kinds of organization are being tested to free the libraries from the chains of standard administrative procedure. The same holds true for new library construction.

Guidelines for the people's "literary provisions" have existed for some time. In Berlin there is the Library Development Plan, laid down in 1995. The Henning-Evaluation of 1993 offered suggestions for sites and volume of construction. Yet to this day the upkeep of public libraries falls under the jurisdiction of the district authorities voluntary services. The decentralized main and branch libraries of Berlin's 23 districts are largely autonomous in their work, but dependent on state-level funds for building investment. When, where, and how much is built thus depends less on demand and more on fiscal policy.

The three new libraries introduced here were built where there was a need for construction and renovation: for the preservation of historic monuments, for the renovation of old buildings and for the development of a local center in a large-scale housing project. As various as the conditions were, so too were the planning procedures.

The Library at the Luisenbad
This library endured the classic, tried-and-true, but lengthy administrative procedure. The owner was the city-state of Berlin, the contract awarded to an independent architecture office. From the project's announcement to the start of building, a construction investment-and-planning period of at least 5 years is called for by state budgetary regulations. The most important intermediate step at the specialized level is the compilation of a public requirement program, which is then set down into a construction planning paper, acting as binding regulations for ratification procedures, calls for bids, selection, and construction. The city-state of Berlin closely regulates the contents and course of each step in the procedure through the Construction-Directive (A-Bau). Each step has to be financially secured through parliamentary resolution. In this interaction of parliament and administration, the project is processed, split up among construction, financial, and specialized administrations. The specialized administrations are the offices responsible for culture at the district and municipal levels. Extensive and often time-consuming voting procedures are necessary. But once they have been politically secured, the results can be immediately put into

planning, because authority vis-à-vis architects and construction firms exists in the contracts.

In 1984, a motion in the city council, demanding a utilization concept for the historic emsemble around the Luisenbad, provided the impetus for the planning. The Luisenbad developed out of the long outdated Gesundbrunnen, a spa facility turned bathing area, which then became a restaurant and dancefloor, before finally being used as a movie theater and partly torn down in 1980. Local protest saved the picturesque foyer and wing, which are now under protection as historic landmarks.

Test designs resulted in the 1985 resolution to house the library on this site; the budgetary procedure was set in motion, an approved public requirement program existed by 1987. The sophisticated construction job foresaw a competition which was won in 1988 by the office of Chestnutt + Niess. Their design was recommended for execution, but with one revision. Due to an order by the finance administration, the children's and youth section had to be omitted from the program. Construction began in February 1992 and was completed at the end of 1995.

The library can be reached from the

Badstrasse through the entranceway of a typical turn-of-the-century Berlin apartment block or from a riverbank path along the Panke, past a colorful brick apartment house, which recalls old bathing and recreation facilities. Embedded in the riverbank promenade is the former office building and the "foyer" of the torn-down festival halls. Both old structures are freestanding, two-story buildings, narrow as coachhouses. With their irregular floor plans, they adjust to the boundaries of the diagonal allotments. These picturesquely grouped stucco and brick buildings are augmented by additions that show distinct contrasts in volume and material.

The office building accomodates administrative workplaces and is connected underground with the main building. It is approached first from its rear side, which is closed off partly by a new wall of dark brick with little porthole windows and big glass-block surfaces. The remains of the Marienbad together with the coffee kitchen have been luxuriously restored. On the upper floor lies the splendid Puttensaal, which today is used on public occasions. Unfortunately, most of the building, which was restored all the way to its wood-beamed ceilings, cannot be used as a library, due to fire regulations.

The library hall is located as a slightly slanted semicircular space before the old building's still-visible wall line. A wedge-like skylight emphasizes this seam. The hall floor lies one story lower than the old building and was able to be expanded with spaces set beneath the lawns. Also, a sunken and walled-in garden was made, to which opens the glass-covered, rounded base area. Strong pillars following the semicircle support the flat roof.

A ramp and a glass elevator mediate between the old and new building levels. In the middle of the hall, they lead up from a gallery which has been placed in the room like a square table. On this table is located the news and information center. The open stacks area below is densely filled with shelves. Unfortunately, there is not much room left for reading areas. But the entire interior design lay in the hands of the architects, to lend both building and decor the same high design standards.

Library in the
Former Industrial
Courtyard
Architects   Renate Abelmann +
                    Walter Vielain, Berlin
Client   Hanns Rauch, München,
                    Flurstück GmbH, Berlin
Usable Area   2,200 sq. m
Opening   June 10, 1996
Building Costs   DM 4 million
Address   Brunnenstrasse 181,
                    Berlin-Mitte

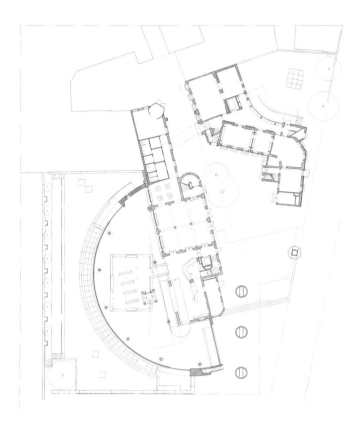

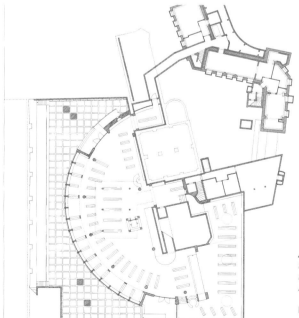

*All photos of
the library at
the Luisenbad:
Reinhard Görner*

**Floor plans
1:500**

The Library in the Former Industrial Courtyard

The industrial courtyard (Gewerbehof) at Brunnenstrasse 181, in the north of the Mitte district, has housed a library since the 1920s. After World War Two the library had to cede a good deal of its space to a furniture builder, and a planned new building was never constructed. The property's restitution to private ownership created an entirely new situation. The library gave up its traditional space on the second floor of the front house, in favor of securing far greater space long-term in a courtyard building.

The building's owner was the sole principal in the courtyard's reconstruction. This eliminated a lengthy budgetary approval procedure for investors as well as the district's administrative duty for architects and building firms. Construction costs were covered by the owner; thus the city-state of Berlin pays rent as periodic payments on the overhead costs. Since paying for library furnishing was beyond the city budget, the owner assumed these costs as well and added them to the rent.

As a tenant, the library had no direct influence on design or execution, even if the building were erected especially for the library's purposes. The building adminis-

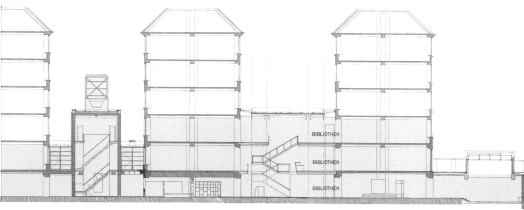

tration responsible can only advise and indirectly influence construction through negotiations with the owner. The position of public tenant is improved through their preference for long-term leases as well as the security of their payments. In this case, the library was granted a fair amount of say, and thanks to the special involvement of the private owner, a tailor-made expansion and interior remodeling was possible for the district library.

In 1990, the restitution to the old owner in Munich took place, and he commissioned an architect of his choice that same year. The Phillipp-Schaeffer-Bibliothek—the name recalls a former colleague and resistance fighter against the Nazis—was opened to the public in the spring of 1996, even before all construction was completed.

The complex of buildings on the Brunnenstrasse is a well preserved Berlin courtyard ensemble from the period immediately before World War One. It consists of a front building with three rear buildings, which are joined by wings into tracts with a U-shaped floor plan. There are cellars beneath the courtyard surfaces.

In its new location, the library extends through all three rear buildings in the basement, first, and second floors. The public areas are joined into a long tract,

a two-story entrance hall with a glass wall to the courtyard connects the second and third rear buildings, and between both front wings the "sawdust bunker" of the former furniture builder became the staircase and connective unit. Opposite the entrance hall, in the side wing, lie the administrative offices on the first and second floors. They are linked to the complex through stairs and a freight elevator which also serves disabled people.

The entrance hall presents a generous foyer with the staircase and the information and circulation desk. The hall opens to both sides, to the youth and to the adult libraries, both on two levels. The entrance areas offer easy orientation, with densely arranged book shelves off to the side. All rooms have generous reading spaces which, like all the furniture, were painstakingly designed. The new buildings, the interior remodelling, and the furniture all share the same sense of design. The architecture of the renovated courtyard becomes a robust and sober frame into which the new elements in all their variety are self-confidently, yet modestly arranged.

Of special interest is the children's library in the basement. Openings in the courtyard ceiling create spaces with natural lighting, and an atrium-like, glass-

roofed yard at the end of the rooms almost achieves an outdoor quality. The low ceilings and existing pillars and niches have been cleverly used to create various playrooms for different age groups.

The Trendbibliothek (trend library) is completely different. It was conceived as a pilot project with a varying selection of multi-media and is intended as a meeting place, information center, and forum for discussion among young people. Through its forward position on the ground floor it appears to be the library's calling card, and so perfectly complements the mixture of private and cultural uses for a Berlin commercial courtyard.

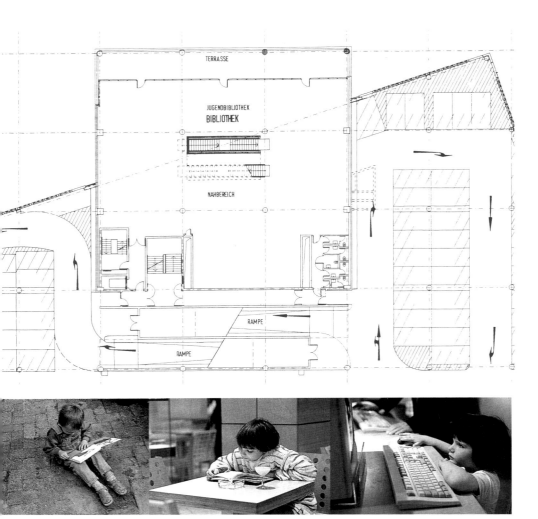

Library in the
Lindencenter
Architects   J.S.K. Perkins & Will,
                    Braunschweig
Developer   Immobilien-KG
                    Schnermann & Co.,
                    Hamburg
Usable Area   2,860 sq. m
Opening   October 26, 1995
Building Costs   approx. DM 7 million
Address   Prerower Platz, Berlin-
                    Hohenschönhausen

The Library in the Lindencenter

In the case of the Anna-Seghers-Biblio-thek in Hohenschönhausen, which was integrated into a shopping mall, the private investor was the sole principal of construction. The city-state of Berlin had a legal claim to the accomodation of a library. The planning procedure was carried out within the shopping mall's development process, such that both, the developer and library administration, were navigating organizationally and artistically uncharted territory.

The first step was the selection procedure for a developer. Firms applied with concepts for the use, construction design, and financing of building investments on publicly-owned property. Parts of such construction programs often consist of public-use areas. A committee evaluated whether and to what extent the submitted applications fulfilled functional, artistic, and economic criteria. The most acceptable proposal — modified by further nego-tiations, if need be — becomes the basis for a contract between the private devel-oper and the public financier. The contract regulates ownership and usage rights on the property, regulates planning and building procedures, and determines the building's design. Since the design and the financing concept are offered simul-

taneously, the selection of an architect is made with the selection of a developer, unless a realization competition has been agreed on.

The developer selection procedure is organized by the responsible building administration or by an office it has com-missioned. For the "nuts and bolts," how-ever, political resolutions are needed. These, in turn, are based on recommenda-tions by the finance administrations. It is a matter of course that future public users should play a decisive role in determining the building's layout, but the relatively short time for preparation — if one takes standard budgetary procedure as a yard-stick — often proves to be a problem.

The large housing project Hohen-schönhausen in former East Berlin was planned from the beginning as an inde-pendent district, but plans could be only partially realized up to 1989. A library, as part of several loosely arranged apart-ment blocks in the main center, already existed. But the expansion into a "mid-center" first and foremost called for retail space. So the new library building was torn down to make room for a compact shopping mall. There, in turn, space had to be set aside for the replacement library.

In 1991, on the basis of an urban con-struction framework plan, the developer

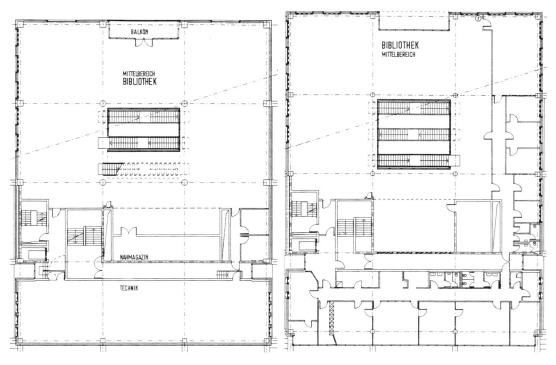

Photo of the library in the Lindencenter from the author. Photos of readers: Erik-Jan Ouwerkerk

Floor plans 1:500

selection procedure was begun for the Lindencenter. The selection commission gave the nod to the sole acceptable proposal in 1992, and the planning and building procedures were set in motion. A realization competition did not take place because the developer had committed himself to the wished-for construction concept. The library itself did not take part in the selection procedure, but through subsequent negotiations could attain the expansion of its assigned space through rental space. In 1993, the application for expansion passed through the district council, and the lease could be signed in 1994. The old library was torn down in the same year, construction was approved and began soon afterwards. In October 1995, the Lindencenter was finished and the library opened to the public.

The Lindencenter lies at the intersection of Hohenschönhausen's tram lines, on the housing project's main street axis toward the commuter rail station. Retail spaces fill three floors, from the basement to the second floor. Above lie two parking levels, interrupted by department store and library levels. The slightly trapezoidal floor plan is almost diagonally bisected by a walkway. At right angles to this, side walkways lead to the rest of the building.

Three main spaces emerge from the main building: a department store at the corner of the street intersection, the cube-shaped library at the opposite corner, and the cylinder of the parking-deck ramps. The library walls are positioned according to the walkways axes, and thus bisect the main building. In front of the library is a newly designed square as a transitional space to the residential area.

The library is connected to the walkways only through a side hallway. The main entrance leads into a narrow, artificially-lit stairwell with elevator. On the second floor there is a row of rooms for library administrators. On the third floor, one reaches the public levels of the library, occupying three floors and connected by a central staircase with a glass roof. This recalls the spatial typology of the old library. But here, the minimal entranceway and generous open stacks form a surprising contrast.

At the entrance level, a loggia with reading spaces outside spreads out before the visitor along the entire length of the facade facing the square. The three square-shaped library levels are of equal size and furnished alike: walls and ceilings correspond to the building standards throughout the shopping mall, carpeting and the serial shelving system are color-

coordinated. Only the space-defining staircase in the center, which allows views from floor to floor, is a special design. With this library a space has been created, which appears both tranquil and easy to navigate. It offers much reading area and roomy furnishings to accomodate growth. Its spaciousness and clear arrangement of rooms are the special qualities of the Lindencenter library.

Oliver Hamm
Westkreuz – Ostkreuz

The Changing Face of Berlin along the Inner-city Train Line (S-Bahn)

Once it was the famous subway "Linie 1" which every Berlin visitor was inevitably invited to take, if he or she wanted to feel the city's atmosphere and get to know its various peoples. On the other hand, the city's panorama unfolded best if the visitor bought a ticket on the famous boat line and took a trip from Kottbusser Tor to Charlottenburg Palace via Kemperplatz, observing how often the city turns its back to the waterfront. But today insiders recommend their visitors take the S-Bahn from Westkreuz to Ostkreuz via Zoo and Mitte, if they really want to have a close view of the city's changing face. There is no need to wait at any of these stations, because the route is covered by four different S-Bahn lines: S3 – S5 – S7 – S9. The glimpses of the cityscape offered by the train windows are explained on the following pages.

Westkreuz S-Bahn Station
An intersection of road and rail, from here day visitors scurry away towards the trade fair grounds, the Deutsch-landhalle, or the International Congress Center (ICC). After the long journey through the city's Grunewald forest park, we pull into the low-lying S-Bahn station. The view here still seems suburban and green, but above it, hidden from sight, there's a whole lot of building going on. Despite temporary delays caused by the city's budgetary problems, the fair ground's new exhibition halls continue to expand. The complex consists of the new Hall 7 parallel to Messedamm and three two-story halls perpendicular to it. Together they will increase the trade fair grounds' gross floor space by 60 % to 160,000 sq. m by the year 2000 (architect: Oswald Mathias Ungers with Walter Noebel).

The halls' exterior is a quadratic grid. The steel girder frame is filled in with ceramic plates or glass. The interior is painted white, giving it an almost museum-like character.
The Deutschlandhalle is classified as a historical monument and needs renovating. But it has been facing an uncertain future ever since two new multi-purpose sports halls were built in the Prenzlauer Berg district. The future of the plot next door, incorporating the Zentralen Omnibus Bahnhof (ZOB = main bus station), is also unclear. Back in 1990, the Swedish firm Skanska planned a 180,000 sq. m office complex with hotel and apartments. But the result of the urban design competition, won by the Berlin architecture firm Ganz & Rolfes, has long since been abandoned.

Meanwhile, a glass, lens-shaped building balances just above the Halensee entrance to the freeway: the new office building by Hilde Léon and Konrad Wohlhage with its double-glazed climate facade. Our journey continues past the Charlottenburg station. Here we have a view of Stuttgarter Platz, which is practically unchanged since 1968. Three almost identical cafés on the corner of Windscheidstrasse still appear to be havens for old student revolutionaries from the Sixties who once sought refuge from military service in Berlin. But this too is threatened: the results of the competition to redesign the square and the station were announced at the end of November 1996. First prize went to Bernd Albers, who proposed arcades along the S-Bahn embankment and a 15 story high-rise next to it.

Photo: Christian Richters

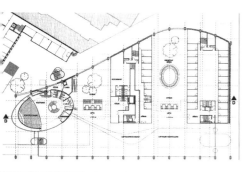

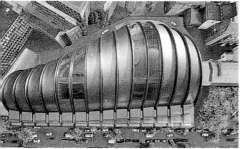

Photos: Hélène Binet

Ludwig-Erhard-Haus
We already have left Savignyplatz behind us—the secret center of old West Berlin. Now, shortly before we enter Zoo Station, two buildings appear to our left: the oddly fanciful Theater des Westens (architect: Bernhard Sehring, 1895/96), and the far more wondrous creation of the nineties, the Ludwig-Erhard-Haus. The latter is home to Berlin's Stock Exchange and the "Communication and Service Center for Businesses in the Berlin Region." The local Chamber of Commerce and Industry is having 30,700 sq. m of gross floor space built here, most of that for offices.

The "armadillo," as christened by its London architect Nicholas Grimshaw, is almost 40 meters high and 100 meters long. It winds between several old buildings, with the floors hanging from fifteen powerful steel arches, which give the building its form. Two deep atria ensure that enough daylight penetrates the "belly" of the stock exchange. The animal's true face is veiled on the Fasanenstrasse side. It was "brought into line" by Berlin's former Building Director Hans Stimmann personally, and so looks like any

other office building complying with the city's maximum eaves height. However, its rounded "spine" rises considerably above this. The unusual architecture has a unique climate concept, complete with a sunlight-distributing-system integrated into the facade, natural ventilation, and glassed atria as climatic buffers.

Kant-Dreieck
Close to Ludwig-Erhard-Haus is another quite unusual building called the Kant-Dreieck, designed by Josef Paul Kleihues. The first thing you notice about the building is the huge sail placed on top of it, high above the eaves of neighboring buildings. It is at once an immediately recognizable emblem, an advertising board, and a protective cover for the cleaner's closet. It weighs heavily on the tower which seems too small—

the local council wasn't prepared to let it be built any higher. Its slightly squashed proportions are underlined still further by the division of the tower into two halves, with the base having five stories and the upper part six, though both are the same height. The building was still considered good enough to win Berlin's annual architecture prize, not least because of its triangular wing, which helps make full use of the plot, and its fine details. The sex

shop next door hasn't disappeared, much to the annoyance of the architect and his client KapHag. In fact the Kantstrasse as a whole has not lost its sleazy image. Just diagonally opposite, on the other side of the railway overpass, Germany's largest chain of sex stores, Beate Uhse, has opened a cool, almost distinguished Erotic Museum …

Photo: Haila Ochs

Zoofenster

For years, Berlin's most famous carpet shop, Teppich-Kibek am Zoo, had occupied the plot where construction of the Zoofenster (Zoo Window) building should long have started. London architect Richard Rogers designed the office tower, complete with conference rooms, restaurants and shops, back in 1991–1992 for the Dortmunder Brau und Brunnen AG. The carpet shop stood firm, refusing to give up its lease, which was due to run until the year 2000. Even a mysterious hit from a crane, which damaged the building in the summer of 1995, didn't stop him — the shop was given emergency support to help keep it standing. This particular David and Goliath fight looks as if it will end in spring 1997. Kibek is clearing out, but certainly not without a handsome compensation. That opens the way for the twenty-two story building with a gross floor space of 34,200 sq. m. At 115 meters it will be Berlin's tallest building after the Television Tower. One day, the skyscraper will open out towards Zoo Station and Hardenbergplatz to the north, turning its back on Kantstrasse, whose prestige the local council had actually hoped to increase. And, much to the council's displeasure, another three high rise projects in the western half of the city center have so far been announced in the wake of the Zoofenster plans. Christoph Langhof, on behalf of his client ITAG, intends to tear down Schimmelpfenghaus, a protected historical building which spans Kantstrasse's entry onto Breitscheidplatz, and redesign the Gloria-Block, crowning it with a new skyscraper as a counterpart to the Zoofenster. The Zentrum am Zoo is to receive a new eastern extension in the form of a narrow high rise building designed by Hans Kollhoff and Helga Timmermann. And one street away, Bremen businessman Thomas Grothe intends to tear down the Ku'damm-Eck building (achitect: Werner Düttmann), replacing it with a small high-rise, a mere 75 meters tall, designed by Hamburg architects von Gerkan, Marg & Partner. And diagonally opposite from that, the so-called Victoria-Areal awaits its fate. Chicago architect Helmut Jahn's winning entry in the design competition, put on ice in 1988, remains unpopular — he intends to place a 55 meter high slab between Kurfürstendamm and Kantstrasse, something which would dwarf the Kranzler-Eck building along with most of the other buildings around the Kurfürstendamm, Berlin's most prestiguous commercial street.

Bolle Areal

After leaving Zoo Station and crossing the Strasse des 17. Juni, the train enters the Tiergarten, Berlin's large inner-city park. The apartment blocks of the Hansaviertel can now be seen. In 1997 they will be celebrating their fortieth birthdays. The S-Bahn stations here, Tiergarten and Bellevue, were only just reopened in November 1996 after being given a complete overhaul. Between them to our left, on the other side of the River Spree, the tall towers of the Bolle Areal (Bolle Area) spring into view. And to our right we can just see the first buildings rise on Potsdamer Platz. Now it really does seem as if both halves of the city are moving closer together.

Shortly before the Wall fell, construction was just being completed for most of ITAG's new Focus Teleport Business Center Berlin (architects: Ganz & Rolfes) on the plot here between the Spree and Alt-Moabit road. No one could forsee the upturn that would hit Moabit. But German reunification, and the prospect that this area would be very close to the future goverment district, made the adjacent plot, which formerly housed the Bolle dairy, quite a coveted location.

What has since been built here is not just another office quarter, but an area mixed with offices, admittedly with an imposing 150,000 sq. m of office space, 100 apartments, a hotel, a supermarket, and several shops. The complex was designed by the Berlin architects Kühn, Bergander, Bley, and Wolf Rüdiger Borchardt. The two wings of the central, U-shaped courtyard rise powerfully above the ensemble. Irritating here is not the scale, which is only fully visible on the Spree side, but rather the cold "splendor" of the mirrored facades.

Photo: Richard Davies

Apartment Developments at Lüneburger Strasse 22 and 14–20

Echoes of the International Building Exhibition from 1984–87 can be found in the urban infill carried out by Mario Maedebach and Werner Redeleit for BEWOGE in 1991–92. The feeling for collage-like layered facades, so dominant in buildings just ten years ago, now seems to be lost in our era of all-too-serious "critical reconstruction." The new building acts as a transition between a building from the 1950s and a more modern one on the corner. Structurally, the street facade is almost symmetrical with sound-proof glass, subdivided by exposed concrete apron walls. Eleven, three-room, state-subsidized apartments, each over 80 sq. m are spread throughout both halves of the house and over all six floors. Just a few steps away and as close to the S-Bahn embankment, its contemporary neighbor, house number 22 quotes modernist vocabulary: bands in white and glass wrap the corner of the apartment house by Jürgen Fissler and Hans-Christoph Ernst. The structure contains 42 state-subsidized apartments and a cleverly integrated child care center. The client is R + W Immobilienanlagen.

Housing Development for State Employees at Moabiter Werder

The Moabit Werder area stretches from Paulstrasse up to Moltkebrücke. It is currently a desolate wasteland with a few remnants of that spontaneous vegetation which took over here after the Second World War, after the southern part of the Hamburg-Lehrter Güterbahnhof freight station was abandoned. In the meantime, most traces of the famous shipping company Hamacher, who carried out its business here until 1995, have been removed. The only building still standing is the red-tiled administration building, a near-perfect example of classical modernism. It is to be converted into an elementary school. Originally, the huge area was due to house a row of five high-rise blocks of state-subsidized apartments, similar to those in the nearby Hansaviertel, built along the railway overpass. But after German reunification, the national government claimed the plot to build 750 apartments for state employees within sight of the new parliamentary district. In 1995, Berlin architect Georg Bumiller won the design competition for the project with a proposal which actually contravened the somewhat conventional conditions of the competition. The body of his building winds several times as it gradually rises from east to west, in a westward continuation of the "Federal Band" (Axel Schultes' and Charlotte Frank's proposal for the new parliamentary district). It has already been nicknamed the "Diätenwurm" ("parliamentary salary worm"). In 1999, the houses and apartments should be ready for tenants.

The Reichstag Building

Continuing with government buildings, the Reichstag is now visible off in the distance. Hardly any other building has suffered as much abuse and structural intervention as this first parliament building of a unified Germany. Kaiser Wilhelm II used to get riled up about this "national ape house," designed by Paul Wallot and officially opened in 1884. It was set aflame by the Nazis on February 27th 1933, and then extensively damaged in the last days of the Second World War twelve years later. Reconstruction followed from 1961 to 1972 under Paul Baumgarten's direction and in accordance with what he called "purified modernism." Nothing was left of the old Wilhelminian architecture except for a few suites of rooms and the building's exterior. The new architectural style was intended to express the then-current understanding of democracy. Practically all traces of this will be extinguished after the buildings current redesigning by Sir Norman Foster, who will transform it into the new home of the Bundestag, Germany's lower house of parliament. Christo's wrappings had only just been removed in summer 1995 when the Reichstag was almost completely gutted to make way for renovations and approximate restoration of Wallot's original interior design. The crowning moment will come when Sir Norman Forster — contrary to his original plans — will top off the Reichstag with a glass cupola. The parliamentarians of Germany's "Berlin Republic" should be able to move in by spring of 1999. At that time, the outlines of the chancellor's office, the buildings for the parliamentary parties and their library will be visible in the background.

Photo: Andreas Schoelzel

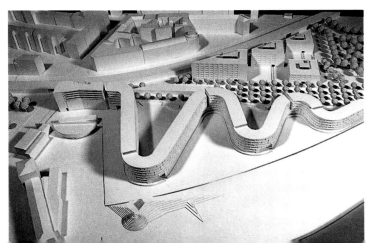

The City Quarter around Lehrter Bahnhof

We are now entering the S-Bahn station Lehrter Stadtbahnhof. This was renovated as recently as 1987 for DM 20 million but will be completely torn down over the next few years. Berlin has major plans for the site. The old Lehrter Bahnhof station, which had stood here since its construction in 1871, was badly damaged in the Second World War and torn down in 1957. In just a few years the new Lehrter Bahnhof (architects: von Gerkan, Marg & Partner, Hamburg), Europe's largest railway station, will be standing on this site. The 400 meter long platform building, itself braced by two massive office blocks, will become the backbone of a whole new city quarter. It is easy to forget that the total volume of construction here is hardly less than on Potsdamer Platz, which is already visible growing on the horizon due south. Architects Oswald Mathias Ungers and Stefan Vieths (Cologne) are planning several blocks and two high rise towers for offices and a hotel between Invalidenstrasse and the Spree, as well as a colonnade around the whole of Humboldthafen. North of Invalidenstrasse, apartment buildings by Max Dudler will go up, combining meandering and block style buildings. Gross floor space, including the surrounding blocks, will excede 350,000 sq. m.

Moving the Spree's Bed

The area around Lehrter S-Bahn station currently looks like a crater landscape smack in the middle of town. The view is dominated by a vast clearing extending from Perleberger Brücke in the north to Potsdamer Platz in the south. The space corresponds to the former border between the two halves of the city, but this middle section wasn't cleared until 1995. In just a few years, the Tiergarten Tunnel will run underneath the clearing, carrying north-south road and rail traffic underneath the new government quarter. Up until just a few months ago, the Grün Berlin GmbH's administration building stood here with its exhibition hall so reminiscent of a ship's hull (architects: Ganz + Rolfes, 1985). Now, in its place, they have broadened the originally bottle-neck shaped branch of the Berlin-Spandau Ship Canal entering Humboldthafen. The Spree river had to be temporarily removed from its natural bed at this point, so that the three tunnels (for cars, trains, and subways) could all be burrowed underneath the former and future river bed using the open construction method. The top of the tunnel will lie just one meter underneath the Spree. As soon as the tunnel's "lid" has been put back on, building can begin for the Lehrter Bahnhof, the Chancellor's Office and the German Parliament's new buildings.

Museum für Gegenwart (former Hamburger Railway Station)

The train is now leaving Lehrter Stadtbahnhof and crossing Humboldt-hafen. The barges can be seen waiting in the harbor, ready to transport some of the 18 million tons of sand extracted to make way for the future tunnel. Behind them appear the twin towers of the facade at the entrance to the former Hamburger Bahnhof station. It has not been used as a rail station since 1884, and for a period starting in 1906 it housed the Museum of Transport and Construction. After World War Two the building entered a long dormancy, being used first by the Allies, and then by the East German State Railway. As such, it was an East German enclave within West Berlin's territory, located right next to the Wall, and closed for decades. The West Berlin government only managed to take over ownership of the building in 1984, provisionally restoring it three years later. In 1988 it first demonstrated its potential as an exhibition space for modern art with Harald Szeemann's exhibition Zeitlos (Timeless). Two years later, Josef Paul Kleihues began conversion work for a newly-founded Museum für Gegenwart (Museum for Contemporary Art). It's 8,000 sq. m exhibition space will serve as a permanent home to the Marx Collection (the private art collection of a Berlin building developer) plus works from the New National Gallery. Kleihues divided up the compact three-story entrance building, built in 1846–47 by Friedrich Neuhaus, into a series of rooms with a variety of shapes and sizes. But he retained the two wings along the front courtyard, which had been added in 1911 and 1916, as three-naved picture galleries. The heart of the building is without a doubt the central hall, erected by Ernst Schwartz in 1906, with its three naves and arched iron girders. The hall is mainly naturally lit through skylights and clerestories. Juxtaposed to this is the narrow, almost 80 meter long East Gallery, the only newly constructed addition to the building thus far (there is still no money for its pendant the West Gallery). Here a barrel vaulted light-ceiling projects artificial illumination into a room, whose cross-section resembles that of a railway car.

Office and Business Building at the Corner of Luisenstrasse and Reinhardtstrasse

Crossing Humboldthafen also takes us over the former border and we enter what used to be East Berlin. We are now traveling past the Charité, an old hospital complex on the edge of the historical city center. Despite war damages and a few ill-proportioned East German additions, the hospital has managed to retain its turn-of-the-century character. On the right, Santiago Calatrava's new Kronprinzenbrücke (Crown Prince Bridge) appears, linking the city area Friedrich-Wilhelm-Stadt with the Spreebogen. On the left, the window is briefly filled with the sight of the two year old business and office building located at the junction of Luisenstrasse and Reinhardtstrasse. The distinguished eight-story glass cube by Dusseldorf architects Eller, Maier, & Walter appears somewhat misplaced among its surroundings with their morbid East German charm.

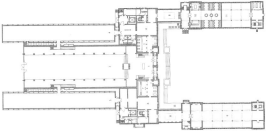

Photos: Christian Richters

Photo: Haila Ochs

Centrum Judaicum

The journey continues between the fire walls and the first precast concrete socialist apartment blocks in Friedrich-Wilhelm-Stadt and on towards Friedrichstrasse station. Just before the train enters the station, the golden dome of the former Neue Synagoge (New Synagogue) gleams in the distance to our left. On May 7th 1995, the eve of the 50th anniversary of the end of World War Two, the building on Oranienburger Strasse, originally built by Eduard Knoblauch and Friedrich August Stüler from 1859 to 1866, was reopened as the "Centrum Judaicum" (Jewish Center), thereby establishing its new cultural importance as the Jewish community's exhibition and assembly center. After being damaged by fire during the Nazi "Reichskristall-nacht" (Night of Broken Glass) on November 9th 1938, and then largely destroyed during air raids in 1942 and '43, the Synagogue was finally demolished in 1958. A partial reconstruction of the building's entrance and the central section together with the former women's galleries was started in the old socialist era in 1988 (under direction of the architect Bernhard Leisering). The women's galleries, used for exhibitions and lectures, provide a view into a large void in the middle of the city. The former dimensions of the prayer room are recalled by both a construction of steel and glass, which protects the remains of the exterior walls against rain and indicates the room's old cross-section, as well as by a ground plan drawn on the floor of the newly built courtyard. Even though the Jewish community has no current plans to rebuild the prayer room, saying that "the past cannot be reversed," it has at least left open the option of doing this at some future time.

Photo: Haila Ochs

Bahnhof Friedrichstrasse

The train is now entering Friedrichstrasse station, the only station in the formerly divided city where people could cross from one side to the other. The border control facilities have naturally long since vanished. Anyone wishing to see how the "Organs of Control" worked can visit a model of an East German Secret Police's station in the German Historical Museum, or search for any remaining traces in the former border control building now converted into the concert venue "Tränenpalast" ("Palace of Tears"). Nevertheless, an abrupt change can be detected at the station: all at once the passengers are completely different, even down to their newspapers, the Berliner Zeitung (formerly an East German daily) instead of the Tages-spiegel. Renovation of the hall, the platforms and the entrance area are still not finished. In autumn 1996 the artist Ben Wargin was allowed to expand his performance "Departure-Arrival" to a temporarily closed platform. The hall is now being reconstructed in a 1920s style. All traces of East Germany's renovations during the 1950s have disappeared, along with the border control facilities. The city's landmark conservationists and architect (Werner Weinkamm, Berlin) were hoping to recreate the original clear spatial structure of the entrance hall, but the recently privatized Deutsche Bahn AG wanted as much shop frontage as possible and shimmering glass tiles on the hall pillars instead of the terra cotta or natural stone tiles normally used in Berlin's inner-city train and subway stations.

A View Down Friedrichstrasse

One thing not visible from the station is Friedrichstrasse's new heart, the Friedrichstadt-Passagen, which was described in detail at the start of this publication. What is visible though, to the east, or left, is the building site for the new Dussmann-Haus designed by Miroslav Volf. The two old buildings next door and the neighboring new building belong to a whole complex which takes up a large part of the block between Mittelstrasse, Friedrichstrasse, and Dorotheenstrasse. On the western side we can see the renovations and addition to the former Hotel Metropol, transformed by Holger Nettbaum into the Hotel Maritim proArte. As with so many other areas of the city, the areas north and south of Bahnhof Friedrichstrasse were subject to a prominent urban design competition in 1993, the results of which are still only virtual. Winners were architects Johanne and Gernot Nalbach with a dense block perimeter construction.

Museumsinsel

The train is now rumbling over the renovated railway arches. Like those at Savignyplatz, these arches are also occupied with shops and pubs. As we cross the Museumsinsel (Museum Island), which is actually only the northern tip of the Spreeinsel, the track is jammed between the noble facades of the Bodemuseum and the Pergamonmuseum. Is there a more tristful place in Berlin than this museum ensemble, left in disrepair, and joined by the neighboring wasteland of the Lustgarten and Schlossplatz, extending as far as the former Staatsratsgebäude (East Germany's State Council Building)? The result of the 1995 Museumsinsel competition has since been revoked. Milan architect Giorgio Grassi's prize-winning proposal will not be built. Instead, the five prize winners have been asked to revise their proposals and re-submit them in the summer of 1997. For cost reasons, only the rebuilding of August Stüler's Neues Museum (New Museum) is currently being considered. The planned museum additions and connecting buildings have been put on ice for now. Renovating the whole of the Museumsinsel would cost around DM 820 million and probably take until 2010.

Hackesche Höfe

Hackescher Markt station is gleaming with fresh splendor (renovated by the architect group Orlando Figallo, Nicole Rottwinkel-Tuncel, Rainer Birkel and Peter-Gregor Rottwinkel). Natural light pours through the skylights in the vaulted ceiling onto the platform and across the original tile walls. Looking north across the square one can see a relatively unimpressive facade. Hiding behind this is Hackesche Höfe (Hackesche Courts), Berlin's largest mixed-use residential courtyard development. It is a complex multi-layered construction from 1906 with a total of eight courtyards in which diverse, old and new tenants seem to co-exist peacefully. For old-established residents in the rear courtyards, who face the former Jewish cemetry and the neighboring buildings along the quiet Sophien-strasse, much has changed. This tran-quil area — admittedly somewhat dilapidated — is being transformed into a proscenium, especially the Hackesche Höfe, for a pleasure and consumer oriented clientele. The lovingly renovated old buildings — particularly August Endell's Art Nouveau facades in the first courtyard — create an ideal stage set for the entrance of a whole range of actors. All the commercial residents here attract their own particular specialist public — the Varieté Chamäleon in the first courtyard, the artificium book shop, the Café and Galerie Aedes East (architectural exhibitions) in the second, and all the other different boutiques and galleries. People from all possible walks of life and all corners of Berlin visit, and might only ever cross paths here. It is a unique experiment by the developer Roland Ernst, a successful blend of apartments, culture and offices. But the unique recipe cannot be reproduced at will. Another factor in its success is the growing popularity of the surrounding Spandauer Vorstadt district, which might sooner or later make it a serious competitor with the area around Kollwitzplatz in Prenzlauer Berg.

Photos: A. Zibel, Jürgen Henkelmann

115

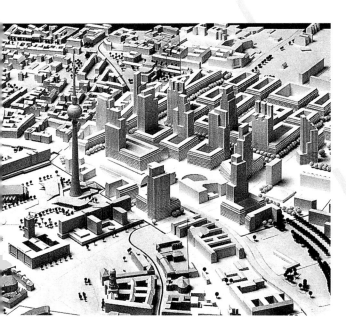

JannowitzCenter

Our journey now continues on to the Jannowitzbrücke (Jannowitz Bridge) station. After the building's general overhaul, and the redesigning and extension of its platform, platform hall and entrance hall, by the architects Wehner—Gaisser—Schulz, the structure once again possesses a clear and airy ambiance with its large glass surfaces and blue steel girders. At the other end of the Jannowitzbrücke, which gives its name to more than just the station, the face of the JannowitzCenter rises skyward. In September 1996 Berlin's Senate Department for Urban Development, Environmental Protection, and Technology, including its three environment subdepartments, moved into 13,500 sq. m of space here.

From the train window one can only guess at the building's true dimensions. This is because behind the freshly plastered frontal buildings along Brückenstrasse (the extension of Jannowitzbrücke), a complete block of buildings stretches into the distance, integrating some protected historic buildings in the process. Vebau GmbH and the Philipp Holzmann BauProjekt AG have had some 45,000 sq. m of total floor space built (28,000 sq. m of offices and shops, 69 apartments, and 220 underground parking spaces). The architects, Hentrich-Petschnigg and Partner, have helped themselves to a few stylistic references to "the white modern," including a few trendy decorations and details, like the lofty winged roof. Questionable, though, is whether the elevated, interior courtyards between the frontal buildings, protected from traffic noise by huge glass panels facing the road, really are an adequate response to the powerful precast concrete buildings of the Berlin Congress Center. It's true that the courtyards optically widen the narrow ravine-like street and pour light onto the pavement, but they cannot offer any further significant contribution to the street front.

Alexanderplatz

The train is now arriving at the Alexanderplatz station, which is still undergoing its facelift by the architects Rebecca Chestnutt and Robert Niess. We are now at the traditional center for the "more humble" Berliners, just beyond the gates into the historical city. But this could change if the local government and several developers have their way. Alexanderplatz was earmarked as a financially strong city district. But that begs the question of how many centers of importance Berlin can handle. In 1993 when Hans Kollhoff proposed a crown of twelve skyscrapers "in the second row" behind a new block-perimeter building complex on the edge of a redesigned Alexanderplatz, demand for office and retail space still seemed boundless.

But developers have become more cautious at Alexanderplatz and elsewhere. Kollhoff's plans included provisions for more than a million square meters of office and retail space combined with a small number of new apartments—partly at the expense of existing residential buildings behind the extension of Karl-Marx-Allee. So far, none of the planned bold skyscrapers has been built. In the meantime, the existing structures on Alexanderplatz have, if anything, become more permanent. Kaufhof (a German department store chain) bought out and redesigned the Warenhaus Centrum (former East German department store), and is now planning an addition. The Hotel Berlin, so far the only high-rise on the square, was exten-

sively renovated. Tearing it down and replacing it with a new building is not an option. The buildings around the hotel's wide base were overhauled and new tenants moved in, including a huge electronic media store. And just recently, the Bankgesellschaft Berlin moved into the Haus Alexander, freshly renovated by Pysall, Stahrenberg & Partner. Peter Behrens originally designed both this and its neighbor, the Haus Berolina. The latter, however, still awaits renovation. Both these wing buildings near the station were the only realized portions of major plans for Alexanderplatz in the 1920s, which were supposed to herald a radical new beginning here.

HOM Office Center Trias

Between Jannowitz-brücke and Michael-brücke, which leads to Strausberger Platz, the tracks run alongside the Spree for a while. Billboard advertisements for films are (still) being painted in the workshop areas underneath the railway overpass, along the river's edge. But these spaces for workshops and warehouses, with their river front view, have long since been attracting a different clientele, partly because of what has happened above their heads. Shortly before Michael-brücke, three glass, shimmering, silver-green, 13-story towers nearly kiss the railway viaduct — together they are the Trias office center. The prow-like buildings with their ellipsoidal floor plans, together with the local thermal power station across the river, create a sort of gateway for rail and water traffic. On the Holzmarktstrasse side, to the north, it appears to be a normal six-story street front building, which really only begins to make sense in the context of

future neighboring buildings. On the ground floor the total depth of the site allows for shopping space. Above and level with the railway tracks, two courtyard roof gardens are linked by a new promenade along the railway arches, like new urban stages. For the moment though, the only life comes from the employees of the Deutsche Bahn rail company and the state privatization agency. But that should change with the developments around the main-line Hauptbahnhof railway station.
The curved glass fronts with encircling bands of windows give most offices magnificent views of the city. The office center, with its more than 30,000 sq. m of floor space, was designed by the "Architektengemeinschaft Holzmarkt" (Luci Beringer & Gunther Wawrik, winners of an internal selection and Zobel & Weber, both of Munich). Bauwert AG was responsible for project planning and construction management.

Photo: Dieter Blum

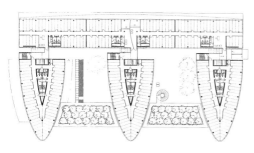

Deutsches Architektur Zentrum

Just after the power station, even closer to the river on the south bank, appears a modernized factory area — immediately recognizable to insiders as the Deutsches Architektur Zentrum (German Architecture Center) or DAZ building. The factory for motor ploughs and spiral drills was originally built shortly after 1900, partially damaged in the Second World War, and then became a part of East Germany's largest textile combine VEB Bekon from 1962 until 1992. After that it was used by around 100 artists and craftsmen and by a disco, until the federal privatization agency sold it to a purchasing group under the direction of the Bund Deutscher Architekten (BDA, German Architects' Association).

Now the building houses not just the national headquarters of the BDA, but also those of the German Landscape Gardeners' Association and of the SRL (City, Regional, and Landscape Planners), as well as a series of architects' offices and branch offices belonging to firms from the construction and furnishing industries. Only a few of the tenant artists managed to survive the change in ownership.
Claus Anderhalten renovated the old five-story red-brick building. Gaps left since the war were filled in — as with the west facade, where the new glass main entrance was added. In the second stage of restoration, the architects Assmann, Salomon, and Scheidt, added an attic story for 18 apartments and another 10 offices. The German Architecture Center was opened on July 1st 1995 with the conference "Changing Metropolises." Since then it has served as an exhibition site, information center and a forum for further education.

Heizkraftwerk Mitte

Over the past few years, BEWAG, Berlin's still state owned electricity company, invested some DM 600 million in modernizing the thermal power station Heizkraftwerk Mitte, in Berlin's Mitte district. Originally built between 1961 and 1964 based on plans by the Dietrich Zimbal Collective, the complex was then renovated by the "Projektgruppe Architektur und Städtebau" (PAS, Jochem Jourdan & Bernhard Mülller of Frankfurt am Main). The power station may have been aestheticized from the outside, but the lion's share of the money was invested in new gas and steam turbines, invisible to passers-by. Among other things, the plant is to produce electricity for the new buildings on Potsdamer and Leipziger Platz. A portion of the

investment, DM 2.5 million (almost one percent), was available for the "art projects," obligatory for publicly funded buildings. These will be clearly visible in the future: Per Kirkeby is designing a promenade along the Spree with areas of greenery, an accessible brick tower, and a brick wall broken in several places. This will serve to cordon off the power plant grounds and yet still allow people to look through. The gas tank near the river bank is to be overgrown with climbing plants. Ayse Erkmen plans to spread out eight steel pipe benches around the site. These can be cooled in summer and warmed in winter. And Dan Graham is to construct an oval pavillion made of glass and perforated steel-sheets along the Köpe-nicker Strasse. It will be a miniature counterpart to the three Trias towers on the opposite side of the river. The area opens to the public in May 1997.

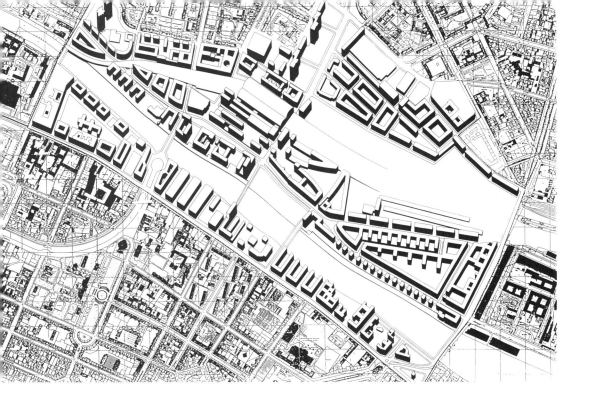

Hauptbahnhof

The train is now approaching Hauptbahnhof, Berlin's largest main-line railway station. Surprisingly, it seems more like a suburban station rather than the capital's largest. Renovations are not quite complete. Before we arrive we can see the site of another city quarter about to be built. It lies on both sides of the track and extends up to the banks of the Spree. The plot's future structure is still not recognizable. Norbert Hemprich and Julia Tophof won the open design competition in 1992. They have since revised their proposals, which now envisage some 500,000 sq. m of total floor space with 2,200 apartments planned to the north of the tracks and along the Spree, accounting for one quarter of new building volume. Between them there will be new buildings for offices, trades and services, a hotel, and a cinema. There is talk of an extra 10,000 (hoped for) jobs. For now though, the view of the surrounding area is dominated by industrial wasteland to the south, and precast concrete high-rise blocks to the north. The density of the suggested new buildings will be hardly any less than it was in the pre-war days of Berlin's former working class Friedrichshain district. But it will have a completely different character: the relation to the Spree, to its bank promenade and to its park have been re-created through the north-south visual axes, the development of squares and terraces, through the planned reconstruction of Brommybrücke, and the building of an additional bridge, forming a link across the Spree between Kreuzberg and Friedrichshain. Further down the river, between Mühlenstrasse and the Spree, lies the East-Side-Gallery, the longest remaining protected stretch of the old Wall. It faces an uncertain future. A special roof is supposed to protect the wall paintings against further erosion, but at the moment there is no money to restore this piece of art.

City Carré

We are now approaching Schilling bridge. The trilor shanty town here which sparked heat-ed debate as recently as early summer 1996, has long since vanished. Just a few scattered relics remain. Diagonally opposite, right next to the railway embankment, the City Carré comes into view. This has been financed by private investors through a real estate fund under direction of Dresdner Bank. The bank itself moved in here in summer 1996 with around 1,000 employees, and maintains a long term lease for 35,000 sq. m of total floor space. The building's upper body is elevated two stories and has a uniform brick facade.

The glass substructure seems almost too delicate for the heavy upper bulk it has to support. But the openings in the facade reveal the outlines of a large inner rotunda, where one discovers that the massive volume is in fact divided in sections. From the rotunda on the ground floor, which is surrounded by shops, you can reach a further, narrow, glass covered courtyard. Surprise. What seemed like such a rationally planned building, is actually a mixture of old and new. The block is over a hectare large, and incorporates an old school house, which is now used as a "boarding house" (138 apartments), taking advantage of the stair wells and room heights from the original use.

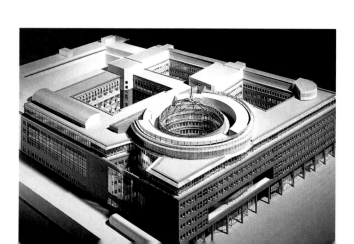

Oberbaum City
(former Narva Factory)
After passing through Hauptbahnhof, the area taken up by the railway track immediately expands. The city retreats, giving way to concrete apartment blocks, industrial buildings and railway sheds. To the north, for one short moment, we can see the towers at Frankfurter Tor. The next S-Bahn station, Warschauer Brücke, has a bustling atmosphere it hasn't had for a long time. This is because of the newly restored interchange with the subway station of the same name, completely rebuilt in its former style. The station has now reclaimed its historical role as the terminus of Berlin's legendary U1 subway line. Just below the track we can see the huge site of the former Narva factory. It is bordered by Warschauer Platz to the west, Lehmbruckstrasse to the east, Stralauer Allee to the south, and railway tracks to the north. Originally an Osram factory, light bulbs

continued to be manufactured here during the East German era, and indeed right up until spring 1995. Most of the original buildings dating from between 1903 to 1908 are still intact, and are currently being restored and filled in to form a dense "city-within-a city." By the year 2000 this business and services center is expected to provide some four to six thousand new jobs. Also planned are 330 apartments in 16 new buildings between Lehmbruckstrasse and Ehrenbergstrasse. They are part of the first phase, which also includes the renovation of the old building complex at the intersection of Rotherstrasse and Ehrenbergstrasse and of the old tower, which will be increased five stories. Architects are Schweger and Partner.

Office Building Warschauer Strasse
The next eye catcher is a former industrial plant for refrigeration elements, which was turned into an office building. This meant remodelling the floor plans and, strangely enough, wrapping the whole building into a white envelope. Now shops and practices inhabit the ground floor; the most important office tenant is the research library for the history of education. Architect is Gerold Otten, Westerstede; and the client is DIM-Deutsche Immobilien Vertriebs mbH.

Ostkreuz S-Bahn Station
The journey ends at the Ostkreuz railway junction. The station is still much the same as it was after it was rebuilt between 1901 and 1902. The original station dated back to 1881. Visible in the distance is the huge reinforced concrete skeleton of the "Treptowers" services complex on the EAW site at Osthafen (200,000 sq. m of office space and 900 apartments). On the other side of the railway embankment, on the peninsula known as the Stralauer Halbinsel, the first apartments in the Rummelsburger Bucht development are nearing completion. Some 4,000 apartments and 180,000 sq. m of office and business space are being built here. The layout follows a so-called "urban collage" which assembles ideas from the three winning entries from the competion of 1993: Klaus Theo Brenner, Herman Hertzberger and Martorell, Bohigas, Mackay.

A further 270,000 sq. m of office space are under construction or have already been rented out at the Ostkreuz service center on the former Knorr-Bremse site just opposite the railway station. Interrupting plans to build another four skyscrapers at Ostkreuz seems a wise decision, bearing in mind the absolutely unbelievable amount of building activity between Hauptbahnhof and Rummelsburger Bucht.
It would seems that "stony Berlin" concludes with the Ostkreuz S-Bahn station and environs, to be replaced by a more picturesque landscape along the Spree and Treptower Park.

11

Architects	Dominique Perrault, Paris
	with APP-Berlin,
	Rolf Reichert & Hans Jürgen
	Schmidt-Schicketanz
Structural	Ove Arup & Partner, Berlin
Engineering	
Steel Roof	Krupp Stahlbau GmbH
Construction	
Contract manager	Walter Habermann
Client	OSB Sportstättenbau GmbH, Berlin
Address	Landsberger Allee
	Berlin-Prenzlauer Berg

Haila Ochs
The Self-supporting Roof

above the Velodrome on Landsberger Allee

"Right now, through Christo's work, Berlin is showing that absence can be more than presence. My model is the landscape, in the broadest sense of the word. With such a model, architecture melts — or at least architectural ambition is put back in its rightful place. That is to say, our relationship to our surroundings has to loosen up, it has to become more open and lighter, so that everything which comprises these surroundings can be included, even the things which are generally said to be ugly ...

When I build in Berlin, or to be more accurate, when I let two enormous buildings disappear under the ground in Berlin — a velodrome and a sports center with an olympic-sized swimming pool — then what's left is nothing more than Manet's 'Déjeuner sur l'herbe'...

My poetic and abstract answer consists of allowing only the metal roofs to be visible. They project just one meter out of the ground and appear to be floating in an orchard with 450 apple trees. They reflect the colors of the day and of the season: during the day, the light of the sky is reflected in the large flat surfaces as if in the water of a lake; at night they exude many different kinds of lights, creating a magical atmosphere. This effect is caused by the metal fabric which is capable of catching the light and making the large geometrical elements float and sway ...

As for the type of structure, this project makes no technical or technological claims; our work sees itself as a sensitive poetic act ..."

Dominique Perrault, 1995

The architectural competition for the Landsberger Allee sports center, complete with velodrome and swimming pool, was decided in July 1992. It was one of the projects intended to help Berlin prepare for the 2000 Olympics. French architect Dominique Perrault took first place with a proposal embedding the two arenas within an arboreous plateau. Despite the rejection of Berlin's bid to host the 2000 Olympics, it was decided to build the planned complex as a sports center for the Prenzlauer Berg district. Together with cycling and swimming halls, a district sports hall and a smaller second pool are also to be built on the same plot.

Groundbreaking began in June 1993. The foundation stone for the project was officially set on September 5th 1995. The first section built was the velodrome, a circular building 140 meters in diameter with room for 10,000 spectators. On January 23rd 1997 the starting pistol was fired to inaugurate the first six-day race on the new track. The swimming pools should be finished by the end of 1997. Only then will Perrault's poetry of disappearing be visible.

The huge circular roof on top of the velodrome, with its central oculus for light, creates a breath-taking space below. Even if Perrault isn't wild about structures, as he claims, in this case the roof really is the architecture.

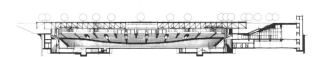

Photos and section: OSB Berlin

The steel structure was erected by the Krupp Steel Company between June 1995 and February 1996. We spoke with Walter Habermann, the contract manager, and Gerhard Mattner, the contractor's site representative.

Who decided how the roof's structure would be? Was it the architect's idea, the engineers', or that of the steel firm?

Habermann   The architect had an idea while drawing up the plans. He wanted a round, self-supporting roof and as large an area as possible free of columns. Ove Arup devised a load-bearing system suitable for his idea. We then suggested solutions for the production and assembly.

Were there any special difficulties during the production and assembly?

Mattner   No. The most important part of the work for the velodrome was the preliminary preparation: the assembly itself wasn't difficult after that. We haven't done anything like this before, so it was exciting to see if everything fitted in the end.

And did it fit?

Habermann   Almost better than we had expected. It isn't normal to have such a high degree of precision required. But with a radius of around 60 meters, a sloping of the rods by just one thousandth means a deviation in height of 6 cm. That's why we also chose a special form of tie rods, ones which enable the forces within the tie rods to be controlled and the distortion of the pull rods to be set exactly.

Please don't go into detail yet. How was the roof constructed?

Habermann   It was quite easy really. The circular roof is like a huge cake divided into 48 segments. The individual pieces of cake are bordered by trussed girders, about 4 meters high and 54.4 meters long, running radially, which are connected to each other by secondary tangential girders. The girders were made and delivered in two parts because of their enormous length and only assembled on site. Each of the 48 radial girders spans from an inner ring structure over a main ring structure, supported on 16 concrete columns, and is cantilevered outwards above this main ring and anchored by a tension element at the other end. 16 of the radial girders lie directly on the 16 concrete columns. Between each of these are another two girders being indirectly supported; in other words, attached only to the inner ring and the outer main ring structure. The inner ring is 10.8 meters in diameter and outlines the central skylight. The ring was constructed as a spatial framework in order to absorb the resulting torsional forces and

The spectator seating
area during construction
and details of the roof:
the truss structure with
primary and secondary
truss girders as seen
from below, the connec-
tion of the secondary
girders, and the wreath
of rodan bars in the inner
ring

All Photos:
Erik-Jan Ouwerkerk
Drawing: Krupp
Stahlbau Berlin GmbH

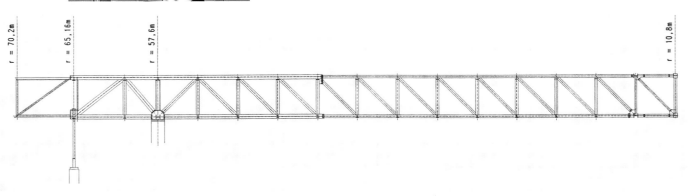

r = 70,2m r = 65,16m r = 57,6m r = 10,8m

DACHMITTE

prevent twisting. In structural engineering terms, load-bearing works through a combination between
a flat framework, supported vertically by the columns under the main ring and anchored at the end by tie
rods, and a point-loaded circular plate with an elastic edge restraint.

How would you have constructed the roof if it hadn't needed to have a skylight?
Habermann   Not much differently. An inner ring would have always been necessary. The head plates of
the radial girders would have had to have been fastened next to each other on a ring anyway.

A further ring is recognizable within the supporting ring. What is its function?
Mattner   That's a ring of rodan bars which isn't connected to the load-bearing structure but to the
skylight supports by means of tie rods. It has no structural function. That's just architecture.

How do you as the builder handle the special requirements which an
architect thinks up without giving too much thought to its execution? Is
the work involved in transmitting an idea into production a hindrance or
a challenge for the firm carrying it out?
Habermann   Certainly we are interested in unusual and complicated tasks. Lots of firms can build
simple structures. Competition in that area is enormous. That's why we devise our own construction
concepts and develop as many of the components as possible ourselves. We can only survive financially
if we make many special suggestions and offer superior technical know-how.

A very diplomatic answer. But here you were cooperating with a world
famous design office ...
Mattner   One feature of a good structural engineer is that he also takes into account the possibilities
of a smooth construction. It shouldn't just look nice but should be able to be assembled reasonably.
Habermann   The solution developed by Arup office fulfilled the static requirements perfectly. But we
had doubts about both its suitability for use and the dimensional accuracy which was required during
construction assembly. Thus, in cooperation with Arup, we developed new solutions for the anchoring
and for the secondary girders.

What exactly did you change?
Habermann   You are asking us to describe something which is normally described by drawings.

The support system and the tension members: the main ring truss of the circular roof is supported by 16 concrete columns. Each radial truss girder is stressed by a group of cables encased in a steel pipe and anchored to the ground

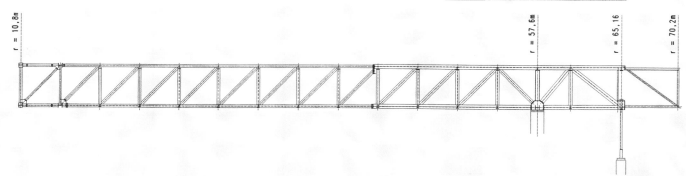

Wouldn't it be worth a try?

Mattner Originally 160 mm thick round steel rods were supposed to take the roof's tension. The disadvantage with this would have been that we no longer would have had the chance to compensate differences in height. That's why we used stressing cables—the sort used in reinforced concrete construction or bridge-building. These cables are encased in a pipe which later, when everything is adjusted and finally pretensioned, is filled from below with concrete so as to protect against corrosion. The tension is created by a hydraulic press which grabs and tightens each individual cable. A bolt is then inserted on the outside of the pipe's mouth and adjusted with a nut. This alternative method of anchoring was our own suggestion. It allowed for corrections and thus for greater precision during construction. Each of the radial girders was prestressed to the theoretical value of 40 tons to put the frame under stress and simultaneously to check that the cables didn't move. After the supporting structure was removed and the stressing cables took the full weight, measurements showed the final result to be within a few millimeters of the pre-calculated values.

Habermann Would you like even more detail?

While we're on the subject …

Habermann We worked with guy cables common in bridge-building. Individual cables were fed into the anchor head and fastened with clamps. The use of anchor boxes with an exterior bolt together with a ring nut enabled an exact adjustment of the given forces. For one tension element, twenty two single strands are arranged in a steel pipe and anchored to the ground plate. The steel pipe is not linked to the radial girder, so the tensile forces are carried by the steel strands alone. These stressing cables are made by a Swiss firm, and are usually used in prestressed concrete construction. They are standard steel stressing cables adapted to suit our needs. Such cables were also used to raise the Hotel Esplanade's Kaisersaal (Imperial Room) on Potsdamer Platz.

You also mentioned something about secondary girders, what was the problem there?

Mattner Ove Arup gave us detailed preliminary plans. These included the complete structural engineering, elevations, and suggestions for connections. Originally, head plate connections were envisaged for the secondary girders, but the division of the circle into 48 sections meant that the head plates would not abut the radial girders at a right angle. They would have required an inclination of 3.75 degrees—but you can't guarantee that kind of accuracy in their production. That's why we settled on a connection

The roof construction begins with the inner ring truss, supported by a working deck. The first radial truss girders are attached. Head plates are bolted onto the inner ring

Photos: Philipp Wolff/OSB

The horizontality of the roof can be seen from the uppermost level. The grand perspective makes the roof appear dome-like

Photo: Erik-Jan Ouwerkerk
Drawing: Krupp Stahlbau Berlin GmbH

using splice plates. With these, the force is directed completely through the web of the girder. The web is fortified in the connecting area so that it can withstand the forces of compression and tension. The advantage here is that the bolt holes can allow some adjustability. In general, we produce these plate connections with 2 mm of play at the holes—thus, giving us room for any possible compensation for inexactness in the production or assembly. With a head plate joint you could never achieve such an exact fit for the girder's tangential links.

Habermann We included 5 mm leeway in our plans for assembling the two parts of the radial girders. The gap is filled with a filler plate—a so-called 'finger filler'. If you have two pairs of screws then you can insert a filler plate over them from above and below, and so compensate for different lengths.

Mattner Such things are part and parcel of steel construction. You can't produce the pieces with absolute accuracy. A steel construction is always calculated a shade on the small side and any difference compensated with filler plates. You can't compare steel construction with other forms of construction— the dimensional tolerances are far smaller. You even have to include the layers of paint in your preliminary calculations: paint makes something thicker and that can make a difference of several millimeters on larger prefabricated parts of a building.

How are the girders connected to the inner ring?

Mattner There it's head plates. The girders are right-angled so it's no problem.

Will the roof structure be covered, and what about sound and fire insulation?

Mattner A sound insulating layer will be included between the steel structure and the roof skin. There is no fire protection. Nothing burns at a height of 16 meters.

Habermann The Building Inspectors' demands had more to do with the escape routes. The whole furnishings and seating were chosen especially so that there is hardly any fire load. Even the wood used for the cycle racing track is hardly flammable.

What are the roof layers above the structure like?

Mattner Above the steel girders there is a Z-joist, which is fastened to the girders, and on top of that corrugated metal roof decking. The Z-joist gives the roof some slope and allows the rainwater to be drawn off. Above the metal roof decking there is flat sheet metal—thus creating a smooth roof area with an appropriate slope. On top of the sheet metal comes the usual roof layers—vapor barrier, insulation and sealant.

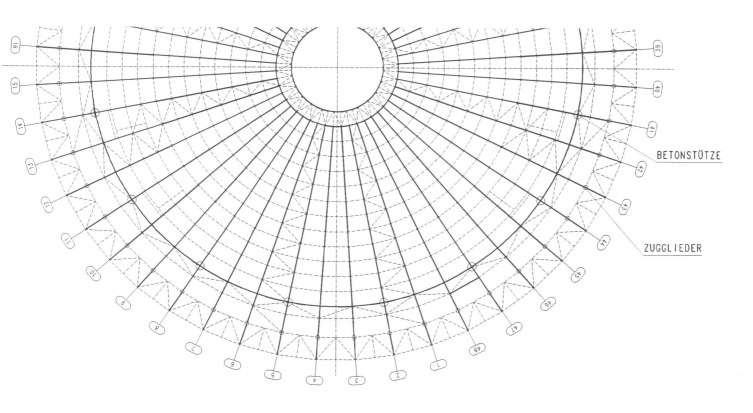

BETONSTÜTZE

ZUGGLIEDER

Habermann   The main construction is really completely flat. The Z-joists on the secondary girders are tapered. You have to imagine it like a fan. First the water runs in the direction of the main trussed girders, and is then led outside from there.

All you can see outside are the shimmering mats ...

> **Mattner**   These stainless steel mats lie about 50 cm above the roofing on their own stainless steel construction. That means that above the roof construction there is another framework on which the mats are fastened. They have been omitted in the area around the skylights. The mats were prefabricated to fit the 15,000 sq. m roof area exactly. They have the same shape as the roof segments, with widths of approx. 7 meters near the outer rim of the roof and becoming narrower towards their pointed ends at the center of the building. The joints between the strips run exactly along the radial beams.

What was the total time it took to assemble the roof structure?

Habermann   We started on August 15th 1995. The first step was constructing a working deck to support the inner ring structure throughout the assembly. The individual segments of the ring were already fitted together and given their last coating in the factory. Then the inner parts of the radial girders—which had been produced in two halves—were connected to the inner ring construction, and simultaneously the exterior parts of the radial beam were put on the main ring girders and screwed down. The inner and outer pieces were then screwed together. The tension elements had to be threaded in at the same time as the outer part of the radial girder was being assembled and linked with the main ring girders.

This was followed by the prestressing. The clamps were pressed into the anchor box using the so-called "power seating method." In a second step, a hydraulic press was again used to subject the tension elements to the set values of 320 or 380 kps kN. The weight was then carried over from the tension elements to the steel construction by tightening the ring nut after the press had been released.

36 hydraulic presses, capable of being controlled simultaneously, were placed around the working deck while it was being lowered below the inner ring. These were first raised, before being continually lowered over the next two hours. They were lowered 134 mm, thus nearly achieving the theoretically calculated figure of 125 mm. After the lowering, the strength in the tension elements was checked again, and once more there was a good correlation with the static calculation.

> **Mattner**   In total the assembly lasted eight months. We assembled the last trussed beam on December 20th 1995. That was two days earlier than planned, despite the fact that part of the assembly fell during the harsh winter. At times we had wind-chill temperatures of up to minus 46 degrees Celsius.

Please tell me some more about the logistics.

Habermann   The parts came from three different factories—from Austria, Belgium, and us. There were unforseeable delays on the construction site but we couldn't change the subcontractors' planning. That meant the first parts were delivered at a time when the building site wasn't really ready for them.

> **Mattner**   The trusses from Belgium were already there in April 1995. They arrived by boat and I had to search the whole of Berlin before I finally found a temporary storage place for them. It was down in the harbor in Königs Wusterhausen. They stayed there for 4 or 5 months. The advantage was that the parts were stored close by and ready for assembly whenever necessary. The 16 sections of the outer ring were brought from Austria by heavy freight vehicles. That was the hardest part of the whole operation. They had to be stored on the building site throughout the summer. We were able to have the smaller secondary girders delivered little by little. That was very advantageous for the assembly.

Habermann   The firms had exact instructions for the assembly, the timetable for delivery dates, and the coating. In order to get a unified color we chose one single paint producer. And yet in the end there were still variations in color because the parts had been lying outside in the open air for different lengths of time.

> **Mattner**   The paint color RAL 9006, silver sparkling with metal particles, weathers very quickly and takes up patina. The color will darken even further later on. It's just very sensitive.

How much steel did you use in total?

Habermann   We used around 3,500 tons of steel for the 140 m wide self-supporting "spoke wheel." That's about ten times as much as is in the Berlin Radio Tower. The inner part of a trussed girder weighs 10 tons, the outer part another 20. The total weight multiplied by 48 makes 1,440 tons for the radial beams. The secondary beams weighed 800 tons. The main ring was delivered in 16 sections each weighing 28 tons—that makes almost another 450 tons. Then another 200 tons came from the eight 25-ton segments of the inner ring, another 500 tons for the various technical rooms and maintenance areas within the roof structure. And that's not including the 86,000 screws.

And the cost?

> **Mattner**   The shimmering mats alone costs almost DM 40 million ...

Habermann   The architectural element so crucial for the architect—the stainless steel mat—is around four times as expensive as our roof construction, which was about DM 10 million.

The stainless steel mats
are elastically fastened
to a separate framework
and can be removed for
cleaning the roof

Photo:
Erik-Jan Ouwerkerk

Chronology

of Building Events from 1989 to December 1996

If anything happens anywhere at any time and if events are competing with each other, then who will be able to remember things later on with any exactitude?

Who will, a year from now, still know when the Galeries Lafayette were opened, returning a bit of the old glamour to Friedrichstrasse; or when construction on Potsdamer Platz actually began; or when the Info Box was finished; or when the question of an international airport for Berlin was decided in favor of Berlin-Schönefeld; or when Philip Johnson's ear was stolen? Who was to blame for the failure of the Berlin-Brandenburg union? When did the emigrant Heinz Berggruen return to Berlin and what was his gift to the city? And since when is Berlin able to relax in the certainty of becoming the nation's capital again?

This last question shows clearly enough that the chronology of this first Bauwelt Berlin Annual could definitely not have started with January first, 1996. Too many crucial events happened before then, too many of the fundamental decisions were made before. The most important planning goals for the city had been formulated; and almost all the federal competitions were decided. Thus the chronology had to go back to the night when the Berlin Wall fell.

From that point on it takes great strides through the interim years 1990, 1991, 1992, 1993, 1994, noting those decisions which are now gradually being realized. In 1995 the density of events increases, and for the year 1996 we have tried, as far as this is possible, to record an entire year, event by event.

The chronology is the backbone of the annual, creating a time line of news reports about the city and its architecture. At times, it's amazing to follow the unedited juxtaposition of events, at times, the crowded facts and figures read like a dreary worship of success. The bulk of the task was organizing the facts from a variety of sources including newspaper reports, press releases, institutions, firms, developers, events calendars, personal knowledge, backed up by untiring research.

In a few instances we decided to include events that appear to belong more directly to the cultural sector, though such distinctions become difficult with events like "Site Seeing Berlin" (entertainment on construction sites), one of the main attractions of last summer. And of course, there were the topping-out ceremonies that resembled something between an open air festival and a feast for 10,000. The Berlin developers proved themselves to be a new breed of promoters bringing the city to the edge of its seat. Their real commitment, however, is registered more concretely in the figures found at the end of most reports.

From time to time, amidst this flood of innumerable facts and figures, essays and quotes turn up in the time line, allowing a brake and offering the reader some literary diversions from the otherwise linear form. Each essay serves to comment on one event, while the quotes for the most part are comments on the whole city.

We offer no index at the end, as we expect by 2001 at the latest, the chronology will be online and facilitated by search commands.
The Editors

6.20.1991

By a vote of 337 to 320, the Bundestag (Lower House of German Parliament) passes the resolution "Toward Completing German Unity" and thereby commits itself to Berlin as the seat of government. Transfer of Parliament to Berlin should take place after four years.

10.30.1991

The Senior Council of the Bundestag decides that the former Reichstag building should be used for plenary sessions of the Bundestag.

12.11.1991

The Federal Government decides: the Federal Chancellory and ten ministries will move to Berlin; those ministries remaining in Bonn shall

8.31.1989

Unification Treaty between the Federal Republic of Germany and the German Democratic Republic; Article 2 specifies Berlin as future seat of the capital.

10.3.1990

Unification of Germany and of the two halves of Berlin.

11.9.1989

Where everything begins: fall of the Berlin Wall.

4.14.1992

Under the title "Housing Construction Strategies 95" the Berlin Senate (the executive cabinet working under the Mayor and accountable to the City Council) decides on an urban development program establishing gigantic projects through the year 2010, both in the form of condensing and making new uses for existing areas, as well as in the form of urban expansion projects in new suburbs. The 11 biggest projects with a high share of new construction add up to a surface area of approx. 1,500 ha. Belonging to

April 1992

Start of urban development planning for the clinical city Buch in the northern part of the Pankow district. The clinical facilities of Ludwig Hoffmann and Hermann Blankenstein, built from 1899 on, and continually expanded via additions of new buildings and residential areas, are supposed to be extended into an urban district for approx. 35,000 residents. The Arbeitsgruppe für Stadtplanung (AGS—City Planning Team) of Edvard Jahn, Wolfgang Pfeifer, and Heinrich Suhr (Berlin) draws up the master plan for the entire site with approx. 134 ha.

6.12.1992

First result of the Bundestag's capital city resolution: the "Spreebogen International Competition of Urban Design." In immediate proximity to the Reichstag, the new parliamentary and government quarter "Spreebogen" is to arise, abolishing the historic rupture between East and West Berlin and corresponding architecturally to the image of a parliament that is close to the people and open to the outside world. The green spaces of the Tiergarten park and the banks of the Spree river are to remain open to the public. From out of roughly 800 works submitted from 48 countries, the design of Axel Schultes and Charlotte Frank, Berlin, is chosen on 2.19.93. The Schultes-Frank design links Friedrich-Wilhelm-Stadt to Moabit by means of a linear buckle and

| 1989 | 1990 | 1991 | 1992 |

each establish a second office in Berlin. On 6.3.92 it is agreed that Berlin will receive, in addition to the Chancellory, Press and Information Office, and Foreign Office, the following ministries: Interior, Justice, Finance, Economics, Labor and Social Welfare, Family, Senior Citizens, Women and Youth, Transportation, as well as Building and Urban Development.

the newly planned centers with dimensions of about 5,000 housing units each are: Karow-Nord (97 ha), Buch (134 ha), Französisch Buchholz (51 ha), Eisenacher Strasse/Marzahn (48 ha), Gartenstadt am Falkenberg (40 ha), Altglienicke (190 ha).
Established as development areas inside the city are: Johannisthal-Adlershof (420 ha), Wasserstadt Oberhavel (206 ha), Biesdorf-Süd (142 ha), Rummelsburger Bucht (130 ha), Eldenaer Strasse/Alter Schlachthof (50 ha). A special role is taken up by the parliamentary and government quarter.

As an urban district of its own, Buch V, with a surface area of 111 ha, is supposed to become a residential and commercial area for about 10,000 people. The structural concept was developed by Mario Maedebach and Werner Redeleit jointly with landscape planner Norbert Müggenburg.

keeps the area within the Spreebogen river bend open as a park. On 6.24.93 the revised version of the design is confirmed once more.

July 1992

The Deutsche Bahn AG opts for the so-called "Mushroom Concept" for completing Berlin's railway paths. A new north-south connection and a new east-west connection for long-distance and regional traffic will lead through the city center. Both lines will cross at the new central rail station, the Lehrter Bahnhof. Only two architectural firms are invited to an insider design compeitition: Josef Paul Kleihues, Berlin, and von Gerkan, Marg, and Partner, Hamburg. For execution, the design of von Gerkan, Marg, and Partner is proposed.

And how did you like the Wall, I asked finally.
Unsightly, said Lambert, too low, architecturally contemptible,
if not worse, insufficiently lit; but as an idea, quite good—two heaps
of the miserable nation, carefully separated by a wall, the one heap
the other one's declared enemy—that is certainly a situation worth
preserving.
Ingomar von Kieseritzky, 1991

...later he saw the thing also from the back, il muro à la Boccaccio,
and then it really appeared to be built of Rabelaisean stuff, with splits
and tears, with holes full of grass, not as stabile as our side, with the
exception of the area around Potsdamer Platz, which I'll come back to,
to confirm the sense of the entirety for you. While you, eternal hero of
classical tragedy, have only managed a wall's inspection in the
Leipziger Strasse...
Fritz Rudolf Fries, 1995

10.20.1992

At the international design workshop for the development area Karow-Nord, the firm of Moore Ruble Yudell (Charles Moore †, John Ruble, Buzz Yudell), Santa Monica/USA is awarded first prize and commissioned to do follow-up work on the master plan. On a terrain of 97 ha on the northeastern edge of the city in the Weissensee district, a new city region with about 5,000 residences and corresponding infrastructure, as well as 13,000 sq. m for industries and services, will be built by the end of 1997. The landscaping plan was worked out by the Berlin planning firm MKW (Cornelia Müller, Elmar Knippschild, Jan Wehberg); over 50 architectural and landscape planning firms are participating in the planning and realization of the buildings and grounds. Developer is the working group Arge-Karow, a merger of the investors Wohnbau Groth & Graalfs GmbH and GEHAG Gemeinnützige

1.21.1993

Decision in the limited international competition for completing the garden city at Falkenberg in the Treptow district. The first prize is taken by the Berlin firm Quick Bäckmann Quick (Klaus and Susanne Quick, Michael Bäckmann) with Hannelore Kossel (landscaping), Berlin. On the approx. 40 ha of fallow land between Altglienicke and Bohnsdorf, in the immediate neighborhood of the "Tuschkastensiedlung" by Bruno Taut (1912–15), about 1,500 residences, 5 childcare centers, an elementary school, an addition to the St. Hedwigs Hospital, and an extended central park are to be constructed. In charge of the project: Wohnungsbaugenossenschaft 1892 eG. together with the Berlin Senate Building and Housing Administration. Construction start for the first phase is planned for April 1997.

March 1993

A master plan and 24 building plans are submitted for the development area Altglienicke in the southwestern part of Treptow district, on the border of the urban districts Rudow, Schönefeld, and Adlershof. The approx. 190 ha area, where around 5,300 housing units with infrastructure and space for commerce and services are planned, is being supervised (since 1992) by LEITPLAN GmbH, Berlin (a merger of PLANWERK and BGMR). Roughly 20 different architectural firms will work on the three subregions: "Town Center Altglienicke," "Residential Area 1/Altglienicke-Süd," and "Alphabetical areas" along the Schönefelder Chaussee.

The palace is so entirely wiped out that it requires a great effort just to conjure it back again, like a Fata Morgana, in the immense area that is now the Marx-Engels-Platz. Only two plane trees remain where the oldest masonry of the palace once fell away steeply to the Spree. … You'd say they'll freeze, so lost in the vastness. … Walking in Berlin, you feel more at ease than anywhere else in Germany, and it cannot be denied that it is pleasant to walk across this square. … Though founded on destruction, it lives from the magnificent views of the urban elements that have made Berlin what it is since the days of Schlüter and Schinkel. To the east, the red tower of the old city hall rises boldly and yet almost delicately above the tribune; to the north on the right is the cathedral … in the west, above the trees of the voice academy, the Pegasus horses on the cornice of the Neues Museum stage a great race toward the sky …; then comes the magistral beginning of "Unter den Linden" with the crudely repaired Wache by Schinkel (the victory angels have disappeared), the Zeughaus before it and the university beyond. There's no disputing it: the square, this gigantic square, is still held in place by an architectural frame, by the very tradition that was supposed to be extinguished with the palace.
Benno Reifenberg, 1951

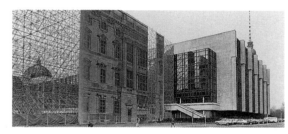

1993

Heimstätten. The city-state of Berlin is supporting residential construction with public funds using its first and second subsidy programs.

12.15.1992

Presentation of the architectural project "Max Reinhardt House" by Peter Eisenman, New York. Clients: Gottfried Reinhardt and Advanta Management AG, Frankfort. On the 6,000 sq. m large property of the former Friedrichstadt-Palast (next to the Berliner Ensemble), Peter Eisenman has designed a multi-story office building in the form of a spiral-shaped, curved bow— 128 m high and exploding every dimension of its surroundings—which if built (according to the Bauwelt) would "presumably sink on the spot into the swampy ground." In October 1995, the heirs to the Reinhardt estate initially abandon their plans.

2.19.1993

The results of the building competition for "Reconstruction of the Reichstag Building for the Bundestag" are announced. Out of 80 works submitted, 15 prizes and 25 purchases are selected; the sum of prize money offered comes to a total of DM 700,000. The competition was nationwide, and 14 foreign firms were invited. The three submissions in the first prize group are: Santiago Calatrava, Zurich (with an overarching new cupola), Pi de Bruijn, Amsterdam (glazed courtyard instead of cupola, main assembly hall and presidential wing as individual building components), and Sir Norman Foster, London (Reichstag under a transparent roof, public forum inside with main assembly hall in the center). On 6.1.93 the Bundestag chooses Sir Norman Foster as architect for the reconstruction of the Reichstag.

4.28.1993

Ceremonial opening: The Berlin House of Representatives resides from now on in the building once home to the Prussian Parliament, built 1893–98 by Privy Councilor Friedrich Schulze, remodeled for its new use by Jan Rave, Berlin, for DM 160 mill.

6.30.1993

A simulated facade of the destroyed "Stadtschloss" painted on 7,000 sq. m synthetic material (artist: Cathérine Feff, Paris, Initiator: Wilhelm von Boddien and promotional committee) is installed in front of the Palast der Republik (the Palace of the Republic, a modern building used by the former German Democratic Republic's legislature from 1976 to 1990)— just in time for Walter Ulbricht's 100th birthday. Through September 1994, the perfect illusion created by the hanging is supposed to seduce Berliners into opting for the reconstruction of the Stadtschloss (the Berlin city residence of the Hohenzollern monarchy, built 1706).

7.4.1993

The development area "Capital City Berlin— Parliamentary and Government Quarter," is formally established.

7.22.1993

Berlin Senate resolution formally declaring the area Alter Schlachthof Eldenaer Strasse in the Prenzlauer Berg district as an urban development region. The "Stadtentwicklungsgesellschaft Eldenaer Strasse" is commissioned with implementation of the project in November 1992. The 50 ha site of stockyard and slaughterhouse, opened in 1881, shall become a residential and commercial district for 7,000 people, with protected status for buildings designated as historic landmarks.

8.23.1993

Briefing for the international urban design competition "Spreeinsel" around the Schlossplatz (at the time still called Marx-Engels-Platz) and Werderscher Markt. The competition is dedicated to the search for an architectural definition for the new Berlin city center. The briefing makes a commitment to tearing down the GDR Foreign Ministry, Staatsrat (GDR executive council) building, and the Palast der

Republik. The procedure has two stages: On 12.15.93, 52 submissions from the first phase of applications (roughly 1,400 participants) will be selected. For the second phase of competition, the stipulations will be changed: the demolition of the Staatsrat building is invalidated. On 5.11.94 the prize jury decides in favor of the design by Bernd Niebuhr, Berlin. Niebuhr proposes an oval-shaped open courtyard (empty center) surrounded by dense block construction.

9.10.1993

The privately organized Bundesbaugesellschaft Berlin mbH (Federal Construction Company Ltd.) is founded. It supervises the four large parliamentary construction measures: remodeling the Reichstag, construction of the Chancellory, erecting the new administrative buildings for the parliamentary parties and the Bundestag in the Dorotheenblöcke, and the new parliamentary buildings in the Alsenblock and Luisenblock.

10.12.1993

The cabinet in Bonn decides to extend the period for moving the federal government to Berlin through the year 2000.

11.25.1993

Competition decided for the 100 ha central area around the underground station Elsterwerdaer Platz in the Marzahn district (Biesdorf). Bernd Albers, Berlin, and the Zurich landscape planner Dieter Kienast are awarded first prize.

12.31.1993

RIAS (Radio in the American Sector), the "free voice of the Free World," loses its contract and is incorporated into the newly founded Deutschlandradio. The counter voice of Karl Eduard von Schnitzler in "Der Schwarze Kanal" ("The Black Channel") has not been heard since 1990.

1.10.1994

Competition announced for the Federal Presidential Office on the northern grounds of the Bellevue Palace. The difficulty for the participants lies not in the use of space (a small administrative building), but in its location and the site's demanding expectations. Its proximity to Bellevue Palace and the dense stock of trees on the grounds of the Tiergarten park have to be taken into consideration; above all, however, the question most at stake is: How representative may — or must — a utilitarian building be for the Federal Republic's head of state? The jury decides on

3.15.1994

Formal establishment of the urban development area Rummelsburger Bucht. For purposes of implementation, the trustee "Entwicklungsgesellschaft Rummelsburger Bucht mbH" had been founded back in June 1992. For the approx. 130 ha area, an international assessment procedure (September 1992 through February 1993) was undertaken; Klaus Theo Brenner was entrusted with drawing up the master plan

4.8.1994

Competition announced for the Federal Chancellory in the western section of the "Spur des Bundes" ("Federal Trail") at the Spreebogen, based on the urban design concept of Axel Schultes and Charlotte Frank (first prize in the Spreebogen competition). On grounds of functionality, protocol, and security, the areas for general administration and the supervisory area will be housed in two different buildings. On 12.13.94 the prize jury decides in favor of two equally ranked works: again for a design of Axel Schultes and Charlotte Frank, Berlin, which draws together the two buildings in a cluster of buildings with raised courtyards, and for the design of the firm of Krüger-Schuberth-Vandreike, Berlin, which emphasizes the supervisory area as a solitary entity in the midst of administrative wings.

1993 | **1994**

9.15.1993

Decision on the second stage of the urban design competition for Alexanderplatz. The first prize is awarded to Hans Kollhoff, Berlin, for a block structure woven through with passages and covered courtyards, towered over by a group of highrises whose equal height of 150 m is ironically proclaimed to be "second Berlin Traufhöhe." (The "Traufhöhe" — literally "eaves height" — refers to the height limitation of 22 m in Berlin midtown quarters.)

9.23.1993

Berlin's application to host the Olympic games in 2000 is unsuccessful. At the second ballot in Monaco, Berlin loses out. Planning for an Olympic village in Ruhleben is immediately halted, while work continues on the cycling and swimming facilities in the Landsberger Allee by Dominique Perrault, Paris, and the boxing arena in Friedrich-Ludwig-Jahn-Sportpark by Joppien Dietz Architects, Frankfurt/Main.

11.14.1993

Reopening of the Neue Wache by Karl Friedrich Schinkel, dedication as "Central Memorial for the Federal Republic of Germany." The new design is based on an idea by Federal Chancellor Helmut Kohl to combine an enlarged statue of the "Mother in Mourning with Dead Son" by Käthe Kollwitz (1937) with Heinrich Tessenow's interior design of 1931.

December 1993

The 140 ha site of Biesdorf-Süd in the Marzahn district is formally declared as an urban development region. For implementation beginning 1994, the "Deutsche Bau- und Grundstücks-AG" is appointed as trustee-developer. The structural concept for the entire region was already submitted on 8.25.93 by the Planungsgruppe 4, Berlin (Peter Dittmer, Jens-P. Kruse, Paul M. Losse). Alongside 5,200 housing units with corresponding infrastructure, 400,000 sq. m of space for shops, offices, and commerce are to be developed.

10.25.94 in favor of the design by Martin Gruber and Helmut Kleine-Kraneburg, Frankfurt/Main, which places a self-contained elliptical building, set off from Bellevue Palace, in the clearing of the grounds' English garden.

and simultaneously required to incorporate the designs of Herman Hertzberger, Amsterdam, and David Mackay (firm of Matorell Bohigas Mackay Puigdomènech, Barcelona). September 1994: groundbreaking for 130 housing units on the southern bank of the Stralau peninsula. Through 2010, approx. 5,400 housing units, with corresponding infrastructural installations and nearly 600,000 sq. m of space for services and commerce are to be developed.

3.16.1994

Competition decided for the restoration of the Neues Museum and the erection of additional buildings on the Museumsinsel (Museum Island). First prize: Giorgio Grassi, Milan. 16 of 18 invited international architecture firms participated.

6.1.1994

The federal government decides, in opposition to its original building intentions, to use mostly pre-existing buildings for the ministries moving to Berlin. The only new buildings will be the Chancellory and the annex to the Foreign Ministry.

10.13.1994

Groundbreaking for the Hellersdorf Municipal Center. One of Germany's largest new housing projects will receive an urban center with a municipal hall, educational, cultural, and athletic facilities, and about 1,000 housing units on a space of around 31 ha. At the heart of the center is a square with shopping arcades and residential as well as business space, with a park on the southern side. As private developer for the DM 2.2 billion project, which should be finished by the year 2000, the Berlin Senate hired the MEGA Entwicklungs- und Gewerbeansiedlungs AG (MEGA Development and Business Settlement Stock Company). The urban design competition had already been decided in 1991 in favor of the office of Brandt + Böttcher, Berlin.

7.1.1994

The Senior Council of the Bundestag comes out in favor of building a cupola for the Reichstag.

10.28.1994

The first building competition within the parliamentary quarters is decided: For the "Parla-

overall floorspace on three adjoining sites, mostly office space, with some for retail and restaurants, a small share of housing, and a gigantic supply of entertainment sites (cinema center, musical theater and the like). The basic order for the urban design results from the International Competition "Potsdamer and Leipziger Platz," which the firm of Hilmer und Sattler, Munich, won on October 2nd, 1991. The architects building here will be: Renzo Piano/ Christoph Kohlbecker, Hans Kollhoff, Lauber + Wöhr, José Rafael Moneo, Richard Rogers, and Arata Isozaki (for Daimler-Benz); Helmut Jahn (for Sony); Giorgio Grassi, Peter Schweger, Jürgen Sawade, and Roger Diener (for A + T).

11.30.1994

Initial groundbreaking in Wasserstadt Oberhavel, Quartier Pulvermühle. Wasserstadt Oberhavel is a development region dating from the time before the fall of the Berlin Wall. Initial designs had already been presented in November 1990 by the Berlin architects Hans Kollhoff/Helga

with the first prize in October 1995.
For the Quartier Pulvermühle, on the eastern bank of the Havel, the urban design concept rests on the prize-winning submission of the Berlin architects Johanne and Gernot Nalbach. Developer: GSW.

procedure 1993) will be carried out by four firms: PAS Jochem Jourdan & Bernhard Müller, Frankfort/Main/Kassel; Hartmut and Ingeborg Rüdiger, Braunschweig; Otto Steidle and Partners, Munich; Hildebrandt Machleidt + Partners, Berlin. The outdoor planning comes from the landscape planners Reuß

mentsneubau Alsenblock" ("New Parliament Building Alsenblock") in the eastern area of the Spreebogen, the first prize goes to Stephan Braunfels, Munich: he designed a block whose rows align with the "Spur des Bundes" ("Federal Trail"), with courtyards opening to the outside, but sealed off by glass walls.

10.29.1994

With a ceremonial cornerstone laying for the debis project, constructions on Potsdamer Platz begin. The three biggest investors — Daimler-Benz, Sony, and A + T (ABB, Terreno, and the Ernst entrepreneurial group) — will erect approx. 560,000 sq. m

November 1994

Start of construction for the Siedlung Rudow Süd in the Neukölln district. Through the year 2000, 1,700 housing units with facilities for infrastructure, shopping, and services are to be constructed. Energy will be provided by a newly constructed decentralized block power plant. The urban design concept for the 45.3 ha project was developed by the Berlin architecture firm Martin + Pächter; different developers and architects are responsible for the individual buildings.

November 1994

Urban design idea competition for an approx. 60 ha site at the corner of Landsberger Allee and Rhinstrasse, in the area of the Lichtenberg, Marzahn, and Hohenschönhausen districts. The first prize is awarded to Daniel Libeskind. By sometime around 2015, a new urban district with 1,000 housing units as well as 130,000 sq. m of office and commercial space will emerge.

Timmermann, Christoph Langhof, Jürgen Nottmeyer, and Klaus Zillich. In mid-1992 there followed a formal designation as urban development area and the foundation of the "TET Wasserstadt Berlin-Oberhavel GmbH" as trustee for the city-state of Berlin. Through the year 2015, on an area of approx. 206 ha, a region previously used mainly for industry will be reshaped into a residential and working quarter for approx. 34,000 people. There are plans for approx. 17,000 housing units with infrastructure (16 child-care centers, 7 elementary and 3 high schools, youth and senior citizen centers, playgrounds and athletic fields), 950,000 sq. m of commercial and service space, as well as two new bridges. The competition for completing the southern bridge was decided in December 1993, the first prize going to Walter Arno Noebel with Martin Krone (firm of Leonhardt, Andrä, and Partners), Berlin. In the competition for the northern bridge, Herbert Fink along with Dörr, Ludolf, and Wimmer, Berlin, are honored

12.7.1994

Berlin Senate issues resolution formally declaring the development area Berlin-Adlershof. Commissioned with project implementation is the "Berlin-Adlershof Aufbaugesellschaft" (BAAG — Berlin Adlershof Building Society), established in August 1993. The urban reconstruction on a total area of 420 ha in southeastern Berlin, with public funding of DM 3 billion, is currently Berlin's largest development project. Between 1995 and 2005, a "City for Business and Science" is to emerge on the site of the former Akademie der Wissenschaften (Academy of Sciences), the DDR-Fernsehfunk (GDR Television Station), and the Johannisthal Airport. The natural science departments of the Humboldt-University, various research institutes, technology-oriented firms, and a media center will form the new city section together with a residential quarter for approx. 15,000 people and a 70 ha scenic park. The overall urban design planning (assessment

+ Riedel, Regina Poly, Stefan Tischer, Berlin. The traffic design includes the remodeling of the rapid transit station Adlershof, after a design by Albert Speer & Partners, Frankfurt/Main, is being implemented since April 1995.

12.22.1994

In the second round of the urban design competition for the City Quarter Lehrter Bahnhof, the jury recommends the design of O.M. Ungers (with Stefan Vieths) as the basis for subsequent revisions. The design of Max Dudler, awarded second prize, is now to form the basis for development in the area north of Invalidenstrasse. Project developer: Tishman Speyer Properties.

January 1995

Winners of two limited building competitions within the development area Berlin-Adlershof: first prize for an environmental technology center received by Jo Eisele and Nick Fritz with Helmut Bott, Darmstadt; the competition for a photonic center is won with two first prizes: Matthias Sauerbruch and Louisa Hutton, Berlin, and Ortner/Ortner, Berlin.

1.9.1995

The federal commissioner for the Berlin move, Building Minister Klaus Töpfer, opens the first office building for the Bundestag and its staff: The former GDR Peoples Education Ministry, Unter den Linden 69–73, which was combined with the older neighboring building at Wilhelmstrasse 60, will in future house offices for members of parliament and a portion of the Bundestag administration. Conversion: Gehrmann Consult, Wiesbaden.

1.25.1995

Dedication of the Mosse-Zentrum at Jerusalemer/ Schützenstrasse in the Mitte district. The corner building for the publishing house in Berlin-Mitte was renovated à la Mendelsohn by architect Bernd Kemper, Hanover.

2.7.1995

As winner of one of the two first prizes from the preceding competition, the firm of von Gerkan, Marg, and Partner is awarded the contract for the new Dresdner Bank building (Pariser Platz 5a/6). This brings the number of architects picked for the reconstruction of Pariser Platz to four. It was previously determined that Josef Paul Kleihues will build the properties on Pariser Platz 1 and 7, formerly Haus Sommer and Haus Liebermann; the Hotel Adlon is assigned as a direct commission to the architects Patzschke, Klotz, and Partners, Berlin. Not until May 1994, after two competitions arranged by its members, did the Akademie der Künste (Academy of the Arts) designate Günter Behnisch, Stuttgart, as architect.

January 1995

Urban design idea competition for the 210,000 sq. m large commercial area in Lichtenberg. The area is to be condensed into a new city section for living and commerce. Developers: District Office and the investors TRIGON, KHR-Projektentwicklungsgesellschaft, und Ruschestrasse GmbH. Seven participants invited from four countries. First prize: Trojan, Trojan + Neu, Darmstadt.

Architect of the new wing on Jerusalemer Strasse: Dieter Schneider, Berlin. Overall concept: Jürgen Fissler and Hans Christof Ernst, Berlin, Developer: Druckhaus Mitte GmbH Hans Roeder.

2.6.1995

Federal Building Minister Klaus Töpfer and the state building company Bundesbaugesellschaft Berlin sign the framework agreement to coordinate the government's move.

Construction has begun in and around Pariser Platz. But it has hardly affected the persistent memory of the "Pariser Platz" in the minds of Berliners. The many debates concerning the square have produced a sort of collective memory. There is hardly a person, who does not consider the Quarré with its strict spatial geometry, exemplary of Prussian rationality and discipline; hardly anybody, who does not delude him or herself that everything here was pulled from the same mold. Wouldn't be nice to have these characteristics back again throughout the city, and particularly on Pariser Platz? Thus the many voices calling for its reconstruction, as though these special virtues could be regained by the old image, just as we remember them to be.

Yet, the dispute was not about rebuilding the enclosed city square "in its spatial geometry and its quietude and concentration." Rather, it was about restoring those distinct, special virtues. The difficulty of such a task manifests itself in the number of expert reports commissioned by the senate: in September 1991, "Pariser Platz. Critical Reconstruction of the Area" by Dieter Hoffmann-Axthelm and Bernhard Strecker; in January 1992, the urban planning evaluation "The Area around the Reichstag and Pariser Platz" by Hildebrand Machleidt, Wolfgang Schäche and Walter Stepp; in September 1993, "Appraisal of the formal principles for Building on Pariser Platz in Berlin" by Bruno Flierl and Walter Rolfes. Accompanying the senate's efforts was the tireless work of the "Society for Historic Berlin" in the Stresemannstrasse. The Society bundles the collective powers believing in the reconstruction of square and virtues. Then came what was intended to be a counter-appraisal: an exhibition organized by the Free Democratic Party (FDP) in February 1995, depicting Pariser Platz in a want-to-be horrifying vision composed of computer-simulations derived from pre-existing plans.

By then the senate had long since evaluated the expert's reports, translating the desired characteristics into set "design regulations" (a written corpus supplementing the Pariser Platz building plan I 200). These included: establishing a building base, a maximum cornice (16.70 m) and eaves (22 m) height, limiting the window area at 30 (later 49) percent of the facade, limiting the materials to natural stone and plaster (later also artificial stone) and the colors to light ochre, yellow and gray. Finally, on February 9th 1995, the Berlin parliament announced: "The design regulations have to ensure the conservation of the square's historic appearance."

The pre-established dimensions, materials, and colors all refer to the Brandenburg Gate, which only a historian knows to have originally been white.

Make The Gate White *Tilmann Buddensieg*

"And to the right between the tops of the venerable Linden trees you were met by the shining soft-hued glow of marble from the magnificent, snow white gate." Such was the praise from the Jacobin republican Georg Friedrich Rebmann in his "kosmopolitischen Wanderungen" (Cosmopolitan Journeys) from 1793, a year after completion of the Brandenburg Gate. A structure we know today only in a yellowish-gray sandstone.

Barely twenty years later Julius von Voß, a popular author in Berlin around 1800, lamented: "The white, a color imitating marble, which shines so ideally against the Tiergarten green, is now besmeared with a repulsive café au lait," thereby, "robbing all dignity from the portal to Europe's most splendid street." Thus, without any doubt, the Brandenburg Gate was conceived by the master builder Carl Gotthard Langhans and by his royal client as a shining "snow white" marble replacement for the Athenian propylaeum, as a Berlin "Marble Arch." As a Greek stranger, it impinged on the square's otherwise uniform rococo style. It contradicted the historic ensemble of noble palaces with their warm tones and similar shapes. It also rejected Philipp Gerlach's courtly "rules of design" from 1740, which provided the standard, so "the neighbors would know how to preserve the city's regularity." In the year of the French Revolution, the Brandenburg Gate brought an end to the court and dynastic traditions of high and low, of public and private architecture. It promoted the enlightenment ideals of Winckelmann, and even the utopia of broad reaching civil liberty.

Investigations from 1991 revealed eight paint layers over the original chalk white, hidden by a disastrous "restoration" of 1956, which defiled the Gate by scraping the sandstone surface and declaring it to be "authentic".

Berlin building officials insist on this egregious surface as the standard for all new buildings on Pariser Platz. Berlin's building director Hans Stimmann confirmed the decision in an interview with Frankfurter Allgemeine Zeitung (FAZ) Magazin on July 28th 1995: "The same material must be used as that used for the Brandenburg Gate, that is, natural stone or plaster." Thus, an authenticity is ascribed to the "dull surface of the natural stone" from 1956, thereby validating false facts, which then justify "political decisions," which, in turn, become the basis for the development plan, that is, for the law.

Blindly the new building designs—save for the new Akademie der Künste by Günter Behnisch—are bowing to the sandstone statute. No one has mentioned plaster. "A hint of natural stone" is so en vogue in new Berlin, the tile industry declares. It is generally misperceived as part of a Prussian/Berlin tradition. But in reality, most of the Berlin facades were covered in colored plaster, stone paint, as well as painted brick. Especially prevalent was the elaborate masonry and ornamental work. Today, it is the natural quality of stone that is supposed to compensate for the loss of ornament and color.

3.1.1995

In the urban design report for a section of the development area Biesdorf-Süd, the approx. 10 ha site of the former Erich-Weinert-Kaserne, Reimar Herbst and Martin Lang, Berlin, receive first prize. In May 1995 the construction plan for the section "Grüne Aue" is also submitted.

3.20.1995

Dedication of the underground memorial on August-Bebel-Platz in the Mitte district by Micha Ullmann, commemorating the book-burning of 5.10.33. The "Library" is a room with empty shelves set in the ground and only visible through a glass sheet from above. In June 1995 the Israeli sculptor and graphic artist receives the Käthe Kollwitz Prize from the Akademie der Künste of Berlin-Brandenburg.

4.7.1995

Start of the exhibition "Hauptstadtplanung für Berlin" ("Capital City Planning for Berlin") in the foyer of the Staatsrat (former GDR executive council) building. The giant model of Berlin will stay on as a permanent exhibition in addition, to rotating exhibits of plans and building competitions for Berlin.

4.8.–7.9.1995

Exhibition "Kino Movie Cinema. Einhundert Jahre Film" ("One Hundred Years of Film") in the Martin-Gropius-Bau, organized by the Stiftung Deutsche Kinemathek (German Cinematic Foundation). At the heart of the exhibit is the estate of Marlene Dietrich, acquired by the city of Berlin for 5 mill. dollars. Exhibition design: Hans Dieter Schaal, Attenweiler.

4.10.–8.23.1995

Exhibition "Berlin 1945" in the former Kunsthalle Budapester Strasse. This

Architectural conservationists will name two reasons for opposing the restoration of the original white of the Brandenburg Gate: first, the composition of the original chalk white is unknown. Second, the history of the diverse surfaces, including the 1956 denigration by natural stone, is part of the building's history. Rather than see the dash, stained surface as a malformation, it is cherished as part of the "natural aging process."

Why is the classical architecture of London, Paris, Washington, Hamburg and Oldenburg predominately white, while the symbols of Berlin—the Brandenburg Gate or Karl Friedrich Schinkel's Altes Museum—seem to us more akin to the building aesthetic of Le Corbusier, in which "relationships are established between raw materials?" Out of misguided respect for natural stone, historic architecture is displaced into modernism. Only a decisively new architecture—reflecting the square formation of the Platz, the building height and the proportions of the Gate—would pay due respect to that which is unattainable, without seeming stylistically obsequious, and without burdening the new buildings with tons of natural stone and by a "Clandestine retreat" (Nietzsche) subjugating them to the principles of some mediocre, imperial "Platz architecture".

One can only reiterate the 1991 demands of Arenhövel and Bothe: Make the Brandenburg Gate white again, forward to the origin of the white gate on the new Pariser Platz! As desired from the outset, it would thereby distinguish itself fundamentally and uniquely from its new neighbors with their stuck-on, screwed-on or self-supporting natural stone walls from all over the world. Then, the small-mindedness of material assimilation would not risk disturbing the Gate's "Pathos of Distance."

3.15.1995

Last night anonymous culprits kidnapped the American architect Philip Johnson—or rather his 170 kilogram, 4 m tall likeness made of cardboard and tin—from the construction site of the American Business Center on Checkpoint Charlie. The ear of the same, together with a demanding written confession (from Nietzsche's Zarathustra), was sent to the news offices of the Berliner Tagesspiegel. A spokesman of the American Business Center GmbH (CEDC) explicitly denied any public relations trick and showed little interest in the figure's "gradual return," as he had already ordered a reproduction of the reproduction right away …

3.24.1995

Official opening of "Haus Pietzsch," Unter den Linden/corner Neustädtische Kirchstrasse. In five upper stories 3,400 sq. m of office space were developed, in the glazed gap between this and the adjoining building the client exhibits his private art collection, and on the ground floor is a branch of Café Einstein. Architect: Jürgen Sawade, Berlin.

exhibit is the core of a series of events entitled "Fifty Years of Peace in Germany" commemorating May 8th 1945. Concerts, public readings, stage and film productions, exhibits, and commemorative ceremonies take place in Berlin and Brandenburg. Within this series of events, the following ceremonies will be observed: groundbreaking for the exhibition and documentation center "Topography of Terror," architect: Peter Zumthor, Switzerland; roof raising ceremony for Jewish Museum in Kreuzberg by Daniel Libeskind; and first exhibit in the Centrum Judaicum (former Neue Synagoge) on "Jewish History in Berlin."

4.28.–7.9.1995

Exhibition on the thirty year-long architectural work of von Gerkan, Marg, and Partner, Hamburg, entitled "Unter grossen Dächern" ("Under Large Roofs") in the Berlinische Galerie.

5.1.1995

After a 20-month building period, the first houses have been completed for the new construction area of Kirchsteigfeld in Potsdam. At the end of 1996, 2,000 housing units out of a planned 2,800 will be ready for occupancy. On about 58 ha of real estate, the small town for around 7,000 inhabitants based on an urban design by Rob Krier, Vienna, will be the largest new construction project in the eastern German states. (Architects' workshop: October 1991.) More than 30 architects are planning the houses on this estate, with an investment volume of DM 2 billion Clients: Fondsgesellschaften der Groth & Graalfs GmbH.

5.7.1995

Reopening of the former Neue Synagoge as "Centrum Judaicum" in the Oranienburger Strasse. Reconstruction of what was once the largest synagogue in Europe (architects: Eduard Knoblauch and Friedrich August Stüler, 1859–1866) went on for seven years. The prayer room for 3,200 persons, demolished in 1958, was not rebuilt; only a remnant of the wall has been secured behind a steel-and-glass construction, while the entrance hall and antechamber to the synagogue were restored. The new building at Oranienburger Strasse 29, which closes the gap between the synagogue and the foundation offices for the Centrum Judaicum, is accessible from all the areas, including the library. Architect for the remodeling: Bernhard Leisering, Berlin.

5.7.1995

The new Berlin landmark preservation law comes into effect. It differs from previous legislation (valid since 1977) in four respects: The constitutive procedure for placement under protection will be replaced by a list reporting procedure, as is already the practice in most other federal states. The landmark list, which will be published in the official bulletin on 9.29.95, is a register of currently known building and garden landmarks,

5.8.1995

Start of demolition work on the former GDR Foreign Ministry in Berlin-Mitte, which will be completed in December 1995. The building at Friedrichswerder, on the property of the former Bauakademie by Karl Friedrich Schinkel, was built in 1967 after the plans of the Josef Kaiser Collective. It was conceived as the western closure to the new inner city area that extended to Alexanderplatz and changed the urban spatial structure of Berlin's Mitte district. Day by day, Berliners can now follow how the silhouettes of the Cathedral and the Friedrichswerder Church re-emerge from behind ever smaller barriers.

May 1995

Construction starts in the urban development area Eisenacher Strasse along the eastern edge of the Marzahn district on the border to Hellersdorf. On the 48 ha grounds of a former collective farm, more than 1,600 housing units with corresponding amenities, as well as 93,000 sq. m of commercial and service space and the green corridor Wuhlepark, are to be developed by 1997. The urban design concept comes from the planning firm of Heribert Wiesemann, Martin Seebauer, Karl Wefers, and Partner, Cologne.

5.16.1995

The master plans for the parliament's biggest and most expensive construction project are presented. For the 1,800 offices of the parliamentary parties and Bundestag administration in the two Dorotheen blocks, five architectural firms are picked in a negotiation procedure following European guidelines: Thomas van den Valentyn, Cologne (expansion of the Reichspräsidentenpalais for the Parliamentary Society and Bundestag Register); Peter Schweger, Hamburg; Pi de Bruijn, Amsterdam; Peter Busmann and Godfrid Haberer, Cologne; von Gerkan, Marg, and Partner, Hamburg.

5.1.1995

As of May, films are being shown again at the Titania-Palast. The highly popular and much frequented public theater (architects: Jacobi, Schloenbach, 1926–27) has often been remodeled, by Hermann Fehling among others. Architects of the most recent remodeling: Gruppe BAUart (Rudolf Bertig, Andreas Herrmann, Volker Nielsen, Elke Schwarz), Mühlheim/Ruhr.

5.2.1995

The St-Canisius-Kirche along the Lietzensee in Charlottenburg, built from 1954–57 by Reinhard Hofbauer, one of the most beautiful churches of the postwar period with its parabolic vaulted interior, is totally burned out. The bell tower has to be demolished in September.

5.5.–5.17.1995

"Berliner Bauwochen" ("Berlin Buildings Weeks") on the theme "City Projects."

and landmark areas, with around 7,500 positions. The list can be updated to account for new findings. Based on the example of the eastern city districts, subdivisions of the landmark protection office will be set up at the district level. The State Archaeological Landmark Office and the Department of Building and Garden Landmark Maintenance will be united into a single State Landmark Office. Responsibility goes to the Senate for Urban Development, Environmental Protection, and Technology.

After 1989, demands were raised to rebuild the Bauakademie, which was pulled down in 1962. The winner of the Spreeinsel competition from May 1994, Bernd Niebuhr, envisioned tearing down all of the buildings on Marx-Engels-Platz but incorporated the outlines of the Bauakademie into his urban design concept.

"I, too, have devised the model of a city from which I derive all others," replied Marco. "It is a city consisting only of exceptions, exclusions, contradictions, absurdities. If such a city is the most improbable there is, then as the number of abnormal elements decreases, the probability increases that the city really exists."
Italo Calvino, 1972

5.17.–7.9.1995

Housing exhibit "Stadt-Haus-Wohnung" ("City-House-Home"). The exhibit with 200 Berlin building projects is erected on a 600 m long open air installation on the median strip of Unter den Linden. It documents residential building in the Berlin of the nineties: completed and planned housing, individual houses and housing estates, modernization and gentrification of residential environment, city projects and investors' projects. According to the catalogue, 71,000 publicly subsidized housing units were approved between 1991 and 1995, 16 urban renewal areas (15 in the eastern part of the city) were identified between 1993 and 1994, and 10 suburban projects were initiated. Responsible for the exhibit: Barbara Hoidn, Hans Stimmann; for the architecture: Gernot Nalbach, Berlin.

… not really to say, why so many, perhaps everyone is waiting, although much of it is already there, or could be there, in the morning another wait at the housing office, keys are available, but have to be picked up in another street, on the map it's about the length of a matchstick = 1.2 kilometers away, arrive, the opening hours have changed, have to return in four days, back to the waiting office to pick up the applications for apartment renovations and, most importantly, for the advice, communicating everything to everyone, as long as you wait obediently in line, what great organisation, at least the waiting numbers give you some shimmer of hope that there is in fact some order…
Bettina Vismann, 1994

Summer 1995

Construction starts in the urban development area Französisch Buchholz. On fallow land once used for farming in the Pankow district, between the historic village center Alt-Buchholz and the rural area Blankenfelde, a residential quarter with roughly 3,000 homes in closed and open building styles is to be developed, in addition to 25,000 sq. m of commercial and service space. The master plan for the 51 ha area was submitted by the planning firm of Johannes N. Müller in June 1992. In 1992, after a competitive assessment procedure, the Berlin firm Wolfgang Engel/Klaus Zillich (together with landscape planner Hannelore Kossel) was commissioned with the overall urban design planning. Planning procedures for individual sections are underway since August 1993.

June 1995

Decision on the construction of the "Gedenkstätte Berliner Mauer" ("Berlin Wall Memorial") on Bernauer Strasse. On 12.19.1994 the capital city committee "Berlin 2000" agreed on the work of Kohlhoff & Kohlhoff, Stuttgart, one of the second prizes. The Federal Ministry of the Interior makes DM 1,7 mill. available. At the same time, American investors announce their intention to build a theme park "The Wall" in Fort Lauderdale, Florida and solicit investors in Germany who can put up 50,000 US dollars each.

May | **June**

5.31.1995

Roof raising ceremony for the block "Hofgarten am Gendarmenmarkt" between Friedrichstrasse, Behrenstrasse, Charlottenstrasse, and Französische Strasse. Josef Paul Kleihues (overall design) building together with Max Dudler, Jürgen Sawade, Hans Kollhoff. To be developed: one hotel (Four Seasons); shops, restaurants, 22,000 sq. m office space and only 45 privately financed housing units. The house containing Restaurant Borchardt on Französische Strasse 47 and the corner house plus the adjoining house on Friedrich-/Behrenstrasse are preserved: An additional house in Friedrichstrasse, artificially embedded by Hans Kollhoff into his design, collapsed in the course of construction and will now be reconstructed. Project development: Hines Grundstücksentwicklung. Estimated construction costs DM 550 mill.

Französische Strasse, at Borchardt *Helene von Nostiz*

Eating oysters at Borchardt after the theater was one of the chic happenings which you could, with a certain smile, put down as a little escapade. When my parents took me there after the opera for the first time in my early youth, I was full of eager anticipation. I was filled with visions of unimagined splendor and unknown sensuality. How astonished I was as we were led through a corridor lined with dark fabrics by the stolid head waiter. We were shown several tables behind gloomy curtains. A harsh light shone down over these from chandeliers of a not exactly tasteful style. No music rang out. There wasn't a window to be seen. A few darkly dressed people sat around …

No playful apprentice waiter fiddled about with bowls in time to a melancholic dance tune. An elder family father in a waiter's tail coat and a wedding ring on his finger stepped slowly and measuredly. He knew his guests, and assessed them, scattering an "Excellence" here and a "Highness" there without ever making a mistake. The oysters, which could only possibly be accompanied by a particular Chablis, were carried out seriously. Here enjoyment received a legitimate face reminiscent of the rituals of ceremonial activities. One had the feeling that the only people who would enter these chambres séparées would be thoughtful men or couples contemplating a solid life-long relationship.

Chance had it that I recently sat at Borchardt again with my brother after many long years of traveling and the chaos of war. We believed we had remained unrecognized. But then the head waiter, now turned gray, stepped up to us: "I've waited on Sir and Madam on an earlier occasion. How are your esteemed parents?" And the atmosphere which had always dominated these rooms was brought back to life at a stroke.

6.1.1995

Construction starts in the urban development region Staakener Felder on the western edge of the Spandau district. In three sections, on an area adding up to 14.8 ha, roughly 1,300 homes — of which about 80 % will be publicly subsidized — will be developed along with two child care centers, an elementary school, and public gardens. In 1993 an overall urban design concept was established, and in the following years framework contracts were set up with three investors (TRIGON, Bauwert/BEWOGE, and Lincoln Property Group), who will also secure financing for the infrastructure.

6.7.1995

Opening of an 11-story office building called "Platinum" on Sachsendamm, between freeway and rapid transit junction. With its 5-story legs, the office building sticks to the so-called "Berliner Traufhöhe" (eaves height) and then grows in pyramidal fashion to a height of 40 m. Architect: Jürgen Sawade; Client: Colonia-Nordstern-Versicherung. Construction cost: DM 134 mill.

6.8.1995

Solidarity demonstration on behalf of Bärbel Bohley, civil rights activist in former GDR. Politicians from all parties gather in front of Bärbel Bohley's house in Berlin-Mitte to protest against the enforcement of a legal decision to pay Dr. Gregor Gysi, chair of the PDS (post-Communist) parliamentary party in the Bundestag, DM 3,500 in libel damages (Gysi was accused by Bohley of cooperating with the Stasi, the East German secret police). Bohley's legal counsel, by the way, is the right-wing cultural policy spokesman for the CDU parliamentary party in the Berlin assembly, Dr. Uwe Lehmann-Brauns.

6.4.1995

Opening of the largest new German hotel under the name "Estrel Residence Hotel" in the Neukölln district, close to the Schönefeld airport. 17 stories high, it offers space for 1,100 rooms with 2,250 beds. Outside: glass and pink granite. There are 14 guest rooms for the handicapped, 50 sq. m large, available at the standard rate. Hence winner of the "Golden Wheelchair" prize. Architects: Heiner Hennes, Waldemar Thielemann, Bonn. Builder: ISB Universale Bau GmbH. Cost: DM 240 mill.

6.13.1995

60th birthday of Jeanne-Claude and Christo in Berlin.

6.17.1995

First wrapping of Christo's Reichstag covering: The first material track is laid (complete wrapping 6.25.–7.9.). Five mill. visitors come to Berlin. Harald Martenstein writes in the Berlin daily paper Tagesspiegel: "The program of events accompanying the Reichstag wrapping is the city itself."

6.19.1995

Reopening of the Steglitz manor on Schlossstrasse. Built as "little Wrangler's Castle" around 1800 according to plans by Friedrich Gilly, 1803–1804 it was remodeled and finished by Heinrich Gentz. On the occasion of Berlin's 750th anniversary, a restoration consistent with its landmark status was decided and realized for DM 16 mill. by Christina Petersen, Berlin. The Steglitz district administration office uses the lower rooms for temporary exhibits, while the two upper floors are rented out to cultural institutions.

6.7.1995

The glass wall commemorating the murdered Jewish citizens of the Steglitz district is unveiled on Hermann-Ehlers-Platz. On an 11 m long, 3.5 m high, and 20 cm thick wall clothed in reflecting plates of refined steel are inscribed facsimiles of pages from the Berlin deportation lists, a chronology of the Jews of Steglitz, photos, and a quotation from the chief prosecutor in the Nuremberg war crimes trials. Architects: Wolfgang Göschel and Joachim von Rosenberg (with Hans Norbert Burkert), Berlin, after a competition won in 1992.

6.10.1995

Opening of the Panorama-Rotunda on Pariser Platz. Three additional rotundas, in which the future Berlin is literally painted out, are erected on Schlossplatz, Alexanderplatz, and Potsdamer Platz. Under the motto "Berlin 2005, City Visions," the illustrated magazine Stern presents Berliners with four round tents of painted illusions after models by the architect Yadegar Asisi. Included in the virtual reality presentation is the reconstructed Stadtschloss.

6.15.1995

Competition decided for new concept and extension of the Swiss embassy in Berlin. 9 works are submitted, the Swiss firm Diener & Diener, Basel, is selected. The house on Fürst-Bismarck-Strasse 4, built in 1870 by Friedrich Hitzig, is the last testimony to the former Alsenviertel. In the year 2000 (in the interim, the embassy will be moved because of work on the Tiergarten tunnel) it will be the only house inhabited by "foreign" residents in the Spreebogen precinct.

6.17.1995

Aedes East, the branch of the architectural gallery Aedes on Savignyplatz, is opened in the Hackesche Höfe on Rosenthaler Strasse with a festival, a symposium, and three exhibits, including "Illusions of Power — National Socialist Buildings in Berlin." Architect of the gallery and café next door: Ben van Berkel, Amsterdam.

6.21.1995

Cornerstone ceremony in the square between the Schützenstrasse, Markgrafenstrasse, Zimmerstrasse, and Charlottenstrasse in Mitte. Architect: Aldo Rossi, Milan, with Bellmann and Böhm, Berlin. Clients: Dr. Peter and Isolde Kottmair, Munich. On the 8,468 sq. m large property, taking up an entire block, eleven individual houses will be built within Berlin's historic pattern which means a system of small lots. The artificial parceling will be conveyed by the different colors of the houses. Perpendicular buildings and side-wings form four large courtyards in the interior of the block. The overall floorspace of 43,000 sq. m is divided into space for offices, shops, and 20% housing.

Prima Pietra with Aldo *Sebastian Redecke*

The red carpet is rolled out on the Berlin sand for the Prima Pietra—the foundation stone ceremony—to Aldo Rossi's DM 400 million multi-purpose complex on the plot between Schützenstrasse, Zimmerstrasse, Markgrafenstrasse and Charlottenstrasse in the city's downtown Mitte district. Hosts once again are the Kottmairs from Munich, the developer pair for both of Rossi's buildings in the capital city. In the closed-off Zimmerstrasse a valet parking service is waiting to discretely park the invited guests' cars, large and small.

The path to the foundation stone is filled with jugglers, people walking on stilts, brass bands and cabaret artists. Kids brought in especially for the event pack the rotating big wheel and the balloon-covered miniature railway. But the advertized clown is missing. Delicacies prepared by Käfer caterers, Munich's finest, are offered from all directions, every step of the way. Whole strawberries swim in the sparkling fruit cocktails.

The Master of Ceremonies warmly receives the special guests at the front. These include not only the Italian Ambassador Vattani, a recognised Rossi connoisseur, but also, complete with a protocol cordon of honor, la sua Eccellenza, the president of the Italian senate Scognamiglio, fresh from the Palazzo Madama in Rome. The Piemont name crosses the MC's lips with surprising ease. Also in attendance is Berlin's governing mayor Eberhard Diepgen. One of the key speakers is the fully liable partner in the investment fund. He diagnoses a lull in the Berlin real-estate market, but this will have no influence whatsoever on the timing of Rossi's colorful block. After wishing the project

moves "deep into the black", Diepgen makes tenuous reference to Michelangelo. This is because the project broschure claims that one building in Schützenstrasse is supposed to be an hommage to the facade of the Palazzo Farnese in Rome. But how can this be? The freestanding palazzo was built by Antonio Sangallo il Giovane starting in 1516. After Alessandro Farnese became Pope Paul III, Michelangelo's contribution was a single loggia above the portal and a mighty crowning cornice. A generous interpretation of Rossi's Michelangelo mutation—the future home of a bank—might even acknowledge similarities with two bays from Farnese's interior courtyard.

An honor guard in traditional Prussian uniforms fires a short gun salute before the band—clad in lederhosen—starts setting the mood for moving into the main marquee. The avantgarde bulldozer ballet, which some people were expecting, has been cancelled. The Kottmairs have kept the marquee and the exhibition room with Rossi's oeuvre completely white. The decor is accented by marbolized column shafts dressed in garlands and small may trees standing in airbricks on the richly laden tables. Our seats are next to the cathedral preacher, who is already noticeably cheery from the fine Käfer pinot blanc. He had previously grabbed the hammer for a short while during the Prima Pietra ceremony.

The smoked brook char with creamed horseradish was followed by Munich Festtag soup. Unfortunately we didn't get to experience the rest of the festivities: including grilled ox with gravy, red cabbage and small potato dumplings; the divertissemento rondo veneziano with dancers from the German State Opera; the noble Augustinian brew fresh from the barrel; the one number "Behind the oven sits a mouse"; the apple strudel with vanilla sauce, the Bavarian G'stanzeln from Fritz Winter, tea and biscuits; Mrs Finczynski from Christies auctioning a 49 x 81 cm watercolor and India ink original from Aldo Rossi for the benefit of the German President's wife's charity "Muko-Hilfe", for which thirty thousand Marks had already been offered and the heavy, long-lasting cloudburst at noon.

"Grüss Gott" everyone.

June

6.22.1995

The parliaments of Berlin and Brandenburg ratify the plebiscite for a merger of the two states; in the Brandenburg State Parliament (Potsdam) with 64 votes out of 84; in the Berlin Parliament with 188 votes out of 233.

6.23.1995

Berlin parliamentary resolution to establish a foundation "Stadtmuseum Berlin—Landesmuseum für Kultur und Geschichte Berlins" ("City Museum Berlin—State Museum for the Culture and History of Berlin") as an organizational merger of the Domäne Dahlem, Ephraimpalais, Knoblauchhaus, the Märkisches Museum, Berlin Museum and Jewish Museum in the Martin-Gropius-Haus (later in the Libeskind building), the Nikolaikirche, the Natural Science Collections, and additional institutions.

6.22.1995

Opening of the exhibit "1945. Krieg – Zerstörung – Aufbau" ("1945. War—Destruction—Building"), as part of the series "50 Years of Peace" in the Akademie der Künste on Pariser Platz. It shows the plans of Albert Speer for the "World Capital Germania" and other German cities—and juxtaposes postwar visions in the East and West.

6.23.1995

Construction start for the "Rosmarin Karee" (Quartier 209a) between Behren-/Charlotten-/Friedrichstrasse in Mitte. The house on Behrenstrasse 46 will be the only house to remain preserved. Architects: Jürgen Böge, Ingeborg Lindner-Böge, Hamburg (offices, shops, restaurants) and Paul Kahlfeldt, Berlin (70 city apartments). Project developer: Hines and Büll & Dr. Liedtke, Hamburg. Estimated construction cost: DM 300 mill.

7.1.1995

Florian Mausbach, formerly head of the Planning Department in Bielefeld, is appointed president of the Bundesbaudirektion (Federal Building Authority). He succeeds Barbara Jakubeit, who takes over a teaching position in design at the TH Darmstadt.

7.1.1995

Berlin's first high-rise, the Borsig-Tower in Tegel, designed by Eugen Schmohl 1922–24, has been faithfully restored and the new owner, Herlitz Falkenhöh AG, moved in. Around the Tower on a total area of 150,000 sq. m Herlitz is planning an office park with a business center, and apartments. The cornerstone ceremony for the business center (Architect: Walter Rolfes, Berlin) and the apartment building (Architect: Norbert Stocker, Berlin) will take place on 9.28.1995. Project completion is scheduled for 1998. Responsible for the urban planning concept is Claude Vasconi, Paris,

6.25.1995

After the dispute over the results of the competition for the Holocaust Memorial, Lea Rosh announces a decision in favor of the design by the group around Christine Jackob-Marks, Berlin. This was preceded by a competition with 528 participants and two first prizes. Christine Jackob-Marks (with Hella Rolfes, Hans Scheib, Reinhard Stangl) designed an inclined concrete plate 10,000 sq. m large, in which 4.2 mill. names would be engraved. (Of

The Politics of Memory *Jane Kramer*

The two Germanys do not much like each other now that they are one Germany, or agree on anything beyond a taste in cars, but they share this: they are determined to settle their crimes into "history." They want to resolve a duty to remember and a longing to forget, as if duty and desire were the thesis and anti-thesis of a dialectic of destiny. They have a stubborn, almost innocent German faith that their past is like their prime rate or their G.N.P.—something that with a good plan and a lot of attention can be adjusted, refreshed, pressed into the service of the new German nation.

After fifty years, they have lost patience with the painful plain truths of recapitulation. They prefer the symbolic simplicities of objectification—the monuments, memorials, and "commemorative sites" that take memory and deposit it, so to speak, in the landscape, where it can be visited at appropriate ceremonial moments, but where it does not interfere unduly with the business of life at hand…

6.27.1995

An underground building project of the third kind is opened up: the Zehlendorf tunnel, which fulfills its mission perfectly as an escape route from the robbery of a Commerzbank branch. Estimated loot: DM 17 mill. The participants in the bank robbery are captured later, peu á peu. Portions of the loot were also recovered. Only the locker contents remain in the dark.

---

the 6 mill. Jews murdered in Europe, only this many names are known.) The competing prizewinners —Simon Ungers, Cologne, with Christina Moss, Christina Alt—had proposed an 85 x 85 m square grid made of double T beams on concrete blocks. The beams will be perforated in such a way as to let sunlight inscribe the names of the death camps on the ground. Severe objections were raised against both designs.

Two years before the Wall fell, a local television-talk-show hostess by name of Lea Rosh announced that Berlin was going to have a memorial to the six million Jews who died in Europe during the Second World War. She had a promise from Chancellor Kohl of a hundred and forty million dollars' worth of Berlin real estate on which to built it—five acres of what was once a no man's land near the Brandenburg Gate, between the Pariser Platz and the Leipziger Platz, and is now the middle of town…

When Kohl presented Rosh with a pricey chunk of central Berlin, he may have been thinking about a nice park, with another sentimental Kollwitz statue—something discreet, something to show the world that, whatever anyone said about Jews and Germans, their relations were tranquil; they had all been liberated on 5.8.1945, and the rest was "history." But Rosh wanted to build a monument that was, as she once said, big like the crime. She wanted a big public. A big budget. Big discussions. Big ideas.

The Senat wanted to hold what could be called a competition as big as the crime, because Berlin has (this is the official term) "a democratic competition culture," and also because the memorial, with a total budget of twelve million dollars, was going to be the most expensive memorial project in Berlin's history, and the city wanted to have a say in whose project it was going to be. Bonn, which had also pledged four million dollars, wanted the same say. And so, of course, did Lea Rosh…

6.28.1995

Federal Chancellor Kohl decides that the new Federal Chancellory will be built following the design of Axel Schultes and Charlotte Frank. He simultaneously determines the cost for the new building should by no means excede DM 400 mill. Originally, DM 280 mill. were planned, but interim calculations raised costs to DM 600 mill. Axel Schultes believes he can fit the restriction to DM 400 mill. by "compressing the building's entire body."

7.1.1995

Opening of the Deutsches Architektur Zentrum (German Architecture Center) in Köpenicker Strasse 48/49. Architect of the first building section: Claus Anderhalten, Berlin. The DAZ opens with an initial conference on the theme "Werk-Stadt Europa. Metropolen im Wandel" ("City-Making [a pun on the German word for 'Workshop'] in Europe—Metropolises in Change"); in anticipation of the 1996 UIA World Congress in Barcelona.

who will also build the department store. The developers are investing a total of DM 800 mill. The architecture offices Axel Schultes and Deubzer-König, Berlin, will also participate in the immense building task.

July 1995

Remodeling begins on the Reichstag: Already during the Christo wrapping, the building had been cleared of asbestos and virtually reduced to a mere building framework. Hardly anything will be preserved from the exquisite remodeling of Paul Baumgarten from the early sixties. In contrast, elements of Wilhelmine building decoration, e.g. rediscovered pillar models, will be "reworked." The spending limit set by parliament for the remodeling: DM 600 mill.

140

Case Beer? *Sebastian Redecke*

For Richard Roger's grand project "Window on the Zoo"—or zoo window for short—construction should have begun two years ago. The Brau und Brunnen AG (Brew and Spring Company), a real-estate company, which also bottles beers such as Dortmunder Union or Schultheiss, made loud-mouth announcements that the Berlin steel and glass tower would be opened in 1995. Today demolition bulldozers instead of building cranes still occupy the property. In the meantime they have done some serious clean up. Buildings from the 50s had to be cleared out. There was major outrage over the exemption from applicable planning laws. Nevertheless, the 20 stories and more than 350 million mark shopping and entertainment center is due to be realized with hardly a modification. It will tower over Eiermann's Gedächtniskirche (memorial church). The investor talks self-assuredly about an anchor in the urban landscape between the train station and the Ku'damm, intended to establish a dialogue with the Gedächtniskirche.

In a corner of the almost entirely cleared plot stands the post-war flat-roofed building housing the salesrooms of an old carpet dealer, who is sitting on his lease until 2000, refusing to budge, not even for

7.2.1995

During dredging work in the foundation trench for the Hotel Adlon on Pariser Platz, six bottles of 1941 red burgundy are discovered from what was once a collection of 250,000 bottles stored in the wine cellar.

July	August		

7.31.1995

Opening of a five-day symposium with 90 film scholars and historians on the theme "Big Cities in Film." It is simultaneously the 16th meeting of the "IAM Hist" (International Association for Media and History). Summary: "All city visions have become equal. The cinema no longer understands the city and can no longer represent it."

8.5.1995

House-Running on the Fischerinsel: On this and the following weekend, anyone who wants can run straight down the 65 m high facade of the house on Fischwinkel 9 supported by a harness and rope. Fee: DM 70; Record: 15 seconds.

August 1995

During site excavation for a residential and commercial building in Alt-Köpenick (developers: TRIGON-Gruppe, architects: Moritz Müller and Götz Keller), the foundation of Berlin's oldest house is discovered. On this site around 1200 there stood a pinewood house that was replaced in 1212 by a larger house, and yet again by a third building in 1246. Owing to the height of the water table in the 13th century, the remnants of all three buildings have been preserved. (All of Köpenick is being archaeologically explored.)

8.15.1995

During construction work for the high-rise "Zoofenster", the building occupied by the firm of Teppich-Kibek on a property adjoining the corner of Joachimstaler Strasse and Kantstrasse is damaged so badly that it has to be closed off due to the danger of possible collapse.

the sweetened offers from the beverage company. The investor seemed cooperative, allowing the building to stay, despite the delays its caused, because it's no problem to prop the building up on stilts and build around it. Suddenly, in mid-August the situation changed entirely. One day after closing time, the demolition ball really got swinging and knocked a little at the walls of its neighbor with the expensive carpets. The accident had consequences. Three supports were rammed and buckled; an intermediate roof collapsed. The local building authority of the Charlottenburg district, Claus Dyckhoff, said it was a miracle that nothing more was destroyed. As a result, the building was closed and fenced off and declared unstable. Makeshift wooden beams now serve as temporary supports for the damaged structure. Naturally, the investor deeply regrets the mistake. Meanwhile, structural engineers are conducting extensive "examinations" and earning a killing on their reports. Whether the demolition man had brew or spring water beer before or, perhaps in quantities, after, remains pure speculation. Police investigators still had left at least "a few questions unanswered." There is "the initial suspicion of a felony." Was there perhaps more involved than just beer?

colored Renault Twingo. It's still the same song, and it's still good, because it still deals with current problems, no matter how old you are. There's always reason for rage. Mick Jagger goes and goes and goes.

Concertgoers vociferously criticized the fact that there were not enough trash containers, that they were forced to throw litter on the ground. Disorder, wildness, chaos, it all has its charm, especially for Stones fans, but the audience would rather see the disorder limited to the stage area. Someone said the female background singers had to sign a statement before the tour promising not to sexually harass the band members. Even if it's not true, it's a great story. It shows that the Rolling Stones still are where they almost always have been, at the peak of the times. The popular accusation of betrayal (the Stones used to be wild and leftist, but now they're just cynical moneybags) is only half true. Society has conformed to the principles of the early Rolling Stones at least as much as the other way around. The song "Time is on My Side" proved them right after all; their "Voodoo Lounge" tour is the victory march of a triumphant lifestyle. Sex, drugs, and rock'n'roll? These days, no problem: kept within reasonable limits, and of course taken with caution and due concern for health. The legalization of marijuana is probably only a matter of time, like changing the legal business hours for stores.

The triumph of the Rolling Stones is so absolute because resistance was so strong at the beginning. Musicians with literary pretensions like Bob Dylan or sensitive guitar wizards like Eric Clapton were accepted relatively quickly by parents and cultural journalists, and for that reason only enjoy a moderate cult following today. The rock-hard Stones, on the other hand, were subjected to such fierce assault from the media that they didn't even have to die like Jimi Hendrix or Janis Joplin in order to be received back into favor. The 1980's—the time of

The Devilish Angels *Harald Martenstein*

First the machine awakes. The empty stage of the Rolling Stones spits fire and smoke. It emits a scraping, metallic sound. An industry awakes and gradually transforms itself into the drummed rhythm of "Not Fade Away." The machine is a six-armed octopus with stairs and runways for Mick Jagger, with towers, cranes, strings of lights—a mixture of Brent Spar and the recent architecture of Friedrichstrasse.

These days the Rolling Stones are something everybody can agree on, like the German national soccer team the day after winning the world championship, or Richard von Weizsäcker after his speech on 5.8.1945. In the Olympic stadium before the beginning of the concert, 75,000 people do "La Hola," the Wave, the most successful Mexican cultural export next to Corona beer and Tequila. All day long every radio station in the entire city has played the music of one and the same band.

Whoever is against them—and of course there's always someone—is suspected of just wanting to attract attention. Still, hats off to Ingrid Stahmer, top candidate of the SPD party, quoted as saying that with all due respect for the band's overall work, many of the Stones' texts have "anti-women undertones." Eberhard Diepgen would never have been so bold.

The Rolling Stones are like the VW Beetle, improved for decades in one detail or another, but still always the same unmistakable Beetle, only now with a vanity mirror and double-chrome trim. Their stage looks like a more successful version of the 1990 "Steel Wheels" tour. The rubber dolls, including an inflatable Elvis Presley, look better than ever. The sound: couldn't be better, a small acoustic miracle. "Satisfaction," puked out anarchistically on the first single I ever bought, sounds full and fat on the "Voodoo Lounge" tour, almost lip-smacking. This is how someone bellows out his pain and rage who dreams of a Porsche 911 SC 3.0 Targa and is forced by society to drive a mustard-

8.19./20.1995

debis summer spectacle presents the open air show: "Beyond the Night" on the construction site of debis on Potsdamer Platz. Arata Isozaki's building shell is used as stage set for the "Pyro Space Ballet."

8.24.1995

Decision for the Tempodrom. According to plans by Jutta Kalepky, Berlin, the new building for the Tempodrom will be developed on the long controversial grounds near Anhalter Bahnhof. Fifteen years ago, Irene Moessinger invested her entire inheritance in a circus tent and erected it in Berlin on the Kemperplatz. Her Tempodrom, which she later moved into the Tiergarten near the Kongresshalle, became one of the most popular entertainment venues in Berlin.

9.1.–11.19.1995

Cy Twombly retrospective in the Neue Nationalgalerie.

9.3.1995

Opening of the exhibition Berlin—Moscow/ Moscow—Berlin in the Martin-Gropius-Bau. It can be seen in Berlin through January 1996, and starting 3.5.96 in Moscow's Pushkin Museum.

peace movements, candlelight demonstrations, and social consciousness—were the most difficult decade for the band. No tour between
'82 and '90, constant conflict between Mick Jagger and Keith Richards,
weak recordings. But the soft water of peace consciousness hasn't
entirely eroded the Stones. Their comeback also has something to do
with a new longing for hardness and immediacy, for unfiltered life.
People don't even like to watch TV quite so much anymore.

The new bassist Darryl Jones gives the Stones of 1995 a dangerously fluent, almost elegant sound. But he does it unobtrusively, as
bassists always have. Jones comes from jazz; he is Bill Wyman's suc-
cessor, and black. A woman might also have been conceivable as the
fifth Rolling Stone, but one of the "Tank Girl" type. The singer Lisa
Fisher will be famous for a while after the tour: during "Miss You" she
is supposed to circle her tongue around Mick Jagger's right nipple,
exactly to the beat of the song (there must be an exception in her
contract). The whole thing is projected in close-up on the giant video
screen at the center of the stage-even a couple of years ago that would
have provoked all kinds of culture-pessimistic clucking. During the
hooker hymn "Honky Tonk Woman," the face of Marlene Dietrich
appears on the video screen for a moment between comic-figures and
other female stars in compromising poses. Marlene Dietrich looks out
over the packed Olympic stadium in the service of a band whose
leader relished being photographed by Leni Riefenstahl.

Charlie Watts, the stoic drummer who recently celebrated his
thirtieth wedding anniversary, is himself celebrated frenetically every
evening this tour in a running gag initiated by the audience. During the
song "Angie," they push Papa Watts and his shooting gallery to the
front of the stage on a pallet. The arrangement almost looks like a
wheelchair and prefigures the triumphant tours of the future.

Art always was expected to be subversive, especially rock music;
otherwise it's just department store Muzak. But nowadays the Stones
are projecting another message from the stage. A message, crazy as it
may sound, that is reminiscent of the last days of the German Democratic Republic. In Prenzlauer Berg the young geniuses fulfilled, to all
outward appearances, the state's demand for loyalty; their opposition
was in their heads and their incomprehensible poems. In 1995 the
Stones, too, are both complicit and subversive. They show off their
success and their riches; they are obviously the cleverest business-
men of all. But all the while they present themselves not as Establishment, but as bank robbers. The Rolling Stones dig a tunnel and siphon
off a few million from Volkswagen Corporation; the audience likes that
sort of thing. The Rolling Stones don't promote Greenpeace and they
don't save baby seals. Or rather: for enough money they would even
save baby seals. Only because they are so unscrupulous can one still
take songs like "Street Fighting Man" and "Sympathy for the Devil" at
their word.

9.8.1995

Groundbreaking for the
Sony-Center on Pots-
damer Platz. Architect:
Helmut Jahn, firm of
Murphy and Jahn, Chica-
go (competition 1992).
Developer: Sony with
TishmanSpeyer and
Kajima. On a triangular
area between Kemper-
platz, Potsdamer Platz,
and Bellevuestrasse,
eight construction sec-
tions are grouped around
an oval public forum
covered with a tent roof.
On the 26,500 sq. m large
property, there will be
132,500 sq. m of overall
floorspace, which will be
divided up into offices,
apartments, retail shops,
restaurants, film house/
"Mediathek," and a
cinema center.

Dominant features within
the dense building struc-
ture will be: the Sony
European administration
at Kemperplatz, the 26
storied high-rise at Potsdamer Platz and the roof
construction (steel, glas,
fabrics) above the public
forum. The halls of the
Grand Hotel Esplanade
designated for landmark
conservation will be
incorporated into the
building on Bellevue-
strasse. This means dis-
placing the Kaisersaal
by 75 m.

9.8.–10.20.1995

"Berlin—In Search for
the Lost Center," an
exhibit in the rooms of
the Chamber of Archi-
tects on Karl-Marx-Allee.

9.15.1995

Opening of the Heinz
Galinski School on the
Waldschulallee in Char-
lottenburg (Eichkamp).
Ceremony with the chair
of the Jewish Community
of Berlin, Jerzy Kanal,
the chair of the Central
Council of Jews in Ger-
many, Ignaz Bubis, and
President Roman Herzog.
Architect Zvi Hecker, Tel
Aviv.

9.16.1995

The competition for the
Volksbank headquarters
on Kaiserdamm in
Charlottenburg (on the
site of the former State
Insurance Office) is won
by Eike Becker, Georg
Gewers, Oliver and
Swantje Kühn, Berlin.

9.18.1995

J.S.K. Perkins & Will,
Berlin receive the com-
mission for one of the
largest railway buildings
of the postwar period.
Bahnhof Papestrasse in
Schöneberg is one of four
newly planned railway
stations, along with
Lehrter Bahnhof, Gesund-
brunnen, and Spandau.

9.22.1995

Eight years after it was
chosen in a competition,
the 15 m high glass "Blue
Obelisk" by Hella Santa-
rossa is erected on
Theodor-Heuss-Platz.

9.25.1995

Cornerstone laid for the
Friedrichsfelder Viertel
in Lichtenberg. On this
quarter between Alt-
Friedrichsfelde, Gen-
singer Strasse, railroad
tracks and Biesdorfer
Kreuz, 565 state subsi-
dized housing units,
offices, and commercial
spaces will be built.

9.26.1995

At a construction site on
Mohrenstrasse, the 28-
year-old painter Käthe
Ebner is killed by a fallen
steel construction beam
serving as the support
for heavy construction
vehicles. It was supposed
to be moved by crane
several meters across
ground in the vicinity
of the building shell of
Kontorhaus Mitte.

9.27.1995

Roof raising ceremony for residential houses on Baufeld 2 in the development area Karow-Nord. Construction start was September 16th 1994. The first homes will be ready for occupancy in December 1995. Arge Karow-Nord, made up of Wohnbau Groth + Graalfs GmbH and GEHAG Heimstätten AG, will supplement the 5,100 homes to be developed by 1997 with a neighborhood center, schools, kindergartens, a church center, athletic facilities, etc. In August 1995, the first new school with 795 places (architects Liepe and Steigelmann, Berlin) was officially opened.

10.8.1995

Competition decided for the DG-Bank on Pariser Platz 3. Architect Frank O. Gehry, Santa Monica, USA, with a design that sticks to 5 stories prescribed for Pariser Platz, but grows to nine stories on Behrenstrasse. The DG-Bank will create 250 jobs here. Investors: Deutsche Genossenschaftsbank and Hines. Construction cost: DM 250 mill.

10.9.1995

Decision in the urban design and landscape planning idea competition for the site of the former Nordbahnhof, Invalidenstrasse. Plans foresee: a winter circus, a city square, athletic facilities, and a park. First prize: Romuald Loegler and Martin Janotta, Cracow/Berlin.

10.13.1995

Competition decided for completing Moabiter Werder. The jury recommends the design by architect Georg Bumiller, Berlin (although originally a special purchase), which arranges the 750 homes for federal employees in a coil ("Diätenwurm") along the avenue leading from the Spreebogen.

10.14.1995

Resumption of the subway connection from Kreuzberg to Friedrichshain over the partially reconstructed Oberbaumbrücke (architect: Santiago Calatrava, Zurich) and the streetcar connection (Line 23) from Prenzlauer Berg to Wedding. Oberbaumbrücke was one of the most frequented checkpoints for crossing the Wall.

10.16.1995

INFO BOX is opened on the still non-existent Leipziger Platz. The architects Till Schneider and Michael Schumacher, Frankfort/Main, erected

10.18.1995

Competition decided for the gatehouses on Leipziger Platz. First prize: Oswald Mathias Ungers with Stefan Vieths, Cologne. Eight firms were invited; Aldo Rossi, Milano, declined to participate.

10.18.1995

Festive opening of a new building for teaching and research in the Rudolf-Virchow University Clinic. Architects: Hannelore Deubzer and Jürgen König, Berlin.

10.22.1995

Berlin's second parliamentary election after reunification results in: CDU (Christian Democrats) 37.4%, SPD (Social Democrats) 23.6%, PDS (post-Communist party) 14.6%, Greens 13.2%, REP (far right) 2.7%, FDP (Liberals) 2.5%. The Grand Coalition between CDU and SPD has to continue. A castling move in the political chess game of urban planning in Berlin: The CDU now gets to appoint Jürgen Klemann as Senator for Building, Housing, and Transportation (previously an SPD portfolio); the SPD appoints Peter Strieder as Senator for Urban Development, Environmental Protection, and Technology (previously run by the CDU). The former Senate Building Director, Hans Stimmann, SPD, shifts into the Urban Development department as state secretary. (In Berlin's city-state government, cabinet ministers are called "Senators.")

1995 — **October**

10.5.1995

The Ring-Center at Bahnhof Frankfurter Allee is opened. Architects: Klaus Eckhard Kuhn and HPP, Dusseldorf, developer Radamco, NL, and Schliebe & Co; construction cost DM 180 mill. The "Kaufhof" shopping center closes its branch in the historic building next door at the Frankfurter Tor and moves into the Ring-Center.

10.7.–1.7.1995

Exhibit "Architectural Models of the Renaissance — The Harmony of Building from Alberti to Michelangelo" in the Altes Museum. The traveling exhibition conceived for the Palazzo Grassi in Venice shows roughly thirty restored wooden models. True-to-scale model building and the competitive system in architecture developed in the early Renaissance.

10.8.1995

Reopening of the Kirche zum Heiligen Kreuz (Holy Cross Church) after remodeling. The parish hall was integrated into the church and a public events hall created. Architects' Group Wassertorplatz. Construction cost DM 18.3 mill. The Kirche zum Heiligen Kreuz is only one example of attempts to expand or find new uses for church spaces. Public housing units are supposed to be built into the Spandauer Lutherkirche; e.g.

10.13.1995

Groundbreaking by Chancellor Kohl signals the start of tunnel work on the intra-city north-south connection for long-distance and regional trains. The tunnel will stretch along 3.3 km, from Gesundbrunnen station through to the long-distance railway station planned at Papestrasse, underneath the site of the former Lehrter station for long-distance passengers and freight trains. A second tunnel for regional traffic will run underneath Potsdamer Platz, a third as street tunnel from the Landwehrkanal to Invalidenstrasse. Anti-Tunnel GmbH, founded to oppose the tunnel construction, organizes demonstrations.

in only three months' time an exhibition pavilion in which the Potsdamer/Leipziger Platz developers present their visions for the largest urban construction site. Through 12.31.2000, debis, Sony, A+T, Deutsche Bahn, Telekom, and BEWAG will explain events on the building site with the aid of models, maps, computer simulations, and video films. The bright red box, which from a distance appears to hover above ground, is a prefabricated steel skeleton. Three large glass surfaces on a loggia subdivide the outer membrane of red steel sheets, and supply — after the virtual images inside — a panorama of the real building site. The construction cost of DM 10 mill. are shared by the Berlin Senate and the developers.

10.25.–12.21.1995

"KranZeit" ("Crane-time"). Paintings and watercolors by Ulrich Baehr. Exhibit in inner courtyard of Berlin Senate Building and Housing Administration at Behrenstrasse 42–45.

10.26.1995

Opening of the Linden-Center on Prerower Platz in the Hohenschön-hausen housing estate. In the middle of a new building area, there are now a warehouse, 86 retail stores, a post office branch, and the main branch of the Anna Seghers Library, which, integrated into the center, was (unusual for a public library) erected by a private investor and rented out to the city. Architects: J.S.K. Perkins & Will, London; investor: ECE, Hamburg; cost: DM 216 mill.

11.1.1995

Provisional list of new street names: Since reunification, nearly 100 streets in the eastern districts have been renamed, not without provoking reactions ranging from amazement to outrage: for example, Wilhelm-Pieck-Strasse is changed to Torstrasse, Hans-Beimler-Strasse to Otto-Braun-Strasse, Clara-Zetkin-Strasse to Dorotheenstrasse, Dimitroffstrasse to Danziger Strasse. The renaming of Niederkirchner Strasse (seat of the former Prussian State Diet, now serving the Berlin Parlia-ment), ardently desired by its president Hanna Renata Laurien, fails in light of the Communist resistance fighter's renown. Ever since, the Berlin Parliament chose to reside at Post Office Box 10111.

Only the Partridge Way is Immortal *Jens Reich*

Street names are the tool we Germans use to help us overcome our past. Mostly in bunches, we dispose of our uncomfortable memories, and at the same time the new names announce the "winners of history".

11.8.1995

Back by popular demand, a map of Berlin showing the course of the Wall is available for purchase again. The map "where the Wall was" costs DM 4.80. Published by Pharus-Verlag.

11.13.1995

Princes Charles in Hellersdorf. The Prince wanted to see for himself what developments looked like in Berlin's youngest district. So he paid a highly personal visit to tenants on the

11.15.1995

Reopening of the historic Alexanderhaus, one of two buildings by Peter Behrens (1930–32) on Alexanderplatz, with 15 shops on ground floor and gallery. After recon-struction of the 6 office floors, the headquarters of the Bankgesellschaft Berlin and Investment Banking will move in here. Architect of the remodeling: Stefan Buthner from Pysall, Stahrenberg & Partners, Berlin. Owner of the building is the Landes-bank Berlin. The Bero-lina-Haus, the counter-part to Alexanderhaus, likewise a property of LBB, is currently being used by the district administration office for Berlin-Mitte. After its planned move into Rat-haus Mitte, the Berolina-Haus will be renovated in similar fashion.

10.27.1995

The longstanding chair-man of the board of Daimler-Benz AG, Edzard Reuter, is elected as the new board chairman of the Bauhaus-Archiv e.V. He succeeds the late Max Bill, a close friend.

In the 1950's, my landlady in Berlin stubbornly refused to accept the new street names. It was a kind of ideological trench warfare. She still spoke of Danziger, Elbinger, Elsässer and Lothringer Strasse, while Dimitroff and Wilhelm Pieck already progressively resided in the street plan. She had problems with the fact that her own Frankfurter Allee had to be written as "Stalinallee" on return addresses—but she wasn't much of a letter writer anyway.

Even officially, the old names, though dying out, persisted stub-bornly in many places. The city center had long been filled with names like Taubenstrasse, Jägerstrasse, Luisenstrasse, Wilhelmstrasse. But they were put to an end: Johannes Dieckmann, Otto Nuschke, and Otto Grotewohl moved in victoriously. Memel yielded to Marchlewski, and Petersburg to Mister Bersarin.

Only Marienburger and Christburger mysteriously survived the street-name massacre. The Marienburger, a gruff symbol of indestruc-tible Germanness on foreign ground, persisting subversively as a street name in socialist Berlin—what a proud national image!

Neither Walter nor Erich made it to a street or a monument. Ulbricht and Honecker merely looked out beneficently over the people of the state from flattering hand-colored photographs in bureaucrats' offices. This made it simple to mop up after the fall. There was no need to reprint countless city maps, letterheads, or business cards, no new stamps had to be cut. Only the pictures were taken down.

They say that in the late Hellenistic period, there were busts and equestrian statues of the emperor where just the head could be exchanged after a successful palace revolution. This could be done as often as was necessary. We accomplish the same thing symbolically by renaming streets.

For years I have passed by the corner of Leninallee and Rebhuhn-weg (Partridge Way) in Marzahn—if only the bureaucrats would finally realize that Partridge Way alone is immortal.

ninth floor of Ernst-Bloch-Strasse 35 and went on to open an exhibit on the future of Cecilienplatz, a square being reshaped by an international team of planners under the lead-ership of the English architect John Thompson and gathering ideas sug-gested by 150 Hellers-dorfers.

November 1995

Decision in the competi-tion for the "Residential and Commercial House on Pariser Platz 6a." First prize: Bernhard Winking, Hamburg (one of the two first prizewinners in the competition for Dresdner Bank, Pariser Platz 6). On the comparatively small property, which also possesses a downright tiny facade fronting the square, an open passage is to be developed for exhibiting automobiles. Investor: Hanseatica.

11.16.1995

Competition decided for the "Südliches Klingel-höferdreieck" ("South Klingelhöfer Triangle"). The prize jury under Max Bächer awarded (from among seven invited offices) the first prize to the Berliners Hildebrand Machleidt, Walther Stepp, and Partners. Between the Landwehrkanal, Klingel-höferstrasse, Cornelius-strasse, Stülerstrasse, and Rauchstrasse, a 5-story block-defining construction is planned. The middle of the quarter will be formed by a large square, surrounded by garden-houses. Develop-er Groth + Graalfs con-siders a usage that com-plements the Northern embassies along the northern part of Klingel-höferdreieck, be they embassy houses, floors of diplomatic missions, restaurants etc. For now, however, the property still belongs to the state of Berlin. Not long ago, the vision to build a World Trade Center (architects Léon, Wohl-hage) on this property collapsed.

Hofgarten am Gendarmenmarkt
Kontorhaus Mitte
Lindencorso
Germaniabogen
Kaiserin Augusta Hof
Zollernhof
Wallhöfe
Minerva Haus

Carré am Gendarmenmarkt
Luisen-Carree
Rosmarin Karree
Schönhauser Karree
City-Carée
fradoo Carée
Prenzlauer Karree

Spree Galerie
Spree Forum
Fenster zur Spree
Spreepark
Spreebogen Plaza
Spreeknie

11.24.–12.10.1995

Exhibit of the ten best designs from the "idea competition for a new building in place of Schinkel's Bauakademie" in the former Staatsrat building in Berlin-Mitte. After the start of demolition work on the GDR Foreign Ministry, Manfred Sack issued a call in ZEITmagazin for an architectural competition to

12.6.1995

With the opening of "Maxwell's Restaurant," the restoration of the former Josty brewery (Bergbrauerei, 1893–94), Bergstrasse 22 in the Mitte district, is completed. Architects of the remodeling: Klaus Lattermann and Barbara Ewardt, Berlin.

12.31.1995

The conversion of the former GDR Ministry for Foreign Trade building, Unter den Linden 44–60, into 410 offices for the Bundestag is finished. A glass attic was put on top. Shops will move into the ground floor; the Egon-Erwin-Kisch-Café will also return to its old spot. The house was gutted, save for the load-bearing structure, and is thus almost a new building. Architect of the remodeling: Alexander Kolbe, Berlin. Construction cost: DM 121 mill.

11.24.1995

Merchants and owners hope to win more customers after changing the name of the "Markthalle am Alexanderplatz" to "Berlin-Carré." In 1996, the old Alex market hall would have become 110 years old.

1995/96 | **November** | **December**

11.24.1995

The biggest landscape planning competition in Berlin to date: for two parks on Potsdamer Platz, is decided. After revision of the two winning designs (two 2nd prizes), the victor, with 13 votes to 1, is a design by Dutch architects Maike van Stiphout and Bruno Doedens, Ouderkerk a/d Amstel. The area planned consists of a so-called "splendid track," a 2.5 ha narrow strip between debis and A+T, and a roughly 1 ha "Kemperpark" between the edge of the Tiergarten, and the Sony and Hertie sites.

Zentrum am Zoo
Köpenick-Center
City-Point-Center
Gesundbrunnen-Center
Jannowitz-Center
Lindencenter
Steinbeis Zentrum Berlin
Goldpunkt-Center-Berlin
Centre Paris-Berlin

Forum Köpenick
Forum Pankow
Forum Friedrichshain

FriedrichstadtPassagen
Plaza Marzahn
Atrium Charlottenburg
Allee-Passage Friedrichshain
Landsberger Arkaden
Checkpoint Arkaden
Leibniz-Kolonnaden
Park Kolonnaden
Kindl-Boulevard

Triangel
Trias
Trigon
Kant-Dreieck
Landsberger Spitze
Pyramide

collect ideas for a contemporary alternative to the reconstruction of Schinkel's building. Over 700 architects requested the documents, 225 submitted their designs by 10.3. The jury selected those examples that they regarded as "new, modern, pointing toward the future, (and) radical … in Schinkel's sense." The discussion about the reconstruction of the Bauakademie, which began after 1989, led in 1991 to the founding of the "Association for the Reconstruction of Schinkel's Bauakademie," which wants the reconstruction to be as true as possible to the original. The opponents of rebuilding started organizing in the autumn of 1995; their strongest argument is to question how it might possibly be used. For the time being, the space is being reshaped after a design by the landscape architects Lange & Grigoleit: the historic outline is traced out using grass and gravel surfaces and hedges.

12.14.1995

The Landeskriminalamt (state police office) on Platz der Luftbrücke is completed. The design goes back to a competition from the year 1987. Architects: Bea and Walter Betz, Munich/ Berlin. Behind the 170 m long facade, one finds on 77,600 sq. m overall floorspace: the management of the office for crimefighting and technical police investigations and a standby court with the division of police custody.

12.31.1995

Effective on 12.31.95, GEHAG (non-profit housing company) sells the 696 apartments in the so-called Artists' Colony in Berlin-Wilmersdorf to the Bochum-based VEBA AG. The colony was erected between 1927 and 1929 by architects Ernst and Günter Paulus as a "garden terrace city" commissioned by the Berufsgenossenschaft deutscher Bühnenangehöriger (GDBA—Professional Cooperative of German Stage Members) as well as the Schutzverband deutscher Schriftsteller (Protective Association of German Writers). In 1955 the GDBA had sold its shares to GDBA (75% state owned) while conceding rights of recommendation for the allocation of apartments to the tenants. This clause was not carried over into the current contract. The sale price is astonishingly low: DM 1,302/sq. m. Newspapers report that the secretary of state of the revenue administration sits on the supervisory board of GEHAG.

January

Berlin is the capital of the United States of Europe. The city lies somewhere equidistant — as a bird flies — from the Neckar, the Rhine, the Elbe and the Danube; from these rivers wreathed in dreary poetry. Or, botanically speaking, overgrown. Why haven't those eminent industrial concerns, otherwise so well practiced in affiliates-daughter, son and grandchild companies, founded the United States of Europe.... Regardless, the capital of the United States of Europe indeed exists.

Berlin is impersonal. The city bears the distinction, that great people have racked their brains over it, which is certainly in the interest of humankind. Architects tried in vain to beautify the city, already so full with all of Bavaria, half of Greece and a portion of Italy. Even the Expressionism of the large and the petty bourgeois art dealers has been applied, but also in vain. In a few weeks Berlin will have digested and forgotten both old and new frauds.
Herwarth Walden, 1923

January 1996

Federal Building Minister and Berlin Moving Commissioner Klaus Töpfer submits a revised moving concept: The Labor Ministry should move into the former GDR Media Ministry building (formerly Reich Propaganda Ministry); the Family Ministry (originally envisioned at that spot) will find a home in the federally owned real estate at the corner Jäger- and Glinkastrasse. In the Bendlerblock on Reichspietschufer will be (as planned) the Berlin branch office of the Defense Ministry as well as the Federal Insurance Office and the Institute for Geodesy. The Interior Ministry is supposed to rent space (the renovation costs estimated at DM 330 mill. for the domicile planned on Mauerstrasse are too high). Remaining unchanged are the decisions concerning the Economics Ministry, which will move into the former government hospital at Invalidenstrasse 3; the Berlin branch of the Transporta-

January 1996

Former AL (Alternative List) city delegate Dieter Kunzelmann is sentenced to five months prison on probation. The background is Kunzelmann's dramatic appearance on 10.10.93 during the groundbreaking of the debis project on Potsdamer Platz. On that occasion he threw one egg onto the car of the Mayor, shattered one windshield, and resisted arrest. His obscenity continued on 12.20.1995, when he threw a (second) egg at subpoenaed witness mayor Eberhard Diepgen in the presence of the court. He continues to be investigated.

1.1.1996

A new mid-point has been found for Berlin, lying at 52.31° northern latitude and 13.25° eastern longitude in Kreuzberg (the district west and south of the old Wall) on the green strip along Alexandrinenstrasse. The State Statistics Office, by contrast, has designated the flagpole on the tower of the Rotes Rathaus (the red-brick building in Mitte restored to its status as city hall for the entire municipality) as the point of coordination for official maps. Berlin's previous mid-points: In 1730, a postmaster's column was erected on the Dönhoff-Platz on Leipziger Strasse to serve as the point from which road distances in kilometers would be measured. Since 1991, distances to other cities are measured from the intersection of Leipziger and Seydelstrasse (Berlin-Mitte). Two additional midpoints lie in Kreuzberg.

January 1996

Demolition of the "Casino" at the corner Leipziger Strasse and Friedrichstrasse (architect: Gerd Pieper, Berlin, who also reconstructed the building across the street with the popular Chinese restaurant). On the site, architect Thomas van den Valentyn, Cologne, is building a 9-story office and commercial building. Project developer: Roland Ernst, investor: DIFA (Deutsche Immobilien Fonds AG).

tion Ministry, which will occupy the former Ministry for Geology next door (supplemented by a new extension); and for the Finance Ministry, which will reside in the former Reich Ministry for Aviation (Goering's Luftwaffe headquarters). The house with the checkered past — it was also the seat of the GDR's Economic Council, its House of Ministries, and finally the seat of the Treuhandanstalt (the trusteeship for privatizing the GDR's state-owned companies) — will be remodeled by the architecture group HPP for DM 700 mill.

January 1996

Competition decided (9 participants) for a new building to house the main studios of ARD (Germany's Channel One radio and television network) on the corner of Wilhelmstrasse and Reichstagsufer. First prize: Ortner & Ortner, Berlin. Planned date of completion: 11.1.98, estimated construction cost: DM 50 mill.

January 1996

Competition decided for a hospital serving Berlin's penal institutions in Berlin-Buch: First prize: Thomas Müller and Ivan Reimann, Berlin, together with landscape planners Kienast, Vogt + Partners and hospital planner Gerhard Schlenzig, Berlin.

1.1.1996

http://cityscope.ict.de: On top of the building of the Verband der Konsumgenossenschaft (Consumer Cooperative Association) on Stresemannstrasse 128, an automatic panorama camera is installed that takes a series of panoramic pictures of Potsdamer Platz. These are processed in the system's computer, electronically archived, and integrated into the Internet via an online connection. This makes it possible anywhere in the world to download any picture one wants from the cityscope archive onto one's own monitor. City-scope is a production of the Berlin multi-media firm "Timeline."

1.2.1996

After 31 years, the Hotel Berolina (architect Josef Kaiser et al, 1963) closes its doors. It was the first Interhotel in Berlin (600 beds/385 rooms) and the second Interhotel altogether (after its Magdeburger namesake "Hotel International"). Along with the "Kino International," the Restaurant Moskau (both buildings also by Josef Kaiser et al), and the much-acclaimed "Mokka-Milch-Eis-Bar," it belonged to the second building segment of the residential block on Karl-Marx-Allee with its conspicuous for its hard-to-overlook bright blue tile facade and 260 windows. The INTERTEC (part of the TRIGON group) will tear down the building in order to build the new Rathaus Mitte (architects: Jan Bassenge, Kay Puhan-Schulz) in its place.

1.11.1996

Charlotte von Mahlsdorf is honored with the very first prize awarded by the "Hellersdorfer Kulturbeirat" (Hellersdorf Cultural Council) for her 50-year work building the Gründerzeitmuseum on Hultschiner Damm. (The "Gründerzeit" was the economic and architectural boom period following German unification in the 1870s.) The award is endowed with DM 4,000. In September 1995, she held her last reception there.

1.13.–1.17.1996

For the first time since it was founded almost 50 years ago, a meeting of the Presidium and Council of the Union of International Architects (UIA) takes place in Germany. The delegates, 40 architects from 35 countries, convene in the Deutsches Architektur Zentrum in Berlin.

1.17.1996

"Leineweber" becomes Erotica Museum. On the occasion of her firm's 50-year anniversary, Beate Uhse opens an Erotica Museum in Berlin in a former department store between Kranzler and Bahnhof Zoo. A more provisional erotica museum already exists in the Hackesche Höfe.

1.18.1996

Competition decided for the renovation and restoration of the Marschallbrücke in Berlin-Mitte (bridge over the Spree extending Wilhelmstrasse). First prize in the new/old group: Pichler Ingenieure and Benedict Tonon, Berlin. This is the solution envisioned for completion. First Prize in the new building group: Arbeitsgruppe Sedlacek and Max Dudler, Berlin.

1.11.1996

The architect Hermann Fehling dies at the age of 86. Together with Peter Pfankuch, he built the FU-Mensa (Free University student cafeteria) in 1952, and with Pfankuch and Daniel Gogel (his partner since 1953) he also built the entrance pavilion for "Interbau 1957." Though conceived as temporary architecture, the pavilion is now celebrating its 40-year existence as the Berlin-Pavilion. The duo's most significant buildings in Berlin: The Lutheran and Catholic parish churches in Schöneberg, two institutes (Max-Planck-Institut for Educational Research, 1965–74 and the FU-Hygiene-Institut, 1966–74), and the first remodeling of the Titania-Palast and the cinema theater Universum.

1.14.1996

The Georg-Kolbe-Museum is reopened with its exhibition space tripled. The new wing's architects: AGP-Architektengemeinschaft Hans Heidenreich, Michael Polensky, Helmut Zeumer, Berlin.

By his very nature, the Berliner is modest and undemanding. He buys his delicatessen at the cheapest shop in town, his clothes at Woolworth's, and his cups and plates from bargain basements. When he really wants to make a day of it he goes to the country on a Sunday and buys a hot dog each for himself and his kids. Major cultural events like the wrapping of the Reichstag or Heiner Müller's funeral leave him unimpressed, fittingly so for the city-dweller he is, who has long imagined himself to be at the center of world wide interest. But at the start of 1996 hordes of Berliners, male and female, went truly crazy. More people turned up for the opening of the Beate Uhse Erotic Museum in Kantstrasse, between Kudamm and Zoo Station, than for any other exhibition opening in a Berlin gallery or for any "absolutemustsee" in one of the city's museum's. Beate Uhse's sales manager, Rüdiger Bründel, said there were "several thousand" on the first day and "around ten thousand on the second," but he didn't want to give any precise figures "because I don't know if that would be in Beate's interest." 'Beate' herself then divulged the secret of her life ("Nobody can be permanently succesful without idealism"), related how she had tens of thousands of her catalogues distributed in the former East Germany after the Wall came down, and had "received carved wooden penises from East Germans as presents" in return. She didn't even lose her composure as she was asked which role sex still played in her life; she just said wisely that different things were important for an older person than for a young one. Meanwhile, ten hostesses from the Ingeborg Albert Erotic Agency in Köpenick were waiting the guests while wearing "historical underwear from the new collection … ."
Henryk M. Broder, 1996

1.25.1996

Topping-out ceremony for the square on Gendarmenmarkt between Markgrafenstrasse, Taubenstrasse, and Mohrenstrasse. The architects of the three new buildings on Gendarmenmarkt: Josef Paul Kleihues (Markgrafenstrasse 34), Max Dudler (BEWAG headquarters, Nr. 35), Hilmer & Sattler, Munich (Nr. 36). The old building with the Jugendstil facade between Mohren- and Taubenstrasse will be remodeled by Regina Schuh, Munich. Project developer: Roland Ernst. The corner house Nr. 34 will be designated as the Markgrafen-Haus since coming into possession of the Hertie Foundation.

Almost as Old as the Century *Julius Posener*

Berlin's university of fine arts, the Hochschule für bildende Künste, was founded after the First World War, essentially by Max Taut. By the time the architecture school had existed fifteen years, it honored the founder with a banquet. Many fine speeches were made, until Max took the floor and stated that if a school is fifteen years old and has not fundamentally changed during that time, then something is wrong with it. I found this, especially on such an occasion, truly magnificent.

At the Hochschule der Künste I was not a design teacher as I had been in Kuala Lumpur, but a historian. I came late to architectural history—I was around sixty. I confess that as a teacher of history I was even more of a dilettante than with design. For German architecture I initially relied above all on the three volumes of Geschichte der Deutschen Kunst (the History of German Art) by Georg Dehio. Choisy, a few Englishmen, and Dehio—a meager foundation for someone who was about to ascend the cathedra to teach students the entire history of architecture. But all my life it has been my custom to pursue some special interest or other with great energy, thereby forgetting the bigger picture. For this method—which is really no method at all—I have even crafted a theory, which says that it doesn't matter from which direction one penetrates to the heart of things, because there, at the center of the sphere of knowledge, the connections will become apparent. In any case, since I have always possessed the gift of compensating linguistically for partial or complete ignorance, these lectures, too, were well received.

It has always bothered me, and bothers me to this day, when I hear scholars talk of architecture as if it were pure form. In architecture form can never be separated from meaning, though to be sure this meaning is first and foremost a constructive one. In this sense I too have tried to teach the history of architecture. Today I am of the opinion that there should be two history courses. The first would be a general one, perhaps organized in such a way that the greatest emphasis would fall on certain things—according to the discretion and preference of the particular lecturer—while others would only be touched upon. The other course would begin around the middle of the 18th century and extend up to the present. At first glance, it may seem as if the 18th century is rather far removed from the problems which occupy us today and which the course is supposed to address. But when one considers that already in the mid-18th century, Laugier described the cathedral of Strasbourg as an example of pure construction, i.e. the foundation of architecture (as Laugier intended it in the best French tradition), and when one is further reminded of the fact that the young Goethe, when he came to Strasbourg, wrote a passionate polemic against this conception in an essay entitled "On German Architecture," in which he faults the Frenchman for his constructivism, it becomes clear that the origins of our own troubles—or shall we say, those that have become visible in our century—lie in that period. A history course beginning around 1750 and dealing with manifestations such as the two Gillys, David and Friedrich (father and son), would be a way back, which could serve even the practicing architect, not merely for the sake of education, but also for understanding what architecture can be and the different ways it has been conceived over the last two to three centuries.

1.29.1996

Julius Posener, the architectural historian and writer, dies at the age of 91 in Berlin. Posener, born in 1904 into an upper middle class family, studied architecture in Berlin with Hans Poelzig. 1933 emigration to Paris, editor with L'Architecture d'Aujourd' hui, afterwards Palestine, entry into the British army there, brief return to Germany as a soldier. Stay in England, then in Kuala Lumpur, where he built up an architecture school. There followed his 1961 appointment to the Berlin HdK (College of Arts), marking his definitive return to Berlin.

1.31.1996

Hans Kollhoff and Helga Timmermann present their expansion concept for the "Zentrum am Zoo." The landmark-protected ensemble, consisting of the Zoo-Palast cinema, the multi-story building on Hardenbergplatz, and the Bikini-Haus (built 1955–57 by Paul Schwebes and Hans Schoszberger), is to be enlarged; planned are 9,000 sq. m of conference accommodations and approx. 2,500 sq. m of cinema halls available for future International Film Festivals. A convention hotel in a multi-story building next to the Elephant Gate, the main entrance to the Zoological Garden, is envisioned. The Zoo management registered protest, fearing too much shade to overwhelm their grounds.

2.1.1996

Matthias Koeppel begins his parliamentary commission to paint a fresco, modified and reduced to a fourth of its original size, and a triptych ("The Opening of the Wall," 31 sq. m) for the parliamentary dining room in the Prussian Parliament building.

2.1.1996

"Zwischen den Stühlen" ("Between Stools"), an architectural piece by Lucius Burckhardt, is presented at the theater in the DAZ (German Architecture Center).

2.2.1996

The Berlin CDU parliamentary party is alarmed and calls a colloquium of building developers in order to evaluate urban planning decisions in Berlin's city center, from Pariser Platz to Schlossplatz, for their historic value.

2.3.1996

Former Senator Dr. Volker Hassemer, CDU, last responsible for the department Urban Development and Environmental Protection, becomes manager of the marketing company "Partners for Berlin" with its seat in the Ribbeck-Haus in Berlin-Mitte.

2.11.1996

Plan for a partial privatization of the Märkisches Viertel, one of Berlin's biggest public housing projects of the sixties. The GeSoBau will sell approx. 150 apartments annually to tenants.

2.13.–2.24.1996

46th Berlin Film Festival. Jack Lemmon receives the "Golden Bear" award for his life's work.

February

Six Sonnets on an Era *Hans Unverzagt*

The Stimmann Era is not yet past.
At first it may've appeared so, though
(where Nagel's gone, will Stimmann go),
in the end the Party's word is last,

and behold, elsewhere something's free quite fast;
if he'd just turn 'round, look to and fro,
he'd find he's back amid the show.
The city knows, before its die is cast,

his expertise is a crucial thing,
though critics and lords of politics grander
for him rarely restrain from their slander,

though they'd much prefer to take it easy.
He's tough from years of honor and enemies.
And this era's song I'm supposed to sing?

I can try, I mean I've just begun;
a people's poet, who from afar
observes the scene, from which the star
artists by him gather, second suns,

state deputies, his selected ones,
he's come to love them, a critics bar
of Scharoun and Hegemann. Modern? Har!
Too late! That utopia we've outrun.

Plot, block, and grid: that's a city.
And European. Easy to understand.
If need be, we'll simulate it on demand.

Missed something, colleague my dear,
from our state offices you shall hear.
That's less aesthetic. What a pity.

After all, with first discovery we'd like to taste
something adequate, t'would be O.K.
Reaching high, risking dismay,
makes little sense, too much paper waste.

Typologies do tend toward haste,
less type, not logic. Goals seldom stay
the reason, rather wrought in a formal way,
so the here and now become less chaste,

in most cases. When designs aren't found,
some image appears a bit too quickly,
to which the functions are strapped and bound,

and if it works, we're joyed by gesture.
If not, that's fine, we let it fester.
Let the image be image unequivocally.

Berlin! Berlinian! Prussian character!
I hear it, and it sounds damn euphemistic.
But truth is much more syncretistic:
a handful of villages, here and there compacter

planned and layed-out, less a factor
for the total picture, not urbanistic,
Berlin is just one large statistic.
Say no more, I'm no benefactor

of cynics. People here love their corner,
despite Hobrecht, Hoffmann, Schinkel, and Lenné
Ice Age geology is what they feel

with Barnim, Teltow at their heel
they come to town by other means. The Spree
Is not the Hudson. Any foreigner

this difference they should see.
People love to talk of the Berlin height,
and yet the projects, which see I might,
are from it a far cry. The devil-tree

of skyscrapers keeps growing. Yet we see
nothing. I'd give anything for a fight!
Birds of a feather stick tight
together. Why can't people think free?

Horizon of the city, stretching flat,
once a trademark, is now almost gone
and will disappear when our hands are done.

Our mania for grand will finally have won.
Sure it'll be big, too big, but not just that.
New York will seem like the neighbor's lawn.

Hans Stimmann! Please come and stop it!
This chance we'll not have for some while,
'cause what we've lost, well, that had style.
And from this new order, you must protect it.

We had a rule, but they came and bent it,
then broke it. Give an inch, they take a mile
and glorify themselves, not accepting the trial
of facing all of us who damn well resent it.

Wishful thinking? Maybe. The poets are dreaming,
beyond this reality so savage.
They see intervention in which to confide

to save the horizon that others elide
and deliver us from Big Men's ravage.
You need only take away the plan they're scheming.

2.23.1996

Senatsbaudirektor
(Berlin Senate Building
Manager) Dr. Hans
Stimmann leaves the
Senate Office for Building
and Housing and throws
a party for good friends
and good enemies. Place:
Sale e Tabacci, the
restaurant installed by
Max Dudler in the taz
(Germany's left-alterna-
tive daily newspaper)
building. He will become
state secretary in the
Senate for Urban Devel-
opment, Environmental
Protection, and Trans-
portation.

1996   February

2.23.1996

Sergius Ruegenberg dies five weeks after his 93rd birthday in his house in Berlin-Kladow. From 1925 to 1931, he was an assistant in the firm of Ludwig Mies van der Rohe in Berlin, and in 1929 he represented Mies in overseeing the work on the German pavilion in Barcelona. Under Hans Scharoun, he worked in the Berlin Magistrate on reconstruction plans 1945–1948. He was only allowed to complete a few buildings, the best known being the school in the Märkisches Viertel. The architecture collection in the Berlinische Galerie acquires the estate of Sergius Ruegenberg and displays a selection of his works from 4.24. to 7.7.1996 in the Gropiusbau.

2.26.1996

Max Dudler, Berlin, wins against 115 fellow applicants in the biggest housing building competition for downtown Berlin: the urban design idea contest for the site "Stadion der Weltjugend" ("Stadi-

2.29.1996

The largest Austrian construction firm with the little prices, Maculan, declares insolvency procedures. Not immediately affected is its daughter firm, Tb Tief- und Verkehrsbau Berlin, which plays a major role in the preparatory work for the Tiergartentunnel.

3.1.–5.1.1996

2 x Africa in Berlin: "Africa—The Art of a Continent," an exhibition in the Martin-Gropius-Bau on Stresemannstrasse. On closing day, the Lord Mayor opens the Africanum in the Friedrichsfelde animal park.

3.5.1996

As of today—beginning with the S7 rapid transit line (Potsdam Stadt to Ahrensfelde)—special customer services are offered under the name "S-presso." 60 workers in bright red anoraks (later 200 federal employment program workers in a non-profit organization) offer snacks, assist with transfers, provide information, and give commuters a feeling of overall security. A cup of coffee costs DM 1.40; a "Schusterjunge" roll with drippings DM 1.50.

3.5.1996

The city Senate announces its program of cuts for publicly subsidized housing in Berlin. In this electoral period, the number of subsidized homes will be reduced from the 60,000 originally planned to 31,000. For 1997/98, mayor Eberhard Diepgen anticipates an entirely new regulation for subsidized housing. The ModInst housing program (Remodeling/Reconstruction) will be cut by 20% annually.

3.6.1996

Ceremonial presentation of the Leipziger Platz project. The 27,000 sq. m area consists of the former Wertheim department store site and the adjoining properties between Leipzigerstrasse, Vossstrasse, and Wilhelmstrasse, neighboring A+T, Sony, and debis. Munich project developers Dr. Peter and Isolde Kottmair have given the DM 1.2 billion construction project to their favored architect, Aldo Rossi of Milan. But it is not Rossi's concrete dome with a span of 70 m that causes a sensation; the real masterpiece are utilization and marketing. A Berlin branch of the famous "Cirque Soleil" is supposed to get an exclusive performance site under the blue dome, the Berlin techno club "Tresor" will move in with a "Tresor-Tower" (techno, pottery studio, and trendy shopping for young people), and the four-star, 300-bed hotel will be marketed by the management of "Traumschiff" ("Dreamboat").

February	March

---

um of World Youth") on Chausseestrasse. The stadium was torn down in 1993 to make room for a sports hall, originally planned for Berlin's failed Olympic application. The design for 200,000 sq. m of residential space envisions six-story block constructions. At the heart of the planning is the Pankepark along the Panke rivulet, which had been canalized for years but is now renaturalized.

2.29.1996

Opening of the Galeries Lafayette (Quartier 207, first new quarter in the Friedrichstrasse) by Jean Nouvel. What no one expected: half of Berlin turned up.

3.3.1996

Opening of the Zentrum für Berlin-Studien (Center for Berlin Studies) in the Ribbeck-Haus on Breite Strasse, which shares the house with the marketing company "Partners for Berlin." The reference library has over 60,000 titles about Berlin from the combined inventories of the Amerika-Gedenkbibliothek (American Memorial Library) and the Berliner Stadtbibliothek (Berlin City Library). The Ribbeck-Haus, built as a residential house in 1624, has a variegated history. In the 18th century it was seat of the High Court of Appeals and of the High Chamber of Audits. After rebuilding the house, severely damaged in the Second World War, it was used by the GDR's League of Architects. And more recently, from 1991 to 1994, it served as the seat of the promotional Olympia GmbH.

Getting into the S-Bahn in Berlin in the mornings, which I normally do in Karlshorst, it sometimes seems as if one is invading the private space of the people who have been sitting in the car for a while. They have already made themselves at home in it: it isn't love that is a house, it's the S-Bahn. It begins with the smell. When people make themselves at home, they are soon surrounded by odor of their stable. They yawn and stretch as if the S-Bahn seat were their bed. They clean the inside of their noses with their fingers. Some sleep and some straighten their clothes, but others are only just getting dressed. Everywhere there is eating; the favorite food is apple, with all the accompanying noises. One doesn't see many retirees in the trains anymore, unlike earlier, when they were the only ones who were allowed to travel to West Berlin. They looked at their simple flower bouquets with a mixture of satisfaction and sadness and pawed frantically through their pocketbooks (where is my passport, where is my wallet, where is the yellow payment card, suddenly the border is so close …). Now there won't be any more retirees like that, unless the Wall …, but let's not get into that. After all, a couple of pieces are still standing. The older people never felt at home in the S-Bahn; the train was a means of transportation between two worlds, an ambivalent thing. They were much too nervous to develop homey feelings. Never once could they be sure that everything was in order, what they did or what they had with them; they could always at least be embarrassed by the uniformed guard at the border. Homeyness has made itself at home again in the train.
Fritz-Jochen Kopka, 1996

In addition, retail (41,000 sq. m) and office (30,000 sq. m) spaces will be offered. Construction start: 1997; completion: 2000.

3.6.1996

The Berlin Senate undertakes the first steps toward setting up an electronic city information system for the state of Berlin. The basis is the data bank previously run by the Senator of the Interior with roughly 16,000 pages in the Btx format. This makes Berlin the second federal state (after Bavaria) at Cebit 96, beginning on 3.14., offering its own page on the Internet under "berlin.de."

Cornerstone laying for a residential construction project in Landsberger Allee, being administered by the two housing agencies WBG (Wohnungsbaugenossenschaft) and WBF (Wohnungsbaugesellschaft Friedrichshain). The existing 8-story prefab buildings get an additional new building thereby creating residential courtyards that are tenant-friendly and protected from noise. There will be 219 new apartments funded by first and second type state subsidies, along with a retail level. Architects: Hans-Peter Harm and Michael Krüger.

3.11.1996

The "Café Einstein Unter den Linden," a branch of the West Berlin parent house on Kurfürstenstrasse, opens in "Haus Pietzsch."

3.13.1996

The Building Commission of the Bundestag decides to build an underground tunnel system between the Reichstag and the nearby government buildings in the Alsen-, Dorotheen-, and Luisenblock. Through the tunnels, which will run 15 m under the Spree river, Bundestag workers will be able to drive into underground garages, restaurant deliveries can be made, and garbage carted away. Estimated costs: DM 60 mill.

trious – images of knights and dragons automatically spring to mind. And a glance at the plans for such a machine reinforces this image. The thing really looks like a steel lindworm. Mr Mönnich is expecting it to arrive over the next few weeks. The components are being brought on several trucks and assembled in front of the Reichstag. It's so big that it will take three months just to do that. The 50 meter monster can then be lowered into the ground and start burrowing. By the year 2002 at least the railway should be able to travel through the tunnel. If Mönnich is delayed, there will be hell to pay: some of the buildings in the new government quarter are to be constructed above part of his tunnel and work has to commence soon.

One thing making life easy for the tunnel builders is the fact that under Berlin's sidewalks lie beaches. Fortunately for them, the last Ice age left loads of sand as it was passing. The machine cuts through it with great ease. Mönnich says that not even the small granite boulders in the sand present a problem for the steel drill: "they are just cracked open." And when it's a large boulder? "Then it's disaster stations." It's more or less the only thing that seems to worry Mr Mönnich. If the drill really were to try and bite off more than it could chew, then it would be pulled back to create a one meter wide space between it's chisels and the earth at the end of the tunnel. Someone would then have to enter this gap and sort things out. Compressed air would be pumped into the gap so that the ceiling wouldn't collapse on top of him. He would be protected by the excess pressure. This would disappear if the air were to escape faster through the porous ground than it could be pumped in. The man would have no chance.

2002: A Tunnel Odyssey *Jakob Augstein*

Its too late to stop now. Mr Mönnich has already reached 18 meters depth. As soon as he makes 22, he'll start burrowing horizontally. Then the Berliners can only hope that the engineers haven't miscalculated with the water table, leaving the Tiergarten—their beloved city center park—to whither once the giant tunnel is finished.

The huge tunnel faced some resistance in Berlin, but not a lot. It is actually a complicated system of eight tunnels lying above, below, and next to each other. It has one primary purpose: to keep the traffic out of the politicians' way. There are three seperate tunnel systems— one for the underground railway (U-Bahn), one for main-line trains, and one for cars. All three of them will lie next to each other when they pass in front of the Reichstag.

But right now Mr Mönnich is directing the activities of the "Berlin Knots" group, which is burrowing in the name of Germany's rail company Deutsche Bahn. Mönnich's men are still tunnelling from the surface downwards in an enormous sand pit stretching right up to the Spreebogen area. Soon, though, they will reach the prescribed 22 meters. Then its the turn of the "shield" to start burrowing forward. The "shield" is a pretty big machine which can cover between six and twenty meters a day. It does this underground, leaving a tunnel in its wake.

Klaus-Dieter Mönnich is from the Rhineland in western Germany. He came to Berlin to dig a very large tunnel, so he ordered two of these machines right at the start. They are made in Baden-Württemberg, where they know a thing or two about manufacturing complicated apparatuses. They are really called shield-burrowing machines, but Mr Mönnich just calls them "the shields." It sounds somewhat illus

Mr Mönnich says that there are no real difficulties in constructing such a tunnel nowadays, only the dimensions are something special: "you don't have a 20,000 square meter underwater concrete sole every day." In the meantime every child in Berlin knows what an underwater concrete sole is. The divers in the artificial lakes on Potsdamer Platz do nothing else all day except build underwater concrete soles. It stabilizes the groundwater level. The principle is the same whether you are building a high-rise block or a tunnel. First you dig a hole. This then fills with water from the ground. This water is then normally pumped out and the hole sealed in all directions. The groundwater level in Berlin would have to be lowered to such a depth that all the trees would wither. The underwater concrete layer helps prevent this.

The scale of the whole building project makes the statistics freaks dizzy. 18 million tons of sand are being dug out to make way for the tunnel. The excavated sand could be tipped out onto a football field until it reached a height of 365 meters. Or it could be loaded onto trucks which would stretch from Berlin to Madrid bumper-to-bumper four times. And what is to be done with the 27 million cubic meters of water which will be pumped out from underneath the Tiergarten? Maybe it could be used to water trees somewhere else.

3.21.1996

Relocation of the Kaiser-
saal: In the middle of the
Sony Center planned for
Potsdamer Platz (archi-
tect Helmut Jahn, Chica-
go), the remains of the
old Hotel Esplanade have
to be preserved, even if
not at the original loca-
tion. The "Breakfast

March

3.15.–3.20.1996

Festival "Film and Archi-
tecture." More than 60
international films pro-
vide an overview of how
film and video deal with
architecture and urban
design. The program
goes back to the inter-
national Architecture
Biennale in Graz; the
films are shown in the
Zeughaus cinema, DAZ
(German Architecture
Center), and the Brot-
fabrik.

Hall" will be divided into
500 parts and put back
together at the new loca-
tion, while the entire
"Kaisersaal" ("Imperial
Hall") is lifted and shifted
75 m away to its desig-
nated spot between the
Palm Court and Silver
Hall. The two-story,
1,300 ton building, whose
walls are propped up
with stress supports and
steel beams and covered
by a temporary roof, will
be tracked along an
installed switching track
resting on air cushions
and guided by computer.
The switching begun on
March 15th had to be
interrupted after a few
meters, but the rest of
the trip and the rotation
of the building by 90
degrees continued 6 days
later without problem.
The "Kaisersaal" stands
at its new location as of
6:46 pm on March 21st.

3.21.1996

An exhibit in the Chamber of Architects presents the first commissions of young Berlin architectural offices.

3.22.1996

Competition decided for a "Place of Remembrance." In the new building of the Barmer Ersatzkasse health insurance fund, built on the site of a former synagogue on Lindenstrasse 48–50, a publicly accessible memorial is to be created at the bequest of the client and architect. The architect Rupert Ahlbaum issued the invitation for a design competition, which was won by Zvi Hecker together with Micha Ullmann and Eyal Weizman. The memorial space in the interior of the new building should by finished by early 1997.

4.10.1996

10 years of "Linie 1" in the Berliner Grips Theater on Hansaplatz. With the Linie 1 play by Volker Ludwig (music: Birger Heymann), the theater toured Denmark, Sweden, Finland, Italy, Greece, Spain, Canada, India, Hongkong, and Korea, today its 750th performance at home on Hansaplatz.

4.10.1996

A section of Lindenstrasse, between Kochstrasse and Spittelmarkt, receives the name Axel-Springer-Strasse after the famous publisher. In the interim, plans are finalized for tearing down the Springer printing press and paper storage facilities to make way for the construction of a new multimedia center and about 500 privately financed housing units. As compensation for the demolition of the landmark-protected printing press building, the publishers have committed themselves to free up the remains of the Jerusalemer Kirche, which is located in the triangle between Koch- and Lindenstrasse.

Line one *Volker Ludwig*

Two tourist guide enter, followed by a group of tourists.

FIRST GUIDE Und jetzt, meine Damen und Herren, der erregende Höhepunkt eines jeden Berlin-Besuchs: Die Fahrt nach Kreuzberg! SO 36! Da brennt die Luft, da haut's dich um, eine Mischung aus rive gauche und Bronx und dennoch einmalig auf der Welt! Dorthin führt nur ein Weg: Eine Fahrt mit der U-Bahnlinie 1! Take the A train, wie der Pariser dazu sagt! Vom Zoo bis in den finstersten Kiez sind es man grade zehn Stationen, deren Namen jedoch dem Berlinkenner Wonneschauer über Leib und Seele laufen lassen!

The second guide repeats—nearly synchronically with the first—word by word in English.

SECOND GUIDE And now ladies and gentlemen, the exciting high point of every Berlin visit; the journey to Kreuzberg! SO thirty six! There burns the air, there are you from the socks, a mixture out of rive gauche and the Bronx and then still singular on the world! There leads only one way: a trip with the undertrain line one! Take the A train, as they say in Paris to it. From the Zoo till into the darkest place of the town are there just ten stations, whose names let each Berlin knower showers of luck over body and soul run.

FIRST GUIDE
Wittenbergplatz
Nollendorfplatz
Kurfürstenstrasse
Gleiiiiiisdreieck
Möckernbrücke
Hallesches Tooor
Prinzenstrasse
Kottbusser Tooor
Görlitzer Bahnhof
Schlesisches Tooor
Das ätzt! Das fetzt!
Das bleibt im Ohr!

Song repeated by all tourists.

FIRST GUIDE And now for our American friends.

Song repeated by all tourists with heavy American accents.
Last Line: "That moves, that grooves, that bleibs in Ohr".

FIRST GUIDE And now a special hello to all our Japanese guests.

SECOND GUIDE
Sate minasama,
konkaino Beruringoryokoo ni okemasu
kuraimakkusu wa, Berurin hokutou sanjyurokku,
Kuroitsuberugu eno tsuaa de gozaimasu,
Krouitsuberugu — — — Tatoete moushiage masureba,
Pari wa seenusagan no ribugooshyu,
nyuyookushi no buronkusukutodemo moushiagematsyou ka
ie, ie sekai korehiroshito iimasliyootomo
hiruimarenaru kuroitsuberugu eno tabi wa,
berurin chikatetsu, yuu ichibansen de,
yurarete mairimasu.
parikko ni iwasemasureba, ei torein de yukoo
todemo moushimashou ka
koko doubutsuenmae, zooeki kara
mimo kokoromo zokuzokuwakuwaku to sasemasu
nadakai ankokugai made wa,
sonokan oyoso toono, ekini, teisha itashite marimasu.
Song repeated by all tourists with overacted Japanese attitude.

154

4.17.1996

Decision in the competition "New housing at the Railway Station Berlin-Staaken." The Munich architects Fink + Jocher are awarded first prize.

4.22.1996

The competition to complete the Berlin branch office of the Federal Transport Ministry, preceded by an EU-wide application procedure, ends with the award of first prize to Max Dudler, Berlin. Since the landmark-protected former State Geological Office on Invalidenstrasse in the Mitte district (remodeling led by the Dortmund architect Eckhard Gerber) did not supply enough room for a future domicile with about 400 employees, an extension proved necessary. DM 200 mill. are available for the new construction planned.

4.23.1996

20 years ago, the Palast der Republik (architects: Heinz Graffunder, Karl-Ernst Swora) was officially opened, after a more than 3-year construction period, with a ceremony of the construction workers.

4.24.1996

Holocaust Memorial. The three sponsors of the competition to erect a "Memorial for the Murdered Jews of Europe"— the Federal Interior Ministry, the Promotional Association, and the Senate of Berlin—agree on further procedures. The sponsors confirm their determination to erect a Holocaust memorial as well as their financial commitment; they also stand to the site in the former Ministerial Garden. The cornerstone for the memorial is supposed to be laid on January 27th (Holocaust Memorial Day) in 1999. Beginning in 1997, experts as well as members of parliament from Berlin and Bonn will be invited to a series of three colloquiums open to the public, to decide anew "on the basis of the first nine prize winners' designs." If necessary, the prize winners should submit modified or completely new designs. The chairman of the Central Council of Jews in Germany, Ignaz Bubis, criticizes the postponement of construction until 1999.

you imagine: 1911?" Hoppe immediately begins to hold forth with an historical narrative. My synopsis. First: Schiller seduced her. Suddenly, in a velour armchair. "The world moved!" she says. "A fateful theatrical seduction!" she emphasizes. It was in Weimar, during a production of The Bride of Messina. There was such a wonderful Donna Isabella, such a marvelous pair of gloriously heroic sons and their so dreadful drama over the sweet Beatrice. Hoppe now gesticulates herself into such a dramatic pose that the café au lait can only barely be rescued. Onward: "Glory, pathos, blazing love, most beautifully metered verse, total tragedy, heart, tears, the end." Second: she was saved by Max Reinhardt's receptionist. It seems Hoppe had hurried from the Weimar commercial school directly to the Max Reinhardt School in Berlin, but the auditions had only just ended. She rolled her eyes crestfallen, but the lady from reception was moved by the little girl. And then: Reinhardt came and Reinhardt saw! And a short while later the little girl was in Reinhardt's famous ensemble in the Deutsches Theater. "Without the receptionist," Hoppe said, "no Deutsches Theater, no turbulent loves, no Horváth, no Giehse either, and certainly no theater history." Hoppe bites into her streusel cake. "Receptionists, my boy, are very important. Always be nice to receptionists." Very well. "Goebbels, his propositions, Hitler and Goering," she mumbles, "I'd have been quite happy to be spared all those monstrosities."

Crumbs on the table. Yes, and what about Herr Gründgens or Madam Privy Councillor? "No, no, I've spent half my life talking about Gründgens, I beg of you! No red pencil please." Hoppe wants a cigarette. "All that," she says, "has to be written down someday." The match now throws light upon her beautiful wrinkles. "Children, I'm going to write my memoirs, pay attention! Rockslide!—A very good title." Hoppe puffs away. "I know them all: Kortner, Fehling, Hellmer, Jessner, Noelte, Stroux, the gentlemen before, the gentlemen there

4.24.1996

Marianne Hoppe, Berlin's
well-known actress, turns
eighty-five.

Café au lait with Hoppe *Moritz Rinke*

Hoppe has awakened, has breakfasted. Open foyer scene, red carpet. The hotel lobby is immediately under her command: "Don't make me wait even a moment for my taxi." Pages hop, all porters to the telephones. Hoppe presses on. Sternly she echoes through the hallways: "You there! Hey! Where's my taxi?" This is her last, great role. That of Lear. Queen Lear. She wants water for the flowers immediately and is completely immersed in giving orders. The hotel manager nods his head unflinchingly; she wanders over the carpet, gesticulating grandly. Then she stops, visibly cross, and calls everything off—no water, no taxi: "It seems to me the whole world is lying fast asleep." That voice! That echo! And so utterly melodic!

Springtime in Berlin, hours later. Meeting place: the New National Gallery. Hoppe stands right in front of a large Beckmann. "I just love Beckmann!" she cries with eyes fixed on the Beckmann. And how tenderly she points her finger at the painting's center! She'd prefer to scratch off the paint to see what's underneath. "And now, young man, Berlin and a café au lait, please." But of course. It's raining in torrents. "My God, three days ago I was still in Ravenna, the most beautiful weather, and now this deluge." Hoppe weaves around the puddles. She wants Wellingtons or Ravenna.

Instead, she gets café au lait and streusel cake. Hoppe talks. "This utter lack of culture!," she says. "That taxi driver," she continues, "didn't have the faintest idea what the national gallery was, and took me God knows where and talked the whole time about Rostock!" Now her eyes are aglow. "Rostock!" she calls out. "I could have embraced that taxi driver," she says, "Rostock is my old home town, you know." She paid the full fare anyway. "Look," she said, "you have to trust all that is fateful." She leans against the window and directs her glance high up into the heavens. Her face catches some rays of sun. "Yes, yes," she sighs, "I'm an April child from 1911. 1911," she whispers, "can

after, Peymann, Zadek, Müller, my films, everything." She recalls that she is famous. Two American women sit at the next table. Suddenly she starts speaking English, generously greets the next table, looks whether all the guests are looking. Now Hoppe in America: guest performances, galas, Hollywood, the President. All are delighted. She memorizes Tennessee Williams. She waves her arms gracefully— always accompanied by the splashing café au lait, a smile behind clouds of smoke, and the wooden floor that creaks with every adjustment of her chair between sentences. She signals the waiter, takes a bite of streusel cake, translates into English, quotes Kleist and leaves crumbs, then counters with Bernhard and greets and laughs, and everyone else's head is spinning. Hoppe loves it this way, it's her profession: sober entrance, epic matter-of-factness, strict diction, dignity, but then the maneuver, slurred into a subordinate clause the incidental, totally unexpected point: final chaos, good-bye diction, heartiness, triumph, the end. This is Hoppe-dialectic. And what about the leaps between sentences! With Hoppe, these leaps are landslides. Whole epochs, styles, and glorias can spill over from one thought into the next. First she stands blonde and blue-eyed with Schiller in front of Reinhardt, then with Hitler, disgusted at his bedroom while she thinks of Horváth, while outside Dreyfus awaits the end of the group tour to bring her back to Gründgens, who is memorizing Mephisto at the moment, which Klaus Mann then... and so on. At first I think: Faust! And then I think: now she'll be swinging into the Dreyfus Affair! And that Horváth was crushed by a tree! Besides that my head starts spinning when I think that she's sitting there, drinking café au lait, and is standing in front of Hitler's bedroom. And then I think: blue eyes and Reinhardt School and Weimar and Prussia and then Bismarck, until the chair creaks against the floor and she says, "What do you think of Dieter Dorn?" And then I think, "Now you have to switch over from Bismarck to Dieter Dorn!"

Outside the wind is blowing. Hoppe's hair is flying. She wants the cathedral, transience, and then an afternoon nap. The drive to the hotel. Hoppe is silent. City traffic. And at some point her inquiry into whatever became of our "King Lear" interview in Frankfurt, of the unclothed incident. "Did you report my obscenity?" Well, the obscenity was like this: I was a student and opened the door to her dressing-room in 1990. And then: Hoppe in ochre-colored underwear! The shorts down to just above the knee and a mere touch of ochre separated one's glance from the venerable breasts. All glances immediately lapsed into ochre. What might Goebbels have given for this view? But —and the knees grew weaker—I simply swept right into Hoppe's dressing-room! "What shall we talk about?" she asked quite dryly and incidentally while removing her make-up, her face turned close to the mirror. Groping for questions, a tape full of stutters. Suddenly she stood up and saw herself completely and finally in the mirror. In the most beautiful ochre! From her breasts to her thighs! And now she recognized: it was not the Lear-robe which clothed her. No, actually nothing did. "Young man, I am practically naked," she called. "Yes, yes," I called back—and then immediately and single-mindedly vanished and headed for the writing-desk.

Hoppe is silent. Her eyes are sparkling and she smiles. She smiles a very long time. She's surely thinking about the obscenity matter. Then back to the hotel. Open second foyer scene. The staff stands at attention, taxi queues at the entrance, the flowers float in water, the hotel manager nods his head unflinchingly. Hoppe waves it all off, rushes past and stands on the carpet's red velvet. She turns around once more, blows a kiss, and now disappears, waving and still smiling at the foot of the stairs. I think: applause. And the curtain drops for the afternoon nap.

4.26.1996

Topping-out ceremony for the Max-Schmeling-Halle in the Friedrich-Ludwig-Jahn-Sportpark, a three-bayed layout with a major athletic and entertainment hall in the middle bay (with 7,000 fixed seats, the number can be increased as needed to 10,000), three triple athletic halls, and a transport center in the side bays. Architects: Albert Dietz, Annett-Maud, and Jörg Joppien, Berlin. Costs DM 205 mill. Chief user of the hall will be the basketball club Alba Berlin.

4.20.–5.20.1996

33rd theater convention in Berlin.

May 1996

Opening of the office and commercial house "TRIAS" in Mitte, Holz-marktstrasse 15–18, right on the banks of the Spree. From the six-story building base along the Holz-marktstrasse emerge three glass 12-story wing constructions on an ellipsoid floor plan. 22,500 sq. m office space; 2,815 sq. m retail space. Architects: Beringer & Wawrik, Munich (1992 winner of competition). Owner: DG Anlage GmbH (DG-Bank Group). Project developer: Bauwert GmbH.

5.5.1996

Presentation of the competition results for the American embassy on Pariser Platz 2: first prize: John Ruble, Buzz Yudell, Cecily Young from the firm Moore/Ruble/Yudell, Santa Monica, with Gruen Associates, Los Angeles. Construction cost approx. DM 100 mill.

5.9.1996

Cornerstone laying for a Shopping-Mall in Gesundbrunnen, corner of Badstrasse/Swinemünder Brücke. Client: ECE Hamburg.

5.10.1996

"Willy-Brandt-Haus": as the first among the major parties to move its seat from Bonn to Berlin, the SPD opens its future party headquarters in Kreuzberg's Stresemann-strasse. Architect: Helge Bofinger, Berlin/Wiesbaden.

5.1.1996

Former Building Senator Nagel starts his job as commercial manager of the Bredero Projekt Berlin GmbH, a subsidiary of Fundus Investment Funds GmbH.

5.1.1996

Reopening of the Berlin television tower on Alexanderplatz with a 13 m long bar on the outlook floor. The elevator travel time of 40 seconds for the 203 m, it is said, has been shorted to 38 seconds after the six-month remodeling period. The work on the technical floors and the antenna pole will last until October 1999. Currently 4 TV and 9 radio stations broadcast from here; later it will be 7 TV and 18 radio stations.

5.5.1996

The fusion of Berlin and Brandenburg is turned down in a referendum: while a majority of West Berlin voters (59%) vote for a merger of the two states, 52% of those in East Berlin and 63% in Brandenburg resist the fusion. The competition announced in April 1995 and decided in November of the same year for a common Parliament building in Potsdam (first prize Krüger, Schuberth, Vandreike, Berlin) is thereby rendered moot.

13.5.1996

On the development area Berlin-Adlershof, the competiton for a 70 ha landscape park on the former airfield of Johannisthal airport, the first airport of Berlin, is decided. Awarded first prize is landscape architect Gabriele Kiefer, Berlin.

The spherical ash tray is the cultural symbol of the GDR. In spite of—or perhaps even better, because of—it's continual placement at the top of the list of those articles not allowed export, it does not disappear—though holy to the nation—in the reliquaries of sacred buildings or in the glass cases of museums. On the contrary, our great cultural policies ensure that hundreds of thousands of copies are available to everyone, in the city and in the air, for the window cleaner high above and the department administrator in the belle étage down below.
Thilo Köhler, 1989

17.5.1996

Four years after the sale of its film studios to the french Compagnie Generale des Eaux, the DEFA (nationalized East German film company) celebrates 50th anniversary. DEFA was founded after World War II, succeeding the famous Ufa film company. Production since amounted to 750 movies, more than 2,000 short films and documentaries, and they dubbed 3,000 films. A poison cabinet is stuffed with forbidden films and reminds of courage, censorship, and self-censorship.

5.23.1996

After more than five years debate over the location of a major airport for Berlin, the city opts for the expansion of Schönefeld Airport. The sites at Sperenberg and Jüterbog are rejected due to inordinate development costs, which the federal government would have to pay. After submission of a binding planning procedure for Schönefeld,

5.29.1996

Groundbreaking for the International Meeting Center of the Alexander von Humboldt Foundation in the development area Berlin-Adlershof. Architects: Fin Bartels + Christoph Schmidt-Ott, Berlin (Competition 1995).

5.31.1996

Topping-out ceremony for the Hotel Adlon, architects: Rüdiger Patzschke, Klotz and Partners, Berlin, on Pariser Platz, Unter den Linden 75–77. On 43,000 sq. m overall floorspace, 346 rooms will be housed. The construction cost is around DM 435 mill. From its opening in 1907 until its destruction shortly after the Second World War, the former Hotel Adlon epitomized the "Grand Hotel".

June 1996

The Max Liebermann Society founded in 1995 would like to transform the Berlin painter's listet country manor (architect: Paul Baumgarten the elder, 1909) along the Grosser Wannsee into a memorial.

6.5.1996

With the largest shareholder Daimler-Benz (95.7 % of the initial capital) voting in favor, the stockholders of AEG pass a resolution that finally dissolves the 113 year-old Berlin company.

6.5.1996

Decision in the last big competition for federal buildings in Berlin: the new building for the Foreign Office. From 419 participants, 57 designs made the first cut. First prize: Max Dudler, Berlin, with two seven-story buildings (17,000 sq. m useable space) connected to each other and via tunnels to the existing Reichsbank building (architect Heinrich Wolff, 1940). In the smaller house a library is planned, with offices in the larger building. DM 125 mill. are allocated for remodeling the old building, DM 329 mill. for the new buildings.

6.7.1996

Architectural competition decided for the Nordic country embassies. A decision had already been reached on a joint embassy complex in the northern section of the Klingelhöferdreieck. In an international urban design idea competition decided in December 1995, the first prize went to architects Alfred Berger and Tiina Parkinnen, Vienna. By early 1999, embassy buildings for Denmark, Finland, Iceland, Norway, along with a community building and public events hall for exhibits, films, lectures etc., will be built on the 7,200 sq. m site. Winner for the Norway mission is the firm Snöhetta, Oslo. The

---

5.13.–9.13.1996

Checkpoint Liberty. The 13.5 m high copy of Lady Liberty stands golden atop an original watchtower. An art event by John Powers in the context of "Checkpoint Charlie Meets Culture" at the site of the former border control station. Organizer: American Business Center CEDC.

5.17.1996

With the opening of its new "Berlin-Flügel" ("Berlin Wing"), the Hotel Berlin on Lützowplatz becomes the third-largest hotel in the city with 701 rooms in the four-star category, of which 210 rooms have fax and computer connections. Originally built by Paul Schwebes and Hans Schoszberger, the Hotel Berlin first had the "Kurfürstenflügel" ("Elector's Wing") added, followed by the "Berlin-Flügel." Architect Michael König, Berlin. Facade design: Walter and Bea Betz, Berlin ("Kurfürsten-Flügel"), Klaus Theo Brenner and Benedict Tonon, Berlin ("Berlin-Flügel").

Tempelhof is supposed to be closed; the closing of Tegel airport is, at the earliest, set for a date sometime after "Schönefeld International" is up and running.

5.24.–8.8.1996

Exhibition "1936. The Olympic Games and National Socialism" in the former Staatliche Kunsthalle, Budapester Strasse 42.

5.25.–5.26.1996

Opening celebration for the "Berliner Prater" on Kastienallee in Prenzlauer Berg, whose history can be traced back to he year 1837. In GDR times the Prater was, among other things, the "District Cultural House." Today's concept mixes a beer garden with music, an art forum, and theater.

5.30.–2.6.1996

"Pot doré" above the Baggersee at Weinhaus Huth. Cartier International has the honor. The 3.5 m high and 2.8 ton heavy golden pot by artist Jean-Pierre Raynaud makes a stop at Potsdamer Platz on its journey to the Great Wall of China. "In their joint exertion, the pot and the construction site unite the entire mystery and vitality of both their fates." In other words: The artwork stays on the crane for three days.

Berlin's director of public gardens at the time, Albert Brodersen, participated in laying out the garden. Since 1972 the Senate-owned building has been used by the German Underwater Club, which Julius Posener lamented many years ago in his essay "Liebermann and the Frogmen."

6.6.1996

Topping-out ceremony for the Kontorhaus Mitte (Quartier 109) on Friedrichstrasse between Mohren- and Kronenstrasse. Four architectural firms are involved: Josef Paul Kleihues, Dörrie/Lampugnani, Klaus Theo Brenner, and Walther Stepp. The Berliner Bank will open its main branch here; all 84 apartments are rented out to the Hamburg-based Company Madison, which will offer the high-rent suites as boarding houses. Clients: Kontorhaus Friedrichstrasse & Co Investitionsgesellschaft, Berlin, Argenta, Jahr, and Hanseatica. Construction cost: DM 320 mill.

Finnish jury decided in favor of the "Kannel" design by architects Rauno Lehtinen, Pekka Mäki, and Toni Peltola. The competition for Sweden was won by Göteborg architect Gert Wingård. For Iceland, construction will follow the plans of Palar Kristmundsson and Gunnar B. Stefansson. The Danish victor is the firm of Nielsen, Nielsen + Nielsen. The community building will be constructed according to the plan of the Austro-Finnish winners of the competition for the overall concept. The entire site will be enclosed by a 16 m high, copper-clad wall, but allowing outsiders to look in. In the context of the exhibit "The World in Berlin" in the Berlin Pavilion beginning 6.21.96, the works will be shown together with plans for new embassy buildings and renovations of other countries.

6.7.1996

The Stadtforum (City Forum) meets for the last time in the Wallhöfen. Starting September, meetings will take place in the Staatsrat building. The roughly 40 member group was equipped with a new steering committee including city personalities from the architectural, cultural, and business communities, among them Berlin entrepreneur Sitki Özdemir.

6.8.–10.13.1996

With a ceremony in the rooms at Hanseatenweg, the jubilee exhibit "Die Kunst hat nie ein Mensch allein besessen" ("Art Was Never Owned By Anyone Alone") is opened on the occasion of the 300th anniversary of the Akademie der Künste (Academy of the Arts) and the HdK (Hochschule der Künste—Arts College). For four years, around 1,000 objects from 156 private and public lenders were collected to document the three hundred year history of the two academies and their differently

6.11.–8.20.1996

Exhibit "Art and Power in the Europe of Dictators, 1930 to 1945" in the Deutsches Historisches Museum (the German Historical Museum in the Zeughaus). The 23rd European Council exhibit, which explores the tense relationship of artist and architects to the totalitarian regimes of this era, accords the DHM a record number of visitors (100,000).

6.13.1996

"Vineria Franzotti" on Kreuzbergstrasse, "Bar Centrale" on Yorckstrasse, "Nola" on Dortmunder Strasse, and the bar "Zur Weissen Maus"

6.14.1996

The Architectural Museum of Basel awards for the first time. This year, the former Senate Building Director of Berlin, Hans Stimmann, is honored for his contributions to the "contemporary building culture." The prize consists in a serie of 25 photos by Christian Vogt, Basel, which are recording places in Berlin, where the "unvisible decisions of the Senate Building Director become visible."

It's Far from Simple to Build a House *Reinhard Lettau*

Where should one build a tower? Several persons appear, point to a particular spot. They unfold blueprints, retrace lines, toss their heads back, sure of victory. "By Jove," they cry, "if that isn't a tower!" Everybody claps, but how will it look afterwards, after it's built?

And this is only an example. It's no different with houses or whole communities. Let's say the architect arrives. Difficulties don't exist for him. His friends are walking behind him, a whole crowd of friends. His best friend is carrying long, thick rolls that look like stovepipes. Now the architect gets down on one knee. The other knee, the one that is sticking up, becomes a support for his arm. He studies a meadow with a brook, a rock. He narrows his eyes, spreads his fingers like a fan, passes them in front of his face several times. Then he bounces back to his feet and cries, "This is where we'll build the house!" His friends shout "Bravo!" Some put their hands on their hips, tilt their heads to one side and seem to be checking the location once more. The architect notices. He nudges them. "Well?" he cries. "Well?" "Yes!" the hesitant now also shout, but God help us once the house has been built here.

But the real architect doesn't just happen on a certain spot, least of all equipped with blueprints. Without friends, without flatterers he explores the countryside. Abreast of him in a single rank walk the workmen, the carpenters, with their tools, the lock-smiths. When a certain spot attracts the architect's attention, he calls, "Halt!" His call echoes down both flanks. But the left and right ends are much further ahead when all come to a halt, because they hear the command later, so much later that, when things have quieted down again, the workmen are standing in an approximate circle. Within this circle lies a plot of land. If there is a forest, or a hill, they cannot see each other and each stays at shouting distance from the next man for reasons

gifted members with pictures, sculptures, photographs, and archival material. A side-observation: On June 29th, following a thunderstorm, moisture drips onto exhibition pieces from the sheds of the specially renovated rain- and lightproofed roof. By July 27th, the cultural history survey can be viewed anew—dry and light-protected.

6.9.1996

17th birthday of the "Ufa-Fabrik" in Tempelhof. The collective (35 adults, 15 children) is today a network of firms with a turnover of DM 5 mill. and supplying around 120 people with work; i.e., a good two thirds of the employees come from outside. The house-owned enterprises include a whole grain bakery, a cultural center, a café, and a neighborhood center.

on Ludwigkirchplatz count among the victors of the open nationwide competition, sponsored by Marcellino's Restaurant Report, for hot spots.

6.14.1996

Groundbreaking for the "Wohnpark Stralau" ("Stralau Residential Park") with 450 housing units in the development area Rummelsburger Bucht. Overall concept: Herman Hertzberger, Amsterdam, with Inken Baller, Berlin, client: VEBA Immobilien AG. In the summer of 1996, additional competitions for segments of the residential park are decided: For apartment houses with a total of 570 homes (client: Ziel GmbH), two first prizes go to the Berlin architectural firms Erstmann and Kehrer, as well as Pudritz and Paul. In the competition for two child day care centers, the first prize is won by the firm Alsop/Störmer, London. The buildings are to be finished by 1997.

6.17.1996

The Berlin writer Reinhard Lettau, who returned to Berlin in 1994 after several years in the United States, dies at the age of 67.

of communication. Then each squats down wherever he is standing, digs a hole in the ground and waits for the architect to have an inspiration. When he has one, he calls it out to the men. For instance he'll call, "Work's begun!" and if the command makes the round and returns unchanged to the architect—which can and does happen quite often—then they start building. But sometimes the command changes on the way around—to "Have some fun!" for instance—and the workmen put their arms around each other and start to dance across the stubble fields, across gushing streams, high reeds, across a nearby market square, and disappear over the horizon. Then construction is delayed.

But let's assume that the order makes the round and comes back to the architect unchanged and the men start building each at the spot at which he is squatting, without paying any attention to the man next to him. With a song on his lips, one jams his spade into the earth. Another is stacking bricks, perhaps prematurely; while across from him, on the opposite side of the circle, pilings are being driven into the earth. One is mixing mortar, another assembling lengths of pipe, still another is tamping the ground flat and breaking off twigs.

Later when they change places—each moving to the left, taking over the working place of his neighbor to the left, creating a circular, clockwise movement—when it's time to change places, each man gains a more detached view of his neighbor's work. If he likes it, he continues in the same spirit, blending the neighbor's—now his own—achievements with his own—now a neighbor's. But if he dislikes it, he tears everything down and starts afresh, if there is still time for a fresh start before the next change of place. Or he may advance to a place that has just been demolished by his predecessor. Then it may happen that he lacks the appropriate materials. He turns on his heels and heads for the next town to fetch them. Sometimes he meets friends there, they stop in at a tavern. They play a hectic game of cards while the construction waits. By the time the gentlemen stagger back, a new change has taken place, they need new material, and building stagnates. Or a man comes back, but another is now in his place, this irritates him, they fight, layers of chalk dust rise, big bricks fly, another interruption.

Now all have made the round once. They are more familiar with the terrain. They have added to it, taken away from it. But where is the architect? The true architect keeps away from the building area. Out of disgust? Impatience? Not at all. He may be lying on a nearby hill, squatting in a bush, climbing a tree, standing in man-high ferns, alone without friends. He is standing in a pond, raises the megaphone to his lips, calls instructions to his men. Like: "This way and no other!" or: "Don't do that, please!" or, more elaborately: "Gentlemen, I'm lying here in the sweet-smelling clover. My eyes are closed. When I open them, I see nothing but the sky. Nevertheless I command you: Nnnnnnnnnnno! No windows please, no windows at all! I won't tolerate apertures! A house must be coaxed into being the way a sculptor coaxes a statue to life-by subtraction, not by adding. One does not add a house to the landscape, one does not assemble it, one deducts it!"

Another incident: after a couple of years the architect arrives in a small village. Immediately all the workmen walk up to the house they built there some time ago. From every story, people are looking out. Some wave, some show signs of fear. "I don't know," says the architect, and asks for a large hammer. Someone calls from a window, "But pictures are already hanging on the walls; ivy is creeping up one side of the house and all that." "That's true," the architect calls back, "ivy is creeping up one side and the geraniums are in bloom." At night he returns. He takes another look at the house. Lights go on in several apartments. People in nightgowns lean out the windows. Some hold children in their arms, to whom they point. Someone throws dishes into the street. Pets escape in long leaps. Down in the street, the architect is making a speech. He puts the megaphone to his lips and yells, "This house is blocking a number of things. Among them star formations." Torches are lit.

The workmen find new encouragement in these instructions. Those who had been about to pick up the trowel, put it aside and reach for the demolition hammer. Or they drop that too, walk over to the architect, and past him, wander off, leaving the ruin behind them.

"That's the spirit!" the architect calls after them. "I'm all in favor of deliberation."

Now a house has been tricked out of the landscape. They stand about the place, every so often somebody lets a couple of bricks drop, they elbow each other, excuse themselves, point out the beauty of the view, express their appreciation of same; all of a sudden a house is standing there. Someone slaps the architect's back, or runs to fetch him from the cave in which he has been resting. He turns, sees the house and cries, "Good Lord! No! Please move the whole thing over to the left!" Tearing down, rebuilding. To work, to work.

Or the architect is standing before a newly finished house. People are moving in. On the second floor curtains are being hung. The architect examines the house, he frowns. "Yes and no," he says, immediately someone reaches for the axe. The roofless residents come out and join the architect.

Again a house is ready. "A water castle," says the architect, "an underwater castle." It takes several summers to change the course of the river; everybody watches the house sinking.

"It's far from simple to build a house," says the architect; behind him the horizon is drowning in flames.

Now the workmen are standing at a different spot, holding pickaxes and bricks. They begin all over again. Suddenly the architect leaps to his feet. He is standing on a mound. One can see his silhouette from the construction area. He waves the workmen over. They approach with hesitant steps, carrying pickaxe, spade, shovel and wobbling mortar trough. "Closer," he calls, "come closer!" "Where? Where do you want us?" "Here, right here!" He points to a spot exactly beside his left foot. The workmen start and the architect vanishes. He is standing inside the chimney, the workmen can still hear him call orders. They begin building the house around the chimney, but soon they become confused, they miss the architect, naturally, they grow disheartened, and by and by, as his voice grows feebler, they abandon the job.

6.17.1996

Topping-out ceremony for the Quartier Fichtelbergstrasse 1–13 in Marzahn; architect: Heinz Weisener, Hamburg (President of FC St. Pauli) with 198 state subsidized apartments and 5,820 sq. m for trade and commerce. Investment total: DM 95 mill.

6.19.1996

Senator Peter Strieder has appointed an Advisory Council for Urban Design and Planning, which convenes for its constituent meeting today. For a provisional period of one year, he picked as his advisors: the architects Hilde Léon and Bernd Jansen from Berlin, Roger Diener from Basel, Werner Durth from Darmstadt, the architectural historian Fritz Neumeyer, city planner Urs Kohlbrenner, and the landscape architect Cornelia Müller from Berlin.

6.20.1996

Decision in the limited competition for the "Lindengalerie an der Komischen Oper" in Mitte. Awarded with first prizes are: Jürgen Sawade, Berlin, Heinz Hilmer and Christoph Sattler, Munich, Augusto Romano Burelli, Udine, and David Chipperfield, London, each of whom will design one of the buildings. The competition was preceded by a dispute among developers: Those applying to build on the expensive property were Hanseatica, Wert-Konzept, and Walter Eder, a machine manufacturer with a not entirely unequivocal past. While

6.23.1996

The Holy Father makes an epiphanous visitation to transubstantiated Berlin.

6.24.1996

Building Senator Jürgen Klemann takes stock provisionally: To fix prefab buildings, DM 1 billion have flown into the renewal of East Berlin housing projects. For 1996 a further DM 270 mill. are budgeted. For improving residential environments, DM 274 mill. were put into the layout and planning of residential courtyards and playgrounds; 18,000 trees were planted. The federal government and housing companies contributed DM 76 mill.

6.26.1996

Topping-out ceremony in Mitte for the apartment house "Luisenresidenz" on Luisenstrasse 47–52, corner of Schumannstrasse. 94 rental apartments, a store for the nearby Deutsches Theater, restaurant, pharmacy, and a grocery store are planned. The private builder is Osnabrück jeweler Egon Geerkens with DM 50 mill. proprietary capital, architect Hülsmeier, Osnabrück.

6.30.1996

On the first nationwide "Architecture Day," the Berlin Chamber of Architects invites Berliners to take tours of construction sites and new buildings. On the same day the DAZ German Architecture Center opens the exhibition "BauPlatz Berlin."

6.30.1996

Funding for the "Historical Commission" (founded 1959) is cut out of the state budget, thereby forcing the closure of the extra-university "Research Center for History."

7.3.1996

One-million visitors at the INFO BOX after only 9 months. Building State Secretary Uwe Schmitt awards a Berliner in early retirement with an "INFO BOX Tart" made from almond-paste. The organizers had counted on 200,000 visitors per year.

7.3.1996

Mosse-Palais on Leipziger Platz 15. The Berlin Administrative Court confirms the immediate construction stop and the demolition ordinance of

June   **July**

6.20.1996

Italian construction workers deprived of their wages occupy a construction site on Jessnerstrasse in the Friedrichshain district. (The builder is the Berlin subsidiary of the Slovenian TWT conglomerate; the Italian subcontractor is the CM.S.R.L. with headquarters in the Calabrian port city Cortone.)

the city, as owner of the properties, has committed the first two investors to mutual cooperation and to the competition's decision (after a brief interlude by Sawade), Herr Eder (supported by August Everding, State Intendant in Munich) is contemplating an "Opera-Forum" (with Käfer specialties and a Schwarzenegger studio) that he commissions Christoph Langhof, Berlin, to design. While a great deal of ink is spilled over the partisanship of the city officials, State Secretary Hans Stimmann quietly places the administrative building of the Komische Oper alongside Unter den Linden under landmark protection.

6.25.1996

Premiere of the two-month city spectacular "Schaustelle Berlin" ("Site Seeing Berlin"). No sooner had it begun— Berlin's "construction site tourism"—than it became impossible to stop, so it was instantly turned into a summer calendar of events, into a nine-week series of concerts, operas, street festivals, exhibits, and tours, of large and small appearances by artists and jugglers at construction sites and many other places in the city. Highlights: Carmina Burana on the Schlossplatz, the Science-Fiction-Musical in the airplane hangar at Tempelhof, the guest appearance of the Théâtre du Soleil in the Arena Treptow, "Anaphase," danced by the Batsheva Danse Company in the rough brickwork by Arata Isozaki on the Daimler-Benz grounds, Potsdamer Platz. 500,000 visitors were counted.

6.27.1996

At the request of Federal Chancellor Kohl, the extension to the Deutsches Historisches Museum is awarded directly to the American architect Ieoh Ming Pei. After a meeting of the Budget Committee, the representatives of the parliamentary parties vote their approval. Christoph Stölzl, Director of the DHM, has gotten his way in this matter.

7.2.1996

Barbara Jakubeit is appointed Senate Building Director by Building Senator Jürgen Klemann. She succeeds Hans Stimmann and concludes a contract running out on 12.31.2000. Between 1990 and 1994, as President of the Bundesbaudirektion (Federal Building Authority), Frau Jakubeit was already working in Berlin (as the major urban design competitions for the federal goverment buildings were organized). Since 1994, she has been a professor at the TH Darmstadt, where she hopes to return after her time in Berlin.

the Mitte District Office. With four unapproved stories in its transverse wing, the first building on Leipziger Platz—on the property of the former home of Berlin publisher Rudolf Mosse—exceeds by far the permitted number of floors. Architect: Hans Strauch, Boston; client: Hans Röder, Hamburg.

7.3.1996

On Paulsternstrasse (Spandau district), the first decentralized and privately financed fire brigade begins service. It is considered a model of fire protection measures in times of an empty public purse. The building was financed (at a cost of DM 5.9 mill., only half as expensive as a publicly financed fire station) by the firm of Siemens. In exchange, 19 men from the disbanded Siemens company fire brigade were taken into public service. Architects: Kny and Weber, Berlin.

7.3.1996

"Gefesseltes Haus" ("Tied-down house"). Greek artist Jannis Markopoulos entangles the landmark building on Dorotheenstrasse 105, near the Reichstag, in 50,000 m of red-orange synthetic cable. The event remains with the city for several weeks and is supposed to have cost the well-meaning sponsors DM 500,000.

7.9.1996

Roof raising ceremony for the new administration of the Dussmann Group at Friedrichstrasse 90/91. The complex consists of five buildings; in the remodeled house at Dorotheenstrasse 41/43 there will be 50 apartments, from the building on Mittelstrasse only the facade will remain, and new buildings are put up next to a cultural department store at Dorotheenstrasse 39 and Mittelstrasse 5/6. Client: Dussmann Group, construction cost DM 200 mill., 15,000 sq. m usable space. Architect: Miroslav Volf, Saarbrücken.

7.9.1996

At the XIXth World Congress of the Union of International Architects (UIA) in Barcelona, Berlin qualifies surprisingly — surprisingly because hardly supported by its own politicians — as host city for the XXIth World Congress in 2002.

7.10.1996

Today, the Allied Airlift memorial is 45 years old. 100,000 visitors were present on May 10th, 1951, when then Mayor Ernst Reuter unveiled the memorial designed by Ernst Ludwig. Alongside the Airlift memorial, two "raisin bombers" provide a reminder of the Berlin blockade from 6.24.1948 to 5.12.1949.

The supplying of West Berlin by air began on the 28th of June 1948. Even the cement clinker was flown in in sacks. Temporary mills ground them to cement. Transportation was difficult and complicated. Carrying that amount of clinker meant a serious threat to the machines. The pilots had to fly with utmost caution — on the climb, gradually increase your altitude, minimizing tilt in the curves, and on the landing, decrease altitude slowly. Too steep a tilt could cause the sacks of cement clinker to slide around, resulting in too much weight on one side, thereby threatening the safety of the plane. The statistics don't say how many tons of cement clinker were flown to Berlin during the eleven month blockade. Nevertheless, since then the "Cement for Berlin" action has become one of the most memorable chapters in the rebuilding of such a large and yet such a horribly destroyed city.
Heidelberger Portländer, 1957

7.3–7.7.1996

Beach volleyball in the city. 76 trucks full of sand from the Mark Brandenburg transform the parking place on Alexanderplatz in Mitte into a playground for the international Beach Volleyball World Cup Tournament, the last test before the Olympic Games in Atlanta. Beach volleyball fever in Berlin began with a tournament in the summer of 1995 on the Schlossplatz.

7.4.1996

The southern part of the "Ludwig-Erhard-Haus" is almost finished; as first tenant, the Berlin Stock Exchange will move in. The new building for the Chamber of Industry and Commerce will be on Fasanenstrasse/corner of Hardenbergstrasse next to the Chamber's old landmark-protected building (Sobotka/Müller, 1954/55). Architects: Nicholas Grimshaw & Partners, London/Berlin, winner of the 1991 competition. From 1991 until the 1994 construction start, the grandiose design — unfortunately — ran through several stages of simplification. What remains is the supporting structure of 15 arches, from which the floors now hang, along with the internal street providing a glimpse into the new stock exchange floor on the ground level. On Berlin's regional stock exchange, more than 700 stocks (with an emphasis on Eastern Europe) are traded. Client: Industrie- und Handelskammer Berlin. 35,000 sq. m of total floor space. Construction cost: DM 160 mill.

7.9.1996

100th anniversary of the death of aviation pioneer Otto Lilienthal, who (together with his brother Gustav) began experimenting with the construction of flying apparatuses as a student. Less well-known is that he had the workers at his firm share 25 % of the profits, that he founded a popular theater, established an orchard colony, and founded the first public library in 1895 as a member of the "Society for Ethical Culture." The "Ankerbaukasten" (miniature construction set) developed by Otto and Gustav Lilienthal was not successful at first, so the brothers decided to sell the rights, making the next owner a millionaire.

When I was 18 years old, my father took me along on a visit to his old friend Otto Lilienthal. Lilienthal had a small factory in Berlin, where he manufactured his inventions: ships sirens, motors, torpedo boat boiler and other complicated machines. He lived with his employees like a father. He was a large and hearty fellow, friendly and full of life. He built his flying machines in his free time together with his brother Gustav. ... It was like a dream. What a contrast to our own life in Chemnitz. Here was freedom, openness and joy. It was revitalizing. Then we went in the factory and from there to Lilienthal's flight hill ... and in no time he was standing on top with a red scarf around his head and he took off. Then he turned the machine over to me for a try. For a moment I felt the wind tug, then it pushed me to the ground. Lilienthal suggested to my father that I should stay with him and learn to fly, but my father didn't think it was a good idea ... I would've stayed with L. in a second, though it was less his enthusiasm for flying that attracted me and more his way of living and his person. But on the other hand, I was too set on becoming a painter ...
Ernst Ludwig Kirchner, 1937

7.11.1996

Cornerstone laying for the seven-story head-quarters of the Hauptverband der Deutschen Bauindustrie (Association of the German Construction Industry) on Kurfürstenstrasse in Schöneberg. The building, estimated at DM 22 mill., should be ready for occupancy in 1998. Architects: Schweger + Partners, Hamburg/Berlin.

7.13.1996

Love-Parade in Berlin. Under the slogan "We Are One Family," 750,000 participants come to Berlin for the world's biggest Love-Parade, leading from Ernst-Reuter-Platz to the Brandenburg Gate and back again to the Grosser Stern. The first Love-Parade began with a few hundred ravers in 1989.

7.15.1996

Cornerstone laying for a residential and commercial building, Grolmanstrasse 39 near Kudamm. Architect: Werner Weitz, Berlin. What is special here is that the builder, Anthony Ettlinger, is a relative of Walter Rathenau, murdered 1922 in

7.22.1996

Groundbreaking for 820 homes in "Quartier Maselake" within the Wasserstadt (Water City) Oberhavel. Urban design concept: Kees Christiaanse, Rotterdam, developer: Siemens. The city company GSW had already begun in November 1994 to build in the "Quartier Pulvermühle" on the opposite shore of the Havel. Cubic houses by the Berlin architects ENNS (Eckert, Negwer, Sommer, Suselbeek) are to be completed in 1996.

7.27.1996

Fifty years ago, Artur Brauner founded his Film Imperium. For the anniversary, the 77-year-old himself leads tours through the historic CCC studios in Spandau. More than 500 movies were filmed here, filling the cash registers of German movie houses in the fifties and sixties.

7.30.1996

Three competitions are decided for new buildings on the sites of former American army barracks; all the winners are from Berlin. On the grounds of the Turner barracks at Hüttenweg in Zehlendorf (21,600 sq. m), there will be 100 housing units in 15 urban villas. First prize: Klaus Theo Brenner with Gabriele G. Kiefer (landscape planning). On the grounds of the McNair barracks in Lichterfelde on Goerzallee, 150 apartments in rowhouses and semi-detached houses are planned. First prize: Eckert, Negwer, Sommer, Suselbeek, with Norbert Müggenburg (landscape planning). On the southern part of the Andrews barracks in Lichterfelde (between Goerzallee and Altdorfer Strasse, 204,000 sq. m), 700 rental apartments and 170 rowhouses are to be embedded in a park landscape. First prize: Assmann, Salomon & Scheidt, with Jäckel and Micke (landscape planning). The three competitions issued by the fede-

8.1.–8.18.1996

"Light Sculpture Potsdamer Platz 1996." On eleven cranes 20 to 68 m high, artist Gerhard Merz mounts 2,200 flourescent tubes separated from each other by only a few centimeters. Between 8 p.m. and midnight, the cranes will be traced by light bands. An homage to the modern era, according to the artist, who had Ilja Ehrenburg's 1921 text "And yet it moves" recited at the opening. Daimler-Benz,

8.2.1996

Diversion of the Spree. In the course of tunnel construction, the Spree is forced to leave its riverbed on the Humboldt-hafen; for the next two years, shipping traffic—regulated by traffic lights—will take a northern detour in an arc around the foundation trench.

7.13.1996

Underground station Hermannstrasse, linking the underground with the rapid transit line. The 168th station in the Berlin underground railway network (total cost: DM 129.2 mill.) is the new southern terminus of the U-8 line (previously at Leinestrasse); the northern endpoint is Wittenau. The tunnel shell between the old and new termini as well as one fifth of the station shell were built as early as 1932. In the 20S, the Nordsüdbahn AG had already planned to extend the line from Gesundbrunnen to Neukölln as far as Hermannstrasse station (with a link to rapid transit's southern ring). Architect: Rainer G. Rümmler.

Grunewald. The family of the former Foreign Minister had previously always refused to invest in Berlin.

7.19.1996

On the 13 ha of fallow land on the grounds of the Stadion der Weltjugend (the GDR's "Stadium of World Youth"), Sportpark Mitte comes into being. Since 4.1.96, initially for just two years (with an option for another two years), a "Public Golf Center in Berlin-Mitte" comes into being, with a driving range, chipping green, and a three-hole short field. Two golfing clubs, the promotional association "Golfpark Schloss Wilkendorf" and the "Volxgolf-Klub" of the KGB (Kreuzberger Golf Bund) manage the facility.

7.27.1996

Opening of the exhibition "urban twist" in the EIGEN + ART gallery. Four architects (Jürgen Mayer, Karl Unglaub, Bettina Vismann, Tillmann Wagner) and four artists (Yana Milev, Carsten Nicolai, Maix Mayer, Jörg Herold) deal with questions of urban space. They are opposed to a "city image of seemingly familiar historic reinsurance." The motto "urban twist" is a summons to turn away from the habitual glance of the specialist; it sees itself as a thread between architecture and art.

ral government and the state of Berlin were preceded by a Europe-wide application procedure. For each of the three sites, 25 participants were invited to compete. The juries recommended using the first prizes as basis for the subsequent investors' competition.

August 1996

Building permission asked for the Victoria areal at Kurfürstendamm, in the rear courtyard of the corner building where the famous Café Kranzler resides. The developer difa, Hamburg, and the architect Helmut Jahn, Chicago (who won the competiton in 1988), argue for their request on grounds of a controversial development plan passed September 1995. At that time, the site was owned by the Victoria Insurance Company who, promising new jobs, forced the city to approve. Since they sold the site to the next investor, the development plan should be revised, for the 160 m long and 55 m high glass bar would dwarf the Kranzler corner building and its surroundings along Kurfürstendamm.

Siemens, BEWAG, and the Max Hetzler Gallery participate in the project. Gerhard Merz became known in Berlin through his prize-winning, if also unloved, design for re-shaping the Lustgarten, which was ultimately rejected.

The former bed—which will continue to be surrounded on three sides by the Spree—will be dredged into another 17 m deep foundation trench. In contrast to the tunnel under the Landwehrkanal, which will be dug underground at a depth of 15 m, the Spree must be tunneled under using an open construction method, since the tunnel roof will only be 1 m underneath the Spree bottom. At DM 25 mill., the diversion of the Spree, the most spectacular part of the tunnel construction, costs only a portion of the 4 billion allocated for the entire tunnel project.

163

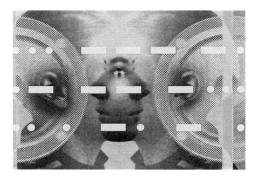

8.7.1996

Cornerstone laying for the new headquarters of the Dresdner Bank on Pariser Platz. The building, after a design by the Hamburg office of von Gerkan, Marg, and Partner, will cost DM 150 mill. and should be ready by autumn 1997.

8.8.1996

Roof raising ceremony in the office and business house "Atrium" on Friedrichstrasse, corner Leipziger Strasse. Architect: Volkwin Marg (von Gerkan, Marg, and Partner, Hamburg/Aachen). Investor: ECE Projektmanagement GmbH, Berlin. Construction total: DM 250 mill.

8.8.1996

Roof raising ceremony for the office and business house "Quartier 106" of the American Business Center on Checkpoint Charlie on Friedrichstrasse. Architect: Philip Johnson, New York. Planned completion: June 1997. Builder: CEDC.

8.16.1996

Opening of the exhibition "Karl Friedrich Schinkel's Bauakademie in Art and Architecture" in the Kunstforum of the Grundkreditbank. Through October paintings, drawing plans, detailed designs, and building fragments of the Schinkel building are on display. The discussion about rebuilding the academy continues.

8.17.1996

Opening of the exhibition "Miracle Economy — GDR Consumption Culture and Product Design in the Seventies" in the Kulturbrauerei/Prenzlauer Berg. Through 1.12.97 the world of merchandise and its advertisement in the period following the end of rationing in 1958 is on view: A thousand and one quotidian objects, from shower caps through clothes made of Wolpyra and Dederon to a chemical-green hi-fi bar.

8.19.1996

In the City Planning Committee for the Charlottenburg district, new plans are presented for the area of the "Schimmelpfeng-Haus" on Kantstrasse (built 1957–61 by Franz-Heinrich Sobothka and Gustav Müller). The design by Christoph Langhof envisions the demolition of the landmark-protected house, to be replaced by a new multi-story building and a shopping passage with a star-shaped, glass-covered room in the middle. The alternative design by Julia Tophof and Norbert Hemprich, by contrast, preserves the Schimmelpfeng-Haus and plans a remodeling of the buildings next door. Charlottenburg's Building Councillor Beate Profé criticizes both plans.

8.19.1996

The Summer Academy of the London Architecture Institute's "Urban Design Task Force" under the sponsorship of Prince Charles takes place for the first time in Germany. In the Villa Kampffmeyer at Glienicker Horn in Potsdam, 22 architecture students from all over the world meet and suggest proposals for the "Dorf Bornstedt" village north of Sanssouci Park and for the "Alter Markt," the old marketplace that prior to its destruction had been the center of Potsdam's old city. On September 2nd, HRH The Prince of Wales makes a personal visit to Potsdam. 4 days later the exhibit of works is opened in the Villa Kampffmeyer. The villa, erected 1923/24 by Adolf and Friedrich Bolle, was restored according to landmark conservation guidelines by the Berlin company Groth & Graalfs so that it may one day

8.21.1996

The sidewalks along the street Unter den Linden are to be widened: on the southern side from 7 to 9.85 m, on the northern side from 8 to 10.85 m. The promenade in the middle and the number of lanes are to remain as they are.

21.–24.8.1996

Surrounded by cranes and excavators, 1,200 visitors experience the dance piece "Anaphase" by the Israeli Batsheva Dance Company, performed in the raw construction of Arata Isozaki's building on the debis site of Potsdamer Platz. Nele Hertling, the director of the Hebbel Theater, came forward with the idea. The performance is part of the serie of events "Dance in August." Daimler-Benz provides DM 600,000 of funding.

8.23.1996

Berlin underground railcars off to Pyongyang! The sale of 120 subway wagons of the type GI (nickname "Gisela") to the North Korean capital city for the price of DM 30,000 apiece is concluded. A few of the wagons, redundant since unification, previously arrived on loan to serve the rapid transit line Piraeus — Athens — Kifissia.

8.9.–9.8.1996

"Sonambiente Festival for Sight and Sound. International Audio Art at the 300-Year Anniversary of the Akademie der Künste." Seventy media works, music performances, tonal projects, tone-space variations, and sound pictures are installed at well-known — Akademie der Künste am Pariser Platz, Staatsrat building, Weinhaus Huth on Potsdamer Platz — and unknown places — Sophiensäle, Postfuhramt Oranienburger Strasse etc. — around the city. Laurie Anderson installs "Whirlwind" in the Max Liebermann Atelier and gives a concert on 9.9. in the Volksbühne at Rosa-Luxemburg-Platz. At the same time: The Hans-Werner-Henze-Festival commemorating his seventieth birthday; the 30-year anniversary of the Berliner Symphoniker.

... according to this theory, when a black hole implodes the information about the objects that have disappeared begins to slid down an infinitely long tunnel. All those numbers and calculations and deviations are swirling around in a huge whirlwind.

So here are the questions: Is time long? Or is it wide? Are things getting better or are they getting worse?
Laurie Anderson, 1996

constitute the centerpiece of the residential site "Arkadien," on which construction began this summer. Ten urban villas with luxury condominiums will be built after a design by the California office of Moore, Ruble, Yudell.

8.21.1996

Cornerstone laying for the shopping center Forum Köpenick in the Bahnhofstrasse. Architects: von Gerkan, Marg, and Partner, Hamburg. Investor: Fundus Group, 40,880 sq.m, investment cost: DM 300 mill.

8.21.1996

Schinkel's homecoming. The bronze statue created in 1869 by Friedrich Drake is ceremoniously unveiled at its original site, Schinkelplatz. The figure had been stored in the Pergamon Museum; the developers Becker & Kries provided DM 100,000 for its restauration.

8.22.1996

Cornerstone laying for the new Rathaus Mitte (borough hall for the Mitte district). The 47 m high elongated disc owes its shape, above all, to landmark conservation, which approved the demolition of the former building on this site, the Hotel Berolina, on condition that the new building would fit in with the landmark-protected ensemble on Karl-Marx-Allee. 21,000 sq.m usable space, construction cost: DM 60 mill. Architects: Jan Bassenge, Kay Puhan-Schulz.

8.22.1996

What everyone has known since the day the jury met on 6.5.96 is now official. Ivan Reimann and Thomas Müller, the 2nd prize winners, and not the victor, Max Dudler, will be commissioned with the new building for the Foreign Office. For the renovation of the old building (architects: Kollhoff & Timmermann, Berlin), DM 125 mill. have been earmarked, DM 329 mill. for the new buildings.

8.25.1996

Open house at the former Reichsbank and future Foreign Office on Werderscher Markt in Mitte. Last opportunity for Berliners to visit the offices of Ulbricht and Honecker in the Central Committee of the SED (East Germany's Communist party) before their traces are erased through renovation by Hans Kollhoff, Berlin. Berliners came in droves.

8.27.1996

Decision in the building competition for the offices of the state of Bremen. The competition among 7 invited participants was won by Léon and Wohlhage, Berlin.

8.27.1996

In the garden of the former Staatsrat (GDR executive council) building, the mosaic fountain is put into operation again to the accompaniment of a brass band and fried fish. The fountain was restored on landmark preservation guidelines by Thomas Widuwilt; building entrepreneur Klaus Groth sponsored the undertaking.

8.30.1996

Premiere of the Reichstag wrapping film "Dem deutschen Volke" by Christo and Jeanne-Claude in the outdoor film theater Waldbühne. Producers: Wolfram and Daniel Hissen, camera Jörg Widmer. The film is the most extravagant documentary of the last 50 years. 14 film teams took part, the length is 105 minutes, and the production cost DM 2 mill. The seven hundred page documentation of the Reichstag wrapping will be available at the Frankfort Book Fair.

9.1.1996

Confusion at the subway station: All those who only yesterday, during the morning rush hour were heading toward the subway station "Rathaus Friedrichshain" find themselves today passing by a sign saying "Petersburger Strasse" at the place where four years ago they entered the "Frankfurter Tor."

9.2.1996

In the "Wolfsschlucht" ("Wolves' Ravine") in Viktoriapark in Kreuzberg (designed 1888–94 by Public Gardens Director Hermann Mächtig), the springs are bubbling again after a two-year restoration (costing over DM 1.8 mill.). The work done on the artificial waterfall, made of limestone and volcanic tuff belongs to the initial construction phase of the Viktoriapark restoration, begun in 1994. Top priority was Schinkel's "Nationaldenkmal" ("National Monument"). The park was placed under the protection of landmark conservation laws in 1979, the first public garden in Berlin to be so designated.

9.6.1996

Opening of the continuing exhibition "Picasso and His Times" in the western Stüler building across from the Charlottenburg Palace. For ten years, provisionally, the Berggruen collection will be on view in Berlin. It embraces roughly 100 works of the classical modern. 25 works of Paul Klee act as a counterpart to Picasso, around whom the collection is grouped, supplemented by works of Cézanne, van Gogh, Braques, and by African tribal art. In his autobiography with the title "Main Road and Side Roads" (after a picture by Paul Klee), the 82 year old Heinz Berggruen, who emigrated to the USA in 1936, explains why he moved back to his native Berlin and left his collection at the city's disposal. His collection is valued at over DM 600 mill.

Main Road and Side Roads *Heinz Berggruen*

Voyage to Berlin. German citizen again. Autumn 1973 …
About this time I reached the long-pondered decision to relinquish my American citizenship and once again take up German nationality. My ideal may have been completely different, that of a federal Europe, to which each land of the Old World could contribute its own culture and tradition; a Europe that would have offered me the possibility of obtaining a European passport. But because back then this Europe was still far off, I had to reach a decision.

I had never felt like an American and I did not feel any urge to go back to America. I felt European. Although I was doing fine in Paris I did not see why I should trouble myself for a French passport. To me it seemed much more sensible to regain the nationality that a barbaric regime had taken away from me half a human life earlier. Language and literature, history and the German landscape tie me to my home country in a way which no thousand-year Reich could ever destroy.

The way I imagined it, giving up American nationality would be purely routine. But re-possessing the German passport I had lost in 1936 was bound to raise certain problems, given the well-known thoroughness of the German authorities. The exact opposite happened. I went to the consulate of the Federal Republic in Paris, filled out a form, attached a notarized copy of my birth certificate and four passport photos, and ten days later I received a German passport. I was German again.

September

8.31.–9.29.1996

The 46th Berliner Festival Weeks present over 140 events on different aspects of the relationship between France and Germany. At the center of the festival lies the exhibition "Marianne und Germania" in the Martin Gropius Building. The period 1798–1898 comes to life in pictures, sculptures, caricatures, literature, and historic pieces of writing from literature and philosophy. Another relationship, reflected in a single person, is given testimony by the 100 photographs of Gisèle Freund, who was born in Berlin, fled to France, and in the early fifties returned to Berlin (at least as a tourist) repeatedly.

9.3.1996

Birthday greetings to the Berliner Funkturm (Berlin Radio Tower): it's 70 years old today! The 150 m high tower on the fairgrounds was erected 1924–26 for radio transmission by architect Heinrich Straumer and is among the landmarks of Berlin. The steel construction weighing 400 tons has a two-story restaurant at 55 m height; at 125 m visitors reach the observation platform.

9.5.1996

In Schloss Bellevue Park 6,000 native and foreign guests of President Herzog meet for a "Festival of Cultures."

9.6.1996

Roof raising ceremony at the Energy Headquarters on Stresemannstrasse, on the corner of Niederkirchner Strasse. From this location, BEWAG (Berlin's city-owned electricity works) will not only supply the buildings on Potsdamer Platz with heat and power, but also with cooling during the summer. Architects: Heinz Hilmer and Christoph Sattler, Munich/Berlin.

It was completely different with the Americans. When at the embassy at the Place de la Concorde I declared that I wished to relinquish my American nationality, the clerk stared at me wide-eyed. Was it clear to me what that meant? Did I know that thousands, no, tens of thousands of people throughout the world endeavored every day to obtain us citizenship? And I wished to give it up so blithely? No, she said, it wasn't that easy. Politely, but determined the lady tried to convince me of the dramatic consequences such a decision might have. At the end, she gave me an appointment two weeks later. I should have time to reconsider. Were I to remain adamant in my wish, I would have to submit a written application for denaturalization with a detailed justification of my request.

"I hope you have thought things over well," said the lady when I returned fourteen days later.

"Yes I have."

"And, you have, I hope, changed your mind."

"No, I haven't."

I handed the lady the form I had filled out; renunciation of nationality, as it is officially known, together with a written declaration with which I justified my intent.

"I have decided," I wrote, "to renounce my American citizenship, obtained through naturalization, because I, once honorably discharged from the United States Army, returned to Europe in 1944, where I have had my permanent residence ever since." I added that my wife was European, that both my children from my second marriage were born in Europe and that all my roots lay here in the Old World.

Newspapers look out for the visionary,
Even in our city. Let us not condemn,
That all around us architects begem
ideas with sketches, filling up the very

Vast. What's lacking is the pecuniary.
Perhaps it's for the best, this stratagem
Of colorcopying the city's fate, let them
Derive the atmosphere from luminary

Illusions. Let it be circus, bread and play
for everybody. Rome did so before,
why not Berlin. We read it day by day

that urban planning is about design,
and ask ourselves, what is the city's line,
what's essence, what is symptom and what for?

Hans Unverzagt, 1996

9.8.1996

Every Saturday from now on, the Berlin daily newspaper Tagesspiegel presents visions of well-known architects for the Schlossplatz in Berlin. The series begins with a report on the mysterious emergence of a previously unknown architectural model for the square that

9.10.1996

One hundred years ago today, construction work began at the Hallesches Tor in Kreuzberg on Germany's first subway, which is actually an elevated railway. In 1902 the six km long stretch between Stralauer Tor and Potsdamer Platz went into service. Today the underground network has a total length of 143 km.

10.9 to 10.20.1996

Opening for the exhibit of the seven winning designs from a competition tendered by the Senate Building Administration for memorials at the intra-city border crossings that have since disappeared. DM 130,000 will be made available for each of the works by Karla Sachse, Gabriele Basch, Susanne Ahner, Thorsten Goldberg, Twin Gabriel, Heike Ponwitz, and Frank Thiel. It is arguable whether 120 bronze rabbit silhouettes and a red plastic bench on the Oberbaum Bridge can keep memories of the Wall and border crossings alive.

9.12.1996

For his Berlin project "Bridges—Power Station —Grain Field" the Munich artist Edmund Piehler has laid out barley fields at twelve locations in the city. Today he mows on Alexanderplatz with a sickle. At the same time, Piehler is showing an exhibit in the Galerie Deschler with the theme "Grain—Earth—Symbol" and delighting the guests there with bread he has baked from his very own harvest.

9.12.1996

Cornerstone laying with Harald Juhnke (well-known comic actor of stage and screen) for the 330-mill.-DM project "Landsberger Arcades." Architect: Aldo Rossi. Developers: Dr. Peter and Isolde Kottmair, Berlin/ Munich. On Landsberger Allee/corner of Storkower Strasse, the service and shopping center will take up an entire Berlin city block by the end of 1997; eight-story buildings enclose a courtyard with greenery, while a towered building on Storkower Strasse is meant to establish an urban accent. The complex will offer 12,000 sq. m of retail space and 20,000 sq. m for services, including a three-star hotel and the Berlin Hotel Academy.

9.13.1996

The "Weiber Wirtschaft e.G." ("Women's Business")—Europe's largest center for company start-ups by women—opens

apparently derives from Karl Friedrich Schinkel. The design envisions a smaller-scale Stadtschloss (the urban residential palace of the Hohenzollern monarchy) along with new buildings for the Prussian Landtag Library, and Academy of Sciences. The political program lurking behind these bourgeois institutions must have been too revolutionary even for Schinkel to present to his king. The designs will be exhibited in January 1997 under the aegis of Bundestag president Rita Süssmuth.

9.8.1996

15 artists are working without compensation, and with the support of private sponsors, on the restoration of their Wall pictures in the East-Side-Gallery. In August 1996 the "Brotherly Kiss" by Dimitri Vrubel, which made the gallery world-famous, was destroyed when sacks of paint were smeared on it. Other paintings in the landmark-protected collection have become weather-beaten or decorated with graffiti. The restoration of the 1.3 km long piece of the Wall is supposed to cost DM 23 mill.

9.8.1996

Opening of the professional gastronomy convention "Arooma" and of the Olympics of chefs in Berlin's convention hall, where (among other things) the German team's lentils with quail slices emerged victorious over the creations of another 30 national crews. At the International Cuisine Exhibition, a total of 331 exhibitors from twelve countries exhibit design trends for kitchens, restaurants, and hotels until September 12th.

It's only when the underground railway tunnels go deep enough that the air stands in them that you get that smell of the special mixture of loam, oil, iron on iron, and ballast dust. The smell is positively redolent throughout the London Tube, but only occasionally in Paris. Its noticeable beneath Alexanderplatz—only on the deepest platforms, of course—and at Gesundbrunnen and Friedrichstrasse stations. But that's about it. As a Berliner I regret this since I breath in the earthy, burnt-smelling aroma only too willingly—even though it's by no means a perfume. There are people who even get queasy from it. It pleases me simply because with it I enjoy the realization of being very deep down in safety. There, where you are protected if a bomb explodes, a fire breaks out, or scaffolding collapses. But I also like the smell as a smell. Its mustiness seems homely to me, and the pungency enticing. Already as a whipper-snapper I wanted to spend all my born days really deep down, and to know how tunnels were excavated, cables laid and sewage system tunnels linked together.
Barbara Sichtermann, 1996

four years after signing the contract to purchase an old East Berlin cosmetics factory. 40 firms currently occupy 5,500 sq. m of commercial floorspace; over 1,000 female shareholders have invested DM 34 mill. in the cooperative since it was founded in 1987. The factory grounds were acquired by the Treuhand (the privatization agency for East German companies) in 1992 for DM 12.5 mill.; subsidies were made available by the commercial and building administration.

9.13.1996

Roof raising ceremony for the first section of a building project in the new construction area of Rudower Felder in Neukölln. Construction began on the housing estate in November 1994. The housing units, of which the first 600 will be ready by year's end (out of a total of 1,700 by 1999), have mostly come about through financing via the first and second methods of state subsidies. The client is Berlin's Gehag. Architects: Martin & Pächter; Schattauer & Tibes; Mussotter & Poeverlein, all from Berlin.

9.16.1996

The press has managed to ferret out a civil servant in the Westend — incidentally an architect — who has actually emigrated voluntarily from Bonn to Berlin. He reports on the considerable trouble his office has given him as a result of his extraordinary step. They have now set up an "Information Center for Berlin" in Bonn to assist the disoriented with advice.

9.18.1996

Exhibition opening in the INFO-BOX: "Campaign Capital City — On This We Are United" displays the building projects of the parliament and federal government — including a model of the Federal Chancellory on a scale of 1:200 — on a 90 sq. m area.

9.19.1996

Opening of the exhibit "Manet to van Gogh. Hugo von Tschudi and the Struggle Over the Modern." Through January 6th, 1997, the acquisitions of Hugo von Tschudi, who became director of the Berlin National Gallery in 1896, will be on display.

9.20.1996

On Schlossplatz, under the direction of the Federal Office for Health Education, the exhibit "LoveLife" opens, intended to reach a mostly young audience with messages about AIDS, sexuality and contraception, love, solidarity, and responsibility.

9.21.1996

Balance sheet on the summer: this season it was far too cold and, at 528 hours, the sun was shining way behind expectations. With the coldest September in 65 years, autumn followed suit.

9.24.1996

Cornerstone laying for the Innovation Center for Environmental Technology at the Science and Business Site ("Wista") Berlin-Adlershof. The building based on designs by Darmstadt architects Eisele, Fritz, and Bott (competition January 1995) will make a total of 33,600 sq. m available to businesses in the environmental sector, 20,000 sq. m by the start of 1998. Investment total: DM 190 mill.; the city-state of Berlin is contributing DM 46 mill.

9.26.1996

With a dreamy Italian buffet for the invited guests, and especially for the construction workers, the roof raising ceremony for the "Quartier Schützenstrasse" is celebrated. The cornerstone was laid for the office and residential complex in Berlin-Mitte on 6.21.96. Architect: Aldo Rossi, Milan. Clients: Dr. Peter and Isolde Kottmair.

9.27.1996

The Bundesrat (German Upper House of Parliament) finally resolves by a vote of 56 to 13 to move to Berlin and thereby nullifies its 1991 decision to remain in Bonn. The former Prussian House of Lords on Leipziger Strasse will now become the seat of the states' chamber. The renovation costs for the old building from 1904 (architect: Friedrich Schulze), which supplies 11,000 sq. m of space, are estimated at DM 185 mill. Architect for the renovation: Peter Schweger, Hamburg.

September

9.18.1996

The environmental departments of the Senate Department for Urban Development, Environmental Protection, and Technology have moved officially into the new building at the JannowitzCenter on Brückenstrasse in the Mitte district. 13,500 sq. m of office space have been leased for 10 years. The office complex, based on a design by the architects Hentrich, Petschnigg, and Partners, should be completely finished by 1997.

His purchase of Manet's "Winter Garden" was the first Impressionist painting acquired by a German museum. This led to conflicts, not only with Wilhelm von Bode, General Director of Berlin Museums, but also with Kaiser Wilhelm II, so that Tschudi left in 1908 for Munich to take over the directorship of the Bavarian State Painting Collections.

9.19.–9.21.1996

For the second time, the "Bauforum Berlin" takes place in the former Staatsrat building in Berlin-Mitte, where 300 participants from every field related to construction discuss future building and assembly methods. Motto: "Building as an integrative process."

9.22.1996

Exhibit of an extensive selection from the painted works of Max Pechstein (1881–1955) in the Brücke-Museum. Through January 1st, 1997, about 80 works by this Berlin Expressionist and early member of the "Brücke" from the period between 1906 and 1945 are shown.

9.22.1996

With the national league game between Alba Berlin and Steiner Bayreuth, the Max-Schmeling-Halle in the Friedrich-Ludwig-Jahn-Sportpark, Prenzlauer Berg district, is officially opened.

9.23.1996

Opening ceremony for the theme restaurant "Planet Hollywood" in the FriedrichstadtPassagen (Quartier 205), Mohrenstrasse/corner of Friedrichstrasse. The restaurant chain's owners are the Hollywood stars Demi Moore, Bruce Willis, Sylvester Stallone, and Arnold Schwarzenegger. After London, Paris, and Helsinki, Berlin now has the fourth European branch.

9.25.1996

After a remodeling phase lasting more than five years, KaDeWe is again free of construction zones. The "Kaufhaus des Westens" — founded in 1907 — is now Europe's largest department store. After the remodeling, in which DM 440 mill. were invested, roughly 2,5000 sales clerks can offer around 380,000 articles of merchandise on about 60,000 sq. m of floorspace. This — not to mention the contingent of paste jewelry — entices 200,000 visitors on opening day.

9.27.1996

In an internal colloquium on "Urban Design Master Planning Alter Markt/former Stadtschloss," the Potsdam City Council presents eight different utilization and structural models developed by the office Topos on a commission from the City of Potsdam. The variations for the Stadtschloss range from a faithful reconstruction to landscaping the area as an interim solution.

9.27.1996

Suitcases — the very emblem of travel — sway above the heads of travelers in the Hauptbahnhof. The installation by the artists Songhak Ky, Hein Spellmann, and Jean-Pierre Theile, initiated by the Deutsche Bahn AG, displays 250 suitcases on steel rods. Later, the collection will be expanded to 12,000 pieces and move to its final destination in the newly renovated rapid transit station at Alexanderplatz.

Impressed, the two men stroke the powerful legs of Karl Marx, squatting as if on a little suitcase next to the standing figure of Friedrich Engels. "Waiting for the travel permit," the old East German joke called the statue. "And that's who those two famous Russians were," a Westphalian next to us explains to his wife …
Renée Zucker, 1995

Dump Porter *Irina Liebmann*

The dump porter — the list of tenants — hangs in the main entrance hall on the ground floor next to the entrance to the stairwell. It was last filled in 1968 — handwritten in black ink, framed but not glassed. Every new tenant has the opportunity to put his name on the board, but only two people have actually stuck a lighter piece of paper with their name on it over that of their predecessor. The names on the list and the letter boxes have long since ceased to correspond with each other. But they have remained the same in their mixture, reading like a chronicle. The Krottkes, Behnkes and Dahlkes are always present. The "ke" ending results from combining a Low German and a Sorbian diminutive. The first people with this family name probably came to the city very early on from its northern or southeastern surroundings — possibly after the abolition of inherited subservience in 1807.

Raddatz and Retzlaff indicate the survival of some Polabic families from the original Slav settlement.

Polish names are the most striking. Since the middle of the last century, and since the completion of the Berlin-Stettin railway line (1843) in particular, masses of agricultural workers and proletarianized craftsmen poured into the city's new industries. This immigration from the eastern parts of Germany has never ceased since then, being reinvigorated by booms and slumps alike. The last two major waves

of immigration into Berlin occured after the Great Depression and after the Second World War. Centuries of immigration can also be read in the differing degrees of assimilation of names: Noack was originally Nowak, and has the same meaning as Neumann or Naumann in German; Gamroth was Gamrodski, virtually unrecognizable after the amputation of the Polish "ski"; Markowski and Kowalski, on the other hand, sound much more Polish; and there hasn't even been any attempt to Germanify Adamowicz and Kowalczyk. Kowalczyk originally meant blacksmith. People coming to Berlin with a skill they could use were often given the description of their job in German as a new surname, resulting in Schmied, Schmidt (or, depending on the official concerned, Schmitt, Schmitz, etc.), Kowalczyk, Kowalski, Kuhfahl, Kusniak or Lefevre, and they gave it on to their offsprings.

I was unable to find any trace of French names from the Hugenot immigration a couple of centuries ago, neither in this house nor in any of the neighboring ones. Maybe the district wasn't noble enough for them. I also could find no more Jewish names.

For decades now Berliners have been witnessing a new wave of immigration. For the first time the immigrants are coming from the south and, for the first time ever, it is not economic pressure which is driving them here. The Saxonians have less impressive names like Graf, Gentsch, Tietze or Voigt. However, someone born as a Gentsch might stand a better chance of becoming a married Lewandowski or a Toussaint in Berlin, quicker than anywhere else.

9.27.1996

In Spandauer Vorstadt, the traditional Jewish quarter in the Mitte district, a bronze sculpture by the Berlin sculptor Karl Biedermann — with a quote from a poem by Nelly Sachs — is dedicated on the newly redesigned Koppenplatz. It marks the new emergence of Jewish life in Berlin.

9.29.1996

At the 23rd Berlin Marathon, which takes 19,532 runners and 148 wheelchair riders from 70 countries straight across town, two newcomers cross the finish line as victors: Abel Anton from Spain and Colleen de Reuck from South Africa.

9.30.1996

In the first nine months of 1996, 4,899 new apartments were completed. Another 846 resulted from modernization work. The Treptow district claimed the most, with 735 apartments. The leader in western Berlin is the Steglitz district with 517.

10.1.1996

Wasmuth loses its lease: After 124 years of history, the art and architecture bookstore Wasmuth on Hardenbergstrasse in Charlottenburg is forced to close shop owing to high rent: DM 13,000 for 530 sq. m. Owner of the landmark-protected store (renovated 1956 by Werner Düttmann) is the Senate of Berlin.

10.1.1996

The first tenants move into a housing complex at Lindenstrasse 28–30 in Köpenick with 127 low-income housing units. Architects: Monika Krebs with Buddensieg/Ockert. Client: Otremba Unternehmensgruppe. Investment total: DM 50 mill.

10.1.1996

The municipal "Residential Building Company Town and Country" sells 700 housing units in the Kissingen quarter in Pankow to the "Bavaria Object and Building Maintenance Company."

10.1.1996

Large parts of the "Residential Park in Staaken" are ready for occupancy: 145 subsidized apartments in 14 buildings. Architects: Dirk-Werner Feige and Rainer Döring, Berlin. By mid-December another three urban villas should be finished in the old center, containing 13 privately financed apartments, office and commercial space. Architects: Kassel office ASP (Nolte, Plaßmann, Reese). Total floor space of the residential park is some 15,300 sq. m. Developer: Bauwert GmbH, Berlin/Munich.

10.2.1996

The German Cathedral (Deutscher Dom) on Gendarmenmarkt is reopened, after a twelve-year restoration, with the exhibit "Questions About German History," previously housed in the Reichstag building. Architects: Jürgen Pleuser and Volker Staab, Berlin. Just like the Französische Kirche, the Deutsche Kirche (1701–08, by Martin Grünberg) got its domed tower in the course of the public square's remodeling 1781–85. After the church was destroyed in the Second World War, work on rebuilding was not begun until 1984 (architect: Manfred Prasser). The steel-reinforced concrete structures completed then have been incorporated into the restoration. Because of a fire on October 24th, 1994, shortly before the project's scheduled end, the vestibule dome had to be partly torn down again.

October 1996

Briefing in the Europewide idea competition for the Federal Garden Show 2001 in Potsdam, from which not only a garden will emerge, but into which a multitude of projects long planned by the city will also be incorporated. The main grounds of the garden show will lie in the giant development region "Bornstedter Feld." On the 300 ha area north of the Sanssouci Schlosspark, used for centuries as military grounds, a new city district for about 18,000 residents will emerge over the next 10 to 15 years. The expansion of the Potsdam Technical College, the construction of 650 housing units as "Solarstadt Kirschallee," and a newly founded technology center are all parts of the ambitious planning concept. Responsible for realization is the Entwicklungsgesellschaft Bornstedter Feld.

10.2.1996

Topping-out ceremony for the Liebermann Haus on Pariser Platz. The new building on the site of the former residence of Max Liebermann is to become a cultural forum for exhibitions and conferences, following the conception of its future tenant, the Bankgesellschaft Berlin. Architect: Josef Paul Kleihues, Berlin. Client: Harald Quandt, Bad Homburg v.d.H. Cost: DM 25 mill.

When you get to the train station, the car drives first to the Leipziger Platz. There you should look to the right and you will see the Wertheim department store; it's the Wronker of Berlin, only much bigger. Then you drive … past the Tiergarten; it's called the Tiergarten even though there aren't any animals in it. It's a park in the middle of Berlin and is so large you could almost put all of Frankfurt in it. Then you go through a beautiful gate, and when you've gone through it you are on a square where there is the most beautiful hotel in Berlin; in the house next to the gate lives the best painter in Berlin, Max Liebermann. Then you drive the entire length of the street "Unter den Linden," the most beautiful street in the world … At the end of the street stands the monument to old Fritz, he was a king (before the emperor there was a king, and before that an Elector, and before that a margrave, just like in the fairy tale of the Fisherman and his Wife, and even the end is exactly the same). … And then you go across a bridge over the Spree and then past the palace to Grandpa and Grandma.
Franz Rosenzweig, 1929

10.3.–10.5.1996

"Idea versus Ideology": Ideas, ideologies, traditional and current views about design, extravagance, chaos, and order —all on the theme of script and typology—are on the agenda of "Typo Berlin 96," the second graphic design conference in the House of the World's Cultures. 30 of the most important typographers worldwide (Neville Brody, David Berlow, David Crow, Kurt Weidemann et. al.) take part in the event.

10.4.1996

Opening of "Kindl-Boulevard" in Neukölln. The name is a link to the over one hundred year history of the site: In 1874 a large beer garden emerged here, in 1927 what was then Europe's largest cinema was built on a section of available ground, and after severe damage toward the end of the war the movie theater was revived in the fifties. Woolworth moved into the landmark-protected building housing the former Kindl Halls

10.8.1996

Roof raising ceremony for five buildings in Köpenick. Four blocks with 128 housing units will be built at Wendenschlossstrasse 103–123, to be ready for occupancy in autumn 1997. Architects: Helga Schmidt-Thomsen and Paul Ziegert, Berlin. Construction cost: DM 40 mill. The fifth house with 33 housing unit at Ottomar-Geschke-Strasse 83–87 will be ready for occupancy in May 1997. Architect: Peter Möhle, Berlin. Cost: DM 11 mill. Client: Köpenicker Wohnungsbaugesellschaft.

October

10.3.1996

Berlin celebrates German Unity Day with a festive parade of the 16 federal states beginning at the Victory Column in the Tiergarten park, proceeding through the Brandenburg Gate, and continuing along the street Unter den Linden to the Rotes Rathaus (City Hall).

And how many friendships are now broken which were once so carefully cultivated in the old East Germany. No longer do I invite plumbers round for an afternoon-long chat over a pot of tea. Now I just cooly make an appointment for one to come round, he comes, hardly even looks at me, and carries out the repair. In the old days I had to cater for him lovingly, and it still wasn't certain he would actually come to carry out the repair. After we all started living in a free market economy, the number of practising workmen in the former East multiplied virtually over night—even though the birth rate has plummetted to new depths. But the old warm relationship between us is no more. I remain silent, no longer so grateful when one of them performs that integral part of repair work, the botched job. It's something which has only gotten a lot more expensive without getting any less frequent.

The collapse of this unconditional love for workmen ran parallel to that of the intimate friendships binding me with anyone who could provide me with things. Practical solidarity, along the lines of 'you provide me with tiles and I'll provide you with cabaret tickets,' has now been replaced by the cold relationship between goods and money. Even paying the rent has changed: now everyone pays who possibly can. In the Communist era, you only paid if you really wanted to. After all, the largest landlord was the state—THEM UP THERE. And it wasn't just dissenters and conscientious objectors who were opposed to them but also non-dissenters and rent-resisters.

My friend the alcoholic, together with the sober idler at work, helped the primacy of fraternal affection win out over economics. And if the economy hadn't collapsed then the love could have lasted forever.
Peter Ensikat, 1996

in 1994. The business center with over 42,000 sq. m of usable space— including a loading alley, a hotel with 216 beds, and an office building— takes up the entire block between Hermannstrasse, Rollbergstrasse, and Mainzer Strasse. The office tower on a star-shaped base rises in graduated steps to a height of ten floors. Architects: Winkler, Effinger, & Partners, Munich. Client: Bauwert. Cost: DM 400 mill.

10.6.1996

52 years after its destruction and 20 years after the start of restoration work, the completion of the St. Nikolai Kirche in Spandau is celebrated. The restoration of the building, which was officially mentioned for the first time around 1240 and has gone through several different phases of expansion and rebuilding, to which Schinkel also contributed, cost around DM 10 mill.

10.8.1996

Cornerstone laying for the Photonic Center on the Technology Park Berlin-Adlershof. Beginning in 1998, young technology firms from the fields of optics, optical electronics, and laser technology will occupy the 19,000 sq. m in an ensemble of three new and two old buildings. Architects: Sauerbruch and Hutton, Berlin (competition January 1995). Developer: Wista.

10.8.1996

Official opening of the "Four Seasons Hotel" in the building segment by Josef Paul Kleihues inside the "Hofgarten at Gendarmenmarkt." On eight floors with around 15,300 sq. m, the luxury hotel offers 204 rooms. Interior finishing in Miami Beach Baroque. Client: Hofgarten Real Estate B.V.; project developer: HINES Grundstücksentwicklungs GmbH, Berlin. Construction cost: DM 200 mill.

10.9.1996

Roof raising ceremony at Branitzer Platz in the city district center of Hellersdorf. 263 low-income housing units in the first construction segment should be finished by the end of 1997. Builder: Wohnungsbaugesellschaft Hellersdorf. Architects: Kny & Weber, Berlin. Construction cost: DM 130 mill.

10.10.1996

Founding of the sponsoring association for an "Allied Museum" in the former American soldier's cinema "Outpost" on Clayallee in Dahlem. In the exhibit "Every object tells a story" from 10.11. to 11.14.96, documents from the history of the once-divided city and the Western Allies are on display. On 6.24.98, the 50th anniversary of the Berlin blockade, the museum will have its definitive opening.

10.11.1996

Sushi and rice sacks, spring rolls and giant shrimp: Festival on Potsdamer Platz with a cornerstone laying for the Sony-Center modeled on Japanese ceremony. With the tapping of a keg of sake (kagami-wari) and ritual drumming, construction on the grounds begins 13 months after the groundbreaking on 9.8.95. With a 26-story glass office tower it will be the tallest house on Potsdamer Platz. In the year 2000 the entire complex — including Sony's European headquarters and film house (design by Helmut Jahn) will be completed.

10.13.1996

50 years ago today, Anja Bremer began creating her famous mixture of art gallery, conversation, and toast-a-glass-of-wine meeting place, initially in her own apartment, since 1955 more permanently at home in the Fasanenstrasse bar designed by Hans Scharoun. A jubilee exhibit there commemorates this starting point.

10.16.1996

Penultimate decision for Pariser Platz: Under direction from Max Bächer, the jury selects the design by the Viennese architects Ortner & Ortner for the northeastern corner of Pariser Platz. The proposal envisions a 6-story office and residential building for the 1,800 sq. m plot, including a total floor space of 9,000 sq. m. Prize sponsors were the Münchner Immobiliengesellschaft ABG (Munich real estate company) and the Bayrische Landesbank. They are planning to invest DM 100 mill. in the project. (2nd prize: Bétrix & Consolascio, Switzerland; no chance for: Helmut Maier, Head of the Society for Historical Berlin). Completion is scheduled for 1999.

10.16.1996

Two sporting goods stores of the department store giant Karstadt are opened: one in the remodeled former Bilka department store building at Kantstrasse/corner of Joachimstaler Strasse in Charlottenburg (the landmark-protected building from 1952 was built by architect Hanns Dustmann, who also designed the Victoria-Areal and the Café Kranzler), the other in Quartier 205 (architect: O.M. Ungers) on Friedrichstrasse.

10.16.1996

Exhibition opening for "The Design of Public Squares" in the DAZ German Architecture Center Berlin. Through November 23rd, outstanding concepts (both completed and planned) for public squares are on display.

1996   **October**

10.9.1996

At Berlin's largest traffic bottleneck, the entrance of the city freeway between Schöneberger Kreuz and Alboinstrasse, traffic is finally flowing without hindrance. Berlin's automobilists have waited 24 years for the opening of the 1.9 km long section.

10.9.1996

Roof raising ceremony for the company startup center "Phoenix," on part of the Borsig grounds at Berliner Strasse 27 in Tegel. There, at the beginning of the new year, around 10,000 sq. m will become available for offices, manufacturing, and service. Construction start was in September 1995. Investment cost: DM 28 mill., more than two thirds of which coming from Berlin's Economics Senate. Architect: Walter Rolfes, Berlin; developer: Herlitz Falkenhöh AG.

10.10.1996

Roof raising ceremony for a "Print Media Center" in the industrial district Plauener Strasse in Hohenschönhausen. When Europe's most modern printing machinery begins to roll at the start of 1997, the entire capital city edition of the "taz" (short for "tageszeitung" — the Berlin-based alternative daily) can be printed within a half hour. Owing to environmentally friendly technologies for the machinery as well as for the building, the enterprise is being promoted with subsidies from both the city Senate and the European Union. Architects: Heiken & Partners, Frankfort/Main. Client: Henke Pressedruck. Cost: DM 30 mill.

10.12.1996

The Archenhold Observatory in Treptow celebrates its 100-year jubilee. Lucky star of the hour: Just in time for the anniversary, the firmament, while under observation, arranges for a partial solar eclipse in celebration. The giant telescope with a length of 21 m was built for the Berlin Industrial Exhibition of 1896, while the building for the Astronomical Museum goes back to the year 1909.

10.13.1996

Flashes of chrome in front of the Olympic Stadium: 5,000 bikers meet up with their companions for a memorial tour on behalf of accident victims from the year gone by, leading from the Olympic Stadium through the city to the Hedwigs Cathedral, where a mass is held.

10.15.–10.18.1996

With "Inno Trans '96," the international professional convention for transportation technology, Berlin presents itself as leader in the field of rail transit. In the convention center and on the grounds of the Wilmersdorf freight train station, new developments in rail, signal, and communication technology by 171 exhibitors from 13 countries are presented. The BVG (Berlin' transport authority) is there presenting its Super-Subway-Train, which — unusually rapid and accessible throughout — is to be built starting 1997.

10.13.1996

90 years ago today: Wilhelm Voigt, by trade a shoemaker, thief, and con artist, exploits the submissive spirit of the time to launch an assault on the Köpenick municipal treasury and arrest the mayor. The event with all its refinements is replayed on its anniversary, although the treasury to be confiscated is empty. A life-sized bronze statue of the self-appointed captain by the artist Spartak Babajan is unveiled in front of Köpenick city hall, cost DM 62,000.

10.16.1996

The largest Israeli Bank "Hapoalim" opens a branch in the Europa-Center. For the first time, an Israeli credit institute is represented in Berlin.

10.16.–10.24.1996

Ars-Digitalis — the media project of Berlin's Hochschule der Künste (Arts College) is commemorating the 300-year anniversary of the Akademie der Künste (Academy of the Arts). With a media competition (prize total DM 50,000), the call went out to submit picture-and-sound sequences for projection onto Berlin architecture. However the opening preview presenting a few selected contributions, projected onto the glass facade of the Peek & Cloppenburg department store on Tauentzien, turned into a view of "virtually nothing" (taz), i.e., there was hardly anything to see. The project director was Jeannot Simmen, the sponsor Vebacom, Dusseldorf. At the award ceremony on 10.24, the Golden ADA (Ars Digitalis Award) was given to the Polish video artist Jacek Szleszynski for his work "In Progress."

10.17.1996

On top of the "Grande Arche" in Paris, German President Roman Herzog opens the exhibit "Berlin —Une capitale en perspectives." A multimedia show and over 150 exhibit pieces (urban and architectural models) on 1,200 sq. m present the future visage of the city. The Berlin show, sponsored by the federal government, Berlin city Senate, the Goethe-Institut, and Partners for Berlin, cost more than a mill. DM. The exhibit stays in Paris until January 1997, and goes on to London, Moscow, New York, Seoul, Tokyo, and Singapore afterwards. Exhibition concept: Wolfgang Schäche and Gerhard Spangenberg.

10.18.1996

Friedrich Hollaender, pianist, conductor, stage and film director, melody inventor, poet, novelist, "exilant," music-hall performer, unrecognized returnee, actor in "One, Two, Three" would be 100 years old today. In his honor the Akademie der Künste (Academy of the Arts) puts on an exhibit and a series of events on the theme "Friedrich Hollaender and the Cabaret of the Twenties."

10.18.1996

First roof-raising ceremony in the "Office Center Treptower Ufer." On around 10,000 sq. m of the 120,000 sq. m large grounds of the former Elektro-Apparate-Werke EAW on Eichenstrasse in Treptow, the "Treptowers" will be erected for the Allianz insurance company, together with two six-story "squares" for Walter Bau AG. The third building segment will be started with the construction of 900 housing units early in 1997.

10.19.1996

The Theater des Westens celebrates its 100th birthday with a big festival. The magnificent building on Kantstrasse in Charlottenburg, built 1895–96 by Bernhard Sehring, looks back on a colorful past. Famous since the sixties for musicals like "My Fair Lady," the theater in its opening years had a program that included serious theatrical and operatic productions, too, or guest appearances by Richard Tauber and Maria Callas.

10.22.1996

"Solar-Infopunkt" opened on Kurfürstenstrasse in the Tiergarten district. The employees of this office, which is run by the Federation for the Environment and Nature Conservation and the Federation of Energy Consumers, advises on all questions having anything to do with the utilization of solar energy.

10.23.1996

The "Hufeisensiedlung" (literally, "Horseshoe Settlement") by Bruno Taut and Martin Wagner celebrates its 70th birthday. The GEHAG housing estate (built 1926) on Fritz-Reuter-Allee in Britz, with its programmatic commitment to creating cheap and healthy living quarters on the city's greenbelt for the industrial workers of Neukölln, counts as one of the outstanding examples of large housing colonies in the Berlin of the Weimar Republic.

10.23.1996

"Hard Core City Berlin"— exhibition opening in the "designtransfer:galerie." 12 student works show urban design visions for Berlin that—as counterdesigns to current thinking in terms of block structures and facades— endeavor to preserve the city as a collection of individual and noninterchangeable places (= "hard cores").

10.24.1996

Roof-raising ceremony in the "Flusspferdhof-Siedlung" (literally, "Hippopotamus Settlement") in Hohenschönhausen. 643 out of 867 housing units between Grosse-Leege-Strasse and Goeckestrasse have been renovated, the remaining housing units should be completed by 1997. The residential area, which was built between 1931 and 1934 in the tradition of Bruno Taut, got its name from the "Zwei Pferde im Fluss" ("Two Horses in the Water") that the sculptor Hans Mettel created for the fountain in the courtyard. Just across from this housing estate—and likewise commissioned by GEWOBAG—a building complex with 120 housing units is going up that is also celebrating a roof-raising today.

October

10.17.1996

Opening of the shopping center "Springfuhlpassage" on Helene-Weigel-Platz in Marzahn. On around 3,000 sq. m a bank, a fitness center, and 14 smaller shops have been established. Architects: Dreß & Wucherpfennig, Berlin. Developer: Wohnungsbaugesellschaft Marzahn. Construction cost: around DM 16 mill.

10.18.1996

The "Peter Joseph Lenné Prize" of the state of Berlin is given to architecture students Lars Peter Dierke, Tobias Gammelin, and Karl Stammnitz for their visions of Tempelhofer Feld. The young talent contest for architects and landscape planners—a pure idea competition—has been sponsored since 1965. More than 228 entries were sent in.

Architects: Kieferle and Partners, Stuttgart. Project developer: Unternehmensgruppe Roland Ernst. Total investment: approx. DM 1.5 billion.

10.18.1996

The Gründerzentrum (Company Startup Center) on Pankstrasse in Pankow is opened after a two-year construction period. The building complex in the district neighborhood of Buchholz puts 5,000 sq. m at the disposal of new company founders. The Gründerzentrum is one part of a business center, comprising a total of eight buildings, that will be finished by the end of 1996 and will house around 110 firms on 34,500 sq. m. The city of Berlin's Economic Administration has a DM 101 mill. share in the construction cost amounting to DM 112 mill. Architects: Heider, Kürten, and Langwagen, Berlin. Client: Gewerbesiedlungs-Gesellschaft, Berlin.

10.21.1996

The modernization of the heating plant Mitte is nearly finished, in spring 1997 final adjustments will be done. BEWAG (Berlin Electricity Company) had to choose a costly "just-in-time"-procedure, keeping the old facilities working while the new ones were installed and tested. The turbine-driven gas generator plant was build 1961–64 by the architect's collective Dietrich Zimbel; architects for the modernization: Jochem Jourdan and Bernhard Müller, Frankfort/M. The facility will be embedded in a park-like surrounding with an artistic note: a brick tower that can be climbed and a wall with lots of corners by Per Kirkeby/Denmark, several steel tube benches heated long-distance from the energy plant by Ayse Erkmen/Turkey, and a water pavilion by Dan Graham/USA. Costs: About DM 600 mill. for the new building and around DM 2.5 mill. for the building's artwork.

10.23.1996

Cornerstone laying for Quartier 201 A at Friedrichstrasse 50-55. Architects: Ulrike Lauber and Wolfram Wöhr, Munich. Project developer: CEDC.

10.23.–10.25.1996

The 13th Logistics Convention meets under the theme "Global Trend" in Berlin's Hotel Inter Continental. The program includes lectures from more than 90 speakers, the awarding of the "German Logistics Prize," and an exhibition.

10.23.1996

A development plan is resolved for the shopping center in the commercial park "Am Borsigturm" in Berlin-Tegel. According to plans by Claude Vasconi, Paris, who, together with Dagmar Groß, also developed the urban design concept for the overall facility, a retail trade center with around 22,000 sq. m of floorspace will be integrated into five old factory halls on the former Borsig company grounds. 120 shops and a cinema multiplex will take up occupancy in autumn of 1998. Cost: DM 500 mill. Project developer: Herlitz Falkenhöh AG.

10.24.1996

A new clock for Berlin: the debt clock in front of the Rotes Rathaus ticks at a speed of DM 193 per second and admonishes—should the pedagogical intention of the Federation of German Taxpayers work out—on behalf of radical savings throughout the public sector.

10.25.1996

The Federation of German Landscape Architects (1,600 members) has officially moved its seat from the Rhine to Berlin. The federal headquarters are now located in the German Architecture Center on Köpenicker Strasse in Mitte district.

10.25.1996

"The cornerstone for the Internal Revenue Office on Joseph-Orlopp-Strasse 58–64 was laid yesterday in the second upper story." (Morgenpost, 10.26.96) Delays in the approval procedure had led to this belated ceremony. Under construction since July 1996, the building with a usable space of 10,000 sq. m is scheduled for occupancy by the end of June 1997. Architects: Axel Liepe, Hartmut Steigelmann, Berlin. Project developer: Trigon Unternehmensgruppe. Investment total: DM 40 mill.

10.26.1996

100 tons of artificial snow along with 50 tons of steel and 15 tons of wood turn Potsdamer Platz into a snowy Swiss landscape. It offers sixteen of the world's best snowboard surfers from eight countries the chance to have a jumping contest in the midst of a total multivision spectacular. Sponsor of "Ballantine's Urban High" is the whiskey brand lending its name.

10.26.1996

First topping-out ceremony on Potsdamer Platz. With a confetti parade, the Golden Gospel Singers, and Daniel Barenboim, who directs

10.28.1996

Anarchic Happening on Potsdamer Platz: There Christoph Schlingensief is shooting his new film "The 120 Days of Bottrop."

10.30.1996

Roof raising ceremony at the "Wilhelmgalerie" in downtown Potsdam. Between Charlottenstrasse, Friedrich-Ebert-Strasse, and Platz der Einheit, a commercial building housing the headquarters of the Deutsche Bank, offices, and retail stores will fill up an entire city block. Architects: Krüger, Schubert, Vandreike, Berlin (competition 1993). Project developer: Deutsche Immobilien Anlagegesellschaft. Cost: DM 120 mill.

10.30.1996

Eleanor Dulles dies at the age of 101. As the official in charge of the Berlin desk at the U.S. State Department in the post-war years, she helped to keep the western part of the city

10.30.1996

Celebration in the festival hall of the Staatsbibliothek Unter den Linden on the occasion of the return of around 100,000 valuable books taken from the state library to Georgia as Soviet plunder. Early in 1997 the precious objects will go home to their original places in different German libraries.

10.30.1996

Opening of an exhibition devoted to political monuments and emblems of the GDR. In the rooms of the gallery Arndt & Partners, French artist Sophie Calle exhibits what she compiled over two years of research: photographed traces of removed emblems and monuments and narrated reminiscences of passers-by and residents, reconstructing and rediscovering what has disappeared. What should and will remain, according to demand, is the little traffic light man as he walks and stands. Working on behalf of his preservation are Jörg Davids and the ultimate committee of sympathizers "Rescue the Little Traffic Light Man."

10.25.1996

Roof-raising ceremony in the "Plaza Marzahn." The residential and business center will grow on Mehrower Allee in Marzahn. The opening for the building, in which commercial space and 50 shops on 8,000 sq. m as well as 110 housing units will be located, is scheduled for February 6th, 1997 after about a year's construction time. Architects: Baasner, Möller & Langwald, Berlin. Developer: Gädecke & Landsberg. Cost: DM 80 mill.

10.25.1996

Roof-raising ceremony in a row of houses with residential and office use at Alte Jakobstrasse 76–80 in Mitte. Completion of the 12,000 sq. m of office and shop space and of the 249 housing units is planned for February 1997. Architects: Planungs AG für Bauwesen, Cologne (Neufert, Mittmann + Graf). Client: Concordia Bau und Boden AG, Cologne. Construction cost: DM 169 mill.

the "Ballet of the Cranes," the construction workers' festival is celebrated—almost two years to the day after the cornerstone laying on 10.29.94. Representing the 19 construction projects of debis on Potsdamer Platz, building crowns are placed on the multi-story buildings of Renzo Piano and Arata Isozaki.

10.27.1996

Only now, so the press is reporting, have 3,000 large-format drawings and sketches of Berlin's Stadtschloss been discovered in the map chamber of the Neues Palais in Potsdam. Two years ago they arrived, unsorted, from Merseburg. The Promotional Committee Berliner Stadtschloss has now gotten them microfilmed for a five-figure sum. These drawings, a building record from the mid-19th century, were made when the Stadtschloss threatened to collapse—what it did not—due to poor foundations. The plans make the recontruction of the palace theoretically possible.

10.28.1996

New city square in Marzahn. Four years after the start of planning and a year and a half after the beginning of construction, "Barnim-Platz" on Havemannstrasse is completed. The 6,800 sq. m grounds consist of a sunken lawn with a water basin and 61 trees. Landscape architect: Heike Langenbach, Berlin. Cost: DM 4.5 mill.

alive behind the Iron Curtain. In America she collected more than a billion dollars for Berlin. The reforestation of the Tiergarten, the building of the Kongresshalle, the clinic in Steglitz, and the Siegmundshof student dormitory all go back to her initiative. In 1990, eager to see a Berlin without a Wall, she celebrated her 95th birthday in the city.

10.31.1996

Roof-raising ceremony for the "Prisma-Haus" on the Platz vor dem Neuen Tor in the Mitte district. The office and residential complex with 4,500 sq. m of office space, 1,500 sq. m of shop space, and 34 housing units, plans by architect Josef Paul Kleihues, will be completed in 1997. Builder: Bayerische Hausbau. Cost: around DM 75 mill.

10.31.–11.4.1996

On the occasion of the opening of the Hamburger Bahnhof, the federation "European Galleries" sponsors an art fair in Berlin—both modeled after and in competition with Art Cologne fair—under the name "European Art Forum Berlin" with the participation of over 100 international galleries. The exhibition site is at the trade fair halls near the radio tower.

November 1996

The construction start, scheduled for 1996, of a gigantic new building complex at Bahnhof Potsdam Stadt triggers vehement protests. The "Potsdam-Center" is supposed to be built on an 88,000 sq. m large property with overall floorspace of 190,000 sq. m (hotel and convention center, shops, offices, restaurants, cinema multiplex). Investors: Deutsche Bahn AG, Landesentwicklungsgesellschaft, and Roland Ernst Group. The project is so controversial—not only in Potsdam and Berlin—that Unesco is threatening to deprive Potsdam of the distinction it only just received in 1991 on Unesco's "World Cultural Heritage" list.

11.2.1996

With the exhibition "Files," which displays the works of 20 young artists on around 600 sq. m, the gallery "Bunker 4th floor" opens its rooms in the landmark-protected Techo-Bunker in the Mitte district.

11.3.1996

The Museum for Contemporary Art opens in the former Hamburger Bahnhof on Invalidenstrasse. Exhibited on permanent loan is the "Marx Collection" left to the Stiftung Preussischer Kulturbesitz (Prussian Cultural Foundation), supplemented by pieces from the Neue Nationalgalerie, Kunstbibliothek (Art Library), Kunstgewerbemuseum (Arts and Crafts Museum), and Kupferstichkabinett (Engraving Cabinet). The design for remodeling and expansion by Josef Paul Kleihues foresaw two Grand Galleries, of which only the eastern one could be realized for the time being.

11.5.1996

In the new building region Altglienicke in the Treptow district, a roof-raising ceremony for the second building segment is celebrated. The project foresees an urban redevelopment integrating the old town center, existing single-family houses and prefab apartment blocks, which were started in the last years of East Germany, but never completed. 2,433 housing units are planned for the new garden city. From four residential areas, the first contains 587 apartments, rented as of January 1996. In the second section, 971 subsidized apartments will be ready for occupancy by January 1997. The third section includes 550 housing units, and is due for completion at the end of 1997, while the fourth, with 320 units, is near completion. Client: Stadt und Land Wohnbauten GmbH, Berlin. Cost: DM 932 mill.

11.7.1996

The Architecture Prize of the Federation of German Architects (BDA) in Berlin is awarded. Decorated with the first prize is the Spruch residential settlement in Buckow by Wolfgang Engel and Klaus Zillich. Also recognized: Hannelore Deubzer and Jürgen König (development of the western side of the Virchow clinic grounds); Rebecca Chestnutt and Robert Niess (library on Luisenbad in Wedding); Petra and Paul Kahlfeldt (Engelhardt-Hof in Charlottenburg); Perpetua Rausch, Heinz Willems (residential development Emstaler Platz in Tegel), Till Schneider and Michael Schumacher (Info-Box on Leipziger Platz). The BDA also awarded the Hans Schaefers Prize for young architects, endowed with DM 10,000, to the offices of Armand Grüntuch & Almut Grüntuch-Ernst (southern bridge Wasserstadt Oberhavel) and

11.7.1996

Today the three-year construction work on the Hackesche Höfe officially comes to an end. The residential and business courtyard facility built in 1906 on the Hackescher Markt between Rosenthaler Strasse and Sophienstrasse in the Mitte district was kept preserved as a result of landmark conservation stipulations having to do with its historic mixture of housing, business, commerce, and art. The Jugendstil facade in the first of the eight courtyards by August Endell was faithfully restored. All in all, DM 100 mill. paid for renovating 80 housing units, 65 commercial units, and 23 penthouse apartments. Varieté and cinema, bookstore and gallery, café and restaurant, designer shops and courtyards with greenery form a colorful mixture attracting tourists and native Berliners. Architect: Stefan Weiß & Partners, Berlin. Clients: Roland Ernst and Rainer Behne.

November 1996

Groundbreaking for a new building complex "Forum Landsberger Allee" on the corner of Landsberger Allee and Storkower Strasse in Friedrichshain. By April 1998 there will be offices, shops, and a hotel on around 26,500 sq. m in the DM 250 mill. project. Architect: RKW, Dusseldorf. Developer: Bauwert GmbH.

11.1.1996

On the 50th anniversary of its founding, the Weissensee Art College shows excerpts from its history in two exhibitions through November 22nd. A photo show traces the careers of former students, the second exhibition is devoted to the Dutch architect Mart Stam (1899–1986), who was head of the College 1950–52 but then left the German Democratic Republic at the end of 1952. Currently at Weissensee there are 580 students enrolled in the departments of architecture, set design, sculpture, painting, textile design, and general design; at the moment, a merger of the College with the HdK in Charlottenburg is no longer being discussed.

11.1.1996

Award presentation: To honor him for his artistic lifework, the American fluxus artist and Berlin resident Emmett Williams (b. 1925) receives the Hannah Höch Prize, newly established by the Senate Cultural Department for promoting artists.

11.4.1996

In the new building region Karow-Nord, the second day-care center is opened. The building on Pfannschmidtstrasse for around 100 children was developed after a design by the Berlin architect Carola Schäfers on a commission from the Senate Building Department. Cost: approx. DM 6.5 mill. Two other "Kitas" in Karow-Nord are to be completed in the next few months.

11.4.1996

In the future residential quarter "Landsberger Tor" in Marzahn, groundbreaking marks the start of construction of around 1,600 housing units for a senior center (corner of Landsberger Allee and Blumberger Damm). On an area of 54 ha, a total of ten buildings with 20,000 sq. m usable space (including two day-care centers, one youth and one senior recreation center, and sports facilities) will be erected by the end of 1997. The Nürnberger Versicherung insurance company has invested a total of around DM 1.1 billion in the facility, DM 80 mill. in the senior center.

11.7.1996

Vaclav Havel and other guests from Brussels, Budapest, Poland, and Germany discuss the theme "Mitteleuropa" ("Central Europe") in the Prussian Parliament building.

11.7.1996

After a careful three-year restoration, it finally became possible—if only the surrounding space could also have been restored—for Berlin's only cinema house organ, still at its original place at Cinema Babylon, to sound its refined special effects. However, the renovation of the motion picture theater, dangerously near collapse, on Rosa-Luxemburg-Platz (built 1929 by Hans Poelzig) is stagnating because of an unsettled restitution suit.

Stephan Höhne & Christian Rapp (daycare center in Karow-Nord). All 56 of the works submitted are on exhibit at the German Architecture Center.

11.7.1996

Decision in the competition for a new building to replace the Catholic Canisius-Kirche on Witzlebenstrasse in Charlottenburg, which burned down in April 1995. The first prize goes to Helga Schmidt-Thomsen & Paul Ziegert, Berlin. 2nd prize Edgar Wisniewski, Berlin; 3rd prize office Büttner—Braun—Neumann, Berlin. For the new building with 350 seats, senior residential facility, daycare center, and parish hall, construction should begin in the summer of 1997. More than DM 10 mill. is available from fire insurance.

11.7.1996

In the Gropius-Passagen on the Johannisthaler Chaussee in Neukölln, Berlin's largest shopping center will be built. On the occasion of the first and most important building segment's completion, the investor, the Munich-based H.F.S: Immobilienfonds GmbH, celebrates an opening ceremony. Out of a total of 60,000 sq. m, 40,000 sq. m are already occupied with 85 businesses. Total cost: approx. DM 400 mill.

11.8.1996

Ceremonious cornerstone laying for the "Park-Kolonnaden," the third major construction project on Potsdamer Platz. On an area of some 16,500 sq. m, several buildings with an overall floorspace of about 76,000 sq. m will rise up along Köthener Strasse. Architects: Giorgio Grassi, Schweger & Partners, Diener & Diener, Jürgen Sawade. Investor: Projektgemeinschaft A+T (ABB Asea Brown Boveri/ Terreno/Unternehmensgruppe Roland Ernst). Investment cost: approx. DM 500 mill. The design envisions a twelve-story semicircular head building and four 6–8-story

11.9.1996

After a 16-month construction period, the first building segment in the landmark-protected industry ensemble on Wilhelminenhofstrasse in Oberschöneweide is completed. The artisan and business center in "Wilhelminenhof" makes 25,000 sq. m of commercial space available in the former factory facilities for diverse users. Sensational rental price: DM 12.50/sq. m. Owing to the required restoration of the grounds, the installation and modernization of the buildings, which were built around 1900 as the automobile factory of AEG, were especially costly. Client: Berliner Landesentwicklungsgesellschaft BLEG. Architect: Ulrich Wolff, Berlin.

11.13.1996

Online for architects: Federal Building Minister Klaus Töpfer gives the starting signal for the Architects Online-Service "BauNetz" with offices in Berlin. The occasion for this online service was the professional convention ACS in Frankfort. At the web address "http:// www.BauNetz.de", architects and planners can receive up-to-date information all about building: products and regulations, competitions and deadlines, along with news reports from the architecture scene. As the

11.14.1996

With the exhibit "Building 1995" and its yearbook "LFW 1996" the Landesverband Freier Wohnungsunternehmen Berlin/Brandenburg e.V. (Federation of Independent Housing Enterprises in Berlin and Brandenburg) uses its annual press conference to present over 100 construction projects by its 260 members. The total number of projects finished in the year 1995 by the building developers, who designate themselves as medium-sized and small businesses, accounts for an investment volume of DM 4.5 billion. For the year 1996 the Federation reckons with 16,800 newly built residential units — more than half of them in Berlin — and around 570,000 sq. m of commercial space.

11.14.1996

The 260 m long underground shopping mile of FriedrichstadtPassagen, which connects Quarters 205, 206, and 207, is officially opened, even though not all the shops have been rented out. For the atrium of the Unger building, American artist John Chamberlain has fashioned the 11 m high "Tower of Klythie" out of colorful compressed junked auto chassis.

U- and H-shaped buildings in adjoining rows, joined together by a trail of green. Originally 70% of floor space was intended for offices (approx. 2,000 work places), 20% for apartments (90 units) and 10% for retail use. Because of the surfeit of office space in Berlin, the developer converted the head building on the Leipziger Strasse into a 1,000 bed hotel with conference center.

11.11.1996

Two inner city rapid stations reopened: Trains on the Zoologischer Garten – Lehrter Bahnhof route are stopping again at the Tiergarten and Bellevue stations after a two-year construction period. Since October 1994 they had been closed owing to renovation of the urban rapid transit viaduct.

11.12.–11.24.1996

Under the motto "Daydreams in Berlin and Elsewhere," Jewish Cultural Week is celebrated for the 10th time with around 50 events (readings, klezmer concerts, film viewings, and for the first time now a theater production: "What's new from the war?"). In the Centrum Judaicum on Oranienburger Strasse on 11.15, the exhibition "Heritage and Mission" (through March 1997) is opened. It tells the 325-year history of the — once and now again — largest Jewish community in Germany.

online service of Bertelsmann Fachinformation, BauNetz is simultaneously an open platform for all important suppliers of information in the construction industry. Its partners include the German Standardization Institute (Deutsches Institut für Normung, author of DIN standards, and its publisher Beuth-Verlag), the German Federation of Architects, and the German Architecture Center, as well as the professional journals Arch+, Bauwelt, and DBZ.

11.13.1996

A memorial stone for Mete Eksi is unveiled on Adenauerplatz. During a violent quarrel among juvenile Berliners on this public square, at the end of October 1991, this Berliner of Turkish descent was beaten up and died two weeks later as a result of the severe wounds inflicted on him.

11.13.1996

The former Volkskaffeehaus on Chausseestrasse 105 in the Mitte district, built 1892 by Alfred Messel in the neo-Renaissance style, has been reconstructed according to the original plans of the architect after a 19-month construction period. The house accommodates 35 rental apartments along with office units and businesses. Client: Gunter Brütt, Hamburg. Architect Gerhard Hoya, Berlin.

11.14.1996

On the grounds of the former stock exchange along the banks of the Spree river in the Mitte district, archaeologists at the construction site for a new office and commercial building have dug up a spectacular find: foundations, pillars, architraves, and ornamental fragments from the stock exchange building torn down in 1958 (and originally built 1859–63 by Friedrich Hitzig) testify to the former splendor of this neo-Renaissance building. But even the foundations of its predecessor, the Itzig palace erected around 1728, were discovered. The new building for the Deutsche Sparkassen Immobilien Gesellschaft (German Savings Banks Real Estate Company) will now have to wait for as long as it takes to document and secure all the archaeological finds.

11.14.1996

Opening of the "Kaufcenter" on Berliner Allee in Weissensee. Barely 2,000 sq. m of shopping space are available; the two upper floors in the three-story building accommodate offices. Architect: Volker Kirsch, Berlin. Building developer: J.F. Müller & Partners, Hamburg. Cost: DM 17.5 mill.

11.14.1996

Cornerstone laid for the new building housing the Federal Presidential Office. The building next to Bellevue Palace is supposed to be finished by July 1998. The four-story oval administration building after a design by the Frankfort architects Helmut Kleine-Kraneburg and Martin Gruber will accommodate 120 offices with 9,500 sq. m of office floorspace. Cost: DM 91 mill.

11.15.1996

The alternative cultural center "Tacheles" on Oranienberger Strasse has been tentatively saved. The forced evacuation threatening an end to the coffeehouse-among-the-ruins has been canceled after week-long negotiations among the owners of the property, the Berlin Senior Finance Management, the potential investor Fundus, and the people running the Tacheles enterprises. A definitive settlement, however, is still pending. For the entire grounds on the area bounded by Oranienburger Strasse, Tucholskystrasse, Johannisstrasse, and Friedrichstrasse, an

11.15.1996

375 documents, files, pictures, and sculptures from the estate of Willy Brandt arrived in Berlin from Bonn. As of December 8th they can be seen in a permanent exhibition in Rathaus Schöneberg.

11.15.1996

Official opening of the City-Carré on Koppen-strasse at the Haupt-bahnhof. The chief tenant with 35,000 sq. m out of a total of 36,000 sq. m of office space is the Berlin headquarters of the Dresdner Bank. The re-maining space is divided into 25 shops and a hotel in the old side wing. Architects: Fischer + Fischer, Cologne/Berlin. Project developer: Philipp Holzmann AG/ Köllmann, cost: DM 450 mill.

11.16.1996

Construction start for the new bridge over the Landwehrkanal at the height of the debis high rise. The link from the Reichpietschufer to the Schöneberger Ufer will become part of the road tunnel project that is going to stretch 2.7 km from here to the Lehrter railroad station. There are plans for an arched bridge weighing 1.140 tons, with a length of 30 m and width of 25 m, the shell of which is meant to be finished by the end of 1997. Total cost: approx. DM 13 mill. Architects: von Gerkan, Marg & Partner.

11.20.1996

Presentation of the design for a luxury senior citizens' residence with 60 maisonette apart-ments near Pariser Platz. Gustav Peichl, Vienna, first prize-winner in the realization competition briefed by the Senate Building Department, presents a nine-story residential and commer-cial house with two sep-arate entrances on the corner of Behrenstrasse and Wilhelmstrasse. Estimated cost: approx. DM 80 mill. Client: Prinz zu Hohenlohe & Bang-hard.

11.21.1996

Major construction site Reichstag: in the gutted middle section, where the plenary hall used to be, "deconstruction" has come to an end. The twelve supporting pillars for the dome will now be put in place. Until the roof is mounted, the sup-ports will be provisional-ly secured by steel cuffs. The heavy glass dome does not rest directly on these supports, but rather on auxiliary con-crete girders. The mount-ing of the dome begins in April 1997.

November

urban development strat-egy had been submitted in June 1996 by Toni Sachs Pfeiffer. It envisions the 23,560 sq. m large prop-erty being developed in small sections with 40 buildings, of which the residential share should be set at 50%. An unusu-al feature: in the block's interior there could emerge a public square. The landmark-protected Tacheles building could be structurally secured and integrated into the project as an art house. It is precisely against this point that protests have been directed by the current occupants, who fear for their autonomy and the wildly romantic demolition atmosphere of this cultural ruin.

11.15.1996

The Berlin city Senate has now approved the necessary funds for a new building to house the documentation center "Topography of Terror," so that it can — as planned — be opened November 9th, 1998. In the course of the austeri-ty debates about Berlin's state budget, a delay in the construction project had been under consider-ation. Vehement protests from the press brought about a reconsideration. Call for donations: Sym-bolic stones (actually, signed drawings by archi-tect Peter Zumthor) could be acquired for the price of DM 100.

11.16.1996

Exactly twenty years ago, on November 16th, 1976, Wolf Biermann was deprived of his citizen-ship by the GDR during a guest appearance in the West. Prominent GDR artists protested at the time, and the "Biermann Case"—the retrospective now tells us—was the beginning of the end for the GDR. The press, radio, and television commem-orate this event with bio-graphical flashbacks, discussions with historic witnesses, and playback from the legendary Cologne concert. Back then, Biermann had just celebrated his fortieth birthday, and today it is already his sixtieth.

11.19.1996

A new market attraction near the subway and rapid transit station Schönhauser Allee in the Prenzlauer Berg district: A 3 m wide and 65 m long "shopping tube" provides space for 28 sales stands. Architects: Architekturw-erk GmbH, Berlin. Client: Kühnwerk GbR. Cost: approx. DM 450,000.

11.21.1996

Construction start for the first building phase in the development region Biesdorf-Süd. BauGrund AG will erect housing units, schools, recreational facilities, daycare centers, and sporting grounds on a 142 ha area. Urban design planning: Bernd Albers.

11.28.1996

Outcome of the urban design competition for Stuttgarter Platz in Charlottenburg. Recipient of the first prize is the planning by Bernd Albers, Berlin, who envisions a 15-story tower house on the corner of Kaiser-Friedrich-Strasse. This is where there is supposed to be space for the entrance area to the Charlottenburg regional train station, and for a hotel and offices. A city square north of the train tracks, a park, a market square, and a transfer of the rapid transit station in the direction of the underground station are all part of the design concept. Investors for the project have not yet been found. Sponsor of the competition brief: Deutsche Bahn AG.

11.29.1996

Presentation of the "Planwerk Innenstadt"—a masterplan proposal for Berlin in the Stadtforum. City Development Senator Peter Strieder and his State Secretary Hans Stimmann have commissioned a comprehensive plan for downtown Berlin. Two teams of planners came up with ideas. For the City-East: Bernd Albers and Dieter Hoffmann-Axthelm, for the City-West: Fritz Neumeyer and Manfred Ortner. The plan is supposed to get a process of development for the next 30 years underway. Guidelines: resumption of the city's historic outline, condensation, rigorous liberation from postwar urban design. The plan as well as the planning procedure are vehemently criticized from all sides.

12.1.1996

The first construction phase of the residential development "Wasserstadt Aalemannufer" in north Spandau is completed. After two years of construction 145 state subsidized apartments in nine buildings are ready for tenants. Architects are the two Berlin firms Martin + Pächter and Feige + Döring. The second phase of construction includes 87 apartments in four buildings and is due for completion within

12.5.1996

The foundation stone is laid for the ARD Media Center on the corner of Wilhelmstrasse and Reichstagsufer near the Reichstag. Starting in 1999 all eleven state broadcasting services will be transmitting from the "Capital Studio Berlin" (Hauptstadt Studio Berlin). The structure offers some 5,000 sq. m of floor space for around 160 employees, including 60 journalists reporting for 51 radio stations, as well as for the public networks first and third channel, and for 3sat and Arte. Chief clients are the SFB and WDR broadcasting networks. Architects are Ortner and Ortner, Berlin.

12.9.1996

Completion and official presentation of the Halensee Office Building along the Berlin city motorway in the Wilmersdorf district. The building is protected from noise pollution by a double-layered glass facade,

12.10.1996

Official presentation of new plans for the Lustgarten. Initial plans by Gerhard Merz, chosen in 1994, met with widespread public protest. A second competition was won by the landscape architect Gustav Lange. The structural elements of his design include rows of trees, two water basins along the central axis from the Altes Museum, and an opening out onto Schlossplatz. Starting in 1997, tubs of plants will be set on the historic plaza of the Altes Museum, whose stone floor dates from 1935. The project will cost some DM 10 mill.

11.22.1996

With a festive concert by the Schöneberg Symphony Orchestra, the new citizens hall in Rathaus Schöneberg is opened. For about DM 3 mill., the former plenary hall of the Berlin House of Representatives was transformed by architect Siegfried Kolbe (office of Kolbe & Sekles, Berlin) into a bright, light-drenched room.

11.28.1996

The "Kino Center Spandau" on Havelstrasse with 1,000 seats was built on a site rich in tradition; from 1911 to 1967, this is where the film theater "Aladin" stood. Client: Günther Mertins and Peter Sundarp. Cost: DM 7.5 mill.

11.29.1996

The artists club "Möwe" ("Seagull") celebrates its 50th birthday and opens its new domicile in the Palais am Festungsgraben. Opened in 1946 at the initiative of the Soviet Military Administration, the Möwe was long a meeting place for prominent painters, actors, writers, and journalist from East and West. It was closed in 1990. The club owes its revitalization as an artists' meeting place in new quarters to an initiative by the actress Renate Heymer.

11.29.1996

The exhibition "The Scenic Eye" stages a dialogue between theater and fine arts in the Haus der Kulturen der Welt (House of World Cultures). Video and sound installations, objects, photographs and paintings, performances by 19 artists put the interactions on display. Through January 1997.

the month. Architects are Kramm + Strigl, Darmstadt, and Feige + Döring, Berlin. Developer for the project (with a total of 478 subsidized and 58 privately financed apartments) is the Bauwert GmbH company, Berlin/Munich.

12.1.1996

The foundation stone is laid for the church and community center in the Potsdam district Kirchsteigfeld. Completion of the church, community library and music school are scheduled for November 1997. Architect is Augusto Romano Burelli, Venice. The clients are the Berlin-Brandenburg Protestant Church, the Protestant-Methodist Church in Northern Germany, the City of Potsdam and Groth & Graalfs. Cost: approx. DM 8.3 mill.

which also allows windows to be opened. The 11-story building is located directly by the road. It was built in an unusual lemon shape, so as not to disturb the views from the adjacent residential buildings. Architects are Hilde Léon and Konrad Wohlhage, Berlin. The developer is Mübau-Grundstücksgesellschaft (Mübau Real Estate Company). Cost: DM 60 mill.

12.9.1996

Foundation stone ceremony for the residential development–including 176 apartments and 48 homes–on Gorkistrasse in the Tegel district. Project completion is expected in 1998. The clients are DeGeWo and the management company Demo-Spreegrund-Verwaltungsgesellschaft. Architects are Gibbins, Bultmann and Partner, Berlin. Cost: DM 50 mill.

12.10.1996

The Berlin Senate votes to consolidate the 23 city districts into only 12. Under the plan, the districts Mitte, Tiergarten and Kreuzberg would be joined as one "Hauptstadt-Bezirk" (Capital District). Despite opposition from the Berlin House of Representatives and from the Council of District Mayors, the Senate is hoping the change will bring more effective administration and annual savings of DM 230 mill.

12.11.1996

Plans for the Palais on Pariser Platz are introduced. The construction site is excavated, the building contract is issued. Completion of the DM 46 mill. office and commercial use building is planned for the end of 1997. Offices, restaurants, cafés and 13 apartments will be spread out over 4,000 sq. m. The architect is Bernhard Winking, Hamburg; client the Allgemeine Hypothekenbank; project developer is Hanseatica/DIAG.

12.11.1996

After much uncertainty the 9,700 sq. m large state owned property between Wielandstrasse and Leibnizstrasse is sold to Hanseatica Immobilien Consulting GmbH for DM 27 mill. The site, formerly

12.12.1996

Construction of the Federal Press and Information Office begins. The building site is located between the Spree river, Dorotheenstrasse and Neustädter Kirchstrasse and will incorporate several historic buildings. Project completion is planned for September 1997. Architect is the firm of KSP, Braunschweig. Cost: DM 220 mill.

12.12.1996

Groundbreaking for the new DG Bank building on Pariser Platz. Architect for the DM 250 mill. project, to be completed by 1998, is Frank O. Gehry of Santa Monica, California. Unique to the building will be an accessible sculpture in the courtyard which can be used as a conference room. The building will be located directly adjacent to the future Akademie der Künste (Academy of Arts) building by Günter Behnisch.

12.16.1996

After two years of restoration work and another two years of standing around silently on the construction site of the New Museum, King Friedrich Wilhelm IV has finally returned to his original place. The great staircase in front of the Old National Gallery had to be entirely renewed to be able to support the 5 m high, 5.4 ton bronze equestrian statue with its four additional pedastel figures. The sculpture was finished in 1886 by Alexander Calandrelli.

12.17.1996

Construction on the "New Hackesche Höfe" begins across from the newly renovated, original Hackesche Höfe on Rosenthaler Strasse in Mitte. The project is being sponsored by the Housing Department Mitte and the Bassmann Group and foresees a residential and office complex of 12 separate buildings. Plans include 100 apartments, plus offices and shops. Architects are Götz Bellmann and Walter Böhm, Berlin. Cost amount to DM 70 mill. The building should be finished in 1998.

12.17.1996

Construction begins on the "Kreditanstalt für Wiederaufbau" (Credit Institute for Reconstruction). The site is at the northern edge of the Gendarmenmarkt in the block formed by the streets: Französische Strasse, Behrenstrasse, Markgrafenstrasse and Charlottenstrasse. By the end of 1998 more than DM 200 mill. will be invested in the new building and the conversions of the historic buidings by Alfred Messel and Heinrich Schweitzer. They will include 700 office work places on 44,000 sq. m of total floor space. The new building was designed by ABB Architekten (Scheid, Schmidt und Partner) from Frankfort/Main. The Swiss architecture firm of Keller, Bachmann and Partners from Bubikon designed the conversions for the historic buildings.

12.19.1996

The exhibition "Stadtgründer aus Leidenschaft" (A City Founder out of Passion) shows documents and photographs on the life and work of the city planner Johann Anton Wilhelm Carstenn, commemorating the 100th anniversary of his death. Carstenn became a millionaire in

used for parking, will be the future location of an office, hotel and residential complex. It will include a 40% allocation for apartments, as well as a playschool on the top floor, and underground parking. Architects are Hans Kollhoff and Helga Timmermann, Berlin.

12.12.1996

A section of the 450 m long tunnel between Stralau Peninsula and Treptow is excavated. The tunnel was originally built as a tram tunnel, which was completed for the 1899 Treptower Park Trade Fair. It lies 12 m under waterlevel at its deepest point. In 1932 the tunnel was put out of use and later served as an air raid shelter in the Second World War, finally closing in 1949. The developer, Entwicklungsgesellschaft Rummelsburger Bucht, now considering reopening the tunnel completely, commissioned a study to find out whether the tunnel poses any threats to the new buildings on the peninsula.

12.13.1996

Construction begins in the Heinrich-Heine-Strasse in Mitte. Within about a year an entire city block between Annenstrasse and Dresdener Strasse will be erected, with 740 apartments and 5,000 sq. m of office space. The Bayerische Hausbau is developing 450 privately financed apartments and an office building by the architects Kny and Weber. The building contractor Viaduct, also working with Kny and Weber, is building an additional 140 partially subsidized apartments. Another 150 apartments designed by the Berlin architects Flöting & Kaufmann will be located on a plot owned by the Salvation Army and should be completed by 1999. Cost: DM 200 mill.

12.16.1996

The worlds largest gingerbread house is exhibited in the "Hotel Berlin." The 6.5 m high structure, made from 1,500 sugary shingles has a chance to get into the Guinness Book of World Records.

12.17.1996

Groundbreaking for the Federal Building Ministry's residential development in Moabiter Werder in the Berlin district Tiergarten. Here 716 apartments are being planned for federal employees who will be working in the future government quarter nearby. In addition to living space, the two sections, a "Snake" and "Atrium Houses," totalling 44,500 sq. m, will provide service and supply facilities. The plans come from Berlin architect, Georg Bumiller, whose design received a "special purchase" award from the jury of the planning competition in October 1995. Co-planners in the project are the competition's second place winners, the Berlin architecture firms of Keil/Pampe and Müller/Rhode/Wandert. Developers for the project are the Gemeinnützige Deutsche Wohnungsbaugesellschaft (Nonprofit German Housing Company) and the Frankfurter Siedlungsgesellschaft (Frankfort Housing Community Company). Cost: approx. DM 240 mill.

12.18.1996

Of the 23 multiplex cinemas being planned in Berlin, "Kosmos Ufa Palast" on Karl-Marx-Allee is the first to open. The historic building, once home to the Kosmos Cinema in former East Germany, was built in the 1960s (architect: Josef Kaiser and Kollektive, Berlin). In the renovated building, nine new theaters were built in a ring around the original theater, which is to be restored in 1997 together with the foyer. Total seating capacity will ultimately be 3,400. Renovations were designed by the architect Konrad Beckmann and the firm RKW, Düsseldorf. The investor is the film company UFA-Theater AG. Cost: DM 55 mill.

Hamburg with the development of the Marienthal Villa area. In 1865 he moved to Berlin and developed the Villa areas of Lichterfelde, Friedenau and Grunewald, complete with access to public transportation systems. The stock market crash ruined Carstenn and he died in poverty on 12.19.1896.

Reggae is Chill-Out for Jungle *Holger Wild*

Winnie knows what's going on. He's always on the lookout for something new, something hip. Winnie is there, where the others aren't. Those white-sock-wearing, penny-pinching, non-smoking, occasional drinkers. Winnie's into excess. Winnie likes Techno. Techno tends toward excess. Techno never stops, never pauses. No breaks between one piece and the next. Techno keeps driving. Techno is now. When Winnie finally heads home in the grey dawn hours, he doesn't remember what he heard. Techno doesn't stick. He can't describe the music in words. Faster, slower, harder, softer, more aggressive, melodic: all insufficient adjectives. Techno is not easy to describe if you're not into the clandestine, not an insider. You've got to "hear-see" it. There's Ambient. That's Trance. This's Hardcore. That's Gabber. It's all measured in beats per minute. Beats are good, the measurement's trivial. Those who aren't part of it, have trouble getting it. But they don't need to. No loss. It actually helps that they think you can't dance to Techno. They help define the otherside, the norm. Techno is all dance. The idea

name is more accurate than they realize. Here Techno becomes ritual, a developed form, stomping in place, hair short, arms akimbo, masses of people. A large red circle pulsates on a screen over their heads. It's halved, crossed through, a symbol changing to the rhythm. Gigantic ring, powerful ring, everyone united below it. Give the mob what the mob wants. The aesthetic is familiar. The joy of Fascism, says Winnie. Tresor (Vault) is another pretty serious place. An old basement with bank safe-deposit boxes like rusty honeycomb along the walls, rythmical white lights, a stroboscope and dry ice fog. The music pumps out, no curlicue, no design, marathon dancing, it's Techno, but not the techno scene. The scene is there where the mob is not. The best clubs are those not yet listed in "Flyer." Neither are they listed in "030," or in "guide," and definitely not in "tip", "zitty" or "prinz." Those no one knows anything about. And you're ahead of the pack, if you do. The Love-WG: candles light the way up the staircase. Upstairs, the air is stale and thick. The windows are covered and nailed shut. I know where it is. You know where. But he doesn't. Nor do they! Cool shirts for sale when it was over. Winnie had one. Drinking cocktails. Not Techno, but cool. Now it's closed. Like The Bunker. Like Friseur and Hirschbar (the best club!). Goa, Trance, Hardtrance, piles of cushions, laying down, stretching out, making out, toking up, exstacy, laserlight circles, laserlight flashes. The more nights, even more ahead of the pack. Does anyone remember the basement in Tacheles? New places, like Ventil, a backyard barrack with a garden, hard to find. Inside under the four corners of the sky, under the lights, a sun beam, a moon ball, green star

is fun, the content is movement. That's why Techno isn't "being," but "becoming." Perhaps, thinks Winnie, that's why Berlin is the Techno metropolis. Berlin is becoming. The past stands around in the city, while the future is being built. Both are stage sets. Life is now; nothing more boring than the established. New clubs are on the cutting edge. In the Mitte district the music is Techno, Jungle and Easy Listening, and whatever else is playing where Winnie ends up. It doesn't always have to be Techno. But nowhere in the world is Techno as present as it is here. Hardly a week goes by without some new club opening. The scene still thrives in east Berlin, where old basements, factories, and warehouses can still be found. City grows here apart from city planning, though the city's authority for factory safety and health control is constantly forcing clubs to close down. This only contributes to the transience of new locations; a club's life expectancy is a source of much speculation. Winnie reads the main Techno magazine "Flyer" with its pocket-size format. Easy to carry, no hassle. Winnie hates hassles. Winnie just needs to know what's going on. The magazine is regularly updated. The layout stays the same; that is, with a few modifications, it keeps developing. Repetition is boring, repetition is for people who know what they're after.

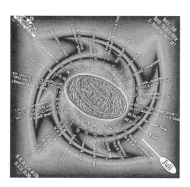

They are stomping in place in E-Werk. It's known in the press as the "Techno-Temple" because of its structure: a huge central hall with smaller side halls. The nick-

spots, white paper north star, bird wings. Tree in the middle: Yggdrasill, a pillar rising up and swinging out, with crinkly branches of steel and green neon. Basement, Blumenladen (Flower Shop), Boogaloo, Ankerklause, Hafenbar (Harbor Bar), Lime Club, Drama, Akba Lounge. Delicious Doughnuts, Boudoir, Knaak Klub, Fix Club, Franz Club, Sophienclub, Kit Kat Club, Silberstein, 90 Grad, Im Eimer (In the Trashcan), Elektrokohle (Electro Coal), Fleisch & Wurst (Meat & Sausage), Aktionsgalerie, Arena, Suicide Circus, WMF, Fischlabor.

And the new music: Easy Listening for example. Came from where? From England? It took over the clubs, that Hammond Organ, off-key lizard lounge sound everywhere, popcorn! The twisted sixties, cheesy campy tunes, splash, patter, burble ... now it's on its way out again. Sexy Sixties, sexy Seventies, sexy Nineties. What's next? Jungle? Jungle is. The Toaster is a good example, a classic cellar disco. Well, not exactly a disco. Is it more like a basement bar? Sounds stupid. Cellar club? Uneasy, cellar cl-, cl-, cl- it catches the tongue after a few beers. In any case, it's got exposed walls, dim lights, bar in the back, lounging corners, reggae. Colorful lights, mellow atmosphere. Reggae is chill-out for Jungle. What was the chill-out for reggae? Chill-out didn't exist back then. Nele works Saturdays at the bar in Toaster. Otherwise she works in Schnabel, Winnie's hang-out. In the Kreuzberg district, not Mitte. The clientele is unpredictable, the music changes daily. They play Jungle In Schnabel. Good. And Abba (Easy Listening II), not so good. What else? Latin junk, Thursday or Friday, hard to tell, "Flyer" gives only cryptic information. So Winnie ends up hearing the stuff every now and then. What's it becoming? Where's the movement going? It's not important where the movement is going. The only important thing: knowing it.

Herr K. preferred City B over City A. "In City A," he said, "they love me, but in City B they were friendly to me. In City A they offered their services, but in City B they needed me. In City A they invited me to dine with them, but in City B they invited me into the kitchen."
Bertolt Brecht, 1967

12.19.1996

Wilhelm von Boddien's Förderverein Berliner Stadtschloss (Berlin City Palace Support Association) introduces a plan for reconstructing the old royal palace. It includes ideas for utilization and financing without government subsidies. Together with the Hamburg developer Hanseatica and the Berlin architects Ralf and Ursulina Schüler-Witte, the association believes reconstruction could be completed in ten years for exactly DM 976.95 mill. Project financing would be a combination of DM 14.6 mill. of income generated through rents, plus money from other sources such as foundations and lotteries. In return the state would have to demolish most of the former East German Palace of the Republic and then convert the property into a hereditary lease holding. The new Palace project would

12.19.1996

The bunker is an old war relic located on the corner of Albrechtstrasse and Reinhardtstrasse in Mitte. It was more recently used as a Techno club until the city's construction supervising authority shut it down at the beginning of the year. In mid-December the hulking structure was closed

12.20.1996

Joseph Beuys's sculpture "Unschlitt/Tallow" arrives at the new Hamburger Bahnhof museum unharmed. This follows months of tug-of-war with the Museum of Abteiberg in Mönchengladbach, where the sculpture had been on display since 1982. The 5.6 ton artwork was moved to the "Museum für Gegenwart" (Museum for Contemporary Art), as part of the Marx Collection. Beuys created the piece in 1977 by making a cast of the hollow space under a road overpass using stearin, paraffin and tallow. The work is said to represent the desolation of such concrete wastelands.

12.20.1996

Renovation of Hackescher Markt S-Bahn station is complete. Renewal of the 115 year old station cost some DM 6.6 mill. The architect was the firm of AS ArchitektenSocietät, Berlin.

12.22.1996

St. Adalbert's Church is reopened after 2 years of renovation work. The catholic church was originally built between 1929 and 1934 after plans by the architect Clemens Holzmeister. The modern brick structure is located in Mitte behind Torstrasse 168. The building's characteristic chancel tower is particularly conspicuous from Linienstrasse. Today is the christening of the new marble altar by the sculptor Joachim Karbe.

12.25.1996

The first restored altar window is unveiled in time for a Christmas Mass in the Berliner Dom. The original stained glass picture "The Birth of Christ" by the historic painter Anton von Werner was destroyed in 1940. The DM 100,000 necessary for the replica was provided by a Berlin donor. Also one of the original eight mosaics in the cupola was finished at the beginning of December after a six month restoration. Likewise, private gifts provided the DM 400,000 needed for the 500,000 piece puzzle.

12.31.1996

The Ku'damm Eck (architect: Werner Düttmann, 1972) is closed. The Berliner Panoptikum and 58 other tenants must vacate the premises. The Bremen developer Hans Grothe is planning to replace it with an office building and hotel.

December

permanently and put up for sale. Even the planned "Final Countdown" farewell parties, with deejays Ziggy Stardust, Mr. Richart, Peyote and the members of Gabba Nation, were prohibited. The adjoining "Ex-Kreuz-Club" will also be closed by year's end.

include a national conference center, state and private office space, a national art museum, a hotel and a library. The architectural plans intend to preserve a small part of the Palace of the Republic, replicating only three facades from the original royal palace.

12.19.1996

After two years of construction, the new Konrad-Zuse-Zentrum for information technology officially opens on Thielallee in Dahlem. The long three-story complex with its round, adjoining building is located in the middle of the Free University campus. Architects are Dähne and Dahl, Berlin. Konrad Zuse, "inventor" of the computer in the 1930s, did not live to witness the opening. He passed away last year.

12.21.1996

After more than two years of construction, the giant working model (on a scale of 1:87) of the Berlin S-Bahn system is complete. The 1.6 km of tracks are shared by S-Bahn trains, long-distance and regional trains, and freight trains traveling between Friedrichsfelde-Ost and Hackescher Markt. The model trains are computer controlled and some have even been sprayed with real graffiti. The whole thing is set in a true-to-life model of Berlin.

12.23.1996

The foundation stone is laid for a privately owned building-service center in Adlershof. The Innovations- und Beratungszentrum (IBZ: Innovation and Consulting Center) at Adlergestell will offer consulting for building technologies, health and environmental protection, and disposal of dangerous waste. The first part of the IBZ, with a total floor space of 9,000 sq.m, should be open by the end of 1997. Architects: Nalbach and Nalbach, Berlin; developer: Rainer Tepasse, Berlin. Cost: approx. DM 40 mill.

12.27.1996

The first partial building permit was issued for the Potsdam Center despite last week's protests. Construction is due to begin after January 6th.

12.31.1996

In spite of icy temperatures around minus 15 degrees Celsius, some 40,000 people turn out for the New Year's Eve party at Brandenburg Gate.

Credits

Photos
Akademie der Künste 164 (bottom)
BauNetz 174
Commerell 138 (middle)
dpa 135 (bottom), 155
Foster and Partners 133 (bottom)
Fundus-Gruppe 175 (photo of model)
Gadi Dagon 164 (top)
Theo Heimann/Der Tagesspiegel 135 (top), 143
Matthias Horn 154
Info Box 144 (middle)
Matthias Jankowiak 158 (top)
Matthias Koeppel 133 (top)
Dr. Peter and Isolde Kottmair 138/139
Luftbild & Pressefoto/Robert Grahn 144 (top)
Mike Minehan/Der Tagesspiegel 162 (bottom)
Stefan Noack/Der Tagesspiegel 131
Erik-Jan Ouwerkerk 130, 147 (bottom), 150, 161, 162
(top), 163 (top and bottom), 170
Reptile 175 (top)
Thilo Rückeis/Der Tagesspiegel 136, 141, 175 (bottom)
Rudolf Schäfer 138 (top), 142, 153, 158 (bottom),
163 (middle)
Andreas Schmidt 138 (bottom)
Bernhard Schulz 144 (bottom)
Architekturwerkstatt, SenBauWohn Berlin 137
Ronald Siemoneit 149
Eleonore Straub & Günter Haring 172
Markus Wächter/Der Tagesspiegel 168
Mike Wolff/Der Tagesspiegel 145, 147 (top)
Zeitmagazin, 11.24.1995 146

Literature
130 Ingomar von Kieseritzky, Der Frauenplan. Etuden
für Männer, Stuttgart 1991
130 Fritz Rudolf Fries, Alexanders neue Welten,
Frankfort/Main 1982
131 Benno Reifenberg, in: Berlin, Hg. Johann Jakob
Häßlin, Munich 1959
132 Johanna Matthieux, 1842, Briefe, in: Berlin,
Hg. Johann Jakob Häßlin, Munich 1975
132 Hans Egon Gerlach, in: Berlin, Hg. Johann Jakob
Häßlin, Munich 1959

134/135 Tilmann Buddensieg, Macht das Tor weiß, in:
Frankfurter Allgemeine, 9.9.1995
136 Italo Calvino, Invisible Cities, London 1979
137 Bettina Vismann, in: Stadtbauwelt 48/1994
137 Helene von Nostiz, Aus dem alten Europa.
Menschen und Städte, Wiesbaden 1950, in: Berlin,
Hg. Johann Jakob Häßlin, Munich 1975
139 Sebastian Redecke, Prima Pietra mit Aldo, in:
Bauwelt 25/1995
140 Jane Kramer, Letter from Germany. The Politics of
Memory, in: The New Yorker, 8.14.1995
141 Sebastian Redecke, Kasten Bier?, Bauwelt
33/1995
142/143 Harald Martenstein, Die teuflischen Engel, in:
Der Tagesspiegel, 8.18.1995
147 Herwarth Walden 1923, in: Berliner Begegnungen,
Ausländische Künstler in Berlin 1918 bis 1933, Berlin
1987
148 Henryk M. Broder, Nackter Hintern mit Feigen-
blatt, in: Berlin – Eine Ortsbesichtigung, Berlin 1996
149 Julius Posener, Fast so alt wie das Jahrhundert,
Basel, Boston, Berlin 1993
151 Fritz-Jochen Kopka, in: Berlin – Ein Ort zum
Schreiben. 347 Autoren von A bis Z. Hg. Karin Kiwus,
Berlin 1996
152 Jakob Augstein, 2002 – Odyssee im Tunnel, in:
Süddeutsche Zeitung, 10.9.1996
154 Volker Ludwig, Linie One, Rock Musical, Text book
Grips Theater Berlin, 1995
156/157 Moritz Rinke, Milchcafé mit Hoppe, in:
Der Tagesspiegel, 4.26.1996
157 Tilo Köhler, Asche zu Asche, in: Deutsche
Demokratische Reise, Hg. Heinrich von Berenberg,
Berlin 1989
159/160 Reinhard Lettau, Obstacles, New York 1965
162 Der Heidelberger Portländer, Werkzeitschrift der
Portland Zementwerke Heidelberg, Sondernummer
Berlin, 1957
162 Ernst Ludwig Kirchner, 1937, in: Berlin, Hg. Johann
Jakob Häßlin, Munich 1975
164 Laurie Anderson, in: Sonambiente. Festival für
Hören und Sehen, AdK Berlin 1996
165 Heinz Berggruen, Hauptweg und Nebenwege.

Erinnerungen eines Kunstsammlers, Berlin 1996
166 Barbara Sichtermann, in: Berlin – Ein Ort zum
Schreiben. 347 Autoren von A bis Z. Hg. Karin Kiwus,
Berlin 1996
167 Renée Zucker, Berlin ist anderswo, Berlin 1995
168 Irina Liebmann, Berliner Mietshaus,
Frankfort/Main 1990
169 Peter Ensikat, in: Berlin – Ein Ort zum Schreiben.
347 Autoren von A bis Z. Hg. Karin Kiwus, Berlin 1996
169 Franz Rosenzweig, Briefe und Tagebücher, 1929,
in: Gert und Gundel Mattenklott, Berlin Transit. Eine
Stadt als Station, Reinbek bei Hamburg 1987
172 Klaus Mann, Der Wendepunkt. Ein Lebensbericht,
1923, in: Berlin, Hg. Johann Jakob Häßlin, Munich 1975
172 Friedrich Sieburg, Wer füttert die Tauben?
(„Die Gegenwart" 7.19.1952), in: Berlin, Hg. Johann
Jakob Häßlin, Munich 1959
179 Bertolt Brecht, Geschichten vom Herrn Keuner,
Frankfort/Main 1967

Berlin's New Buildings 1995/96

Part of the initial idea for the Berlin Annual was to prepare an annual list of the new buildings in Berlin. Berlin seems to be transforming itself over night, and wherever you go, where you drive, where you park, there are construction sites. Architecture experts and amateurs alike would like to know who is building what and for whom. As long as the scaffolding is still up, they could consult the building signs, but their curiosity is really piqued when the scaffolding drops and the new building is revealed. Yet by then, nobody is left to answer their questions. The architecture magazines could not possibly cover the vast quantity of new buildings, and, besides, they tend to cover only those buildings they consider trendy, even though it's them who make up the trends. What other source of information is there for those interested pedestrians and architecture aficionados?

The staff of Bauwelt Berlin Annual, comprised of such devotees, thus came up with the plan for this list in order to satisfy its readers, who presumably are just as architecturally inclined. The idea was well received by the respective Berlin Senate departments, though they were unable to offer assistance. The district departments could not help either, except in one or two cases. The trash collection was the most pleasant, but it has its own way of recording new buildings. The same was true for the district chimney sweeps. The land survey office is conducting a similar sort of survey, but is not yet finished. The State Statistics Office has most of the relevant data, but only for a precious moment until they are recorded and then promptly destroyed: passing on such information is prohibited. Nevertheless, the figure was known: some 1,000 new buildings per year had to be traced.

The task was not an easy one. Ultimately, it meant the arduous compiling of pieces of information from sundry sources. They derived from architects, developers, housing companies, which we knew personally or contacted through Bauwelt advertisements. They also came from books, magazines and information services, particularly those of the ibau planning information. Yet all this still had to be supplemented and confirmed by innumerable letters, faxes, telephone calls and personal testimony.

And even though this final list is not entirely complete—and buildings with less than ten residential or office units were excluded on purpose—we did achieve to collect data on a great number of the new city buildings and to present them in a functional format. The list is ordered according to district and address, and can thus provide quick information on buildings that may have excited interest in passing, and/or facilitate the planning of an architecture tour. Names of architects are accentuated, thereby hopefully satisfying the need for a name index.

A thank you goes out to all project contributors. Those architects or clients, who find their building missing, are kindly asked to give us notice. The list of 1996/97 is open to receive any supplementary information.
Haila Ochs

Charlottenburg

Bismarckstrasse 72,
Fritschestrasse 61
Apartment and Commercial Building
Rainer Autzen, Bernd Reimers, Berlin
Client: B. Prajs Grundbesitz
Urban infill, 7 stories, 27 housing units,
subterranean car park,
4,200 sq. m usable space,
cost DM 10.4 mill.

Bismarckstrasse 101, Weimarer Strasse
Office and Commercial Building
"Die 101"
Kohn Pederson Fox Associates,
London
Client: Férinel Deutschland GmbH
Built 1993–95

Cauerstrasse 18–19
Apartment and Commercial Building
Olaf Gibbins, Jochen Bultmann
and Partners, Berlin
Client: DEGEWO Berlin
Urban infill, 6 stories,
retail spaces, 65 housing units,
gross floor area 8,595 sq. m,
cost DM 14.5 mill.,
built November 1994–September 1996

Haubachstrasse 41
Apartment Building with
Child Care Center
Rolf D. Weisse, Berlin
Client: Charlottenburger Baugenossen-
schaft (apartment building),
Charlottenburg District Authority
(child care center)
Corner building, apartment building
7 stories, 31 subsidized housing units
with approx. 3,130 sq. m gross floor
area, child care center 4 stories,
1,746 sq. m for 128 children,
cost DM 20 mill. in all, built 1994–95

Heckerdamm 204–210
Youth Center
Christian Hartmann, Büro Freitag,
Hartmann, Sinz, Berlin
Client: Charlottenburg District
Authority
Gross floor area 1,280 sq. m,
usable space 690 sq. m,
cost DM 5.5 mill., competition 1990,
built November 1994–April 1996

Heerstrasse 86, Reichssportfeldstrasse
Apartment and Commercial Building
Carl August von Halle, Berlin
Client: Dr. Upmeier Heerstrasse 86 KG
2–4 storied new building with
13 privately financed housing units,
listet villa with 254 sq. m commercial
space, site area 3,085 sq. m,
investment DM 13 mill.

Heerstrasse 135, Scholzplatz
Apartment Building
Kammann and Hummel, Berlin
Client: Volkswagenstiftung Hanover,
repres. by IVA KG, Dusseldorf
7 stories, 44 privately financed
housing units, subterranean car park,
gross floor area 5,000 sq. m,
cost DM 13 mill.

Kaiser-Friedrich-Strasse 96
Secondary School Center (Motor
Mechanics) "Porsche Schule"
Susanne Quick, Michael Bäckmann,
Klaus Quick, Berlin
Client: Education Authority of Berlin
Usable space 3,000 sq. m,
cost DM 17 mill., built 1993–95

Kaiserin-Augusta-Allee 31–32,
Goslarer Ufer 37–39
Office and Commercial Building
"Atrium-Charlottenburg"
Fin Bartels, Christoph Schmidt-Ott
with KMK Architekten, Berlin
Client: R. and J. Gutman, Berlin
Corner building, block alignment,
3 atria, subterranean car park,
site area 10,000 sq. m,
gross floor area 46,250 sq. m, construction cost DM 115 mill.,
built 1993–96

Knobelsdorffstrasse 92,
Königin-Elisabeth-Strasse
Public Insurance Company of Berlin
Karl-Heinz Steinebach,
Friedrich Weber, Berlin
Client: Landesversicherungsanstalt
Office Building, gross floor area
63,000 sq. m, completion 1995

Kurfürstendamm 31
Office and Commercial Building
Fischer, Krüder, Rathai and Partners,
Wiesbaden
Client: BMW Maschinenfabrik
Spandau GmbH
Offices, retail spaces,
site area 1,352 sq. m,
gross floor area 5,494 sq. m,
cost DM 20 mill.

Pascalstrasse 10
Office Building "Spreebogen Plaza"
Jürgen Fissler, Hans-Christof Ernst,
Berlin
Client: Fundus Fonds Verwaltungen KG
5–7 stories, subterranean car park,
site area 20,300 sq. m,
gross floor area 36,500 sq. m,
construction cost DM 75 mill.,
built 1989–95

Rankestrasse 5–6
Office and Apartment Building
Ulrich Findeisen, Frank Sedlacek,
Cologne
Client: Agrippina Lebensversicherung,
Cologne
Addition and conversion of an existing
building, 6 housing units 328 sq. m,
subterranean car park,
office space 6,601 sq. m,
construction period: new building
1993–95, existing building 1993–96

Reichsstrasse 92 A
Apartment and Commercial Building
Klaus Lattermann, Berlin
Client: Grundstückssverwaltungs
Gesellschaft Reichsstrasse 90–93
& Co Wohnbauten KG, Berlin
5 storied heightening on a 1 storied
existing building, 8 housing units,
8 commercial units, subterranean car
park, gross floor area 1,976 sq. m,
cost DM 5.9 mill.,
built 1994–December 1996

Saatwinkler Damm 42–43,
Riedemannweg, Buchholzweg
Office and Commercial Center
"Airport Bureau Center"
Lennart Stange, Berlin
Client: Batiment Baumanagement
GmbH & Co. KG Berlin
6 buildings, 8 stories, offices,
retail spaces, child care center,
gross floor area 60,500 sq. m,
subterranean car park,
cost DM 430 mill., opening October
1995, child care center August 1996

Sensburger Allee 25
Addition to the Georg-Kolbe-Museum
Architektengruppe AGP (Heidenreich,
Meier, Polensky, Zeumer), Berlin
Client: Berlin Senate
Addition to the museum which was
installed 1950 in the former workshop
of Georg Kolbe (built 1927/28),
opening January 1996

Spandauer Damm 115, Soorstrasse 89
Apartment and Commercial Building
Thomas Baumann, Berlin
Client: Bauherrengemeinschaft
Spandauer Damm 115 GbR
Corner building, 7 stories,
18 subsidized housing units,
retail spaces, offices, subterranean
car park, site area 941 sq. m,
gross floor area 7,680 sq. m,
investment DM 30 mill.,
built April 1993–June 1995

Spandauer Damm 148
Students' Residence
Yoshimi Yamaguchi-Essig,
Mathias Essig, Berlin
Client: Studentenwerk Berlin
188 students' apartments,
gross floor area 11,400 sq. m,
cost DM 30 mill., competition 1990,
built 1992–95

Waldschulallee 73
"Heinz-Galinski-Schule"
Zvi Hecker, Tel Aviv/Berlin
Contact architect: Inken Baller, Berlin
Client: Jewish Community of Berlin
Primary school, usable space
4,898 sq. m, cost DM 46.3 mill.,
competition 1990/91, built 1993–95

Warburgzeile 6–16
Child Care Center
Rolf D. Weisse, Berlin
Client: Charlottenburg District
Authority
Free standing building, 95 places,
site area ca. 1,780 sq. m,
gross floor area ca. 1,550 sq. m,
cost DM ca. 5.8 mill., built 1993–95

Friedrichshain

Auerstrasse 27–29
Apartment Building
Eva-Maria Jockeit-Spitzner, Berlin;
Borck, Boye, Schaefer, Berlin
Client: GSW
63 housing units of 74 subsidized
housing units in all,
period of construction: 51 housing units
1995, 1st building phase, 12 housing
units 1996, 2nd building phase

Frankfurter Allee 33–35,
Gabelsbergerstrasse 14–15
Office and Shopping Center
"Alleepassage Friedrichshain"
Gerhard Bremmer, Bernhard Lorenz,
Michael Frielinghaus, Friedberg
Client: Bayerische Hausbau GmbH &
Co, Munich
33 housing units, offices, approx. 22
shops, restaurant, subterranean car
park, site area 12,312 sq. m,
gross floor area 31,164 sq. m,
cost DM approx. 75 mill.,
1st building phase 1995–96

Frankfurter Allee 69, Voigtstrasse 1
Office and Commercial Building
"Quasar"
Shin Takamatsu and Lahyami, Japan
Client: Hübner and Weingärtner GbR
Corner building, 7 stories,
site area 603 sq. m,
gross floor area 4,300 sq. m,
completion 1995

Frankfurter Allee 71–77,
Voigtstrasse, Rigaer Strasse
Office, Apartment, and Commercial
Building "Frankfurter Allee Plaza"
Voidl Tatic, Berlin
Client: Fundus Gruppe
7 stories, 118 housing units,
offices, retail spaces, hotel,
subterranean car park,
gross floor area 90,000 sq. m,
48,761 sq. m usable space,
investment 500 mill.,
built May 1994–September 1995

Frankfurter Allee 105
Shopping Center "Ring-Center I"
Wolfgang Keilholz; HPP Hentrich,
Petschnigg and Partners, Berlin
Client: Deutsche Immobilien Anlage
GmbH, ECE Projektmanagement GmbH,
Rodamco-Gruppe/NL
5 stories, site area 45,000 sq. m,
16,500 sq. m usable space,
investment DM 180 mill.,
built June 1994–October 1995

Friedenstrasse 92–93
Apartment and Commercial Building
"Kontorhaus Friedenstrasse"
von Gerkan, Marg and Partners,
Hamburg
Client: GSW, Grundstücksges. Büll,
Liedtke and Hellberg, Hamburg
Comb-shaped city-block, 7 stories,
143 subsidized housing units,
retail spaces, 22,000 sq. m usable
space, 1st building phase

Friedenstrasse 94–95
Apartment and Commercial Building
**von Gerkan, Marg and Partners,
Hamburg**
Client: GSW
40 subsidized housing units,
supermarket, built 1995–96

*Gubener Strasse 21,
Torellstrasse 7*
Apartment and Commercial Building
Carlos Ewich
Client: PHIDIAS GmbH
7 stories, subterranean car park,
2,400 sq. m usable space,
completion July 1996

Heidenfeldstrasse 13–14
Apartment Building
Gerhard Pfannenschmidt, Berlin
Client: GSW
36 subsidized housing units with
2,300 sq. m, completion 1996

Koppenstrasse, Langestrasse
Office and Commercial Building
"City-Carée"
Fischer and Fischer, Cologne
Client: Merkur Grundstücks-
Gesellschaft, Berlin
Administration center of the Dresdner
Bank, hotel with 133 apartments,
retail spaces, subterranean car park,
site area 10,352 sq. m, gross floor area
72,500 sq. m, investment DM 450 mill.,
built August 1993–November 1996

Lenbachstrasse 19
Apartment Building
Joachim Schmidt, Berlin
Client: GSW
31 subsidized housing units with
1,850 sq. m, 1 commercial unit,
completion 1st building phase 1995,
2nd building phase 1996

Müggelstrasse 19–20
Housing Complex
**Gau and Servais with Hassan Younesi,
Berlin**
Client: GSW
35 subsidized housing units,
1 commercial unit,
usable space 2,454 sq. m,
completion 1996

Neue Bahnhofstrasse 11–17
Office and Commercial Building,
Vocational Academy Berlin
J.S.K. Perkins & Will, Berlin
Client: GbR Neue Bahnhofstrasse,
Frankfurt/Main
8 storied industrial building
from last century with additional story
on top and new building,
gross floor area 33,480 sq. m

Richard-Sorge-Strasse 13
Apartment Building
**Marina Stankovic-Müller,
Clemens Bonnen, Berlin**
Client: Haschtmann Baubetreuungs
GmbH
26 subsidized housing units,
160 sq. m commercial space,
site area 1,204 sq. m,
investment 12.6 mill.,
completion 1995

Rigaer Strasse 29
Apartment Building
**Brenne/Kny and Weber/Betow/
Schäfers, Berlin**
Client: GSW
87 subsidized housing units,
9 commercial units, built 1994–96

Rigaer Strasse 57, Waldeyerstrasse 8
Apartment Building
Axel Schulz, Berlin
Client: Trigon Consult GmbH & Co
Corner building, 7 stories,
24 subsidized housing units,
retail spaces on ground floor,
gross floor area 3,183 sq. m,
floor space index 3.92,
completion 1995

Simplonstrasse 27, Seumestrasse 31
Apartment and Commercial Building
**Klaus W. Grashorn,
Engelke Grashorn-Wortmann, Berlin**
Client: Alte Leipziger
Versicherungs AG, Oberursel
48 housing units with 3,866 sq. m,
3 shops with 575 sq. m, subterranean
car park, gross floor area 6,850 sq. m,
cost DM ca. 17 mill., completion 1995

*Warschauer Strasse 31–32,
Revaler Strasse 100*
Office and Commercial Building
Gerold Otten, Westerstede
Client: Deutsche Immobilien
Vertriebs GmbH
Conversion and addition of an old
industrial building, 6 stories,
site area 1,407 sq. m,
gross floor area 7,200 sq. m,
cost DM 39 mill., built 1994–95

Hellersdorf

Akazienallee 31
Housing Complex
**Rolf Backmann, Eugen Schieber,
Berlin**
Client: Kettler Liegenschaften GmbH
6 apartment blocks with 32 housing
units, gross floor area 2,650 sq. m,
construction cost DM 6.9 mill.,
completion 1995

Chemnitzer Strasse 148–152
Apartment and Commercial Building
**Michael König,
Michael von Möllendorf, Berlin**
Client: BOTAG Bodentreuhand- and
Verwaltungs-AG
24 subsidized housing units ,
1,116 sq. m commercial space,
site area 3,600 sq. m,
investment DM 21 mill.

Dorfstrasse 33
Apartment Building
**Ursula Steinhilber, Stuttgart;
Otfried Weis, Karlsruhe**
Client: Steinhilber GmbH, Heidenheim
16 housing units,
gross floor area 1,099 sq. m,
built January–December 1996

*Henny-Porten-Strasse 10/12,
Janusc-Korczak-Strasse 23/25,
Stendaler Strasse*
Apartment Building, Block 3,2 of
Hellersdorf District Center
**Axel Liepe, Hartmut Steigelmann,
Berlin**
Client: MEGA Entwicklungs- and
Gewerbeansiedlungs-AG
Block defining structure,
48 housing units, commercial spaces,
subterranean car park, built 1995–96

Hönower Strasse, Ridbacher Strasse
Apartment and Commercial Building
**Andreas R. Becher,
Elmar L. Rottkamp, Berlin**
Client: Penz & Pleß GbR, Berlin
29 subsidized housing units,
5 commercial units,
subterranean car park,
built October 1993–October 1995

Wernerstrasse 6–10, 26–36
Housing Complex
**Casa Nova – Dietmar W. Reinhold,
Klaus-A. von Lengerke, Frank Schulze,
Berlin**
Client: WBG Hellersdorf mbH
16 apartment blocks,
63 subsidized housing units,
gross floor area 8,463 sq. m,
floor space index 0.4,
cost DM ca. 17.5 mill.,
built 1994–95, completion 1996

Hohenschönhausen

Grenzgrabenstrasse 6
"Shopping Center Hohenschönhausen"
Jockers and Partners, Stuttgart
Client: Sto AG
Commercial building with areas
for production, storage, training,
and administration,
gross floor area 3,103 sq. m,
construction cost DM 6.9 mill.,
built February 1996–December 1996

Grevesmühlener Strasse 22–34
Apartment and Commercial Building
Gerhard Pfannenschmidt, Berlin
Client: WBG Hohenschönhausen
3 building sections with 51 subsidized
housing units, 16 shops

Indira-Gandhi-Strasse
Sports Complex with Hall for Thrower
Training "Lilli-Henoch-Hall"
Jochen Jentsch, Berlin
Client: OSB Sportstättenbauten GmbH
Triple Sports hall, audutorium with 200
seats, construction cost DM 18 mill.,
built August 1994–August 1995

*Konrad-Wolf-Strasse 3–7,
Suermondtstrasse 37A*
Apartment and Commercial Building
Jürgen Schulz, Berlin
Client: WBG Hohenschönhausen
52 subsidized housing units,
6 privately owned apartments,
retail spaces, practices

Konrad-Wolf-Strasse 13
Housing Complex and
Commercial Building
Baasner, Möller, Langwald, Berlin
Client: WBG Hohenschönhausen
5 buildings, 3–5 stories,
93 housing units, 7,504 sq. m in all,
3,764 sq. m commercial space,
cost DM 30 mill.

*Konrad-Wolf-Strasse 28–29,
Roedernstrasse 73–74*
Housing Complex
Architekturbüro PUB, Berlin
Client: WBG Hohenschönhausen
30 subsidized housing units,
22 privately owned apartments in
2 urban villas, 5 commercial units

*Konrad-Wolf-Strasse 61–64,
Altenhofer Strasse*
Apartment and Commercial Building
**Axel Liepe, Hartmut Steigelmann,
Berlin**
Client: Trigon Consult GmbH, Berlin
5–8 stories, 136 housing units,
ground floor commercial area,
gross floor area 16,000 sq. m,
cost DM 130 mill., built 1995–96

*Konrad-Wolf-Strasse 104,
Werneuchener Strasse 34*
Apartment and Commercial Building
Rolf D. Weisse, Berlin
Client: WBG Hohenschönhausen
Corner building, 6 stories,
17 privately owned apartments,
3 commercial units, subterranean
car park, site area ca. 3,000 sq. m,
gross floor area ca. 2,980 sq. m,
cost DM ca. 7.8 mill., built 1995–96

Landsberger Allee 217–219
Housing and Commercial Complex
Klaus Pudritz, Bernd Paul, Berlin
Client: Immobilienfonds Ziel 8 GbR
4 apartment blocks, 207 subsidized
housing units, site area 13,200 sq. m,
investment DM 127 mill., built 1993–95

*Liebenwalder Strasse 25/31,
Heiligenstädter Strasse*
Apartment and Commercial Building
Hans-Jürgen Mücke, Berlin
Client: WBG Hohenschönhausen
61 subsidized housing units,
6 commercial units

Neustrelitzer Strasse 67/77
Housing Complex
Kirsch and Mösing, Berlin
Client: WBG Hohenschönhausen
24 subsidized housing units,
24 privately owned apartments

Prerower Platz, Falkenberger Chaussee
Commercial Building and Service
Center "Lindencenter"
J.S.K. Perkins & Will, Berlin
Client: ECE Projektmanagement GmbH
3 stories, addition of the Anna Seghers
Library, post office, retail spaces,
gross floor area 18,000 sq. m,
investment DM 210 mill.,
built July 1994–October 1995

Wartiner Strasse 23
Primary School
**Dieter Steinebach, Friedrich Weber,
Berlin**
Client: Hohenschönhausen District
Authority
Four sided primary school and
gymnasium, usable space 9,573 sq. m,
cost DM 37.5 mill.,
built October 1993–May 1995

Zechliner Strasse 5, 7, 8, 24
Housing Complex
Paul Hoppenbrink, Werkfabrik, Berlin
Client: WBG Hohenschönhausen
141 subsidized housing units,
585 sq. m commercial space

Zingster Strasse 1
Apartment and Commercial Building
Baasner, Möller, Langwald, Berlin
Client: WBG Hohenschönhausen
30 subsidized housing units,
branch of a bank

Köpenick

Bölschestrasse 2, Müggelseedamm
Apartment and Commercial Building
Bernhard Winking, Berlin
Client: Multicon Bau & Boden
Investitions- and Immobilien GmbH
22 subsidized housing units,
retail spaces

Bruno-Wille-Strasse 21
Apartment Building
**Mario Maedebach, Werner Redeleit
and Partners, Berlin**
Client: BB-Grundfonds-Gesellschaft
9 housing units,
construction cost DM 2.7 mill.

Friedrichshagener Strasse 5 E–K
Housing Complex
**P.A.I. Architekten, Rosie Grässler,
Uwe Stolt, Berlin**
Client: KÖWOGE
3–5 stories, 49 subsidized housing
units, gross floor area 5,640 sq. m,
floor space index 0.6, built 1995–96

Fürstenwalder Damm 274,
Ahornweg 1
Apartment Building
Klaus Pudritz, Bernd Paul, Berlin
Client: Fürstenwalder Damm GbR
Free standing apartment block,
4 stories, 13 housing units,
site area ca. 1,100 sq. m,
construction cost DM 3 mill.,
built 1995–96

Grünauer Strasse 117–125
Housing Complex
Feige and Partners, Berlin
Client: W. Graf and Maresch GmbH,
Augsburg
1st building phase: 3 apartment blocks
of 11 in all, 160 subsidized and privately
financed housing units in all,
completion 1996

Grünauer Strasse 129–135
Housing Complex
Heinz A. Hellermann, Berlin
Client: Grünauer Strasse 129–135 GbR,
Dr. Görlich GmbH
Block-defining structure, 3–6 stories,
99 housing units, 6 studios,
housing space 6,980 sq. m,
1 commercial unit 143 sq. m,
site area 7,500 sq. m,
construction cost DM 27 mill.,
built 1994–95

Lindenstrasse 28–30
Housing Complex
Monika Krebs, Berlin
Client: Otremba Unternehmensgruppe
5 apartment blocks, 127 subsidized
housing units, office building,
subterranean car park, cost DM 50 mill.,
built 1995–96

Lüderstrasse 2–8, Freiheit 9
Apartment and Commercial Building
Michael Kny, Thomas Weber, Berlin
Client: GbR Lüderstrasse/Freiheit
Corner building, 21 subsidized housing
units, retail spaces, gross floor area
3,674 sq. m, floor space index 1.8

Mühltaler Strasse 18–31,
Egersfelder Allee
Housing Complex
Klaus Pudritz, Bernd Paul, Berlin
Client: Grundreal Vermögens-
verwaltungs-GmbH
Urban villas, 99 subsidized housing
units, subterranean car park,
site area ca. 9,364 sq. m,
usable space in all 8,056 sq. m,
investment DM 57.7 mill.

Wattstrasse 24
Apartment Building
Jochen Dreetz and Partners, Berlin
Client: GbR Wattstrasse 24
2 apartment blocks,
19 subsidized housing units,
gross floor area 1,684 sq. m,
cost DM 3.6 mill.,
built March 1994–March 1995

Wendenschlossstrasse 103–109 A
Apartment and Commercial Building
**Helga Schmidt-Thomsen,
Paul Ziegert, Berlin**
Client: KÖWOGE
40 subsidized housing units,
3 commercial units, built 1995–96

Kreuzberg

Alexandrinenstrasse,
Ritterstrasse 38–48
Housing Complex with
Child Care Center
**Andreas Brandt, Rudolph Böttcher,
Berlin**
Client: bewoge
154 subsidized housing units,
13,000 sq. m housing space,
2,000 sq. m commercial space,
subterranean car park, cost DM 60 mill.,
competition 1991, built 1994–95

Axel-Springer-Strasse 48–50
Office Building "Barmer Ersatzkasse"
Rupert Ahlborn and Partners, Berlin
Client: Barmer Ersatzkasse Wuppertal
(Health Insurance Company)
Gross floor area 12,690 sq. m,
cost DM 38 mill., start of planning 1993,
completion 1996

Boppstrasse 7
Apartment and Commercial Building
"Die Zickenhöfe"
Gutzeit Beyer Architektur GmbH
Client: Voigtländer Grundstücks- and
Verwaltungs GmbH
5 storied new office building in the
courtyard of a modernised existing
building, 3,504 sq. m office and
commercial space, subterranean car
park, site area 2,961 sq. m,
completion 1995

Brachvogelstrasse 1
Office Building
Rupert Ahlborn and Partners, Berlin
Client: Private Developer
Gross floor area 4,871 sq. m,
cost DM 32 mill., completion 1995

Dresdener Strasse 116
Apartment and Commercial Building
**tgw: Markus Torge, Sebastian Gaa,
Klaus Wercker, Berlin**
Client: bewoge
Urban infill, 12 subsidized housing
units, 1 commercial unit on ground
floor, gross floor area 1,530 sq. m,
cost DM 3.3 mill., built 1995–96

Friedrichstrasse 45, Zimmerstrasse 23,
Charlottenstrasse 81
Office and Commercial Building
"Checkpoint Arkaden"
Josef Paul Kleihues, Berlin
Client: KapHag, Berlin
7 stories above ground, 4 underground
stories, offices 11,900 sq. m,
retail spaces 1,400 sq. m, 30 housing
units, subterranean car park,
site area 3,832 sq. m,
gross floor area 20,000 sq. m,
floor space index 4.96,
cost DM 82 mill., built 1994–96

Hasenheide 23–31
"BIC – Office Center in the City"
Manfred Pechtold, Berlin
Client: KapHag, Berlin
9 stories, commercial space, offices,
rooms for festivities, subterranean car
park, site area 12,000 sq. m,
gross floor area 21,000 sq. m,
cost DM 190 mill., completion 1995

Kochstrasse, Lindenstrasse
Axel Springer Editorial Building
**Stössner and Fischer, Berlin;
Karres, Hartmeyer, Dreyer, Hamburg
(Facade)**
Client: Axel Springer Verlag AG,
Hamburg
20 storied additional building,
conference halls, offices,
gross floor area 15,300 sq. m

Lindenstrasse 40–41
Youth Center
Marion Drews, Berlin
Client: Kreuzberg District Authority
Conversion of a former fire station and
new building, usable space 1,351 sq. m,
cost DM 10.3 mill., built 1992–95

Oranienstrasse 50–57
Apartment and Commercial Building
**Thomas Langenfeld, Markus Torge,
Berlin**
Client: GSW
46 subsidized housing units,
ground floor and 1st floor commercial
use, gross floor area 12,022 sq. m,
cost DM 34 mill., competition 1990

Oranienstrasse 110
Apartment and Commercial Building
**Mario Maedebach, Werner Redeleit
and Partners, Berlin**
Client: bewoge
15 housing units, ground floor
commercial use, completion 1995

Riemannstrasse 1,
Zossener Strasse 22–24
Apartment Building with
Child Care Center
Krogmann & Co, Berlin
Client: Immobilienfonds Zossener
Strasse GbR
39 subsidized housing units,
2 welfare stations,
site area 2,582 sq. m,
main floor space 3,534 sq. m,
investment 30 mill.

Schlesische Strasse 27
Industrial Courtyard
**Wolfgang Scharlach,
Wolfdietrich Max Vogt, Berlin**
Client: Gewerbesiedlungs GmbH, Berlin
Conversion and addition,
approx. 11,000 sq. m usable space,
built 1992–96

Schlesische Strasse 27 A
Hostel for Homeless Men
Meyer-Rogge and Partners, Berlin
Client: Kreuzberg District Authority
Addition, usable space 1,805 sq. m,
cost DM 6.3 mill.,
built May 1994–April 1996

Stresemannstrasse 28,
Wilhelmstrasse 140–141
SPD-Headquarters
"Willy-Brandt-Haus"
**Helge Bofinger and Partners,
Wiesbaden/Berlin**
Client: Verwaltungs GmbH Bürohaus
Berlin, Bonn
7 stories, offices and conference rooms,
retail spaces, restaurant, subterranean
car park, gross floor area 24,000 sq. m,
cost DM 105 mill., built 1993–96

Stresemannstrasse 35–37,
Grossbeerenstrasse 94–96
Apartment and Commercial Building
Ulrich Grünberg and Partners, Berlin
Client: GSW
72 subsidized housing units,
8 commercial units,
cost DM approx. 21 mill.,
competition 1989, built 1993–95

Tempelhofer Ufer 8–9
Office Building "Tempelhofer Ufer"
Manfred Pechtold, Berlin
Client: KapHag Renditefonds 46
Urban infill, new building and
modernized existing building,
subterranean car park,
site area 1,652 sq. m,
gross floor area 6,670 sq. m,
investment DM 42 mill.,
completion 1995

Wrangelstrasse 55
Apartment and Commercial Building
Koch and Gräfe, Berlin
Client: CRE Real Estate GmbH
Urban infill,
5 stories plus attic story,
14 subsidized housing units,
134 sq. m commercial space,
site area 601 sq. m,
investment DM 6.2 mill.

Lichtenberg

Alfred-Kowalke-Strasse 39,
Kurze Strasse 1
Apartment and Office Building
Uwe Pompinon, Klaus Beyersdorff,
Berlin
Client: R & W Immobilienfonds 76 GbR
Two 4 storied buildings on the site area
of a listed "Ackerbürgerhaus"
remodelled for office use,
52 subsidized housing units,
1,513 sq. m commercial space,
site area 4,507 sq. m,
investment DM 34 mill.

Bornitzstrasse 73–75, Ruschestrasse
"Office Center Bornitzstrasse"
Hans Kahlen and Partners, Berlin
Client: KHR Projektentwicklungs GmbH,
Objekt Bornitzstrasse KG
1st building of the office center
development, 7 stories,
subterranean car park,
15,200 sq. m usable space

Dolgenseestrasse 1 A,
Sewanstrasse 174
Housing Complex
Ute Frank, Georg Augustin, Berlin
Client: WBG Lichtenberg mbH
2 buildings, 4–8 stories,
215 subsidized housing units,
housing space approx. 15,470 sq. m,
subterranean car park, ground floor
and 1st floor retail spaces and offices
with 1,600 sq. m, site area 16,835 sq. m,
investment DM 136 mill., built 1995–96

Drachenfelsstrasse 5
Apartment Building
Heiko Rößger, Berlin
Client: Drachen – Immobilien GmbH,
Berlin
13 privately owned apartments,
subterranean car park,
gross floor area 1,100 sq. m,
cost DM 2.7 mill.

Rheingoldstrasse
Apartment Building
Sabine Puche, Berlin
Client: Puche and Partners, Berlin
Urban infill, 3 stories,
12 subsidized housing units

Rummelsburger Strasse 63
Apartment Building
Christian Kühnel, Berlin
Client: Grundstücksges. Berlin
Rummelsburger Strasse 63 GbR
30 subsidized housing units,
site area 2,476 sq. m,
investment DM 16 mill.

Schreiberhauerstrasse
Service Center Ostkreuz on the site
area of the former Knorr-Bremse,
J.S.K. Perkins & Will, Berlin
Client: GbR DLZ Ostkreuz, Frankfort/ M.
8–13 stories, administration building
of the Public Insurance Company,
office and commercial space,
gross floor area 84,000 sq. m,
built 1995–96

Schulze-Boysen-Strasse
Primary School St. Maurizius
Arno Weber, Berlin
Client: Lichtenberg District Authority
Opening February 1996

Spittastrasse 15
Apartment and Commercial Building
Peter Busch, Berlin
Client: CRE Real Estate GmbH
Urban infill, 18 privately financed
housing units, 264 sq. m commercial
space, site area 436 sq. m,
investment DM 5.4 mill.

Wotanstrasse 16–18,
Gotlindestrasse 49, 49 A – B
Center for Integrated Housing and
Workshop for the Disabled
Gutzeit Beyer Architektur GmbH,
Berlin
Client: Grundstücksges. Wotanstrasse
GbR/Gutzeit Beyer Fonds Nr. 4
50 subsidized housing units,
1,744 sq. m commercial space,
3,071 sq. m workshop for disabled
persons, subterranean car park,
site area 4,437 sq. m,
investment approx. DM 54 mill.,
completion 1995

Marzahn

Ahrensfelder Chaussee 140–150 A
Apartment, Office, and Commercial
Building "Ahrensfelder Passagen"
Carl Serrin, Berlin
Client: Grundwert Handelszentrum
GmbH & Co, Berlin
Shopping center, offices, subterranean
car park, 48 subsidized housing units,
7,400 sq. m usable space in all,
site area 8,400 sq. m,
investment DM 45 mill.,
built May 1995–September 1996

Grabensprung 198,
Klara-Schabbel-Strasse 1
Apartment Block
Thomas Wagner, Limburg
Client: Henke Systembau & Jödicke,
Bauconsult GbR
3 stories, 11 housing units

Havemannstrasse
Apartment, Office, and Commercial
Complex "Havemann-Center"
Lindner, Roetting, Klasing and
Partners, Berlin
Client: Medico Fonds Nr. 32
Site area 6,800 sq. m,
gross floor area 10,400 sq. m,
built 1994–October 1995

Helene-Weigel-Platz 13–14
Shopping Center
"Springpfuhlpassage"
Dreß and Wucherpfennig, Berlin
Client: WBG Marzahn
New building and conversion
of an existing shopping mall,
4,129 sq. m commercial space in all,
investment DM 16 mill., built 1995–96

Klandorfer Strasse 2 A
Apartment and Commercial Building
Wolf-Dieter Borchert, Klaus Hendel,
Planungsgruppe H3, Berlin
Client: WBG Marzahn
Urban infill,
18 subsidized housing units,
3 commercial units with 340 sq. m,
built 1994–96

Köpenicker Strasse 234, Geraldstrasse
Apartment Block
Helmut Grothe, Salzkotten
Client: Fortline Projekt GmbH,
Bad Lippspringe
10 housing units

Landsberger Allee, Alte Rhinstrasse,
Rhinstrasse 140
Office and Commercial Center
"Die Pyramide"
Regina Schuh, Munich
Client: Fundus Gruppe, Immobilien
Anlagen Nr. 27 KG
5–24 stories, 44,000 sq. m usable
space, gross floor area 73,000 sq. m,
investment DM 285 mill., built 1993–95

Märkische Allee 230 A–244 A
Apartment and Commercial Building
Karl-Manfred Pflitsch, Berlin
Client: WBG Marzahn
1st building phase with 74 subsidized
housing units, 6 commercial units with
450 sq. m, completion December 1996

Mehrower Allee
Apartment, Office, and Commercial
Building "Plaza Marzahn"
Baasner, Möller and Langwald, Berlin
Client: Gädecke & Landsberg
110 housing units,
site area 14,000 sq. m,
subterranean car park, cost DM 80 mill.,
start of construction 1995,
completion of the 1st part 1996

Ringelnatzstrasse,
Hans-Fallada-Strasse,
Mettlachstrasse,
Dudweiler Strasse
Housing Development
"Ringelnatz-Siedlung"
Frank Dörken, Volker Heise, Berlin
Client: WBG Marzahn
220 subsidized housing units,
completion November 1995

Wolfener Strasse 36
Commercial Center Marzahn
Dybe and Partners, Berlin
Client: Gewerbesiedlungs GmbH, Berlin
Usable space approx. 33,800 sq. m,
completion 1995

Mitte

Alexanderplatz 2
Office and Commercial Building
"Alexanderhaus"
Pysall, Stahrenberg and Partners,
Berlin
Client: Bavaria Objekt- and Baubetreu-
ung GmbH
Addition to and reconstruction of the
listed building by Peter Behrens (1929),
site area 3,850 sq. m,
usable space 34,000 sq. m

Alte Jakobstrasse 83–84
"Geschäftsresidenz Alte Jakobstrasse"
Neufert, Mittmann and Partners, Berlin
Client: Concordia Bau and Boden AG,
Cologne
Office and commercial building,
5,333 sq. m usable space

Anklamer Strasse 38–40
Commercial Center "WeiberWirtschaft"
Inken Baller, Berlin
Client: Weiberwirtschaft e.G.
Apartment and commercial building,
7 stories, commercial, production,
and service center in an old industrial
courtyard, 13 housing units,
retail spaces, site area 3,800 sq. m,
gross floor area 9,200 sq. m,
cost DM 18 mill., conversion 1993–96

Behrenstrasse 26
"Hofgarten at Gendarmenmarkt"
Office Building
Josef Paul Kleihues, Berlin
Client: Hofgarten Real Estate B.V.
Amsterdam
Developer: HINES Grundstücks-
entwicklungs GmbH, Berlin
Block-defining structure,
9 stories, 2 shops, 16 offices,
gross floor area 2,765 sq. m,
built 1993–96

Behrenstrasse 27
"Hofgarten at Gendarmenmarkt"
Apartment and Commercial Building
Max Dudler, Berlin
Client: Hofgarten Real Estate B.V.
Amsterdam
Developer: HINES Grundstücks-
entwicklungs GmbH, Berlin
Block-defining structure, 46 housing
units, retail spaces with 472 sq. m,
gross floor area approx. 8,500 sq. m,
built 1993–96

Brückenstrasse 6
Office and Commercial Building
"JannowitzCenter"
Hans J. Erdmann, HPP Hentrich-
Petschnigg and Partners, Dusseldorf
Developer: Philipp Holzmann BauPro-
jekt AG, Frankfort, Vebau GmbH, Berlin
Building section 4, offices, 4 shops,
restaurant, subterranean car park,
gross floor area 16,061 sq. m,
built 1994–96

Brunnenstrasse 31, Anklamer Strasse
Housing Complex
Birgit Hansen, Barbara Kellig, Berlin
Client: Trigon Consult GmbH
21 housing units, ground floor
commercial use, subterranean car park,
completion 1996

Brunnenstrasse 181
Main Library Berlin-Mitte and
Industrial Courtyard
Renate Abelmann, Walter Vielain, Berlin
Client: Hanns Rauch, Munich
Reconstruction with additional links,
library use on ground floor, 1st floor and
basement, 2,200 sq. m usable space,
approx. 8,000 sq. m in all, construction
cost of library approx. DM 4 mill.,
built January 1995–June 1996

Charlottenstrasse 49
"Hofgarten at Gendarmenmarkt"
Hotel "Four Seasons"
Josef Paul Kleihues, Berlin
Client: Hofgarten Real Estate B.V.
Amsterdam
Developer: HINES Grundstücks-
entwicklungs GmbH, Berlin
Block-defining structure,
204 rooms incl. 42 Suites

Charlottenstrasse 80,
Zimmerstrasse 77
Office and Commercial Building
Arno Bonanni, Klaus Lattermann, Berlin
Client: Hübner & Weingärtner GbR
8 stories, commercial space
5,500 sq. m, subterranean car park,
gross floor area approx. 7,600 sq. m,
cost DM approx. 22 mill.,
built December 1992–February 1995

Französische Strasse 48
"Hofgarten at Gendarmenmarkt"
Office and Commercial Building
Jürgen Sawade, Berlin
Client: Hofgarten Real Estate B.V.
Amsterdam
Developer: HINES Grundstücks-
entwicklungs GmbH, Berlin
8 stories, 2 shops,
gross floor area 6,183 sq. m,
built 1993–96

Friedrichstrasse 66–70, Taubenstrasse,
Charlottenstrasse, Mohrenstrasse
"FriedrichstadtPassagen", Quartier 205
Oswald Mathias Ungers,
Cologne/Berlin
Client: Tishman Speyer Berlin GmbH &
Co Friedrichstrasse KG, Berlin
Block-defining structure, retail spaces
16,000 sq. m, offices 33,000 sq. m,
36 housing units, subterranean car park,
site area 8,325 sq. m,
gross floor area 94,600 sq. m,
competition 1991, built 1992–95

Friedrichstrasse 71–74, Jägerstrasse,
Charlottenstrasse, Taubenstrasse
"FriedrichstadtPassagen", Quartier 206
Pei, Cobb, Freed & Partners, New York
Client: Jagdfeld-Friedrichstadt-
Passagen Vermögensverwaltungs KG
Block-defining structure, block
addition, retail spaces 6,885 sq. m,
offices 11,760 sq. m, 12 housing units,
subterranean car park,
gross floor area 48,600 sq. m,
cost DM 750 mill., built 1993–95

Friedrichstrasse 76–78,
Französische Strasse, Jägerstrasse
"FriedrichstadtPassagen", Quartier 207
Jean Nouvel, Paris
Client: Dresdner Bank, Roland Ernst,
SGE Société Générale d'Entreprise,
CBC Compagnie Générale de Batiment
et de Construction
Developer: Galeries Lafayette,
Roland Ernst
Block-defining structure, department
store Galeries Lafayette, retail spaces,
offices, 19 housing units, subterranean
car park, site area 5,139 sq. m,
gross floor area 56,450 sq. m,
cost DM 460 mill., built 1994–95

Friedrichstrasse, Französische Strasse,
Charlottenstrasse, Behrenstrasse
"Hofgarten at Gendarmenmarkt"
Josef Paul Kleihues, Berlin
Client: Hofgarten Real Estate B.V.
Amsterdam
Developer: HINES Grundstücks-
entwicklungs GmbH, Berlin
Block-defining structure, concept of
unit construction system, co-ordination
and basement stories, subterranean car
park, site area 8,392 sq. m, gross floor
area 50,000 sq. m, floor space index 5.9,
investment DM 550 mill., built 1993–96

Friedrichstrasse 79–80,
Französische Strasse
"Hofgarten at Gendarmenmarkt"
Office and Commercial Buildings
Hans Kollhoff, Berlin
Client: Hofgarten Real Estate B.V.
Amsterdam
Developer: HINES Grundstücks-
entwicklungs GmbH, Berlin
2 buildings, 8 stories, shops with
920 sq. m usable space, offices with
approx. 8,653 sq. m usable space,
gross floor area approx. 10,000 sq. m,
built 1994–96

Friedrichstrasse 150–153,
Dorotheenstrasse, Mittelstrasse
Hotel Metropol/Maritim proArte
Holger Nettbaum and Partners, Berlin
Client: Hotel Metropol Berlin Grundstücks GmbH
Conversion and addition of the
former Hotel Metropol (built 1977),
gross floor area 32,300 sq. m,
period of construction: 1st building
phase 1993–95, 2nd building phase
1996–97

Gipsstrasse 23 B
Apartment and Commercial Building
Karin Kupsch-Jindra, Berlin,
Udo Wittner/HPP, Dusseldorf
Developer: Philipp Holzmann
BauProjekt AG, Frankfort
Urban infill, 6 stories,
12 housing units, 2 shops, 1 office,
subterranean car park,
gross floor area 2,079 sq. m,
built November 1993–January 1995

Hausvogteiplatz 2
Office and Commercial Building
Pysall, Stahrenberg and Partners,
Berlin
Client: Industrie- and Wohnbau GmbH
Groth & Graalfs
New building and modernization,
7 stories, 12 office units with
4,167 sq. m usable space, retail spaces,
site area 1,183 sq. m, gross floor area
5,240 sq. m, built 1993–96

Holzmarktstrasse 15–18
"Trias-Büro-Center"
Lucia Beringer, Günther Wawrick,
Munich
Client: DG Anlage GmbH, Bauwert
GmbH, Munich/Berlin
Office Building and service center,
22,500 sq. m office space,
2,818 sq. m commercial space,
subterranean car park,
site area 6,000 sq. m,
investment DM 250 mill.,
urban design competition 1992,
built May 1993–1996

Köpenicker Strasse 48–49
DAZ German Architecture Center
Claus Anderhalten, Berlin
Client: Owners Community Köpenicker
Strasse 48–49
1st building phase: new building
and conversion of a former factory
(built 1902), office and studio spaces,
Federal Office of the BDA,
9,430 sq. m usable space,
cost DM 35 mill.,
built January 1994–June 1995

Köpenicker Strasse 48–49
DAZ German Architecture Center
Assmann, Salomon, Scheidt, Berlin
Client: Owners Community Köpenicker
Strasse 48–49
2nd building phase: additional story on
top with housing units and office
section towards the Spree,
9,430 sq. m housing space, 2,200 sq. m
office space, cost DM 19.5 mill.,
built August 1995–July 1996

Legiendamm 2, Heinrich-Heine-Platz
Apartment and Commercial Building
Klaus Lattermann, Berlin
Client: Eckart-Trautmann Grundstücksgesellschaft GbR, Munich
Urban infill, 7 stories, 22 housing units,
6 commercial units,
gross floor area 2,893 sq. m,
construction cost DM 8 mill.,
built September 1995–December 1996

Legiendamm 14–16
Apartment and Commercial Building
Klaus Lattermann, Berlin
Client: Eckart-Trautmann Grundstücksgesellschaft GbR, Munich
Urban infill, 7 stories, 24 housing units,
7 commercial units,
gross floor area 2,804 sq. m,
construction cost DM 8 mill.,
built September 1995–December 1996

Leipziger Platz
Info-Box
Till Schneider, Michael Schumacher,
Frankfort/Main
Client: Developers Potsdamer Platz
Exhibition area 1,135 sq. m,
gross floor area 2,200 sq. m,
cost DM 10 mill.,
built June–October 1995

Luisenstrasse, Reinhardtstrasse 39
Office and Commercial Building
Eller, Maier, Walter, Dusseldorf
Client: Private Developer
8 stories, 1,882 sq. m usable space

Luisenstrasse, Schumannstrasse
Apartment and Commercial Building
"Luisenresidenz"
Werner Hülsmeier, Osnabrück
Client: Egon Geerkens, Osnabrück
5 stories, 94 housing units including
22 subsidized units, retail spaces,
1,000 sq. m storage space for the
German Theatre, site area 4,700 sq. m,
cost DM 50 mill., completion 12.1.1996

Markgrafenstrasse 34,
Mohrenstrasse 45
Commercial and Apartment Building
"Markgrafenhaus",
Josef Paul Kleihues, Berlin
Client: Unternehmensgruppe
Roland Ernst
9 housing units, 80 offices,
approx. 591 sq. m commercial space,
gross floor area 5,665 sq. m,
site area 954 sq. m, built 1994–96

Markgrafenstrasse 35
Commercial and Apartment Building at
Gendarmenmarkt
Max Dudler with Manfred Kunz, Berlin
Client: Bewag Berlin Electricity
Company
Office space 4,190 sq. m,
11 housing units, retail spaces,
site area 1,466 sq. m,
gross floor area 9,980 sq. m,
built 1995–96

Markgrafenstrasse 36
Commercial and Apartment Building at
Gendarmenmarkt
Heinz Hilmer, Christoph Sattler,
Munich
Client: Unternehmensgruppe
Roland Ernst
2,150 sq. m office space, 8 housing
units with 550 sq. m usable space,
615 sq. m retail spaces,
site area 905 sq. m,
gross floor area 5,200 sq. m,
built 1994–96

Neue Grünstrasse, Seydelstrasse
Apartment and Commercial Building
Günter Stahn, Berlin/
Storr Consulting, Munich
Client: Concordia Bau- and Boden AG,
Cologne
21 housing units with 1,000 sq. m,
office space 1,160 sq. m,
retail spaces 270 sq. m,
subterranean car park

Oranienburger Strasse 19–20
Apartment Building
Feddersen, von Herder and Partners
Winkelbauer, Berlin
Client: Berliner behinderte Kinder
Immobilien Fonds 7 GbR
Urban infill, 6 stories,
10 subsidized housing units,
4 housing units for disabled persons,
gross floor area 3,725 sq. m,
cost DM 15 mill., built 1993–95

Oranienburger Strasse 65
Apartment, Office, and Commercial
Building
Sadowski and Lebioda, Berlin
Client: Colonia Lebensversicherung AG,
Bauwert AG, Munich/Berlin
5 housing units with 551 sq. m usable
space, 4,658 sq. m offices and retail
spaces, subterranean car park,
site area 1,273 sq. m, cost DM 43 mill.,
built May 1994–October 1995

Rungestrasse 15–16
Apartment and Commercial Building
Michael König, Berlin
Client: Bauwert GmbH, Berlin/Munich
39 subsidized housing units
with 2,891 sq. m usable space,
commercial space 75 sq. m, site area
977 sq. m, investment DM 23 mill.,
built October 1994–December 1995

Schützenstrasse 18–25,
Jerusalemer Strasse, Zimmerstrasse,
Markgrafenstrasse
Media House "Mosse-Zentrum"
**Jürgen Fissler, Hans-Christof Ernst,
Berlin; Bernd H. Kemper, Hanover;
Dieter W. Schneider, Berlin;
Hans G. Strauch, Boston**
Client: Druckhaus Mitte GmbH,
Hans K. Roeder
Reconstruction, conversion and
additional buildings (printing house,
offices, retail spaces, housing units,
exhibition), subterranean car park,
reconstruction of the facade built
by Erich Mendelsohn (1921/22),
site area 13,700 sq. m, gross floor
area 69,159 sq. m, floor space
index 5.05, investment DM 350 mill.,
built 1993–95

Taubenstrasse 26
Office Building Taubenstrasse
**Jürgen Fissler, Hans-Christof Ernst,
Berlin**
Client: BIG Investment Gesellschaft KG,
Potsdam
Urban infill, 7 stories,
gross floor area 2,180 sq. m,
construction cost DM 5.5 mill.,
built 1992–95

Torstrasse 6
Office and Commercial Building
**Pysall, Stahrenberg and Partners,
Berlin**
Client: Grundstücksgesellschaft
Wilhelm-Pieck-Str. 6–8 GbR/
Groth + Graalfs
7 stories, 8 office units
with 4,444 sq. m usable space,
subterranean car park,
site area 1,554 sq. m, built 1992–95

Unter den Linden 42
Office and Commercial Building
"Haus Pietzsch"
Jürgen Sawade, Berlin
Client: Unter den Linden 42 GbR,
Wert-Konzept GmbH Berlin
3,400 sq. m office space,
900 sq. m commercial space,
subterranean car park, light-well as
exhibition area for the private
collection Pietzsch, cost DM 25 mill.,
built September 1992–March 1995

Wallstrasse 23–24
Office and Commercial Building
"Die Wallhöfe"
Giffey and Thüs, Hamburg
Client: Deutsche Immobilienfonds AG
New building behind the protected
facade built 1910, 6 stories,
8,000 sq. m usable space,
cost DM 80 mill.

Neukölln

Albulaweg, Kalksteinweg etc.
Housing Development "Spruch"
Wolfgang Engel, Klaus Zillich, Berlin
Client: Haschtmann Baubetreuungs
GmbH
84 houses, 525 subsidized and
privately financed housing units,
side area 8.3 hal, gross floor area
54,000 sq. m, floor space index 1.0–1.3

Housing Development "Spruch":
Strasse 621, Nr. 111
Child Care Center
**Wolfgang Freitag, Christian Hart-
mann, Reiner Sinz, Berlin**
Client: Haschtmann Baubetreuungs
GmbH
147 places, gross floor area 1,930 sq. m,
main floor space 1,160 sq. m,
cost DM approx. 5.7 mill.,
built January 1994–May 1996

Drusenheimer Weg 43,
Gerlinger Strasse
Apartment and Commercial Building
**Axel Liepe, Hartmut Steigelmann;
Helmut Stingl, Hans Wehrhahn, Berlin**
Client: WIR Wohnungsbau GmbH in
Berlin
3 stories, 121 subsidized housing units,
2 commercial units, subterranean car
park, cost DM 450 mill.

Gerlinger Strasse 52 etc.
Apartment and Commercial Building
**Heiss/Machleidt/IBUS (Hillmann,
Nagel, Schreck, Lütkemeyer), Berlin**
Client: WIR Wohnungsbau GmbH in
Berlin
87 subsidized housing units,
2 commercial units,
subterranean car park

Gerlinger Strasse
Child Care Center
**Peter Bendoraitis, BGM Architekten,
Berlin**
Client: Neukölln District Authority
Built 1994–96

Grauwackeweg 17–19
Housing Complex "Hofje"
**Baufrösche Kassel with Stadtwerk-
statt Berlin (Lutz Stanke, Michael
Wilberg)**
Client: Stadt and Land, Wohnbauten
GmbH, Berlin
15 integrated housing units,
part of the modernized housing
development from the 1950s
"Am Schlierbacher Weg",
March 1996: Design Award by the
Wüstenrot-Foundation

Hermannstrasse 214–219,
Rollbergstrasse, Mainzer Strasse
Office and Commercial Building
"Kindl-Boulevard"
Winkler, Effinger and Partners, Berlin
Client: Bauwert GmbH, Berlin/Munich
11 stories, rooms for festivities,
hotel with 211 rooms, cinema,
restaurant, subterranean car park,
site area 12,460 sq. m, gross floor area
52,000 sq. m, investment DM 400 mill.,
built 1994–96

Jeanette-Wolff-Strasse 8, 10, 16, 18,
Lieselotte-Berger-Strasse 23
Housing Development
"Rudower Felder"
**Jutta Schattauer, Constanze Tibes,
Berlin**
Client: GEHAG
4 urban villas, 1 row house, 4–5 stories,
44 subsidized housing units with 3,000
sq. m usable space,
built August 1995–December 1996

Karl-Marx-Strasse 272,
Juliusstrasse 1–2
Apartment Houses
Hafezi and Vahlefeld, Berlin
Client: Grundstücksgesellschaft
Karl-Marx-/Juliusstrasse bR
2 buildings as urban infill,
additional stories on top,
20 privately financed housing units,
2,875 sq. m commercial space,
site area 1,455 sq. m,
investment DM 36 mill.

Lahnstrasse 86
Office Building
**Rolf Backmann, Eugen Schieber,
Berlin**
Client: Bauherrengem. Lahnstrasse
Urban infill, subterranean car park,
gross floor area 2,200 sq. m,
investment DM 5.7 mill., built 1995–96

Landreiterweg
Apartment Buildings
Rainer Oefelein, Berlin
Client: Stadt and Land Wohnbauten
GmbH
Apartment blocks, 106 subsidized
housing units, subterranean car park,
cost DM 55 mill., 1st building phase
completion September 1995

Landreiterweg
Apartment Buildings
Rainer Oefelein, Berlin
Client: Stadt and Land Wohnbauten
GmbH
Apartment blocks,
98 subsidized housing units,
subterranean car park, cost DM 44 mill.,
2nd building phase, completion 1996

Landreiterweg
Child Care Center
Rainer Oefelein, Berlin
Client: Neukölln District Authority
Built 1994–96

Malteserstrasse, Hanielweg
Housing Develompant
**Klaus Baseler, Bernhard Schmidt and
Partners, Berlin**
Client: ITAG Aktiengesellschaft
187 subsidized housing units,
commercial space,
gross floor area 22,700 sq. m

Michel-Klinitz-Weg
Child Care Center
**Jan-Christoph Bassenge, Kay Puhan-
Schulz, Walter Schreiber, Berlin**
Client: Neukölln District Authority
Completion 1996

Mohriner Allee, Koppelweg
Apartment Buildings
Peter Berten, Berlin
Client: Stadt and Land Wohnbauten
GmbH
Apartment blocks, 46 subsidized
housing units, investment
DM 20.6 mill., completion
2nd building phase September 1995

Rollbergstrasse 20
Apartment Building
Architekturbüro ASA, Berlin
Client: Stadt and Land Wohnbauten
GmbH
Urban infill, 12 subsidized
housing units, 1 commercial unit,
cost DM 5 mill.,
completion September 1995

Sonnenallee 192
Apartment Building
**ELW (Georg Eyl, Werner Willi Weitz,
Joachim Würmle), Berlin**
Client: Groth & Graalfs, Berlin
5–8 stories, 100 subsidized
housing units, commercial space,
gross floor area 5,024 sq. m,
completion 1996

Sonnenallee 225
"Estrel Residence Hotel"
**Heiner Hennes, Waldemar Thilemann,
Bonn**
Client: Estrel Hotel-Betriebs-GmbH
17 stories, 1,125 rooms, conference
rooms, 5 restaurants, subterranean car
park, 40,000 sq. m usable space,
construction cost DM 240 mill.,
opening June 1995

Waltersdorfer Chaussee, Knollstrasse,
Schönefelder Strasse
Housing Development
"Rudower Felder"
**Martin and Pächter, Berlin
Schattauer and Tibes, Berlin**
Client: GEHAG Fonds 19 GbR
Apartment blocks, 4 stories,
82 subsidized housing units,
5,860 sq. m usable space,
built 1995–96

Waltersdorfer Chaussee, Knollstrasse,
Schönefelder Strasse
Apartment and Commercial Building
"Rudower Felder"
**GEHAG; Martin and Partners, Berlin;
Schattauer and Tibes, Berlin**
Client: Bavaria Immobilien
Beteiligungs GmbH & Co;
Objektverwaltung KG – LBB Fonds 5
Apartment blocks, 4–5 stories,
153 subsidized housing units,
10,505 sq. m usable space,
6 commercial units with 600 sq. m,
built 1995–96

Waltersdorfer Chaussee, Knollstrasse,
Schönefelder Strasse
Housing Development
"Rudower Felder"
Mussotter and Poeverlein, Berlin
Client:Grundstücksgesellschaft Rudow-
Süd GbR, repres. by GEHAG
Apartment blocks, 4 stories,
64 subsidized housing units,
4,365 sq. m usable space,
built 1995–96

Wissmannstrasse 31
Child Care Center
Joachim Ganz, Walter Rolfes, Berlin
Client: Neukölln District Authority
218 places,
construction cost DM 14 mill.,
built 1993–96

Pankow

Blankenfelder Strasse,
Rosenthaler Weg
Residential Area
"Französisch Buchholz"
Richter Architekten, Berlin
Kammann and Hummel, Berlin
Project Managing: Berliner
Eigenheim GmbH
1st building phase, 9 houses,
416 subsidized housing units,
completion 1996

Blankenfelder Strasse 30/32
Residential Area
"Französisch Buchholz"
Feddersen, von Herder and Partners
Winkelbauer, Berlin
Client: Dr. Upmeier Buchholz West GbR,
Berlin
Apartment building, 4 stories,
15 subsidized housing units,
gross floor area 1,642 sq. m,
cost DM 2.9 mill.,
built January–December 1996

Blankenfelder Strasse 34
Residential Area
"Französisch Buchholz"
Feddersen, von Herder and Partners
Winkelbauer, Berlin
Client: Dr. Upmeier Buchholz West GbR,
Berlin
Home for 30 mentally handicapped
persons, 5 housing communities (6
persons), 4 stories, gross floor area
1,610 sq. m, cost DM 3 mill.,
built January–December 1996

Blankenfelder Strasse 36/38
Residential Area
"Französisch Buchholz"
Bernd Faskel, Berlin
Client: Dr. Upmeier Buchholz West GbR,
Berlin
Apartment building, 34 housing units,
completion 1996

Blankenfelder Strasse 40/42
Residential Area
"Französisch Buchholz"
Carl August von Halle, Berlin
Client: Dr. Upmeier Buchholz West GbR,
Berlin
Apartment building, 34 housing units,
completion 1996

Blankenfelder Strasse 28,
Calvinistenweg 37–41,
Schweizer Tal 9, 11
Residential Area
"Französisch Buchholz"
Krüger, Schubert, Vandreike, Berlin
Client: Dr. Upmeier Buchholz West GbR,
Berlin
Apartment building, 64 housing units,
completion 1996

Blankenfelder Strasse 108–111
Residential Area
"Französisch Buchholz"
Jutta Schattauer, Constanze Tibes,
Berlin
Client: R & W Immobilienfonds 80 GbR
4 apartment blocks, 3 stories plus
attic story, 66 subsidized housing units
with 4,822 sq. m usable space,
built 1995–96

Blumenthalstrasse 31–37
Housing Complex
Kiewning, von Sass and Partners,
Berlin
Client: GbR Blumenthalstrasse
7 urban villas with 59 subsidized and
privately financed housing units,
site area 6,500 sq. m,
investment DM 20 mill.

Dietzgenstrasse 66–68
Apartment Buildings
Bernhard Ailinger, Berlin
Client: Immobilienfonds Dietzgenstrasse GbR
6 apartment blocks, 74 subsidized
housing units, 6 commercial units
with 950 sq. m usable space,
subterranean car park,
investment DM 50 mill.

Eddastrasse 17/19
Apartment Buildings
Klaus Felder, Berlin
Client: Dr. Upmeier
Eddastrasse 17/19 KG
Urban villa with 9 housing units,
1 subsidized duplex house,
site area 946 sq. m,
investment DM 6.6 mill.

Eichstrasse 51
Apartment Building
Hans-Jürgen Mücke, Berlin
Client: CWI CONVESTA Wohnbau &
Immobilien GmbH
4 stories, 720 sq. m housing space

Eschengraben 40
Primary School
Spree Architekten, Axel Heueis, Berlin
Client: Pankow District Authority
Addition of a 5 storied tower to an
existing 19th century school,
cost DM 1.4 mill., built 1994–95

Galenusstrasse 60
Hospital Kitchen Building
Beyer and Hafezi, Berlin
Client: Caritas-Krankenhilfe Berlin e.V.
2 stories, gross floor area 2,022 sq. m,
cost DM approx. 12 mill., built 1995–96

Garibaldistrasse 24–26,
Hielscherstrasse 17
Apartment Building
Ewald, Graf, Neumann, Berlin
Client: R & W Immobilienfonds 77 GbR
2 apartment blocks,
35 subsidized housing units,
site area 2,065 sq. m,
investment DM 17 mill.

Germanenstrasse 25
Apartment Building
Michael König, Berlin
Client: Bauwert GmbH, Berlin/Munich
12 subsidized housing units,
1,016 sq. m usable space,
investment DM 7.5 mill., built 1994–95

Görschstrasse 13
Apartment Building
Barbara Opperskalski, Berlin
Client: GbR Görschstrasse
Urban infill, 6 stories,
gross floor area 1,275 sq. m,
cost DM 4 mill., built 1996

Hauptstrasse 21
Apartment, Office, and Commercial
Building
Hans-Peter Fetz, Berlin
Client: Private Developer
7 housing units, 2 shops,
1 commercial unit,
main floor space 986 sq. m

Hauptstrasse, Hertzstrasse,
Niederstrasse
Apartment Buildings
Andreas Köhne, Berlin
Client: Hertzstrasse 9–11 KG
7 houses, 63 subsidized housing units,
880 sq. m commercial space,
site area 2,563 sq. m,
investment DM 44.3 mill.

Hauptstrasse 173
Apartment Building
Hans Schröder, Winfried Ringkamp,
Berlin
Client: GEWOBAG
88 privately owned apartments,
built April–December 1996

Herthaplatz 5, Buchholzer Strasse 9,
Wackenbergstrasse 31–37
Housing Complex
Ewald, Graf, Neumann, Berlin
Client: R & W Immobilienfonds 78 GbR
Block-defining structure,
4 apartment blocks, 4–5 stories,
92 subsidized housing units,
6,487 sq. m housing space,
site area 4,688 sq. m,
investment DM 40.7 mill.,
built January 1995–March 1996

Hugenottenplatz 1–4
Residential Area
"Französisch Buchholz"
Frank Friedrich, Berlin
Client: R & W Immobilienfonds 80 GbR
Apartment and commercial buildings,
59 housing units,
3,014 sq. m commercial space,
completion 1996

Idastrasse 22
Apartment Building
Wolf and Kreis, Berlin
Client: Vero Verwaltungs GmbH
16 subsidized housing units,
1,414 sq. m usable space,
site area 804 sq. m,
investment DM 9.7 mill.

Kastanienallee 105 A–107, Eschenallee
Apartment Buildings
Rainer Oefelein, Berlin
Client: ARCA, Berlin; Becon Grundstücksgesellschaft Berlin
5 urban villas, 4 stories,
65 subsidized housing units,
gross floor area 6,017 sq. m,
floor space index 1.3,
investment DM 39.2 mill.

Körnerstrasse 35–37
Housing Complex
Helmuth F. Schröder, Berlin
Client: Dr. Upmeier Körnerstrasse KG
Two 5 storied apartment blocks,
30 subsidized housing units,
site area 2,382 sq. m,
investment DM 16.7 mill.

Nesselweg
Housing Complex
Wolf von Horlacher, Gabriele Ruoff,
Architekten LINIE 5, Berlin
Client: CITY 7B
8 row houses, 2 stories plus attic story,
24 housing units with 2,235 sq. m
usable space, site area 13,216 sq. m,
gross floor area 8,897 sq. m,
cost DM 4.8 mill.,
built November 1994–June 1996

Neumannstrasse 3
Apartment and Commercial Building
Fin Bartels, Christoph Schmidt-Ott,
Berlin
Client: Neumannstrasse 3 GbR
56 subsidized housing units,
ground floor 820 sq. m retail spaces,
gross floor area 6,075 sq. m,
construction cost DM 14.2 mill.,
built 1994–95

Pankgrafenstrasse,
Wolfshagener Strasse
Housing Complex
Manfred Schiedhelm and Partners,
Berlin
Client: DEGEWO
4–6 stories,
69 subsidized housing units,
built 1995–96

Pankgrafenstrasse,
Wolfshagener Strasse
Housing Complex
Manfred Schiedhelm and Partners,
Berlin
Client: DEMOS
4–6 stories,
102 subsidized housing units,
built 1995–96

Pankstrasse 8–10
Commercial Center Buchholz
Heider, Kürten, Langwagen, Berlin
Client: Gewerbesiedlungs GmbH, Berlin
Commercial space for 110 companies,
site area 57,300 sq. m,
34,500 sq. m main floor space

Parkstrasse 17–23
Apartment Buildings
Rolf Eggenweiler, Berlin
Client: GbR Parkstrasse
7 urban villas, 67 subsidized
housing units, site area 7,057 sq. m,
investment DM 36.8 mill.

Platanenstrasse 25
Apartment Building
Barbara Opperskalski, Berlin
Client: GbR Platanenstrasse
Block-defining structure, 2 buildings,
3 stories plus attic story,
38 housing units, gross floor area
2,900 sq. m, cost DM 12 mill.,
built 1994–95

Schillerstrasse 2–6,
Waldowstrasse 22–23 A
Apartment Buildings
Winfried Brenne, Joachim Eble, Berlin
Client: GSW
57 subsidized housing units
of 114 housing units in all

Schönhauser Strasse 100–102 A
Apartment Building
Jochen Dreetz and Partners, Berlin
Client: Kontext GmbH, Berlin
36 subsidized and privately financed
housing units, gross floor area
2,498 sq. m, cost DM 6.3 mill.,
built December 1994–June 1996

Schonensche Strasse 29–30
Apartment Building
Ewald, Graf, Neumann, Berlin
Client: R & S Grundstücksges.
Schonensche Str. GbR
Block-defining structure,
29 subsidized housing units,
site area 1,464 sq. m,
investment DM 14 mill.

Schweizer Tal 10/12, Tiriotstrasse 1/5
Residential Area
"Französisch Buchholz"
Bernd Faskel, Berlin
Client: Dr. Upmeier Buchholz West GbR,
Berlin
Apartment buildings, 56 housing units,
completion 1996

Schweizer Tal 13
Residential Area
"Französisch Buchholz"
Ewald, Graf, Neumann, Berlin
Client: Dr. Upmeier Buchholz West GbR,
Berlin
Apartment building, 14 housing units,
subterranean car park,
completion 1996

Schweizer Tal 15/19
Residential Area
"Französisch Buchholz"
Meyer, Ernst and Partners, Berlin
Client: Dr. Upmeier Buchholz West GbR,
Berlin
Apartment buildings, 56 housing units,
subterranean car park, completion 1996

Schweizer Tal 21
Residential Area
"Französisch Buchholz"
Ewald, Graf, Neumann, Berlin
Client: Dr. Upmeier Buchholz West GbR,
Berlin
Apartment building, 14 housing units,
subterranean car park, completion
1996

Schweizer Tal 55/65, Matthieustrasse
Residential Area
"Französisch Buchholz"
Ewald, Graf, Neumann, Berlin
Client: R & W Immobilienfonds 80 GbR
Apartment buildings, 59 housing units,
completion 1996

Wackenbergstrasse 57,
Charlottenstrasse
Apartment Building
Siegfried Rauba, Berlin
Client: Grundstücksgem. Wacken-
bergstr. 57 GbR, Dr. Gerhardt, Berlin
2–3.5 stories, 14 housing units
with 993 sq. m usable space,
cost DM 2.8 mill.

Winkelwiesen, Kastanienallee 47/49
Housing Development "Winkelwiesen"
**Jutta Schattauer, Constanze Tibes,
Berlin**
Client: Immobilienfonds Winkelwiesen
GbR
5 building types, 426 subsidized
housing units,
urban conzept: Schattauer/Tibes,
apartment blocks: Schattauer/Tibes;
Liepe/Steigelmann, Berlin;
Eble/Kalepky, Tübingen;
Thomas Schindler, Freiburg;
competition 1991, built 1993–95

Am Friedrichshain 34,
Greifswalder Strasse 2
Apartment and Commercial Building
**Lennart Stange,
Wolfgang Rautenbach, Berlin**
Client: Oldenburg GmbH & Co Am
Friedrichshain KG
Urban infill, 23 subsidized housing
units, 258 sq. m commercial space,
site area 1,058 sq. m,
investment DM 17 mill.

Bergener Strasse, Ibsenstrasse,
Andersenstrasse
Apartment Building
Horst Pasch, Berlin
Client: WIR Wohnungsbaugesellschaft
in Berlin mbH
94 subsidized housing units,
subterranean car park

Bornholmer Strasse 82,
Schönfliesser Strasse 9
Apartment Building
Gerd Neumann, Berlin
Client: wip Wohnungsbaugesellschaft
Prenzlauer Berg
18 subsidized housing units,
1 commercial unit,
cost DM 9 mill., built 1995–96

Bornholmer Strasse, Stavanger Strasse
Apartment and Commercial Building
**Mario Maedebach, Werner Redeleit
and Partners, Berlin**
Client: GbR Bornholmer Strasse
7 stories, 20 housing units,
236 sq. m commercial space,
site area 1,250 sq. m, cost DM 11.5 mill.,
built 1995–96

Cantianstrasse 24
"Max-Schmeling-Hall"
in the Jahn-Sports Center
**Albert Dietz, Anett-Maud and Jörg
Joppien, Frankfurt/M. with Weidle-
plan Consulting GmbH**
Client: OSB Sportstättenbauten GmbH
Boxing hall, main audience with
10.000 seats, 3 triple sports halls,
approx. 35,000 sq. m, cost DM 200 mill.,
competition 1992,
built June 1993–December 1996

Fritz-Riedel-Strasse
Velodrome
Dominique Perrault, Paris
Structural Engineering: Ove Arup,
London
Client: OSB Sportstättenbauten GmbH
Velodrome with 5,800 seats,
gross floor area 44,120 sq. m,
completion 1996

Kollwitzstrasse 4
Apartment Building
**Feddersen, von Herder and Partners
Winkelbauer, Berlin**
Client: wip Wohnungsbaugesellschaft
Prenzlauer Berg
Urban infill, 7 stories,
15 subsidized housing units,
cost DM 7.6 mill., built 1994–96

Metzer Strasse 4
Apartment and Commercial Building
Klaus Lattermann, Berlin
Client: Haschtmann Baubetreuungs
GmbH, Berlin
7 stories, 22 subsidized housing units,
1 commercial unit, subterranean car
park, gross floor area 1,391 sq. m,
cost DM 4.9 mill.,
built 1995–January 1996

Rodenbergerstrasse 25–27
Apartment Building
Gerd Neumann, Berlin
Client: WIR Wohnungsbaugesellschaft
in Berlin mbH
44 subsidized housing units,
subterranean car park

Schönhauser Allee 181,
Fehrbelliner Strasse 100–101
Apartment and Commercial Building
**Feddersen, von Herder and Partners
Winkelbauer, Berlin**
Client: WIR Wohnungsbaugesellschaft in
Berlin mbH
Block-defining structure, 7 stories,
45 subsidized housing units,
1 commercial unit, gross floor area
6,022 sq. m, subterranean car park,
cost DM 10 mill., built 1995–96

Torstrasse 49, Schönhauser Allee
Office and Commercial Building
"Schönhauser Tor"
**FFNS and Giese-Bohne Planungs-
gesellschaft mbH, Dusseldorf/Berlin**
Client: Schönhauser Tor B.V.
Complete conversion of a listed
building, 8 stories, subterranean car
park, site area 4,500 sq. m,
15,000 sq. m usable space,
cost DM 70 mill.,
completion December 1995

Torstrasse 33/35, Strassburger Strasse
Office and Commercial Building
**Pysall, Stahrenberg and Partners,
Berlin**
Client: Industrie- u. Wohnbau
Groth & Graalfs
Corner building, 8 stories, 20 office
units, 2 shops, subterranean car park,
gross floor area 9,039 sq. m,
site area 2,527 sq. m, built 1993–95

Alt-Lübars 24 A
Branch of a Bank
**Jürgen Fissler, Hans-Christof Ernst,
Berlin**
Client: Köpenicker Bank
Free standing building complex
adapted to historic building relics,
2 stories, gross floor area 450 sq. m,
construction cost DM 2.3 mill.,
built 1993–96

Alt-Wittenau 48 A–D
Apartment Building
**Lothar Eckhardt, Georg P. Mügge,
Berlin**
Client: GSW
71 subsidized housing units

Amendestrasse 40–41
Child Care Center
Werner Wentzel, Berlin
Client: Reinickendorf District Authority
Child care center for 179 children,
connected to a neighborhood center,
cost DM 10 mill., competition 1990,
built April 1995–November 1996

Bernauer Strasse, Emstaler Platz
Housing Complex "Tegel-Süd"
Bernd Müller-Guilford, Berlin
Client: GEWOBAG
Apartment building with 100 housing
units and retail spaces

Blunckstrasse 9
GSW-Offices
Gerhard Pfannenschmidt, Berlin
Client: GSW
Office Building

Bottroper Weg
Housing Complex "Tegel-Süd"
**Otto Steidle and Partners, Munich/
Berlin, with Kress, Kara, Almesberger,
Berlin**
Client: GEWOBAG
Comb-shaped building, 4–5 stories,
192 housing units

Büchsenweg 25 A, 29 A
Apartment Building
Gerhard Pfannenschmidt, Berlin
Client: GSW
20 subsidized housing units

Emstaler Platz
Housing Complex "Tegel-Süd"
Perpetua Rausch, Heinz Willems, Berlin
Client: GEWOBAG
Addition to a high-rise building,
26 housing units, supermarket

Fürstendamm 17–18
Apartment and Commercial Building
Bernd Reinecke, Berlin
Client: Kastner & Partners Bau-Projekt
GmbH, Berlin
Urban villa with 7 housing units and
339 sq. m commercial space,
cost DM approx. 2 mill.,
built April 1995–December 1995

Hoppestrasse 18
Apartment Building
L. Schaffhauser, Berlin
Client: Onnasch Baubetreuung GmbH,
Berlin
Urban infill, 16 subsidized housing
units, site area 785 sq. m,
investment DM 7 mill.

Kieselbronner Weg 2–8 A
Apartment Building
**Ingeborg and Friedrich Spengelin,
Hanover**
Client: GSW
52 subsidized housing units

Klixstrasse, Zobeltitzstrasse
Housing Complex
Feige and Döring, Berlin
Client: Bauwert GmbH, Berlin/Munich
Comb-shaped building structure
and urban villa, 268 subsidized
housing units, commercial space,
gross floor area 26,920 sq. m,
floor space index 2.1

Otisstrasse 50, 50 A–D
Apartment Building
Müller and Rhode, Berlin
Client: WIR Wohnungsbaugesellschaft in
Berlin mbH
80 subsidized housing units,
subterranean car park

Sandhauser Strasse 72–74
"Wohnen am Forst"
Hans-Peter Störl, Berlin
Client: Bassmann Bau AG
Urban villas, 22 privately financed
housing units, site area 5,225 sq. m,
usable space 2,026 sq. m,
investment DM 14 mill.

Schlossstrasse 33
Office Building
Siegried Rauba, Georg Wiesner, Berlin
Client: Bauherrengem. Schlossstrasse
Oberhuber + Böttcher GbR
5 stories, 919 sq. m usable space,
cost DM 3.1 mill.,
completion January 1995

*Schorfheidestrasse,
Dannenwalder Weg 70–72 C*
Apartment Building
**Stefan Scholz in Bangert Scholz
Architekten, Berlin**
Client: GeSoBau/Grundstücks-
gesellschaft Rundling
78 subsidized housing units
with 5,420 sq. m usable space,
2 commercial units, subterranean car
park, site area 11,780 sq. m,
gross floor area 14,666 sq. m,
cost DM 33.7 mill.,
competition 1990, built 1993–96

*Senftenberger Ring 3 A–5 A,
Wilhelmsruher Damm*
Office and Service Center
"Märkisches Zentrum"
Waldemar Poreike, Berlin
Client: Märkisches Zentrum KG
Site area 8,000 sq. m,
gross floor area 9,000 sq. m,
cost DM 43 mill.

*Sommerstrasse 15–25,
Klemkestrasse 102/104*
Housing Complex
**Günther Grossmann, Zsuzsa Dámosy,
Berlin**
Client: DEGEWO
100 housing units, 100 apartments for
old people, child care center,
subterranean car park,
gross floor area 20,310 sq. m,
cost DM approx. 55 mill.,
competition 1990, built 1993–95

Sterkrader Strasse 45 A–F
Apartment Building
Georg Augustin, Ute Frank, Berlin
Client: GEWOBAG-Fonds III
70 subsidized housing units,
built May 1995–December 1996

Triftstrasse 3–4
Apartment Building
Georg P. Mügge, Berlin
Client: GSW
2 buildings with 16 subsidized housing
units, 3 stories, part of the housing
complex "Wohnen am Triftpark",
competition 1990, completion 1996

Schöneberg

Augsburger Strasse 12
Child Care Center
Ursulina Schüler, Ralf Witte, Berlin
Client: Schöneberg District Authority
4 stories, 182 places,
cost DM 11 mill., built 1993–96

Feurigstrasse 64
Apartment and Commercial Building
**ELW (Georg Eyl, Joachim Würmle),
Berlin**
Client: WIR Wohnungsbauges.
in Berlin mbH
18 subsidized housing units,
2 commercial units,
subterranean car park

Hauptstrasse 6
Apartment Building
Planungsgruppe Urbane Baukunst
Client: Stadt and Land Wohnbauten
GmbH
Urban infill, 30 subsidized housing
units, 4 commercial units,
subterranean car park, cost DM 13 mill.,
completion September 1995

Hauptstrasse 65
"BCI – Office Center Innsbrucker Platz"
Lothar Eckhardt, Berlin
Client: ImmobilienINVESTMENT DMS-
Vermittlungs GmbH
Low energy building, 9 stories,
office space 7,000 sq. m,
retail spaces 1,640 sq. m,
subterranean car park, cost DM 50 mill.

Kolonnenstrasse
Office and Commercial Building
"Schöneberger Tor"
**Peter Kreuzinger with Marlies Haase,
Berlin**
Client: Deutsches Institut für
Bautechnik
1st building phase:
offices, supermarket,
2nd building phase: boarding offices,
13,500 sq. m usable space,
start of construction summer 1994

Kurfürstenstrasse 130, Einemstrasse 11
Office and Commercial Building
Rainer Autzen, Bernd Reimers, Berlin
Client: Berlinhaus GmbH
Corner building, 7 stories,
parking on 2 subbasements,
5,700 sq. m usable space,
cost DM 18.6 mill.

Sachsendamm 2–7, Werdauer Weg
Office and Commercial Building
"DLZ Platinum"
Jürgen Sawade, Berlin
Client: Colonia-Nordstern Versicherung
Developer: UNITEC Ingenieur-
gesellschaft für Hochbau
11 stories, 17,341 sq. m usable space,
cost DM 134 mill., opening June 1995

Spandau

Aalemannufer 1–5, Rustweg
"Residential Park
Wasserstadt Aalemannufer"
**David Chipperfield, London;
Kramm and Strigl, Darmstadt;
Feige and Partners, Berlin;
Martin and Pächter, Berlin**
Client: Bauwert GmbH, Berlin/Munich
1st building phase (Martin and Pächter/
Feige and Partners): 9 buildings,
145 subsidized housing units,
built 1994–96; 2nd building phase
(Feige and Partners/ Kramm and Strigl/
Chipperfield): 4 buildings,
87 subsidized housing units,
built 1994–96

Aalemannufer 1–5, House 3, 10, 28
Apartment blocks
David Chipperfield, London
Contact architekt:
Carola Schäfers, Berlin
Client: Bauwert GmbH, Berlin/Munich
70 subsidized housing units,
main floor space 6,000 sq. m,
cost DM 15 mill., built 1995–96

Am Schlangengraben, Freiheit 7
Office Building and "Hotel Senator"
**Herbert and Siegfried Gergs,
Stuttgart**
Client: Gottlob Auwärter GmbH + Co KG,
Developer: Neoplan
8–16 stories, offices, exhibtion areas,
subterranean car park,
5,600 sq. m usable space

An der Kappe 126, 126 A
Apartment Building
L. Schaffhauser, Berlin
Client: Onnasch Baubetreuung
GmbH, Berlin
27 subsidized housing units,
site area 2,670 sq. m,
investment DM 13 mill.

Cosmarweg 91–121
Residential Park Staaken
**Schiedhelm and Partners;
Reinhard Müller; Hansen and Kellig;
Georg Heinrichs; Bernhard Winking;
Barna von Sartory; Bendoraitis,
Gurt, Meissner, Berlin**
Client: Grundstücksgesellschaft
Cosmarweg 91–121 mbH & Co
Beteiligungs KG
580 housing units, completion 1996

Falkenhagener Feld
Apartment Building
GSW Planungsabteilung
Client: GSW
Block-defining structure,
46 subsidized housing units,
gross floor area 5,022 sq. m,
floor space index 1.3

Falkenseer Chaussee 242–256
Apartment Building
**Feddersen, von Herder and Partners
Winkelbauer, Berlin**
Client: WIR Wohnungsbaugesellschaft in
Berlin mbH
1st building phase: street alignment,
85 subsidized housing units,
2 communities (6 persons),
subterranean car park,
gross floor area 11,227 sq. m,
cost DM 16.5 mill.

Falkenseer Chaussee 242–256
Apartment Building
**ELW (Georg Eyl, Werner Willi Weitz,
Joachim Würmle), Berlin**
Client: WIR Wohnungsbaugesellschaft in
Berlin mbH
2nd building phase: street alignment,
43 subsidized housing units,
gross floor area 5,024 sq. m

Földerichstrasse 40
Apartment and Commercial Building
**Wolf and Kreis, Architekturbüro
GmbH, Berlin**
Client: BKatz Baubetreuungs GmbH
Corner building, 5 stories,
25 subsidized housing units,
323 sq. m commercial space,
site area 1,727 sq. m,
investment DM 16.8 mill.

Gartenfelder Strasse
Apartment Building
Rüdiger and Partners, Berlin
Client: Deutsche Immobilien
Investierungs-AG
Corner building, 122 subsidized
housing units, 8,655 sq. m usable
space, site area 5,754 sq. m,
investment DM 63 mill.

Goltzstrasse 70–71
Apartment Building
**ELW (Georg Eyl, Joachim Würmle),
Berlin**
Client: WIR Wohnungsbaugesellschaft in
Berlin mbH
18 subsidized housing units

Kellerwaldweg 2 A, B, Knüllweg 6 A, B
Apartment Building
Stefan Feist, Brigitte Saar, Berlin (GSW)
Client: GSW
42 subsidized housing units

Kulbeweg 24 A
Apartment Building
Hans-Ulrich Eggers, Berlin
Client: ARWOBAU, Berlin
Free standing building,
5 stories, 59 housing units,
usable space 3,051 sq. m,
cost DM 21 mill., built 1995–96

Lüdenscheider Weg
Apartment Building
Gerd Brand, Berlin
Client: GEWOBAG
60 housing units,
built April–December 1996

*Nauener Strasse 70,
Seegefelder Strasse 105*
Apartment Building
**Wolfgang Scharlach,
Rainer Wischhusen, Berlin**
Client: WIR Wohnungsbaugesellschaft
in Berlin mbH
54 housing units,
gross floor area 6,063 sq. m,
floor space index 1.59, cost DM 22 mill.,
competition 1989, built 1992–95

Nennhauser Damm, Hauptstrasse 34,
Bergstrasse 29–91,
Erna-Sack-Strasse 2–46,
Käthe-Heinemann-Weg 1–33
"Residential Park Staakener Felder"
Feige and Partners, Berlin; Büro ASP
(Nolte, Plaßmann, Reese), Berlin,
Kassel, Leipzig
Client: Bauwert GmbH, Berlin/Munich
14 houses, 145 subsidized housing
units (Feige), 3 urban villas,
13 privately financed housing units,
265 sq. m commercial space (ASP),
built 1994–96

Neuendorfer Strasse 1
GSW-Offices Spandau
bauart, Berlin
Client: GSW
Office Building

Niederneuendorfer Allee 35–40
"Residential Park
Wasserstadt Aalemannufer"
Feige und Partners, Berlin
Client: Bauwert GmbH, Berlin/Munich
5 urban villas, 81 subsidized housing
units, gross floor area 8,330 sq. m,
built 1995–96

Parkstrasse 1 A–C, 2 A–F
Apartment Building
Peter Lehrecke, Berlin
Client: GSW
63 subsidized housing units

Pulvermühlenweg
Residential Park
Wasserstadt Oberhavel
Nalbach Architekten/Eckert, Negwer,
Sommer, Suselbeek/Betow, Berlin
Client: GSW
Apartment buildings, 70 subsidized
housing units of 183 units in all,
1st building phase completion 1996

Pulvermühlenweg, Haus 5
Residential Park
Wasserstadt Oberhavel
Carola Schäfers, Berlin
Client: GSW
Apartment building,
14 subsidized housing units ,
gross floor area 1,280 sq. m,
main floor space 900 sq. m,
cost DM 2.7 mill., built 1995–96

Pulvermühlenweg, Grützmacherweg
4 Bridges in Wasserstadt Oberhavel
Hans Kollhoff, Berlin
Client: TET Wasserstadt Oberhavel
16–27 m length, reinforced concrete
composite construction,
completion 1996

Schönwalder Allee 26
"Simonshof", Johannesstift
Günter Plessow, Reinhold Ehlers,
Peter Krop, Berlin
Client: Ev. Johannesstift Spandau
5 apartment buildings with
35 subsidized housing units,
gross floor area 6,500 sq. m

Siemenswerderweg 27
Boathouse at Stössensee
Saskia Schleifer-Kühnel, Berlin
Client: Technical University Berlin
1–2 stories on 300 sq. m,
cost DM 2.7 mill.,
completion August 1996

Sollingzeile 1 A–B,
Frankenwaldstrasse 14 A–c
Apartment Building
Jens Freiberg, Paris
Client: GSW
43 subsidized housing units

Weissenburger Strasse 57 A–c
Apartment Buildings
Rolf Reymer, Berlin; TEBECO Ing.
GmbH
Client: BB-Grundfonds 14 GbR
Three 5 storied houses,
30 subsidized housing units,
site area 2,459 sq. m,
usable space 2,590 sq. m,
investment DM 19.3 mill.

Steglitz

Ahlener Weg 10, 12, 16–20
Apartment Building
Joachim Grundei, Architekten PSP,
Berlin
Client: WIR Wohnungsbauges.
in Berlin mbH/ Hanseatica
55 subsidized housing units,
subterranean car park

Bäkestrasse 15 A, 16
Apartment Buildings
Patzschke, Klotz and Partners, Berlin
Client: Bassmann Bau AG, Berlin
2 apartment blocks, 3 stories plus
attic story, 26 housing units,
site area 3,528 sq. m, built 1995–96

Bassermannweg 17/19
Apartment Building
Gert Eckel, Berlin
Client: Private Developer
3 stories, 24 privately owned
apartments, subterranean car park,
gross floor area 2,400 sq. m,
built 1995–96

Belssstrasse, Lüdeckestrasse
Apartment Buildings
Baufrösche Kassel, Berlin
Client: GSW
5 urban villas completing a housing
development, 64 of 115 housing units
in all, completion 1996

Bergstrasse 6–7
Apartment and Commercial Building
Assmann, Salomon, Scheidt, Berlin
Client: Grundstücksgesellschaft
Bergstrasse GbR
Block-defining structure,
28 subsidized housing units,
ground floor 197 sq. m commercial
space, site area 760 sq. m,
investment DM 17 mill.,
completion 1995

Berlinickestrasse 5–7
Apartment Building
Gertrud Margomenos, Berlin
Client: Garant Controlling,
Unternehmensberatung,
Gesellschaft für Beteiligung mbH
Building addition, 6 stories,
32 subsidized housing units,
subterranean car park

Bürgipfad 24–36 A
Housing Development
Klaus Wiechers, Christian Beck,
Berlin
Client: GSW
14 houses, 2 storied duplex houses
and 3 storied row houses,
48 of 84 subsidized housing units in all,
gross floor area 10,934 sq. m,
floor space index 0.57, built 1992–95

Celsiusstrasse 64, 70, 72
Apartment Buildings, Addition to
"Thermometer-Siedlung"
Ingrid Hentschel, Axel Oestreich,
Berlin
Client: GSW
Celsiusstrasse 72: new building,
34 subsidized housing units,
2,400 sq. m usable space;
Celsiusstrasse 70: conversion of a
garage, Celsiusstrasse 64: new
commercial building with GSW-office,
2 shops, and 2 housing units,
cost DM approx. 17 mill.,
built April 1994–December 1995

Gravelottestrasse 10
Housing Complex
Faber and Krebs, Berlin
Client: Immobilienfonds
Gravelottestr. 10 GbR
34 subsidized housing units,
830 sq. m commercial space,
site area 2,453 sq. m,
investment DM 23.3 mill.

Kaulbachstrasse 63–67
Old Peoples' Home
Rolf D. Weisse, Berlin
Client: Steglitz District Authority
Free standing structure, 84 individual
rooms, 28 double rooms,
site area approx. 8,390 sq. m,
gross floor area approx. 6,940 sq. m,
cost DM 27 mill., built 1993–95

Leonorenstrasse 18/22
Apartment and Commercial Building
Hans-Peter Störl, Berlin
Client: Grundstücks GbR Berlin-
Lankwitz/Bassmann Bau AG
4–5 stories, 44 housing units with
3,197 sq. m, 5 commercial units with
774 sq. m, cost DM 26.8 mill.,
built 1994–March 1996

Lepsiusstrasse
Consulate and Apartment Building
J.S.K. Perkins & Will, Berlin
Client: WPE West LB Immobilien,
Dusseldorf
Urban infill around existing last
century villa, subterranean car park,
gross floor area 3,500 sq. m

Manteuffelstrasse 11
Child Care Center
Hans-G. Rogalla, Berlin
Client: Steglitz District Authority
3 stories, approx. 1,500 sq. m usable
space, cost approx. DM 10.5 mill.,
built September 1993–September
1996

Schlossstrasse
Department Store "Galleria"
Quick, Bäckmann, Quick, Berlin
Client: Ingeborg and Peter Fritz, Berlin
8 stories, 40 shops, 2 penthouses,
subterranean car park,
7,830 sq. m usable space,
cost DM 17.5 mill.

Südendstrasse 48
Apartment Block
Harald Kuhn, Berlin
Client: GbR Südendstrasse
10 subsidized housing units,
2 privately financed housing units,
site area 918 sq. m,
usable space 833 sq. m,
investment DM 6.1 mill.

Tempelhof

Borussiastrasse 61,
Neue Strasse 7, 7 A, 9, 11
Apartment Building
Manfred Pechtold, Berlin
Client: IKAR Immobilienfonds 23 GbR
Block-defining structure,
67 subsidized housing units,
site area 3,291 sq. m,
investment DM 39.6 mill.,
completion 1995

Buckower Damm 259
Apartment and Commercial Complex
Stadtplan Architekten, Berlin
Client: Buckower Damm 259 GbR
New building:
12 subsidized housing units,
conversion of an existing single-family
house and a coach-house to
3 commercial units, site area
1,652 sq. m, investment DM 8.5 mill.,
completion 1995

Culemeyerstrasse 2
Office Building
Pechtold, Rupprecht, Schlicht,
Schulze-Rohr, Berlin
Client: M.O.S.P.E.S. Wohnungsbau
GmbH
Developer: Groth & Graalfs
33 office units, 1 housing unit,
office and service spaces 10,216 sq. m,
gross floor area 13,019 sq. m,
site area 8,003 sq. m, built 1992–95

Germaniastrasse 1, 1 A
Housing Complex
Volker Kranz, Berlin
Client: Immobilienfonds Germaniastrasse GbR
31 subsidized housing units,
site area 1,379 sq. m,
investment DM 18 mill.

Gersdorfstrasse 73 A
Apartment Building
Schröder and Ringkamp, Berlin
Client: GEWOBAG Immobilienfonds
2 GbR
14 subsidized housing units,
usable space 1,162 sq. m,
site area 1,590 sq. m,
investment DM 7.6 mill.

Goldschmidtstrasse 2–4,
Schichauweg 31–35, Gestorffstrasse 1
Housing Complex
Peter Fink, Berlin
Client: Baubetreuungen-Eigenheimbau
GmbH
4 buildings, 54 subsidized housing
units, site area 5,602 sq. m,
investment DM 24 mill.,
completion 1995

Im Domstift
Housing Complex
Georg-P. Mügge, Berlin
Client: Petrus-Werk GmbH Berlin
3 storied buildings,
38 subsidized housing units,
gross floor area 4,128 sq. m,
completion 1996

John-Locke-Strasse
Housing Complex
**Dreß and Wucherpfennig, Berlin;
Peter Rudolph, Berlin**
Client: Stadt and Land Wohnbauten
GmbH
6 urban villas, 92 subsidized housing
units, subterranean car park,
cost DM 49 mill., built 1995–96

*Marienfelder Allee 160–170,
Hildburghauser Strasse*
Housing Complex
**Klaus Meier-Hartmann, Moritz Müller
and Götz M. Keller, Cologne**
Client: NOSTRO Grundstücks-GmbH
& Co Marienfelder Allee oHG
23 apartment blocks with
248 subsidized housing units,
2,625 sq. m commercial space,
site area 14,536 sq. m,
investment DM 119 mill.

Marienfelder Allee 212–220
Housing Complex "Marienfelder Tor"
Carl August von Halle, Berlin
Client: Ärzte-Treuhand Vermögensverwaltungs GmbH
234 subsidized housing units,
3,000 sq. m commercial space,
site area 19,342 sq. m,
investment DM 131 mill.,
completion 1995

Tempelhofer Damm 12
Criminal Investigation Authority
Bea and Walther Betz, Munich
Client: Berlin Department of the Interior
Block-defining structure, pavilion
for a cafeteria in the courtyard,
gross floor area 77,600 sq. m,
construction cost DM 406 mill.,
competition 1987,
built 1989–December 1995

*Ullsteinstrasse 114–142,
Mariendorfer Strasse 1–3*
Office and Commercial Building
Johanne and Gernot Nalbach, Berlin
Client: Becker & Kries Grundstücks
GmbH
Addition to the listed "Ullsteinhaus"
(built by Eugen Schmohl, 1923–26),
usable space 6,766 sq. m,
site area 33,159 sq. m,
investment DM 25.5 mill.,
built 1991–95

Werner-Voss-Damm, Hoeppnerstrasse
Apartment and Commercial Building
**Arthur Numrich, Werner Albrecht and
Partners, Berlin**
Client: Stadt and Land Wohnbauten
GmbH
38 subsidized housing units,
2 commercial units,
subterranean car park,
cost DM 20.2 mill., completion 1995

*Weskammstrasse 15/19,
Hildburghauser Strasse*
"Apartment and Commercial Building
Marienfelde"
Wilfried Schuh, Berlin
Client: KapHag Renditefonds 47 "Wohn-
and Geschäftshaus Marienfelde"
5 stories, 1,225 sq. m office space,
505 sq. m retail spaces, 12 subsidized
and privately financed housing units,
subterranean car park, site area
3,634 sq. m, investment DM 28.8 mill.,
completion 1995

Tiergarten

Alt-Moabit 59–61, Beusselstrasse
Planning and Design Center
"Spree Forum"
Kleihues and Kleihues, Berlin
Client: Hanseatica Unternehmensgruppe Berlin
7 stories, offices, restaurant,
retail spaces, subterranean car park,
gross floor area 20,000 sq. m,
site area 2,900 sq. m,
built May 1994–February 1996

*Bayreuther Strasse 37/38,
Keithstrasse 7, Kleistrasse 22*
Office Building GEMA
Rupert Ahlborn and Partners, Berlin
Client: GEMA Munich
New building:
gross floor area 6,360 sq. m,
modernisized existing building:
gross floor area 6,626 sq. m,
cost DM 60 mill.

Carnotstrasse 4–7
Office Building "Gemini Quay"
Jürgen Sawade, Berlin
Client: Grundag Grundbesitztreuhand-
and Wohnbauten AG, Berlin
Two identical 6 storied buildings,
approx. 19,000 sq. m usable space,
subterranean car park, site area
8,959sq. m, investment DM 163 mill.

Invalidenstrasse
Museum of Contemporary Art
"Hamburger Bahnhof"
Josef Paul Kleihues, Berlin
Client: Berlin Senate for Building,
Housing and Traffic, SMPK Berlin,
National Gallery
Conversion of the former railway
station (built 1843–47 by Friedrich
Neuhaus), and additional wing,
exhibiton area 8,000 sq. m,
opening November 1996

*Jonasstrasse, Turmstrasse,
Bredowstrasse*
Apartment and Commercial Building
Mirjam Blase, Osman Kapici, Berlin
Client: DEGEWO
Block-defining structure, 32 housing
units, 900 sq. m commercial space,
gross floor area 5,010 sq. m,
site area 1,357 sq. m, cost DM 20 mill.,
competition 1991, built 1993–96

Kurfürstenstrasse 53–55
School Extension and
Duplex Sports Hall
**Carola Schäfers
with Klaus Theo Brenner, Berlin**
Client: Tiergarten District Authority
Gross floor area 8,156 sq. m,
main floor space 3,275 sq. m,
cost DM 26 mill., built 1994–96

Kurfürstenstrasse 83 A, 84
Office and Commercial Building
Kammann and Hummel, Berlin
Client: Rheinspree-Parfümeriewaren
Handels GmbH & Co KG, Berlin
Addition of a 10 storied stairwell
and 3 storied new building,
cost DM 15 mill.

Lehrter Strasse 39–40
Apartment and Commercial Buildings
**Jörg Pampe; Steidle and Partners;
PUB – Bernhard Strecker; Werkfabrik
(H. Herzberg, M. Winkes, P. Winkes),
Berlin**
Client: Gehag; SPI; Erbbauverein
Moabit
180 subsidized housing units,
cost DM 66 mill.

Lehrter Strasse 46, Perleberger Strasse
Office and Commercial Building
Wilfried Bete, Berlin
Client: Haberent Grundstücks GmbH,
Berlin
7 stories, offices, shops,
storage space, subterranean car park,
site area 1,971 sq. m, gross floor area
5,202 sq. m, cost DM 42 mill.,
built December 1994–1996

*Lehrter Strasse 47–48,
Perleberger Strasse 64–66*
Apartment and Commercial Buildings
**T. Wiesner, E. Meik, G. Procakis,
W. Kneffel, Berlin**
Client: Haberent Grundstücks GmbH,
Berlin
Four 5 storied apartment blocks
with 60 subsidized housing units,
ground floor 600 sq. m commercial
space, investment DM 36.5 mill.

Lehrter Strasse 47
Apartment Building
Georg Procakis, Joachim Ramin, Berlin
Client: Haberent Grundstücks GmbH,
Berlin
23 housing units,
gross floor area 3,155 sq. m,
built 1994–95

Pohlstrasse 20
Office and Commercial Building
Patzschke, Klotz and Partners, Berlin
Client: librum Buchhandelsforum
GmbH & Co, Berlin
6 stories, office, commercial and
exhibition space, subterranean car
park, 7,775 sq. m usable space,
site area 2,805 sq. m,
investment DM 51 mill.,
completion May 1995

Wiebestrasse 39
Child Care Center
Inken Baller, Berlin
Client: Tiergarten District Authority
85 places, cost DM 4.3 mill.,
built 1995–96

Treptow

Dörpfeldstrasse 40/42
Apartment and Commercial Building
**Paul Panter, Thomas Kemmermann,
Berlin**
Client: LBB-Grundstücksgesellschaft
3–6 stories, shops, offices,
savings bank, 20 housing units,
gross floor area 4,400 sq. m,
cost DM 15 mill., built 1995–96

Dörpfeldstrasse 43
Apartment and Commercial Building
Werner Wentzel, Berlin
Client: Onnasch – Baubetreuungs
GmbH, Berlin
Urban infill, ground floor commercial
use, 1st/2nd floor offices, 3rd/4th floor
7 housing units, site area 688 sq. m,
investment DM 5.9 mill., built 1994–95

*Elsenstrasse 5–8, Am Treptower Park,
Puschkinallee*
Apartment and Commercial Buildings
Patzschke, Klotz and Partners, Berlin
Client: Grundstücksges. Elsenstrasse
5–8 GbR, Berlin
Block-defining structure, 3–5 stories
plus staggered story, 75 housing units,
3,956 sq. m commercial space,
site area 5,684 sq. m, built 1994–96

Elsenstrasse 45–49
Housing Complex Elsenstrasse
**Planungsbüro P & R, Michael Reinelt,
Brigitte Kreutel, Berlin**
Client: Trigon Grundstücks GmbH
200 subsidized housing units,
subterranean car park, completion 1995

Elsenstrasse 102–105
Housing Complex
Kippel, de Biasio, Scherrer, Berlin
Client: Elsenstrasse 102–105
Grundstücksges. GbR
2 buildings, 5–6 stories,
125 subsidized housing units,
480 sq. m commercial space,
subterranean car park,
usable space 10,575 sq. m,
site area 6,247 sq. m,
investment DM 74.6 mill.

*Grabowstrasse, Lohmühlenstrasse,
Lexisstrasse, Harzer Strasse,
Schmollerstrasse, Onckenstrasse,
Bouchéstrasse, Mengerzeile*
Completion of an Existing
Residential Complex
**Arthur Numrich, Werner Albrecht
(Städtebau); Numrich, Albrecht,
GAGFAH, Bernhard Nowottnick;
Liepe, Steigelmann, Berlin**
Client: Stadt and Land; GAGFAH;
Trigon Consult
316 subsidized housing units,
gross floor area approx. 33,000 sq. m,
floor space index 0.9–1.84

Gross-Berliner Damm 72
Administration and Office Building
Baumgartner and Falkenberg, Munich
Client: Grundstücksgesellschaft Filser,
Munich
Office spaces, subterranean car park,
18,500 sq. m usable space,
gross floor area 29,700 sq. m,
construction cost DM 58.9 mill.,
built August 1994–August 1996

Handjerystrasse 24–24 A
Apartment Building
**Heerwagen, Lohmann and Partners,
Berlin**
Client: BOTAG Bodentreuhand- and
Verwaltungs-AG
Urban infill, 26 subsidized housing
units, subterranean car park,
site area 1,164 sq. m,
investment DM 14 mill.

Kiefholzstrasse 408–410 A
Housing Complex
**Axel Liepe, Hartmut Steigelmann,
Berlin**
Client: Grundstücksgesellschaft
Kiefholzstrasse bR
6 houses with 73 subsidized housing
units, site area 4,225 sq. m, investment
DM 36.7 mill., completion 1995

Ortolfstrasse 180
Old People's Housing
HOPRO, Berlin
Client: Stadt and Land Wohnbauten
GmbH
Addition to existing prefabricated
housing complex, 37 subsidized
housing units, cost DM 10.7 mill.

Ortolfstrasse 194
Old People's Housing
HOPRO, Berlin
Client: Stadt and Land Wohnbauten
GmbH
Addition to existing prefabricated
housing complex,
36 subsidized housing units,
cost DM 10.7 mill.

Ortolfstrasse, Siriusstrasse
Apartment and Commercial Building
Manfred Pflitsch, Altmann, Berlin
Client: Stadt and Land Wohnbauten
GmbH
Addition to existing prefabricated
housing complex, 102 subsidized
housing units, 7 commercial units,
subterranean car park,
cost DM 35.9 mill.

Puschkinallee 52, Bouchéstrasse 10
Office Blocks
"Am Schlesischen Busch",
Bewag-Headquarters
**Axel Liepe, Hartmut Steigelmann,
Berlin**
Client: Grundwertfonds Büropark
Am Schlesischen Busch GbR
6 stories, gross floor area 66,200 sq. m,
site area 23,130 sq. m,
investment DM 270 mill., built 1993–95

*Schmollerstrasse 1–4,
Schmollerplatz 21–23,
Bouchéstrasse 34–36*
"Housing Complex at Schmollerpark"
**Axel Liepe, Hartmut Steigelmann,
Berlin**
Client: Grundstücksgesellschaft
Schmollerplatz bR
118 subsidized housing units,
ground floor commercial use,
subterranean car park, completion 1995

Schnellerstrasse 99–102 A
Housing Complex
**M. Müller; Günter Plessow,
Reinhold Ehlers, Peter Krop, Berlin**
Client: Stadt and Land Wohnbauten
GmbH
Apartment blocks, 105 subsidized
housing units, 2 commercial units,
subterranean car park, cost DM 36 mill.

*Residential Area Altglienicke:
1.1 Cologne Quarter*
Housing Development
**Frank Dörken, Volker Heise;
Friedrich Karl Borck, Matthias Boye,
Dietrich Schaefer; Dieter Rühle
and Partners; Büro Joachim Ramin,
Berlin**
Client: Stadt and Land Wohnbauten
GmbH
1st building phase,
587 subsidized housing units,
investment DM 208.5 mill.,
completion December 1995

*Residential Area Altglienicke:
Porzerstrasse 33–37, 67–79*
Apartment Buildings
**Axel Liepe, Hartmut Steigelmann,
Berlin**
Client: Stadt and Land Wohnbauten
GmbH
89 housing units, completion 1996

*Residential Area Altglienicke 1.1:
Weidenweg, Holunderweg; Rebenweg*
Apartment Buildings
Georg Procakis, Joachim Ramin, Berlin
Client: Stadt and Land Wohnbauten
GmbH
78 housing units,
gross floor area 9,855 sq. m,
cost DM 16.5 mill., built 1994–95

Wedding

Antonstrasse 10
Primary School
Michael Oppert, Berlin
Client: Wedding District Authority
Addition to a school built by
Ludwig Hoffmann for 500 pupils,
5 stories, cost DM 8.1 mill.,
opening November 1996

Augustenburger Platz 1
Teaching and Research Facilities for the
University Clinic Rudolf Virchow
**Hannelore Deubzer, Jürgen König,
Berlin**
Client: Senate for Science and
Research, Berlin
Cost DM 800 mill., built 1994–96

*Badstrasse 35–36,
Travemünder Strasse 2*
Jerusalem-Library at the Luisenbad
**Rebecca Chestnutt, Robert Niess,
Berlin**
Client: Berlin Senate,
Wedding District Authority
Building around a listed ensemble,
gross floor area 3,255 sq. m,
cost DM 31.6 mill., competition 1988,
built September 1991–October 1995

Grüntaler Strasse 39–41
Apartment Building
Gisela Schneidewind, Berlin
Client: GESOBAU
28 housing units,
gross floor area 4,200 sq. m,
construction cost DM approx. 8 mill.,
built 1994–96

Luxemburger Strasse 26–28
Apartment Building
Klaus Effenberger, Berlin
Client: GSW
Corner building,
49 subsidized housing units,
gross floor area 5,100 sq. m,
floor space index 3.56

Osloer Strasse 100
Office Building
**Jürgen Fissler, Hans-Christof Ernst,
Berlin**
Client: RCeGe GmbH, Berlin
Urban infill with front building
and side wing, 6 stories,
gross floor area 4,420 sq. m,
construction cost DM 7.8 mill.,
built 1991–95

*Reinickendorfer Strasse, Uferstrasse,
Wiesenstrasse, Bornemannstrasse
"Rotaprint-Block"*
**Beatrix Wuttke, Bernd Albers u.a.,
Berlin**
Client: GESOBAU
6 stories, 230 subsidized housing units,
commercial space, child care center,
gross floor area 27,000 sq. m,
floor space index 1.9

Steegerstrasse 43–61
Apartment and Commercial Building
Mösing and Partners, Berlin
Client: Ärzte-Treuhand
Vermögensverwaltungs GmbH
72 subsidized housing units,
1 commercial unit 96 sq. m,
site area 3,340 sq. m,
investment DM 34.6 mill.

Triftstrasse 67
Students' Residence
Helmut Galle, Berlin
Client: Bürgermeister-Reuter-Stiftung
8–10 stories, 290 housing units for
326 students, subterranean car park,
roof-terrace, cinema, cost DM 42 mill.

Weissensee

*Achillesstrasse 1, Karestrasse 2/8,
Pfannschmidtstrasse 2/18, 1/23,
Röländerstrasse 47*
Residential Area Karow-Nord
**Eckert, Negwer, Sommer, Suselbeek;
Dörr, Ludolf, Wimmer;
Krüger, Schubert, Vandreike;
Burgmayer, Berlin**
Client: WBG Weissensee
442 subsidized housing units,
built 1994–96

Achillesstrasse 24/26
Residential Area Karow-Nord
**Joachim Dörr, Axel Ludolf,
Josef Wimmer, Berlin**
Client: Bavaria-Immobilien Beteili-
gungs GmbH & Co – LBB-Fonds 5
2 apartment blocks, 46 subsidized
housing units, built 1995–96

Achillesstrasse 31
Residential Area Karow-Nord
Primary School
**Hartmut Steigelmann, Büro Liepe and
Steigelmann, Berlin**
Client: Weissensee District Authority
Usable space 5,940 sq. m,
cost DM 40 mill.,
built August 1994–September 1995

*Achillesstrasse 30, 42;
Teichbergstrasse 19, Matestrasse
23/27; Teichbergstrasse 1,
Busonistrasse 90/94*
Residential Area Karow-Nord
**Feddersen, von Herder and Partners,
Berlin**
Client: Groth + Graalfs, Berlin
4 subsidized apartment blocks

*Achillesstrasse 32, 40;
Teichbergstrasse 5/7, Rutenzeile 9;
Teichbergstrasse 13/15, Rutenzeile 11*
Residential Area Karow-Nord
Helmut Ferdinand and Gerth, Berlin
Client: Groth + Graalfs, Berlin
4 subsidized apartment blocks

*Achillesstrasse 34, 38;
Busonistrasse 106/110,
Am Elsebrocken 1, 3, 19;
Teichbergstrasse 3, 17*
Residential Area Karow-Nord
**Stephan Höhne, Christian Rapp,
Berlin**
Client: Groth + Graalfs, Berlin
7 subsidized apartment blocks

*Achillesstrasse 36;
Am Elsebrocken 5/9; 11/15; 17*
Residential Area Karow-Nord
**Jakob Schulze-Rohr, Hans-Jürgen
Ruprecht, Wolfgang Schlicht, Berlin**
Client: Groth + Graalfs, Berlin
4 subsidized apartment blocks

*Achtrutenberg 38/43; 44; 46+48, 53/55;
Gewanneweg 3*
Residential Area Karow-Nord
Bernd Faskel, Uwe Becker, Berlin
Client: Groth + Graalfs, Berlin
5 subsidized apartment blocks

*Achtrutenberg 18, 30; 32; 34/36, 47/51,
Gewanneweg 7*
Residential Area Karow-Nord
Moore, Ruble, Yudell, Santa Monica
Client: Groth + Graalfs, Berlin
6 subsidized apartment blocks

Albertinenstrasse 4, 5, 5 A
Housing Complex
**Georg Brzezinski, Gerd Kehrbach,
Berlin**
Client: Kastanienhof GbR
50 subsidized housing units,
328 sq. m commercial space,
subterranean car park,
site area 3,039 sq. m,
investment DM 34.6 mill.

Beerbaumstrasse 1/3,
Busonistrasse 138
Residential Area Karow-Nord
Klaus Wiechers, Christian Beck,
Berlin
Client: Bavaria-Immobilien Beteili-
gungs GmbH & Co – LBB-Fonds 5
Apartment block,
29 subsidized housing units,
built 1994–96

Beerbaumstrasse 5/9, 11/15
Residential Area Karow-Nord
Stefan Scholz, Berlin
Client: Bavaria-Immobilien Beteiligungs GmbH & Co – LBB-Fonds 5
2 apartment blocks,
60 subsidized housing units,
built 1995–96

Beerbaumstrasse 17/29
Residential Area Karow-Nord
GEHAG Techn. Dept.
Client: Bavaria-Immobilien Beteili-
gungs GmbH & Co – LBB-Fonds 5,
Apartment block,
89 subsidized housing units,
built 1994–96

Berliner Allee 62–66
Office Building and Shopping Center
"Kaufcenter"
Volker Kirsch, Berlin
Client: GbR Berliner Allee/J. F. Müller &
Partners, Hamburg
department store with 2,000 sq. m
commercial space, 1,150 sq. m office
space, cost DM 17.5 mill.,
built January–November 1996

Busonistrasse 113/117
Residential Area Karow-Nord
Carola Schäfers, Berlin
Client: Bavaria-Immobilien Beteiligungs GmbH & Co – LBB-Fonds 5
2 apartment blocks,
23 subsidized housing units,
gross floor area 3,300 sq. m,
main floor space 2,415 sq. m,
cost DM 6.7 mill., built 1995–96

Busonistrasse 81/85
Residential Area Karow-Nord
Alexander Williams, Berlin
Client: Bavaria-Immobilien Beteiligungs GmbH & Co – LBB-Fonds 5
2 apartment blocks,
21 subsidized housing units,
built 1995–96

Busonistrasse 119/125;
Busonistrasse 135/Achillesstrasse 28;
Achillesstrasse 16/
Röländerstrasse 38/40
Residential Area Karow-Nord
Jürgen Fissler, Hans-Christof Ernst,
Berlin
Client: Bavaria-Immobilien Beteili-
gungs GmbH & Co – LBB-Fonds 5
3 apartment blocks,
66 subsidized housing units,
built 1995–96

Busonistrasse 127/131,
Achillesstrasse 18/22
Residential Area Karow-Nord
Johannes Wiesermann, Berlin
Client: Bavaria-Immobilien Beteiligungs GmbH & Co – LBB-Fonds 5
6 apartment blocks,
42 subsidized housing units,
built 1995–96

Busonistrasse 136; Achillesstrasse 44;
Busonistrasse 118/130
Residential Area Karow-Nord
Kammann and Hummel, Berlin
Client: Groth + Graalfs, Berlin
3 apartment blocks, 3 stories,
110 subsidized housing units

Busonistrasse 140/144,
Pfannschmidtstrasse 52/58
Residential Area Karow-Nord
Heinz Hilmer, Christoph Sattler,
Munich/Berlin
Client: Bavaria-Immobilien Beteili-
gungs GmbH & Co – LBB-Fonds 5
2 apartment blocks,
80 subsidized housing units,
built 1994–96

Charlottenburger Strasse 52/53
Apartment Building
Achatzi Architekten, Berlin
Client: Grundstücksgemeinschaft
Charlottenburger Strasse GbR
Subsidized housing units,
gross floor area 2,094 sq. m,
cost DM 4.2 mill.

Falkenberger Strasse 13/14
Child Care Center Integrating Disabled
and Severly Disabled Children
Werner Wentzel, Berlin
Client: Weissensee District Authority
Cost DM 4.3 mill.,
built February 1994–October 1995

Gustav-Adolf-Strasse 130
"DGZ-Office-City Berlin-Weissensee"
Günther Stahn, Berlin/
Storr Consulting, Munich
Client: Concordia Bau- and Boden AG
Apartment and commercial buildings,
inside an existing chocolate factory
complex, 152 housing units, offices,
retail spaces, child care center,
restaurant, gross floor area
88,000 sq. m, cost DM 350 mill.,
built 1993–96

Hamburger Platz-Süd
Apartment Building
Gerd Neumann, Berlin
Client: WBG Weissensee
83 subsidized housing units,
completion July 1996

Hansastrasse 65–149
Housing Complex
Feddersen, von Herder and Partners
Winkelbauer, Berlin
Client: Groth & Graalfs, Berlin
Block-defining structure and single
houses, 3–5 stories, 452 subsidzed
housing units, subterranean car park,
gross floor area 35,000 sq. m,
cost DM 100 mill., built 1993–95

Jacobsohnstrasse 30/32
Apartment Building
Alfred Grazioli, Berlin
Client: GbR Jacobsohnstrasse
Subsidized housing units,
site area 1,471 sq. m,
main floor space 1,919 sq. m,
investment DM 13.2 mill.

Liebermannstrasse 128–144
Housing Complex
Christian Faber, Klaus D. Krebs, Berlin
Client: BbK Immobilienfonds 8 GbR
2–3 stories, 69 subsidized housing
units, 2 apartments for mentally
disabled, site area 6,528 sq. m,
main floor space 5,257 sq. m,
investment DM 35.2 mill.

Orankesee
Apartment Building
Werkplan, Berlin
Client: WBG Weissensee
150 subsidized housing units,
completion April 1996

Pfannschmidtstrasse 2
Residential Area Karow-Nord,
Child Care Center
Carola Schäfers, Berlin
Client: Weissensee District Authority
100 places, gross floor area 1,285 sq. m,
main floor space 497 sq. m,
cost DM 6 mill., built 1994–96

Pfannschmidtstrasse 24/30, 44/50;
Ballonplatz 1–4, 5–8;
Achillesstrasse 15/21, 23/29
Residential Area Karow-Nord
Jan Rave, Rolf Rave, Berlin
Client: Bavaria-Immobilien Beteili-
gungs GmbH & Co – LBB-Fonds 5
2 apartment blocks, 213 subsidized
housing units, 3 commercial units,
built 1995–96

Pfannschmidtstrasse 33/37, 39/43,
57/59/63, 65/69/71
Residential Area Karow-Nord
Eckert, Negwer, Sommer, Suselbeek,
Berlin
Client: GEHAG-Fonds 16 GbR
4 apartment blocks: 2 buildings
with 74 subsidized housing units,
built 1994–96; 2 buildings with
74 subsidized housing units,
built 1995–96

Pfannschmidtstrasse 61, 67
Residential Area Karow-Nord
Dietrich Bangert, Berlin
Client: GEHAG-Fonds 16 GbR
2 apartment blocks,
36 subsidized housing units,
built 1994–96

Pfannschmidtstrasse 73/79, 53/55
Residential Area Karow-Nord
Joachim Dörr, Axel Ludolf,
Josef Wimmer, Berlin
Client: GEHAG-Fonds 16 GbR
2 apartment blocks,
90 subsidized housing units,
built 1994–96

Prenzlauer Promenade 47/48
Apartment and Commercial Building
Fin Bartels, Christoph Schmidt-Ott
with Hansen, Wiegner, Ebert, Paçati,
Berlin
Client: D11 Fonds B 100
Block-defining structure, 7 stories,
210 subsidized housing units,
13,500 sq. m housing space,
2,573 sq. m commercial space,
site area 12,900 sq. m,
gross floor area 19,620 sq. m,
construction cost DM 65 mill.,
built October 1995–December 1996

Röländerstrasse 28/30;
Gewanneweg 5;
Achtrutenberg 31/33; 20/22; 26; 24 + 28; 57
Residential Area Karow-Nord
Joachim Ramin, Berlin
Client: Groth + Graalfs, Berlin
6 subsidized apartment blocks

Röländerstrasse 32/36; 12/26;
Achtrutenberg 52; 50 + 54; 16;
Gewanneweg 1
Residential Area Karow-Nord
Andreas Brandt, Rudolph Böttcher,
Berlin
Client: Groth + Graalfs, Berlin
6 subsidized apartment blocks

Röländerstrasse 44, 47,
Pfannschmidtstrasse 21/23, 25/31
Residential Area Karow-Nord
Casa Nova, Berlin
Client: GEHAG-Fonds 16 GbR
2 apartment blocks,
102 subsidized housing units,
built 1995–96

Röländerstrasse 39/45,
Pfannschmidtstrasse 12/18,
Achillesstrasse 3/13
Residential Area Karow-Nord
Krüger, Schubert, Vandreike;
Dámosy; Wiechers and Beck, Berlin
Client: KapHag Fonds 49
"Wohnen in Berlin-Karow" KG
Five 4 storied buildings with
164 housing units, 12,266 sq. m
housing space, cost DM 86 mill.,
completion May 1996
(Thorsten Krüger, Christiane Schubert,
Bertram Vandreike: building C2, D2;
Zsuzsanna Dámosy: building D1, D4;
Wiechers and Beck: building D3)

Röländerstrasse 46
Residential Area Karow-Nord,
Child Care Center
Horst Hielscher, Berlin
Client: Berlin Senate for Building,
Housing, and Traffic/ Weissensee
District Authority
100 places, cost DM 6 mill.,
completion 1996

Roelckestrasse 152
Youth Training Center/ Building
Professions
Gerhard Münster, Ralf Sroka; Berlin
Client: Zukunftsbau GmbH
Administration and workshop building
as urban infill, 5 stories, 1 storied
workshop and storage building,
4,100 sq. m usable space,
cost DM 13 mill., built 1994–96

Schönstrasse 80
Park-Clinic Weissensee
Thomas Baumann and Schnittger,
Berlin
Client: Park-Klinik Weissensee
GmbH & Co KG
5 stories, 350 beds,
gross floor area 30,000 sq. m,
cost DM approx. 180 mill.,
built 1994–96

Streustrasse 68
Apartment and Commercial Building
Paul Panter, Thomas Kemmermann,
Berlin
Client: LBB-Grundstücksgesellschaft
Urban infill 4 stories,
garden building 3 stories,
savings bank, office space,
4 housing units,
gross floor area 1,400 sq. m,
cost DM 5 mill., built 1995–96

Streustrasse 117
Office Building of the
Housing Company Weissensee
Rolf D. Weisse, Berlin
Client: wbg Weissensee
Block-defining structure,
site area approx. 730 sq. m,
gross floor area 1,600 sq. m,
cost DM 7 mill., built 1994–95

Streustrasse 120, Börnestrasse 5–7
Apartment and Commercial Building
Rolf D. Weisse, Berlin
Client: wbg Weissensee
Corner building, 29 housing units,
3 commercial units, subterranean car
park, site area 2,522 sq. m,
gross floor area 3,755 sq. m,
cost DM 13 mill., built 1994–95

Wilmersdorf

Cicerostrasse 23–25
Office and Commercial Building
Bogensberger and Schlusche, Berlin
Client: Industrie- and Wohnbau
Groth + Graalfs GmbH
Office space 8,906 sq. m,
subterranean car park,
site area 4,512 sq. m, built 1993–95

Cunostrasse 54–56,
Orberstrasse 10–16
Child Care Center
Axel Liepe, Hartmut Steigelmann,
Berlin
Client: Wilmersdorf District Authority
Freestanding structure in the courtyard,
140 places, construction cost
DM 8 mill., built 1994–96

Halenseestrasse, Kronprinzendamm 15
Office Building
Hilde Léon, Konrad Wohlhage, Berlin
Client: Münchner Baugesellschaft
Berlin
11 stories, gross floor area 13,880 sq. m,
subterranean car park, cost DM 38 mill.,
competition 1990, built 1994–96

Hohenzollerndamm 187,
Sigmaringer Strasse 18–19
"Apartment and Commercial Building
at Emser Platz"
Arno Bonanni, Berlin
Client: Emser Platz Grundstücks GmbH
& Co., Berlin
8 stories, 3,000 sq. m usable space,
subterranean car park, cost DM 22 mill.

Kurfürstendamm 115 A+B,
Georg-Wilhelm-Strasse
Apartment and Commercial Building
Hinrich Baller, Doris Pieroth, Berlin
Client: Prinz zu Hohenlohe & Banghard
Developer: PHIDIAS GmbH
Offices, shops, 20 housing units,
subterranean car park,
gross floor area 4,500 sq. m,
cost DM 45 mill., completion May 1996

Kurfürstendamm 119
Office and Commercial Building
"KU 119"
Helmut Jahn, Chicago
Client: "Zürich" Versicherungs-GmbH
Developer: VEBAU GmbH, Berlin
8 stories, offices, shops, café,
subterranean car park, 184 bicycle
stands, site area 4,694 sq. m,
gross floor area 15,240 sq. m,
investment DM 160 mill.,
built 1993–96

Lietzenburger Strasse 67–71,
Fasanenstrasse 33
Office and Commercial Building
"Lietzen Ensemble"
Moritz Müller, Götz M. Keller with
Werner Stutz,
Collectif Architecture, Berlin
Client: Fasane s.c.c.v.,Paris/GESTIMO
7 stories, offices, shops,
17 housing units, subterranean car
park, gross floor area 9,600 sq. m,
cost DM 140 mill.

Pariser Strasse 42–43,
Sächsische Strasse 71
Apartment and Commercial Building
Feige and Partners, Berlin
Client: Bauwert GmbH, Berlin/Munich
Corner building, 7 stories,
19 housing units, site area 872 sq. m,
gross floor area 3,850 sq. m,
cost DM 35 mill., built 1993–95

Prinzregentenstrasse 25
Office Building
Jan Rave, Rolf Rave, Berlin
Client: Bavaria Objekt- and Baubetreuung GmbH
Corner building, 5–7 stories,
subterranean car park,
site area 900 sq. m,
usable space 3,958 sq. m

Richard-Strauss-Strasse 37
Apartment and Office Building
Thomas Baumann,
Kirsten Baumann, Berlin
4 stories, subterranean car park,
gross floor area approx. 1,000 sq. m,
cost DM approx. 5 mill., built 1994–96

Sigmaringer Strasse 18–19,
Hohenzollerndamm 187
Apartment and Commercial Building
Arno Bonanni, Klaus Lattermann, Berlin
Client: Delta Bauträger GmbH/
Hennig v. Harlessem
Corner building, 6 stories plus
attic story, new apartment, office and
commercial building, additional story
on top of an existing building,
16 subsidized housing units,
2,170 sq. m commercial space,
gross floor area 8,042 sq. m,
cost DM approx. 11 mill.,
built December 1993–February 1995

Uhlandstrasse 88–90,
Fechnerstrasse 12
Apartment, Office, and Commercial
Building
Rainer Autzen, Bernd Reimers, Berlin
Client: CIVIS Immobilien
Corner building, 7 stories,
subterranean car park, 15 housing units,
4,300 sq. m usable space,
gross floor area 5,715 sq. m,
cost DM 12 mill.

Uhlandstrasse 134
Apartment and Commercial Building
Hasso von Werder and Partners,
Berlin
Client: GbR Uhlandstrasse 134
6 stories, 29 subsidized housing units,
631 sq. m commercial space,
site area 1,248 sq. m.
Modernized existing building with
additional story on top built by
Norbert Schwinski, Berlin,
investment DM 6 mill.

Wiesbadener Strasse 25–28
Johannes Wiesermann, Berlin
Apartment Buildings
Client: Eisenbahn-Siedlungs-GmbH
4 row houses, 5 stories,
52 housing units, subterranean car
park, main floor space 3,981 sq. m,
built 1994–96

Zehlendorf

Berlepschstrasse 6–8
Saab Showroom and Service Center
Rolf Backmann, Eugen Schieber,
Berlin
Client: Martin Weber
Cost DM 5.5 mill., built 1995–96

Charlottenburger Strasse 4
Office Building of a Software Company
Ulrike and Georg Höing, Berlin
Client: Abriko GbR, Berlin
Free standing building with 4 flexiblel
levels, gross floor area 660 sq. m,
cost DM 1.2 mill.,
built February 1995–January 1996

Düppelstrasse 1,
Potsdamer Strasse 27–28
Apartment and Commercial Building
Rolf Backmann, Eugen Schieber,
Berlin
Client: Fam. Deutscher, Berlin
4 stories, offices, penthouses,
subterranean car park,
gross floor area 1,100 sq. m,
991 sq. m usable space, cost DM 3 mill.

Gimpelsteig 3–5
Hospital Zehlendorf,
Local Dependance of Behring
Gottfried Böhm,
Friedrich Steinigeweg,
Client: Berlin Senate
First aid and teaching clinic, 435 beds,
main building opening September 1995

Kaiserstuhlstrasse 32
Apartment Building
Spree Architekten, Udo Schendel,
Berlin
Client: GbR Kaiserstuhlstrasse 32
Free standing apartment building,
10 housing units,
usable space 1,100 sq. m,
cost DM 3.2 mill., built 1995–96

Sachtlebenstrasse 53, 53 A, 53 B,
Ringelsteinweg 3–8
Housing Complex Goerzallee
Gehag Technik, Ronald v. d. Starre,
Berlin
Client: Grundstücksgesellschaft
Goerzallee GbR, Gehag-Fonds 15
9 apartment buildings, 2–3 stories
plus staggered story, 80 subsidized
housing units with 5,500 sq. m usable
space, subterranean car park,
built 1995–96

Teltower Damm 87–93
John-F.-Kennedy School Center,
Addition
Harald Deilmann, Münster/Potsdam
Client: Bezirk Zehlendorf
School building and sports hall,
complete modernization of the
complex, gross floor area 18,000 sq. m,
cost DM 90 mill., built 1987–96

FSB

FSB Franz Schneider Brakel
http://www.fsb.de
Fax (0 52 72) 60 83 00

FSB

FSB Franz Schneider Brakel
http://www.fsb.de
Fax (0 52 72) 60 83 00

HEWI

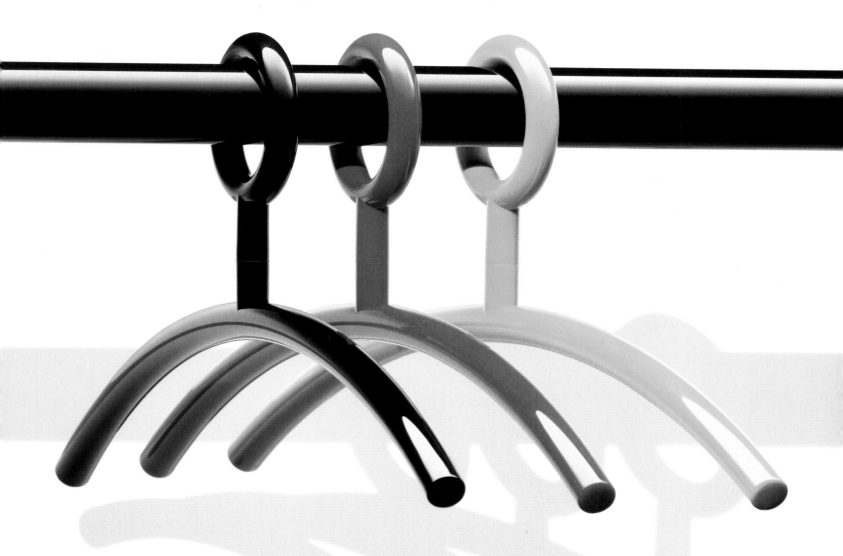

Dress Code
Coat hanger, polyamide, Arolsen 1996
Tidies up every wardrobe. Different coloured hangers for every member of the family mean mother and daughter, father and son, brother and sister, uncle and aunt, will never again need to fight over what belongs to whom.
For more information, contact HEWI, D-34442 Arolsen, Germany, tel. +49 (0) 56 91/82 0

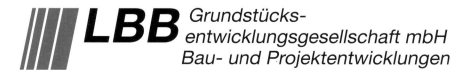

imamumzum...*

Auf Deutschland bauen
Die Hypothekenbank, die Zeichen setzt

Die Berlin Hyp:
Die Hypothekenbank mit Heimvorteil.

Berlin ist als Hauptstadt auch das Gesicht des modernen
Deutschlands. Viele Bauwerke dieser Stadt sind mit der
Berlin Hyp finanziert worden – Zeichen, die das Image der
Stadt prägen. Und das wird auch in Zukunft so sein. Durch
unsere Kapitalkraft und unsere kompetenten Mitarbeiter
sind wir in der Lage, Bauherren und Anlegern überall in
Deutschland hilfreich zur Seite zu stehen, und das nicht
nur finanziell: Wir kennen das Geschäft der Immobilien-
finanzierung seit über 125 Jahren!
Mit der Berlin Hyp wird Architektur in die Tat umgesetzt,
in der Hauptstadt und mit unserem bundesweiten Geschäfts-
stellennetz in ganz Deutschland, denn die Berlin Hyp baut
auf Deutschland.

Berlin Hyp
Berlin-Hannoversche
Hypothekenbank AG

ein Unternehmen der
Bankgesellschaft Berlin

Budapester Straße 1
10787 Berlin
Besucher: Keithstraße 45
Telefon (030) 25 999-0
Telefax (030) 25 999-131

Landschaftstraße 8
30159 Hannover
Telefon (0511) 30 11-0
Telefax (0511) 30 11-384

im Provisorisches Leitsystem im Flughafen Düsseldorf.

MetaDesign für den öffentlichen Raum

am

Immobilienmarketing am
Willy-Brandt-Haus, Berlin.

um

Orientierungssystem in und um den U-Bahnhof herum
(Berliner Verkehrsbetriebe).

Wir geben Orientierung im Gebäude oder auf dem Gelände.
Wir vermitteln den besten Eindruck von der Immobilie oder
dem Verkehrssystem. Wir machen Architektur übersichtlich
und komplexe Systeme verständlich – mit Design.

MetaDesign Berlin
Bergmannstraße 102
D-10961 Berlin

+49·30·695 79 200
fax +49·30·695 79·222

mail@metadesign.de

www.metadesign.com

MetaDesign London
5–8 Hardwick Street
GB-London EC1R 4RB

+44·171·520 1000
fax +44·171·520 1099

mail@metadesign.co.uk

MetaDesign San Francisco
350 Pacific Avenue
USA-San Francisco CA 94111

+1·415·627 0790
fax +1·415·627 0795

mail@metadesign.com

zum

Zum Notausgang
des Gebäudes.

1928

DAIMLERBENZ

Potsdamer Platz

Projekt:

Medienereignis und Gesprächsthema: Der ehemals verkehrsreichste Platz Europas soll wieder zum lebendigen Mittelpunkt Berlins werden. Eine Vision wird Wirklichkeit: der neue Potsdamer Platz.

Betreten der Baustelle erwünscht.

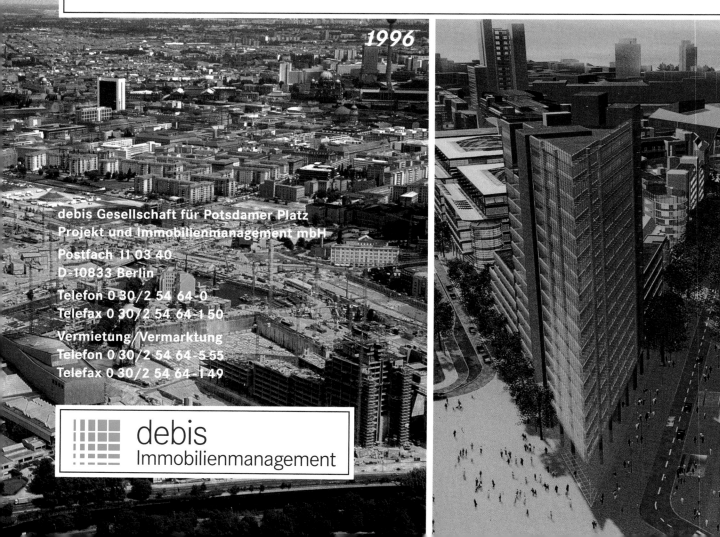

1996

debis Gesellschaft für Potsdamer Platz
Projekt und Immobilienmanagement mbH

Postfach 11 03 40
D-10833 Berlin

Telefon 0 30/2 54 64-0
Telefax 0 30/2 54 64-1 50

Vermietung/Vermarktung
Telefon 0 30/2 54 64-5 55
Telefax 0 30/2 54 64-1 49

▚▚▚▚ **debis**
▚▚▚▚ Immobilienmanagement

We didn´t want the effect to be too dazzling.

Berlin Transport Department´s new bus stop column. It had to be elegant, tough and highly visible. The solution was to streamline: bright and glare-free illumination with only 4 lamps. A few parts, more efficiently used. Less means more.

The columns, designed by Communication Consulting Berlin, consist of a twist free aluminium framework, 3.6m in height. Despite the low power requirement of 144 W they attain a luminance of 850 cd/m² at a distance of 1 m. In the flat version of the column the special internal diffusers ensure extremely even light distribution. If you want to know more about light, ideas and systems from se'lux, please write or call for our interior and exterior catalogues.

se'lux®

Light. Ideas. Systems.

Semperlux GmbH Lichttechnisches Werk · Motzener Straße 34 · D - 12277 Berlin · Tel. (030) 720 01-0 · Fax (030) 721 30 05

"Wir machen Bauwerke zu Bauwerten"

Seit 1983 baut die Bauwert mit an der Zukunft Berlins. Z.B. das Forum Landsberger Allee: 35.000 m^2 repräsentative Nutzfläche in exponierter Lage für Büros, Läden und ein internationales Hotel. Eine faszinierende Architektur, ideale Verkehrsanbindungen und ein qualifiziertes Raumkonzept schaffen optimale Arbeitsbedingungen. Bereits im April 1998 können Sie Ihre Mieträume beziehen. Insgesamt sind schon 75% dieses Gemeinschaftsprojektes mit der BB Immobilien Service GmbH vermietet.

The development corporations
Rummelsburger Bucht and Wasserstadt
Berlin Oberhavel are offering prime
residential and office sites
on the banks of the Spree and Havel
rivers. Here, a fresh breeze blows gently
on the shore and floods are unknown.

Just discovered a further
12.65 km
of shoreline

„Wow, Berlin has waterfront sites!"

At former industrial and harbour sites
apartments, bridges, roads, jetties, child
daycare centres, schools and environmentally
suitable workplaces are under construction.
And there is still plenty of room for innovative
concepts and good architecture.

Lots

Close to the heart of the capital...

for Innovation

...and along the city's leafy edge on the Havel and the Spree rivers.

For more information on
how to rope your
project to our banks
contact Uli Hellweg,
Bernd Cronjaeger
or Juergen Nottmeyer.

Entwicklungstraegergesellschaft Rummelsburger Bucht mbH
Am Koellnischen Park 1A   Telefon: 49 • 30 • 23 19 82 50
10179 Berlin   Telefax: 49 • 30 • 23 19 82 80

Wasserstadt Berlin Oberhavel GmbH

Wasserstadt Berlin Oberhavel GmbH
Eiswerderstraße 18   Telefon: 49 • 30 • 35 59 01 11
13585 Berlin   Telefax: 49 • 30 • 35 59 01 99

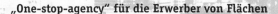

Bauen in Berlin und Brandenburg mit Groth + Graalfs

Groth + Graalfs zählt zu den führenden Berliner Wohnungsbauunternehmen und hat seit 1982 mit einem Investitionsvolumen von rund 4,2 Milliarden DM über 9.000 Wohnungen in Berlin und Brandenburg gebaut. Kompetenz, Erfahrung und das sichere Gespür für Timing und überschaubares Risiko ließen das Unternehmen von den Turbulenzen am Immobilienmarkt nahezu unberührt.

Die Tätigkeit des Unternehmens findet sich in der Mitgestaltung Berlins in den letzten 15 Jahre wieder. Ein Beispiel für den Wohnungsbau der ersten Jahre ist das im Rahmen der internationalen Bauausstellung (IBA) durchgeführte Bauvorhaben Rauchstraße in Berlin-Tiergarten.

Im Bereich der Bürogebäude wurden mit der Zentrale der GrundkreditBank in der Budapester Straße architekto-

Im Nordosten Berlins realisiert Groth + Graalfs das größte private Wohnungsbauvorhaben in Deutschland: Karow-Nord. Bis Mitte 1998 werden 15.000 Menschen hier eine neue Heimat gefunden haben.

Für beide Vorhaben wurden mit der öffentlichen Hand städtebauliche Verträge geschlossen.

Potsdam-Kirchsteigfeld   Foto: Flaskamp

Karow-Nord   Foto: Heinrich Herm

Ob beim Wohnungsbau, dem Bau von Bürogebäuden, Gewerbeobjekten oder Dienstleistungseinrichtungen – alle Leistungen rund um die Immobilie werden aus einer Hand angeboten, vom Grunderwerb über die Fondsverwaltung bis hin zum Stadtteilmanagement einschließlich Haus- und Objektverwaltung.

nische Zeichen gesetzt.

Mit der Gründung seiner Tochtergesellschaft im Herbst 1996, der Groth + Graalfs in Potsdam GmbH mit Sitz in der Potsdamer Innenstadt, setzte Groth + Graalfs deutliche Zeichen für sein verstärktes Engagement im Land Brandenburg.

Besonderes Know-how besitzt Groth + Graalfs bei der Entwicklung großer, zusammenhängender Bauvorhaben im Rahmen von Public Private Partnership, dem Zusammenwirken der öffentlichen Hand und dem privaten Dienstleister. So wächst im Süden von Potsdam das Kirchsteigfeld. Auf knapp 60 Hektar wurden dort 2.000 Mietwohnungen und 400 Eigentumswohnungen errichtet; weitere 100 Eigentumswohnungen und 250 Reihenhäuser werden bis Ende 1999 gebaut.

Zukünftig wird sich Groth + Graalfs noch stärker in den Sparten Stadtentwicklung, Modernisierung und Instandsetzung, Gewerbebau und freifinanzierter Wohnungsbau engagieren. Neben dem Bau ausländischer Vertretungen und Wohnungen für deren Angehörige gewinnt die Errichtung von Gebäuden für die öffentliche Hand und für selbständige Interessenvertretungen an Gewicht.

Groth + Graalfs hat daher sein Dienstleistungsangebot erweitert und bietet neue Wege in der Finanzierung und Zusammenarbeit an: Leasing, Bestandsverwaltung, Führen selbständiger Betreibergesellschaften oder die Übernahme von Sanierungsträgerschaften.

GrundkreditBank Berlin   Foto: J.A. Gonzalez

 GROTH + GRAALFS

Kurfürstendamm 207-208
10719 Berlin
Tel: 030 / 8 80 94-113
Fax: 030 / 8 80 94-119

Schöner bauen –
besser wohnen

Wir sind für unsere Mieter da

Der schöne Norden Berlins

SoBau – Gesellschaft für sozialen Wohnungsbau gemeinnützige Aktiengesellschaft, Wilhelmsruher Damm 142, 13439 Berlin, Tel. (030) 4 07 78-0

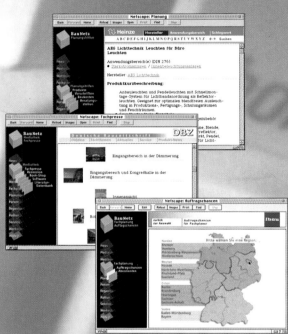

Qualität zu tragbaren Kosten –

Altglienicke Wohngebiet 1.1

Rechts der Bahn: Vordergrund, Wohngebiet 1.1; Hintergrund, Wohngebiet 1.2; links der Bahn: Wohngebiet 1.3

Altglienicke, Wohngebiet 1.1

Werner-Berndt-Siedlung

John-Locke-Siedlung

John-Locke-Siedlung

Werner-Berndt-Siedlung

Florian-Geyer-Straße 104

Schnellerstraße 99–101

Siriusstraße/Ortolfstraße 208–210

für STADT UND LAND
eine Verpflichtung

Mit 43.000 Wohnungen und einer bald 75jährigen Tradition in der Bereitstellung von Wohnraum zu angemessenen Preisen ist die STADT UND LAND ein kompetenter Partner für den Bau von Eigenheimen und Eigentumswohnungen
– für den öffentlich geförderten Wohnungsbau,
– die Verwaltung von Wohnanlagen des eigenen Bestandes und im Auftrag Dritter.

Die STADT UND LAND hat langjährige Erfahrungen als Sanierungsträger in verschiedenen Stadtteilen Berlins, sie hat städtebauliche Aufgaben von der Projektentwicklung bis zur Erschließung. Seit der Gründung im Jahre 1924 setzt die STADT UND LAND ihr Know-how im Sinne der gemeinnützigen Wohnungswirtschaft ein und versorgt Wohnungssuchende in Berlin und dem Umland von Berlin mit Wohnraum.
Dazu gehören Stadtteilentwicklungen in Altglienicke im Bezirk Treptow genauso wie Neubauprojekte sowie Sanierungs- und Instandsetzungsmaßnahmen.
Die Fertigstellung von Qualitätsbau zu tragbaren Kosten ist sichtbar im gesamten Berlin. Dazu stellt die Gesellschaft einige Bauvorhaben vor.

STADT UND LAND

WOHNBAUTEN-GESELLSCHAFT MBH

Werbellinstraße 12 · 12053 Berlin · Sammelrufnummer: 68 92-0 · Telefax: 68 92-206

Grafik **Büro**
Adler & Schmidt GbR

Visuelle Kommunikation

Broschüren
Präsentationen
Ausstellungen

Grafische Erscheinungsbilder

Informationsgrafik
Plandarstellungen

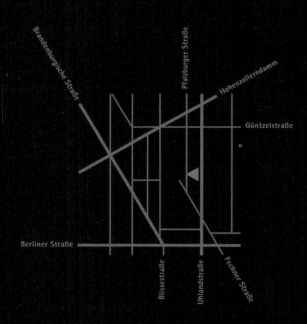

Pfalzburger Straße 43–44
10717 Berlin (Wilmersdorf)

Telefon 030. 860 007-0
Telefax 030. 860 007-20